"We Come to Object"

JOHNS HOPKINS STUDIES IN ATLANTIC HISTORY AND CULTURE
RICHARD PRICE AND FRANKLIN W. KNIGHT, GENERAL EDITORS

"We Come to Object"

THE PEASANTS OF MORELOS
AND THE NATIONAL STATE

Arturo Warman

Translated by Stephen K. Ault

The Johns Hopkins University Press
Baltimore and London

This book has been brought to publication with the generous assistance of the Andrew W. Mellon Foundation.

Originally published as . . . *Y venimos a contradecir: Los campesinos de Morelos y el estado nacional,* copyright © 1976 Centro de Investigaciones Superiores del INAH, Ediciones de La Casa Chata

The Johns Hopkins University Press, Baltimore, Maryland 21218
The Johns Hopkins Press Ltd., London

Library of Congress Cataloging in Publication Data

Warman, Arturo.
  "We come to object."

  (Johns Hopkins studies in Atlantic history and culture)
  Translation of Y venimos a contradecir.
  Bibliography: pp. 309–19
  1. Land tenure—Mexico—Morelos—History.
2. Morelos, Mexico—Rural conditions. 3. Peasantry—Mexico—Morelos. I. Title. II. Series.
HD329.M67W3713   305.5′6   80–8092
ISBN 0–8018–2170–3

CONTENTS

ACKNOWLEDGMENTS

Writing this book has been a complex task in which many people and institutions have taken decisive parts. To acknowledge their cooperation is one of the most difficult parts of the process. Having failed to find a new way to do it, I am resorting to the tried and true formula. I really have a great deal to be grateful for, and I am sorry for any omissions.

In the first place, I wish to express something more than gratitude to the peasants who received us in the Morelos *oriente* with almost infinite courtesy and patience and with true affection. I have always admired their tolerance and cosmopolitan attitude toward strangers who demonstrate curiosity, respect, and politeness, as if they had lived all their lives with the most extraordinary types of people. I remember one conversation: "And you, professor, what work do you do?" "I am an anthropologist from the Iberoamerican University, and I'm trying to. . . ." "Yes, you already told me that, but you haven't told me what work it is you do." If only this book could answer not only his uncertainty but mine as well! But even more than for the acceptance, I would like to offer them my gratitude for their conceptual and theoretical teaching. This book attempts to gather together those lessons, and I offer them thanks as teachers.

The research from which this study and others by my colleagues emerge was a collective undertaking of the Seminar on Peasant Societies of the Center for Advanced Research of the National Institute of Anthropology and History. I am grateful to Guillermo Bonfil and Ángel Palerm for something more than the institutional support that they made possible: the interest and the shared ideal of making research the central activity in anthropological training. I have to thank the people who made up the seminar or who were associated with it for many things: the use of information; the ideas that arose in our lengthy collective and personal discussions; the shared experiences and anxieties of work; and their friendship and camaraderie—all essential in making this book possible. An alphabetical list of the colleagues who took part is certainly not the happiest solution for suggesting the importance of their contribution. I beg pardon for the lack of inspiration, and for their participation in the experience of the seminar and in the collective act of learning I thank: Alfonso Alfaro,

Jorge Alonso, Elena Azaola, Alfonso Corcuera, Laura Helguera, Esteban Krotz, Sinecio López, Roberto Melville, Germán Neira, Patricia Nettel, Armando Pereyra, Alfredo Pintos, Ramón Ramírez, Mireya Rubio, and Alejandra Valenzuela.

The process of writing the book was shared by Sidney Mintz, John Murra, Ángel Palerm, and Eric Wolf, who read the manuscript. Their criticisms were more than merely useful: they were true lessons in the art and office of being an anthropologist. The experience, clear thinking, and professionalism that they contributed may not, perhaps, be recognized because of my failings. They also gave me a lesson in respect for ideas, so that any blunders must be attributed to me.

Teresa Rojas provided historical materials and contemporary commentary: Thank-you very much. Guillermo Palacios helped me in the final correction of the manuscript. I am very grateful for his fierce collaboration, and I cite him by way of carrying out a threat. Mary P. Oliver turned the messy manuscript sheets into clean pages—an almost impossible task—with dedication, patience, and kindness. Even more than that, she allowed me to scrawl all over them again and again and always repeated the feat. I am profoundly grateful to her.

The John Simon Guggenheim Commemorative Foundation made it possible for me to set aside my teaching obligations in order to analyze the enormous quantity of material and to prepare the draft of the book. This experience, so difficult to explain adequately, was very important. The Institute of Advanced Studies at Princeton welcomed me as a member during the academic year 1974/75. There, in an atmosphere of almost inconceivable freedom and with all the facilities not only desirable but imaginable, the final version was drafted. But it provided more than that: its School of Social Sciences, directed by Clifford Geertz, is a place where one can learn a great deal every day.

In short, to all those who made this study possible: Many thanks.

INTRODUCTION

In this book I attempt to tell about the persistence of peasant groups in Mexico and to analyze some of the factors that made it possible, or more strictly speaking, inevitable. The narrative begins in the colonial era and continues almost up to our own time. However, I do not believe that this is a history book in the conventional sense. This search through the past originates in the present and seeks to understand the evolution of the processes that today seem most relevant to an explanation of the persistence of the peasants, the *campesinos*. Moreover, almost the entire history is reconstructed on the basis of the memory of the peasants of eastern Morelos, the protagonists of this book. Precise, personal memories and the stories parents told childern about how life was when they were young—the oral tradition—are in this case the principal sources for the knowledge of the past. Documents and the books based upon them are used in a secondary way to confirm what the people tell, to make it more specific at times, and to locate local events and village histories in a broader context. The fidelity of memory is surprising in its detail, in the enormous stress on exact, concrete fact. People recall the prices of things thirty or fifty years ago; the names of people dead before the revolution and the names of their kinfolk; the exact site of events of nearly one hundred years ago; the boundaries of their lands, set in some instances four centuries ago.

This prodigious memory is not gratuitous. For the people of the *oriente*, the eastern region, the past offers a lesson, teaching that is valid for confronting the present, an arsenal of strategies for survival. The past also takes root in the peasant and marks him; it links him to the land and its secrets. The people know what uses and whom their territory serves and how they made it fruitful. They also recognize what was theirs, what they lost through plunder, and what they recovered through struggle. To put it in a rather incongruous fashion, from the past emerges peasant citizenship, specific mastery of the earth and the plants, roots in the territory and with the people who occupy it, and possession through labor and permanence. That living past, still in effect and brought up to date, is what I tried to embody in this study.

The peasants' link with their past does not make them conservative or

1

antiquated people, much less archaic, as is so often and so arrogantly suggested. Their actions are shaped by their participation in a broader and more powerful system, the same one that puts people on the moon, fights colonialist wars, suffers from inflation or profits from it, and worries about the energy crisis, demography, and ecology. The peasant activities originate or extend outside the local framework and even outside the country. Thus, the description often goes beyond the area, and the analysis centers on this complex network of relationships between the rural villages and the urban centers with their cosmopolitan pretensions—both in the end merely contemporaneous provinces or regions of one single, complex reality and without clear boundaries. The peasants of the *oriente* are a vital part of our time, of daily existence in the factory, at the university, or on the stock exchange, although we might not know it or, more frequently, might not care to admit it. They, on the other hand, know that their destiny is fulfilled and at times decided outside their environment, their control, and, often, their knowledge; they act, then, more from pressure than from choice.

The peasant's performance of his job, in general and in specific terms, is added to the immense currents through which economic goods, commodities, and capital flow limitlessly. All these currents empty into the world capitalist industrial system in its broadest sense. But before blending into the total abstraction that rules this system in absolute anonymity, this job is led through visible channels and strikes against specific obstacles that the peasants know and identify. The description and the analysis, which to a certain extent are shaped by the peasants' perspective, rarely go further than these visible limits, submerged within the borders of a Mexican state. The book deals with peasantry and capitalism in Mexico and only occasionally ventures broader generalizations. I never asked myself whether the facts outlined here and their explanation were representative of Chihuahua, Ecuador, or medieval Spain. Only now, at the end, do I wonder how relationships established with the data of the *oriente* situation will develop in other contexts. I have no clear answers but certainly plenty of curiosity.

I have attempted to allow the people of the *oriente* and their job to appear in all their complexity. The result is scarcely a pale reflection of the true, enormous diversity that this space contains, however small and limited it may be in comparison with the nation. I sought to find what was specific, or particular, about that job. I found not typical peasants but specific peasants. Yet, I do not explain the peculiar as such, as a unique case, more or less curious or even exotic, but as one mode among the many available for adapting to general conditions. The concrete job of the peasants of the Morelos *oriente* cannot be generalized; however, the relations that mold that action are not specific but have a validity that goes beyond the limits of the region in which we are working. I attempted to advance in the understanding of a complex reality by starting from specific actions in order to discover the significant aspect, the general importance, in these unique facts. There is no claim of originality—far from it—but simply anthropological work as I understand it. As a colleague once told me, the problem we anthropologists have is to explain something as sonorous and serious as class struggle with data like the increase in the price of soap. The people who receive us buy less in order to wash the same clothing, which remains clean but a little less white, a bit soiled. To go on about whiteness and cleanliness is not dramatic, but how important it is!

A good part of the history I want to tell is made up of data of just this type, taken from daily life and lacking dramatic and rhetorical flair. These things are done with simplicity and do not serve the ends of inflammatory discourse. Yet, for me, the combination of these daily events has an epic character; it constitutes an almost implausible accomplishment. The objective of this feat is not very rhetorical either and would certainly be intractable material for epic verse: to survive, to go on being peasants, to continue here obstinately, permanently. At times, the epic of daily survival becomes an heroic poem made manifest in battles, in sacrifices. It happened that way in Morelos with Emiliano Zapata and the rebel Army of the South. I do not claim to have written an epic book, but the peasant persistence has just this spirit, expressed in daily acts, always repeated and at the same time always new.

If the book is not history or descriptive monograph or heroic romance, it runs the risk of nonexistence. It must, then, have some label. Let us say—adding at once, modestly—that it is an anthropological study, an attempt at theoretical interpretation of a concrete, graspable reality. The research sought to answer earlier questions and doubts, to speak to theoretical arguments previously established. The questions that I tried to resolve can be grouped into just a single, large question that ultimately guided the preparation of this book. That effort can be expressed as an attempt to clarify what the sources of structural change in Mexico are, which forces are most powerful and what their most acute contradictions are, and who the strongest, most important protagonists in this process are. The question is as valid for the past as for the future, but I posed it to myself in reference to the present. Obviously, a question so general and indefinite was broken down into many more concrete, specific questions, each, accordingly, with viable answers as to the why, the how, and the when of specific actions. These last questions helped structure the book and are in some way expressed in its text. To a great extent, the subtitled divisions are specific questions and essays at an answer.

Clearly, each chapter has a different structure, derived not only from the abundance and nature of the information but also from the linking of different questions, which I assume better suited to a changing reality. This difference also corresponds to my notion that the level of abstraction can increase as the accumulation of information progresses. Thus, for example, in the last chapter, the specificity of facts is more diluted, and processes come to be the protagonists, something that would not be possible in earlier chapters without the risk that the concepts would turn out hollow, merely empty words.

The broadest question is not expressed in the essay, however, although it ventures to offer an answer that is scarcely more than a crude hypothesis, primary and problematic, which poses more related questions. The answer suggests the presence of two principal actors in the process of the most profound change: the peasants and the State. They are the bearers of the most critical contradiction, central in the process of a capitalist industrialization that is dependent and tardy, if not, indeed, posthumous and unfinished. Obviously, these forces are not the only ones, nor do they act in a void; they are not even homogeneous, but, on the contrary, complex and contradictory. Mexican "development" is a sort of mass spectacle with a multistellar cast, one in which everyone wants to steal a scene in the service of his own private interests. Moreover, it is needless to say that the producers do not appear in the work, and only occasionally do we recall that they are the owners of the scenery, the dressing room, and the seats. But this study suggests that the central contradiction, the one on which the survival of the whole depends, is posed between these forces. One, the State, has the longest part, and its entrances are frequent to the point of repetitiveness; to bring off the part, one has to be a good actor and have plenty of experience on the boards. The other, the peasantry, does not speak in the play but never leaves the stage. The peasants are always present, and they are the majority; the rest move about in their vicinity or stumble into them.

In this book I try to define these complex protagonists concretely. Here it is only worthwhile to note that from my point of view each one is defined in terms of the other, and both are mutually modified. The process of "development" can be narrated and understood as the adjustment between these two forces. Fixed, invariable formal and functional characteristics cannot be attributed to the peasants or to the State. Their forms are constantly changing, dissolved only to be reshaped, always through different people. The peasants and the State change profoundly, but they do so on different patterns. These are differentiated though interdependent structures with distinct purposes that require specific forms of organization that are not interchangeable. Obviously, the interdependence is not egalitarian but, on the contrary, a relationship

of dominance and of complex exploitation with many diverse beneficiaries, who are often in competition.

It is possible for the peasant to plant onions, tomatoes, or sorghum
for the market, to emigrate as a seasonal farmhand, *bracero,* or calmly
to become a Protestant, certainly not very "traditional" activities,
without ever ceasing to be a peasant. This does not depend so much on
the concrete job as on the nature of the relationships that regulate it.
The symmetrical, redistributive relations that the peasants practice among
themselves make it possible and necessary for them to produce commodities for the capitalist market without having the labor, the essential
commodity of the system, bought or sold or even constitute a cost of
production. This combination creates a surplus that is appropriated,
accumulated, and reproduced far from the peasants. They keep, but
only with great difficulty, enough to live on in the most frugal manner,
without the possibility of saving or accumulation.

This surplus, created by millions of persons, which can be measured
only with difficulty but is clearly perceived and can be analyzed, is the
real, effective sustenance of industrial capitalism. To satisfy the demands
of "growth and development," the peasants have intensified their
activity; they have made it more diverse, complex, and strenuous in
order to pay a higher rate of exploitation, which is at once more ubiquitous and rigorous. In order to be "modern" and to plant grafted fruit
trees, to fertilize with chemical mixtures, to harvest products that are
too expensive for them to consume themselves, the peasants have had
to make themselves more "traditional." They have to plant the corn
they are going to eat, meet ceremonial expenses, make one another co-
parents, establish reciprocal relations for direct, noncapitalist exchange
of work and productive resources. They have even had to grow, reproducing themselves in order to enlarge the size of their work force, which
contributes the surpluses. A demonic dialectic indeed.

The principal agent of the exploitation of the peasants is the State,
which imposes the general conditions for the distribution of resources,
their circulation and valuation, for the dominance of capitalism and its
preservation. With its protection, the specific agents who share the
spoils of the peasant surplus thrive. The Mexican State has also changed
radically. The landholding oligarchs, the *hacendados,* no longer dominate
it—or at least not all of them. It is a nationalist, populist state brought
forth by a revolution of enormous proportions. It is this State that distributed the land and expropriated the oil companies; it supported the
Spanish Republic and received its refugees, never broke relations with
revolutionary Cuba, and today welcomes those exiled by the fascist
coup in Chile. The principal agents in the exploitation of the peasant,
those who confront him in an acute and unadorned contradiction, are

the good and the patriotic, the promoters of dependent industrialism, of "modernization" at any price, of the establishment of growth as an objective in itself, at the expense of the people who produce the wealth. These same people have converted agrarian reform, which was conceived as a process leading toward the establishment of justice and well-being, into a mere instrument for the growth of the industry that makes oppression even more grave.

Neither the peasants nor the State is an autonomous entity. Both are associated with other complex dependencies, with other forces and pressures. Both are stratified within and divided by interests that often contradict each other. The contradiction between the peasants and the State is not the only one in the country, and thanks to a coalition of many interests, it is not even the most apparent. However, it is the essential one in the sense that the changes that would radically and basically affect the entire situation can only be generated within it. It seems to me that other groups or sectors can realize important changes internally and even in many of their external relations without modifying the basic direction of the development of the national whole. We have seen private industries pass into the hands of the State without essentially altering the capitalist industrial model; foreign industries have come into national hands, and, much more actively, vice versa, with the same result. I am not trying to ignore or minimize the importance of these changes and of many others that take place; I am only suggesting that any revolutionary change, in the sense of basically altering the structure, will involve the *campesinos* and the State in a central way and will drag down the constellation of forces and interests that put pressure on the system.

The formulation of this hypothesis has no prophetic value. In recent years the contradiction between the peasants and the State has become more acute, but the lessons of the past do not suggest that this will lead immediately to a confrontation. When this happened in the case of *la bola grande,* the Big Brawl, with which the Zapatistas upset everything, the structural contradiction was combined with conjunctural conditions created not only by the peasants. The detonator itself, Madero's uprising, was an urban mutiny. What seems clear is that the political revolt, the coup, became a revolutionary struggle through intervention of the *campesinos,* who had demands of their own; then the central contradiction became explicit and acquired preeminence. It is unlikely that history will repeat itself, and the lessons of the past are only that, not a crystal ball for soothsaying. But it is still less probable that the contradiction between the peasants and the State will remain immobile, frozen. If the hypothesis does not permit prophecy, neither does it give grounds for optimism or for pessimism; it simply contributes to underscoring some facts and to interpreting them in a certain way.

However, while the hypothesis can be "neutral," the book does not want to be. I did not write it seeking an uncommitted, distant, or cold stance. I strove to be faithful to the facts, neither to hide nor to disguise information, but I did take sides. In colonial times, when the Spanish crown was distributing the Indian lands among the *conquistadores*, in order to take physical possession the new owners had to pass along the boundaries of their new property without meeting any objection. The Indians were always there with their trumpets and flags. In the old colonial documents, they start their declarations with this sentence: "Y venimos a contradecir"—"And we come to object." It did them little good, and they lost their land piece by piece, almost clod by clod. From that time on, the peasants have always been present to object, to denounce injustice, and to defend their right to cultivate the land and retain its fruits. The peasants continue to be there, objecting through their presence and their job to the new exploiters, those who promote "development and modernization" based on exploitation imposed through violence and justified with the arrogance—and at times the stupidity— of the powerful. I have tried to add my voice to that presence. I, too, would like to object.

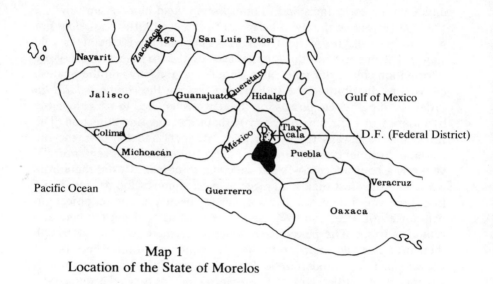

Map 1
Location of the State of Morelos

Map 2
The State of Morelos

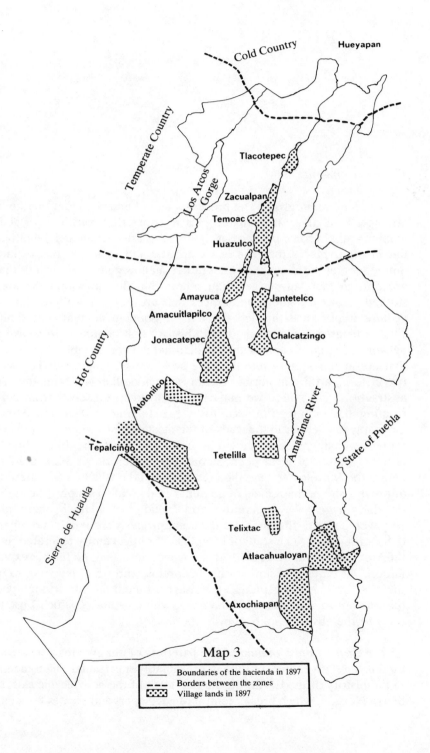

Cold Country

Hueyapan

Temperate Country

Los Arcos Gorge

Tlacotepec

Zacualpan

Temoac

Huazulco

Amayuca

Jantetelco

Amacuitlapilco

Jonacatepec

Chalcatzingo

Hot Country

Atotonilco

Amatzinac River

State of Puebla

Tepalcingo

Tetelilla

Sierra de Huautla

Telixtac

Atlacahualoyan

Axochiapan

Map 3

——	Boundaries of the hacienda in 1897
- - -	Borders between the zones
▨▨▨	Village lands in 1897

I   ORIGINS

The Environment

The Geographic Area. The processes and phenomena that this study attempts to analyze are situated in a territory that constitutes a geographic area. In some instances its boundaries are obvious and definitive, but in other places they are less emphatic and seem to dissolve into minor geographic unevennesses: a rather shallow gully or some hills that are not, in fact, any larger than others that do fall within the area studied. However, these differences that are not physically definitive acquire importance through the human phenomena that they limit. Thus, our area is also shaped by a history that continues to weave a network of relations among the people; that network establishes borders that are at times more real than the accidents of geography. To these two criteria, a third important one must be added: *area* is ultimately an abstraction, a resource we make use of to keep ourselves from confronting the infinite, the successive, real linking of phenomena that inevitably lead either to the study of the most distant antiquity or to Wall Street, which are, especially the first, ultimately the true (though remote) causes of local phenomena. The three criteria were used to define the Morelos *oriente,* the area under study, which in the interests of brevity and perhaps even of grammar is also called simply "the area" or "the *oriente.*" We reserve the term "region" for a larger sphere, not very well defined, that includes the area, properly speaking, and others that border on it. The state of Morelos, a political entity federated into the Mexican Republic, is defined in advance and needs no further explanation. At times it is simply called Morelos, and when referring to it, the word *state* is not capitalized, a usage adopted not for orthographic reasons but to distinguish it from *State,* with a capital *S,* which I use to refer to the abstract political institution.

The Birth of the Mountains. The paternity of our area must be attributed to a relatively recent though presumably spectacular phenomenon in the history of the Earth: the surging forth of the neovolcanic axis, or Sierra Nevada, which breaks central Mexico apart and creates ferocious

10

unevennesses between the plains, piedmonts, and valleys where human activity developed. The rise of the Sierra Nevada brought forth the volcano Popocatépetl, the impressive northern boundary of the area. The volcano contributed enormous quantities of materials: lava, ashes, and alluvia that spread out southwest of the peak into a broad piedmont area that further south opens into a plain four thousand meters lower than the crater of its aristocratic ancestor (Bataillon, pp. 160–70). To the south, the plain runs into the Sierra de Huautla, part of the Sierra Madre del Sur, older and more worn down than the still haughty Sierra Nevada, yet a more formidable obstacle to communication among the people: an endless chain of mountains, less lofty than the imposing cones at the northern end of the zone but far more hostile, without a single important stream to ease the aridity.

Between these two obvious physical boundaries is situated the area of the Morelos *oriente.* Its form vaguely suggests a triangle with a very elongated base that runs from north to south. Its northern vertex can be located on the peak of Popocatépetl, and its southern extreme in Tlancualpicán, where the Nexapa River begins to carve its path through the Sierra Madre del Sur on the way to the Las Balsas River. A sizable number of gorges, *barrancas,* issue from the volcano. One of them, the Tezozongo, can serve as the western boundary of the area, starting at its origin in the slopes of Popocatépetl. Tezozongo becomes the Los Arcos Gorge before joining the La Cuera *barranca,* which after a long journey contributes its intermittent torrential flow to the Chinameca River. The Tezozongo Gorge changes its name to Los Arcos because an aqueduct constructed on it diverts its waters, so that instead of contributing to the Chinameca and then to the Amacuzac, they are channeled toward the Amatzinac River and then to the Nexapa, if any volume has remained after use of the water for irrigation (see map 3). A few kilometers from where the *barrancas* of Los Arcos and La Cuera meet is the village of Tlayecac, where the western vertex of the triangle is established.

South of Tlayecac, mountains rise from the *cerro* ("low mountain") La Cruz to El Cacalote and, together with the Sierra de Huautla, form the border of the area in its descent toward Tlancualpicán. Between the Las Limas *cerro,* the last of the mountains that originate south of Tlayecac, and the rise of the sierra the plain runs westward to the Chinameca River without major obstacles. At this point the border necessarily becomes imaginary, and yet it functions. The Sierra de Huautla draws the rest of the boundaries quite neatly to Tlancualpicán, rather extravagantly underlined by the Tepalcingo River, which runs almost parallel to the mountain chain.

Above Tlancualpicán, toward the north, the Nexapa River joins the *barranca* of Los Arcos, another Los Arcos *barranca* that, unfortunately for the narrator, bears the same name as the one in the north. That gorge, running from north to south, serves as a border for the zone along the east and is also, conveniently, the political border between the states of Morelos and Puebla. At the latitude of the Jantetelco peak the Los Arcos Gorge ceases to mark the border, which follows instead the Amatzinac River, the only perennial stream of importance, to its origin in the high slopes of Popocatépetl.

Thus, these features shape the perimeter of what we call the Morelos *oriente*. Its maximum length is seventy kilometers, the base of the triangle that runs from north to south; its maximum breadth is twenty kilometers, along the triangle's altitude, between Tlayecac and the peak of Jantetelco. This implies an area of approximately seven hundred square kilometers, if one follows the most elementary geometry and if all the complex outlines of the borders become perfect straight lines.

The area is structured by various congruent phenomena. The slope of the land descends from north to south along the whole length of the Morelos *oriente*. Consequently, all the gorges and streams go in the same direction—that is, they flow toward the Nexapa River, whether naturally or, as in the case of the northern Los Arcos *barranca*, because of human effort—and they constitute a single system.

The entire hydrographic system of the Morelos *oriente* runs through very narrow gorges with high, almost vertical walls that in some spots exceed twenty meters in depth. The principal source of sustenance for this system is harsh, torrential water, which makes the volume irregular, even extreme: great avenues of water during the rainy season and total drought during the rest of the year. Some permanent springs also crop up in the area: the one at Atotonilco, the most important, surges into a spa and then irrigates small areas; the one at Jonacatepec, not to be outdone, will be devoted to another spa; the spring at Las Pilas creates great concern over who irrigates with its waters; and there is also the slender trickle at Huazulco, which came forth miraculously during a severe drought in the last century. The people use all the spring water before it can get to the *barrancas*.

The thawing of the perpetual snows of Popocatépetl gives rise to the only permanent stream of importance: the Amatzinac river or gorge, which develops north of the village of Hueyapan and runs along a route to the south. Its importance is enormous, and because of its position and functions, it can be compared with the spinal column of an organized being.

The mountainous formations and their consequences—the downward slope, the drainage, and the gorges—all congruent in direction, give the landscape of the Morelos *oriente* a more or less clear organization. In this pattern we can distinguish three zones or subareas: the sierra, or cold country; the piedmont, or temperate country; and the plain, or hot country.

The Cold Country. The cold country can be characterized by its rough, mountainous nature, with its great slopes and an absence of valleys or plains. In fact, it belongs to the sierra of Popcatépetl. To move from the peak of the volcano to the point where the slope becomes less sharp, which coincides with the contour line at 1,750 meters, takes scarcely 25 kilometers towards the south, a straight line along which the altitude descends more than 3,500 meters. The first ten kilometers, the highest, are unpopulated and almost unused by man. There one finds the perpetual snows; sandy places; scant, sparse grasslands; and occasionally some mountaineers. It is cold, and frosts and snowfalls are common.

At the altitude of around three thousand meters the forest of pines and hemlocks and some more substantial grasslands begin. The first traces of human activity appear there: lumbering, less intense today than seventy years ago; meager flocks of sheep and some cows; some paths; crosses that crown some mountains and serve equally for orthodox worship of the Catholic saints and for magic control of the rain and hail that make agricultural activity possible a bit further down. The Amatzinac River with its cold, crystalline waters already runs here, although its volume is still slight.

Below three thousand meters the natural landscape of a pine forest in which oaks already begin to appear competes with another form of landscape, one shaped by the agricultural activity of the inhabitants of Hueyapan. The critical problem in making this activity possible was conquering the slope, creating and retaining the soil. It was necessary to break into the sides of the mountains in order to level off the soil in stepped terraces and then to protect their borders by planting maguey plants and fruit trees. On these terraces, which cover whole mountainsides, the cornfields grow among fruit trees: peach, pear, plum, and thorn apple; today, the more daring experiment with cherry trees. The maguey plants that protect the edges of the *repado,* or terrace, also produce, and wineskins for pulque are seen in almost all the houses. The width of the terraces is defined by the slope, which is so severe that they rarely exceed five or six meters. Their length, also defined by the topography, tends to curve, following the mountain. New terraces are built each year in a difficult struggle against the forest.

Others factors limit agriculture—above all, the cold, the frosts, and even the excess humidity. The rains, frequent and abundant, continue through ten months of the year, and average rainfall reaches two thousand millimeters. For the peasants, the problem is lack of heat, of sunshine. The growing cycle for corn takes almost ten months at this altitude.

The village of Hueyapan, the only one in the area that is located in the cold country, occupies a hollow where the incline smoothes out. The house lots are large, and corn, wheat, and other crops for domestic consumption are raised in them; lately, fodder and flowers are also being planted. With these last species, it was necessary to introduce irrigation to permit cutting in the winter and to protect the plants from frosts. Built by local cooperative groups, the watering system, a veritable spiderweb of rubber hoses, takes advantage of even the slightest trickles of water.

The villagers speak Mexican, and many of them wear traditional woolen garments that are woven locally. The houses are adobe with gabled roofs that rise with a slope as pronounced as that of the mountainsides.

South of the village, below 2,250 meters, the mountains become smaller, although their grade does not diminish very much. The vegetation is stunted, and shrubs dominate. It is not unlikely that at one time this landscape was a forest of evergreen oaks, for some of these are still seen. The terraces here become a bit wider and more specialized. Along with corn alone, a variety of fruit is raised, especially peaches. The Hueyapan *ejido,* communal land, is located here. The temperature, though still cold, becomes less harsh, but, in turn, the rains are scantier and concentrated in a shorter period. This is the border with the temperate country.

The cold country is linked with the rest of the area by a good dirt road —which can become a wretched path during the rains—that joins Hueyapan and Tlacotepec. Another path ties Hueyapan to its municipal seat, Tetela del Volcán, passing through Alpanocan, a village forced into the political realm, for it belongs to the state of Puebla, not to Morelos. Strictly speaking, no clear boundary exists between Hueyapan and the other villages of the cold country; however, its connection with the rest of the area and its position at the headwaters of the Amatzinac River justify its inclusion in the *oriente* and offset the arbitrariness of its isolation.

The Temperate Country. Almost coinciding with the contour line at 1,750 meters, the mountainous slopes of the volcano seem to be worn down to open out toward the south in a piedmont that is smooth, though with a clear, gentle slope. Whereas in the cold country used by the people of Hueyapan the altitude drops a thousand meters within scarcely thirteen kilometers, in the temperate zone it takes eight kilometers to descend two hundred fifty meters. Here level land surface is abundant. The forest has disappeared completely, and in the few spots where the vegetation is not the result of human activity, low brush, some of it already thorny, and grasslands dominate. The rains, which are statistically sufficient for dry farming, appear irregularly and in a concentrated period: from December to April it almost never rains; in May and in October it rains occasionally only in good years; the rainy season tends to fall between June and September; and dogdays, or Indian summers, which can endanger the sown fields, do appear.

However, in the temperate country the Amatzinac River already attains an important volume, which the mild slope moves along efficiently. The management of the water makes it possible for this zone, the smallest in area, to have the highest concentration of human settlement. Within scarcely ten kilometers, six villages are crowded upon the edges of the Amatzinac Gorge: four on the right side—Zacualpan, Temoac, Huazulco, and Amilcingo—and two on the left—Tlacotepec, which has its best lands on the right side, and Popotlán, the smallest of all. The left bank of the river is protected by a perpendicular, rocky wall that offers almost no openings; however, the right side, also vertical, offers an extremely tiny plain where water can be drawn off. Even so, taking water must be done well above the lands to be irrigated in order to use gravity to avoid the *barranca* walls that enclose the river.

Irrigation is the dominant phenomenon of the temperate country, and all its villages are united in a single system of canals and reservoirs that, because of their limited capacity for storage, serve, above all, to regulate the distribution of water. The flowing water gives rise to orchards, the characteristic element of temperate-country agriculture. Surrounded by fences of piled-up rocks, which serve both to define boundary lines and to encourage the formation of soil, the orchards are the site of habitation, which leads to a semidispersed pattern for the villages. With the exception of the principal streets, in which houses are crowded one next to the other, the villages seem deserted, the houses hidden behind the orchard foliage. Now only Spanish is spoken in these villages, and modern buildings, which still seem a little out of place, are beginning to appear.

The traditional orchards are complicated vegetal associations of plants organized by levels in accord with their requirements for sunlight. Pecan trees occupy the highest level, almost twenty meters from the soil; the middle level is occupied by guava, avocado, plum, and quince trees as well as by other varieties that are experimented with; the lowest, shadiest level shelters coffee plants. All these are combined to obtain almost continuous production: in June and July, quinces, avocados, and guavas ripen; in August, nuts; in January and February, plums. . . . The lack of water, the speculative qualities of the market, and the appearance of a blight possibly brought on by introduction of chemical products into farming have encouraged the specialization of some once-complex orchards in a single crop, like quinces or sugar cane in small areas where it is intended exclusively for making rum. Technological miracles must take place in this industry with its three rustic factories, the only ones in the temperate country, since there is no clear relation between the enormous volume of rum production and the cane fields, productive surely, but still only tiny.

Other land with access to the flowing water, the *ejido* land that previously belonged to the hacienda, is given over, as is that of some orchards that were cleared, to short-cycle crops like tomatoes, onions, and green beans, which are commercial and speculative, as well as to other, more secure crops like rice and sesame, or *alegría,* which is made into the candy of the same name in Huazulco.

The dry-farming lands that were never irrigated or that the water never reaches are dedicated to corn in combination with beans and squash—*la milpa,* the "cornfield"—and, more recently, to rain-fed tomatoes and onions. The lands that are still covered by the extensive canal system but receive no share of water are considered half-irrigated, since during the rainy season they can make use of the surplus from the irrigation further up and of the runoff of rainwater that passes through the ditches, called *achololes.*

The temperate country offers the greatest variety of crops, obtained from very small parcels of land. The population density and the scarcity of water and land also result in a higher frequency of territorial conflicts between the villages.

The temperate country is politically organized as a single *municipio,* or "municipality," which has its seat at Zacualpan, although according to the 1970 census the villages of Temoac and Tlacotepec have more inhabitants. In all, ten thousand people live in the *municipio* of Zacualpan. Communication in this zone is maintained by a recently asphalted road that joins Tlacotepec, Zacualpan, and Temoac with the Amayuca cross-roads; dirt roads branch off from it, leading to other settlements.

The Hot Country. Along the south, the temperate country gradually becomes the great plain of the hot country, without a clear-cut border to separate them. Between the village of Huazulco, to the north, and Jantetelco and Amayuca, the orchards give way to the aridity of the plain. The contour line at fifteen hundred meters, which we will use as a boundary, crosses between these villages. We will consider Jantetelco and Amayuca, located below this altitude, part of the hot country.

On this great plain the slope downward becomes imperceptible and is hardly interrupted by two solitary *cerros.* The peak Jantetelco is a rocky mass that reaches about 1,850 meters in height—sufficiently proud, so legend tells it, to fall in love with Ixtaccíhuatl, The Sleeping Woman, which proudly rises more than 3,000 meters above the romantic peak. This love stirred the jealousy of Popocatépetl, who began duels of thunderbolts, storms, and hail with his diminutive but bellicose rival. A little more to the south of that peak stands the Tenango *cerro*, also exceeding 1,800 meters at its summit. This is a more complex *cerro*, or even three *cerros* linked together: La Cantera, El Coyote, and Tenango, which were sometimes called the Los Halcones *cerros*. The great rocky masses recreate the landscape of the Wild West idealized in *los westerns*, a coincidence that could not be passed up, and thus some U.S. films have been made among these mountains.

On the plain the dominant note is aridity. Uncultivated vegetation is sparse, low, and thick-stemmed, with scanty foliage and a generous share of thorns. The acacias, gourds, *casahuates*, and cacti, along with an isolated pepper tree or *pirul*, the tallest among the shrubs, stand out like dark blotches in a landscape dominated by drab tones during almost the entire year. The rainfall is quite concentrated, occurring in a short spell of less than four months—from the feast of San Juan, at the end of June, until the feast of San Miguel and the *cordonazo* of San Francisco* at the end of September and beginning of October. The few heavy squalls that come outside this season do not penetrate the hard crust of the dried-out, sun-baked earth. Although the average precipitation exceeds the seven hundred millimeters necessary for dry farming, the rains are irregular, and Indian summers occur, endangering the planted fields. It gets hot, and the sun beats down intensely, so that the humidity evaporates rapidly.

Under such conditions, the risk of practicing dry farming is high. But such farming does cover great portions of the hot country and is, in fact, its most important activity. According to the type of soil, corn, sorghum (though recently introduced, the crop that occupies the largest area), and peanuts are planted; all these have a certain resistance to drought. Plants that require great investment and involve enormous risks, like rain-fed tomatoes and onions, have also been introduced lately; in addition to their vulnerability to natural phenomena, they enter an obviously speculative market and must take their chances there.

Irrigated lands are scarce in this zone. Thin streams of water taken from the Amatzinac arrive at Jantetelco, Amayuca, Jonacatepec, Chalcatzingo, and Tenango. These meager volumes enable a small part of the land to be cultivated as semi-irrigated, and under exceptional conditions as totally irrigated, thus palliating some of the risks of dry farming. On these lands the hacienda used to plant cane, which has now vanished. Atotonilco's own spring enables it to establish a small irrigated

* The last rains of the season, occurring near the saint's feast day.

area; this also happens in Tetelilla and Tepalcingo, which receive water from the canal drawn off the Huautla River many kilometers from the area. Rice, tomatoes, onions, chiles, and even bananas, intensive crops that with water offer high returns, are planted on these lands. Other villages, like Amacuitlapilco, Telixtac, Atlacahualoyan, and Quebrantadero, do not have irrigation water available. Under the sonorous title of Benito Juárez Plan, retention dams are being built at various points of the region in order to irrigate small areas. Further south, in Atlacahualoyan and Quebrantadero, the Ministry of Hydraulic Resources is constructing an irrigation system with water from deep wells with the aim of expanding commercial crops.

The hot country is the largest and most populated zone, although it has a lower population density. The villages are separated from one another by great stretches of farmlands. They are compact villages with small houselots on which almost nothing is grown, although they contain some fruit trees, and pigs and chickens are kept in them. Axochiapan, at the southern extreme of the area, is the largest village, indeed a small, active commercial city. However, almost all its activity is directed toward commerce with people from the sierra and from the state of Puebla; thus it does not exercise much influence on either the hot country or the Morelos *oriente*. Jonacatepec, the judicial seat, and Tepalcingo, the largest villages, serve more as small-scale administrative and commercial centers. Tepalcingo is the site of the celebration of the fair on the third Friday in Lent, the most important in Morelos and perhaps one of the principal ones in the country. Axochiapan, Tepalcingo, and Jonacatepec are municipal seats, so that the other villages are attached to them.

The hot country is well connected by highways. In the north, the federal highway that links Cuautla with Izúcar de Matamoros, in the state of Puebla, crosses it from east to west. At the crossroads at Amayuca this road joins one that comes from the north, crossing the temperate zone, and another that runs through Jonacatepec, Atotonilco, Tepalcingo, and Quebrantadero, reaches Axochiapan, and goes on to Atencingo after crossing the hot country from north to south. Another road, not asphalted, also crosses the zone in the same direction: it branches off from the Cuautla-Matamoros highway and links Tenango, San Ignacio, Atlacahualoyan, and Axochiapan. Roads that turn off these highways link the other villages of the hot country. An interoceanic railway branch that unites Cuautla with the city of Puebla also crosses this zone.

The most important remains of what was the great estate of Tenango and Santa Clara are in the hot country. They have had varied fates: The elaborately reconstructed settlement at Santa Clara de Montefalco houses

Opus Dei, which has established a retreat for its rich members and schools for the local population there. Tenango, partially restored, is still the property of the descendants of the owners of the hacienda, who use it as a vacation home. San Ignacio, rather carelessly rebuilt, is also a recreation home, but it may possibly be converted into a hotel with a strong, indeed very strong, colonial flavor. The little estate of Atotonilco, or San Nicolás, is in ruins, and a prodigious fig tree has taken root in its buildings. Other ranches of the hot country are also in ruins. Times have certainly changed.

The Area and Its Neighbors. The area defined and christened as the Morelos *oriente* is a rural, agricultural zone. Almost all its people live by cultivating the countryside, whether the land is their own or someone else's. Corn is the only constant crop from the lowest zone up to the last terrace won from the slopes of Popocatépetl. Almost no resource outside agriculture is present in the area. According to what the villagers say, some iron deposits were exploited in Tlacotepec and Alpanoca during the colonial era, and the Galván ironworks, the first in New Spain, was on the *cerro* of Cacalote (Diez, 1 : xlvii). None of these lasted. The only nearby silver mine, exploited from the sixteenth century up to our time, is at Huautla; no other sufficiently attractive vein has appeared in the vicinity.

The forests of the north, brutally exploited for hundreds of years, have lost their most valuable timber species. Memory of this exploitation and the consequences it had for the people have hindered the entry of sizable new forestry enterprises. The only industry of the area, with the exception of the three temperate-country rum distilleries, is found in Axochiapan: eleven lime factories make use of nearby deposits.

The area is not, then, the site of industrial centers or of cities of provincial importance that extend their influence beyond its limits; moreover, it is not the seat of any administrative center or any important market, with the exception of the Tepalcingo fair, which lasts less than a month. On the contrary, its people and institutions have to leave in order to supply themselves with goods, services, and even guidelines. Markets for the products of local agriculture are also sought outside the area. Because of that, it pays a tribute for its dependence and establishes a set of asymmetrical relations with neighboring areas and zones as well as with other areas that exercise a definitive pressure on the Morelos *oriente* without strictly being neighbors.

To the northeast, the area is linked first with Tetela del Volcán and from there with Ocuituco and Yecapixtla. By other roads, one reaches Jumiltepec, Ecatzingo, and San Juan Tepecoculco, all in the state of Mexico. These villages form a rural, peasant environment that in many ways can be considered an extension of the area. But at the same time, it is through this zone that various areas of Morelos connect with the Valley of Mexico through a relatively low mountain pass, Amecameca, at an altitude of about twenty-five hundred meters.

The Valley of Mexico, at an altitude of 2,240 meters, is the site of the greatest human concentration in the country and has been for almost a millenium. It is also the seat of the national State, the political authority, which is based in Mexico City. It is also the largest industrial center, and one of every five Mexicans lives in its metropolitan area; consequently, it is the greatest nucleus of production, of consumption, and of exchange in the nation. Between the village of Jonacatepec, the center of the Morelos *oriente,* and Mexico City, it is scarcely ninety kilometers on a straight line, and about one hundred twenty following the principal roads.

The difference between the average altitudes of the Morelos *oriente* and the Valley of Mexico makes possible a differentiation in agricultural production, even as the distance makes exchange desirable. This combination encourages the establishment of many crops in the *oriente* expressly for supplying the metropolis. A great deal, indeed almost all, of the luck of the local cultivator is tied to the capricious behavior of the gigantic urban market, La Merced, which is controlled by a few immensely powerful monopolists, *acaparadores.* Another bit of luck depends on federal-government decisions regarding credit and the prices of basic products. Some luck also depends on the rainy season, plagues, and hail. Many other decisions that will affect the life of the area's inhabitants emanate from Mexico City. Innumerable products that the peasant buys come from the city—things that are made there or that pass through it as a distribution center, as well as many services that cannot be obtained in the area or in neighboring regions. The interaction between the Morelos *oriente* and the Valley of Mexico is one of the phenomena that characterize the area.

Along the west, toward the south-central section, the area is adjacent to the valley of Las Amilpas, which is formed around the Cuautla and Chinameca rivers. This valley shelters an organization parallel to that of the Morelos *oriente.* The environment and activity of the two areas fail to complement one another because of a lack of diversification. However, the valley of Las Amilpas, with more water available for irrigation, is more densely and more heavily populated. This difference permitted the rise of a center for services, the city of Cuautla, which has created its own dynamic of growth by harnessing village resources to the point of becoming a provincial center whose attractions draw people from the rural villages of the Morelos *oriente.*

In Cuautla, a rustic-looking business center that is in fact quite diversified and efficient has grown up; it encompasses both a large weekly market and a good daily market, where it is possible to buy the week's provisions, pottery, clothing, and even furniture at prices lower than in the area. Around the market and in conjunction with it, more or less specialized stores have been established—hat shops, pharmacies, hardware stores in which farming equipment can be acquired, as well as stores for fertilizers, insecticides, and seed. These types of products are attractive to the inhabitant of the *oriente* not only because of their price but also because he cannot acquire them locally. Moreover, services have appeared—from inns and saloons to doctors' offices, banks, and specialized workshops, as well as public services and offices, hospitals, an agency of the Ejidal Bank, and even church confirmations. From the point of view of the area, Cuautla is the regional center *par excellence,* the one most frequently visited. It is also the first step on the way to Cuernavaca, the capital of the Free and Sovereign State of Morelos.

Although Cuernavaca is a complex city, to the point of having a pretentious plan for industrial development, it does not serve directly as a supplier for the area, since it is effectively almost as far away as Mexico City. Its presence is felt in politics, the sphere in which it represents an unavoidable stage for the formalization of life in the *oriente.*

Toward the northeast the area comes near the state of Puebla. The high villages, compared with those of the temperate country, show an obvious difference from them since they have no access to irrigation. To complement their dry farming, the Puebla villages have developed an active specialization in pottery, and their products are widely distributed. Since all the roads that link the pottery villages connect with those of the area, the village supplies depend in good part on the weekly market at Zacualpan. By going through the pottery villages, the inhabitants of the cold and temperate zones of the Morelos *oriente* used to get to Atlixco, an important regional center in the state of Puebla, which is almost as far away as Cuautla but better supplied. The highway system broke this link, and to get to Atlixco today it is necessary to travel almost a hundred kilometers.

To the east the area borders at its center and south with the fertile valley of Atencingo and Izúcar de Matamoros, in the state of Puebla. This valley also shows a structure parallel with the Morelos *oriente,* but here a combination of factors preserved the large sugar-cane enterprise (see Ronfelt). Izúcar de Matamoros is an important regional market that occasionally becomes an alternative to Cuautla, but exchange is slowed down by the political barrier between the two states, which is translated into assessments and local and state taxes that affect the movement of commodities. To some extent this has favored the growth of Axochiapan as a secondary commercial center.

Toward the southwest rises the Sierra de Huautla, and toward the south, the Sierra Madre del Sur, which form severe obstacles for communication and exchange. Rough paths scarcely pierce them, although the new railway that will cross to the state of Guerrero keeps trying to break down the isolation. Yet, almost-hidden trails abound, trails used when the few ranchers of the sierra dedicated to raising live-stock—and, incidentally, to illicit "gathering" activities like cattle-rustling—come down to stock up. Some rather occasional communica-tion with the state of Guerrero was established through the sierra but now moves along the modern highways that go around it. But the importance of the sierra should not be discounted merely because of the little use made of it or because of the scarcity of traffic. It is and has been a refuge, a territorial reserve that serves only those who know it. Even today, when it is said of someone that he has fled to the sierra, it seems like a definitive, irreversible act.

The Remote Past

The First Owners of the Land. The Morelos *oriente* retains numerous traces of ancient human occupancy. Many of the villagers' chats turn to treasures uncovered: the imaginary pots full of gold coins and the actual little pre-Hispanic masks or figurines that crop up in turning over the soil or that are scratched out of overgrown mounds. In Chalcatzingo, deprived of natural resources in modern times, harvesting the past has overcome important crises more than once: the people there inherited an archeological deposit. The area's most important ancient grouping rises on their lands, and digging up and selling of pre-Hispanic figurines were significant factors in the economy. Even today, the ruins having been controlled by national institutions, the villagers find work and even entertainment in the archeological excavations.

The main street of Zacualpan is bordered by stone fences that at one point begin to grow and grow until they exceed five meters in height. In that spot the street cuts through a big pre-Hispanic mound, so large that its owner plants corn on its extensive surface. Associated with the mound is a group of ancient terraces that descend toward the river and are planted with fruit trees in full production. Between Tenango and San Ignacio stands a set of weed-covered pyramids that serve as a land-mark for a good place to hunt pigeons. In the mountains of the cold country, ruins that suggest fortresses appear. On the Cacalote *cerro* a group of tumble-down terraces hides a sizable number of bas-reliefs carved as profusely and carefully as those that have brought fame to Chalcatzingo. To get to them, it is necessary to cross other mounds.

Many such mounds stand on the eastern face of the Tenango *cerros.* Another important ancient grouping, Las Pilas, at the Jonacatepec Spring, has been restored to serve as an attraction for the resort being built there.

Very little is known about all these ruins. We have no idea about the first human occupancy of the territory. The most ancient ruins dated belong to a complex, developed farming culture, the one at Chalcatzingo, which flourished in the mid-formative period, between fifteen hundred and six hundred years before our era (Sanders and Price, p. 15). It has been considered an extension of Olmec culture or a regional culture with Olmec influence (Sanders and Price, p. 119).

Beginning with the flourishing of Chalcatzingo, two factors appear critical in the development of the area: the presence of an irrigated agriculture and a high level of interaction between the area and the high valleys of Mexico and of Puebla-Tlaxcala, which formed, in William Sanders's terminology, the symbiotic central region of Mexico. These factors have retained their strategic importance up to our own times—almost thirty-five hundred years later.

Occupation of the area seems uninterrupted from the formative period, when Chalcatzingo and the Cacalote *cerro* groups arise, until the arrival of the Spanish *conquistadores* in the sixteenth century. By then, the area and the neighboring zones of what is today the state of Morelos were subjugated by the Aztecs. As tribute, they used to demand a good part of the produce of the low, hot valleys that could not be obtained in high valleys like that of Mexico, where the metropolis of the Aztec empire was established.

In the area, the principal product for tribute was cotton, which was cultivated in the irrigated sections of the hot country, called *Tlalnahua,* or "the land within," and of the temperate country. This product was also exchanged with other villages of the highlands that were supposed to pay tribute in the form of blankets but did not produce cotton. The hot country also offered *guajes,* or vessels made of dried gourds, and honey, both gathered products. In the Tlalnahua, corn, tomatoes, and chile were also raised, the last two with irrigation, for local supply and perhaps for exchange. Besides cotton, the temperate zone produced corn; chile; *huauhtli,* or amaranth; and a great variety of fruits in the irrigated orchards. In the cold country, the maguey for pulque appeared, and forest products were exploited (*Libro de Tasaciones,* p. 46; and Títulos, 4 : 19 [*see* Bibliographical Note]).

The pre-Hispanic ruins and the earliest colonial documents suggest that agriculture was carried out on terraces on the mountain slopes or in closed orchards protected by walls on the level lands, in small niches retrieved from the aridity or from the slope by human effort. These sources also suggest the existence of a widespread, complex system (or several systems) of irrigation that extended throughout the area. This combination, based on very intensive, organized use of human labor, not only permitted but demanded a high concentration of population. With those characteristics, the Morelos *oriente* represented attractive booty for the conquerors.

The Black Legend. The Aztec empire collapsed in the first quarter of the sixteenth century and was replaced by Spanish colonial subjugation. In the Morelos *oriente* there was no military conquest; its incorporation was accomplished in indirect fashion when the Spaniards mastered the centers the area was attached to: first Yecapixtla and Tlayacapan, and then Tenochtitlan, the capital of the Aztec empire.

The first effect of the conquest was brutally destructive. Epidemics, hunger, and uprooting by slavery and forced labor shaped a panorama in which the overriding phenomenon was death. It is not too daring to estimate that during the first fifty years after the conquest at least half the native population disappeared. In Chalco, a city quite near the area and one to which it was attached sometime during the pre-Hispanic epoch, nearly half the population died in scarcely a year in consequence of an epidemic between 1563 and 1564 (Gibson, p. 461). The demographic decline would last yet another century, ultimately signifying a total loss perhaps nearing 90 percent of the pre-Hispanic inhabitants.

We have no specific information about the area, but to give an idea of the general demographic movement, we can use data from the Cuernavaca jurisdiction of the Marquesado del Valle, the marquisate of the Valley of Mexico, which included the Tlalnahua. The accounts are unlikely and have been much debated, since the data are fragmentary, of questionable reliability, and almost always expressed in numbers of tributaries that produced income or work for the benefit of the census takers. The following data are drawn from Bernardo García (pp. 166–67), who multiplies the number of tributaries by four in order to obtain the total population. Around 1560, perhaps already past the worst moment of demograhic decline, some twenty thousand tributaries, or eighty thousand inhabitants, were recorded for the entire jurisdiction. In 1571 a count by López de Velasco, which is considered trustworthy, indicated that there were 24,750 subjects, or 99,000 inhabitants. Fifty years afterward they had been reduced to 8,084 tributaries, or 32,336 inhabitants; in 1636, sixteen years later, 5,395 tributaries, or 21,580 inhabitants, were left.

This means that in sixty years the indigenous population was reduced by more than three quarters. Barrett (p. 10) confirms this general process of decline from the conquest until the middle of the sixteenth century, so that in 1681 the Marquesado del Valle had scarcely one third the tributaries of a century earlier. During the last part of the seventeenth century the process reversed itself, and generalized demographic growth began. Only in 1800 did the total population of the state of Morelos reach the figures of the indigenous population of 1571, and it took perhaps until 1950 to reach a demographic load similar to that of the pre-Hispanic era.

In the Morelos *oriente* the demographic catastrophe was harshly felt. Historical documentation presents in abundance the testimonies in which the Indians, referring to the lands, say, "that they are unploughed for many years in this region, and the elders have been heard to say that from the time of the great *cocoliztli* ["pestilence"], more than forty years ago, they have remained idle because of the death of the natives to whom they belonged" (Títulos, 3 : 11). This evidence, given in 1617, seems to refer to the great epidemic that affected the indigenous population between 1576 and 1581 (Gibson, p. 461).

In the area, the demographic decline started the deterioration of the native agricultural system. This system was, apparently, intensive and hydraulic and thus involved enormous amounts of human labor, with almost no machinery, to obtain very high yields for each area unit culti-vated. The physical disappearance of the labor force opened the way to introduction of European-style extensive-farming systems, in which with the aid of draft animals a relatively skimpy work force could cover a large farming area and there was a greater yield per unit of work invested. The slope and orchard agriculture was moved to the plains, where the soils were "so weak and thin that they cannot be planted except every third year, so that, having rested, they might bear fruit again" (Títulos, 5 : 3). With the fallow period, the index of land necessary to make European agriculture viable for the grower rose.

Along with the extensive system, European seeds and crops were introduced, in some cases replacing native crops. Just this seems to have happened with cotton, the most important crop for exchange in Indian agriculture. In 1550, in Zacualpan, four *fanegas** of wheat were sown, since on its quite well-irrigated lands "all the fruits of Castile and of the earth give forth; in this village is the great orchard of Solís," and in Huazulco, three *fanegas* of wheat "in the midst of a great deal of cotton" (*Libro de Tasaciones*, p. 55). In 1618 a Spaniard in the hot country demanded that he be given water to irrigate a wheat field that was about to be lost (Títulos, 4 : 1); the Indians from Chalcatzingo tried in vain to protect "the water with which we irrigate our plots of chile and cotton"

* Each a unit equaling, as a measure of volume, 90.814 liters; as a measure of land, 3.566 hectares.

(Títulos, 4 : 19). This is the last recorded mention of raising cotton, which was initially displaced by wheat.

Along with wheat, other European crops were introduced. In 1617 pomegranates were planted in Solís's irrigated orchards, and one of the enterprising friars at Zacualpan, perhaps motivated by nostalgia and certainly in hope of a good business, had a field of anise among some Indian cornfields (Títulos, 3 : 3). All these products were commercial, destined for a market in the hope of turning a profit; with this goal, Spanish agriculture, entrepreneurial and capitalist, was setting itself further apart from the indigenous peasant agriculture, based on self-sufficiency. The pursuit of profit augured the most important agricultural phenomenon in the area: the appearance and expansion of sugar cane, introduced in Zacualpan and Tlacotepec between 1580 and 1590 (Sandoval, p. 48). Cane slowly replaced the fields of wheat, a grain that was considered a primary necessity and had regulated prices, so that it was subject to requisitions that severely limited the profit margin in raising it (Chevalier, pp. 62–63).

The New Owners of the Land. With the conquest, the land acquired a new owner: the Spanish crown. Unable to exercise direct domain over the conquered territories, it conceded its rights to individuals eager for wealth. Before 1550 the entire Morelos *oriente* had been distributed: Tetela and Hueyapan, the cold country, were bestowed in *encomienda*, in trust, on María Estrada, a daring Spanish woman who fought distinguishedly in the battles of Yecapixtla and La Noche Triste. Once settled, she got married for the second time, to Alonso Martín Partidor, who succeeded her as trustee and was perhaps the first Spaniard accused of being a *latifundista* (Chevalier, p. 112; Diez, 1 : lxx). Tlacotepec, Zacualpan, Temoac, and Huazulco, the temperate country, were given in trust to Francisco de Solís (Diez, 1 : cxx; *Libro de Tasaciones,* p. 53). The fourteen villages of the Tlalnahua, the hot country (which were surely more than fourteen and about which no two lists agree), remained within the Marquesado del Valle, which Carlos V bestowed on Hernán Cortés in 1529 (Barrett, p. 109; García, p. 158).

In the first two cases, the concession did not grant ownership of the land, but only the right to collect the tributes of vassalage, whether in kind, money, or work, and to retain a commission (Chevalier; Zavala; Simpson). Almost invariably the trustee, or *encomendero,* received as personal property by royal grant an area of land, where he could use the Indian labor in some productive activity for his own benefit. In the area a gift was made to Lady Juana de Carcamo of four *caballerías** within

---

* Each a unit of land equaling 42.795 hectares.

the village limits of Temoac "beyond those that she has there" (Títulos, 2 : 25). By then the destruction of the indigenous culture was already so severe that "some little hills which seem hand-made" served as boundaries for the land (Títulos, 3 : 62). Grants on crown lands were also bestowed on individuals who were not *encomenderos:* on Pedro de Neira, Esteban Ferrofino, and Pedro Ledesma in the Temoac limits (Títulos, 3 : 25–27). It is quite probable that the beneficiaries of royal grants were straw men for the *encomenderos* or for other property holders who wanted to increase their patrimony. Pedro Ledesma sold his land almost immediately to Miguel de Solís (Títulos, 2 : 70), heir of the *encomienda* of Lady Juana de Carcamo and apparently her husband.

Not only land was granted, for the water was given away with the same generosity. In order to complete the task of evangelization, the Augustinian fathers were established in the Morelos *oriente,* with monasteries at Zacualpan, Jantetelco, and Jonacatepec and vicarial or visited churches in other villages. In the interest of a greater guarantee for the permanence of their work, they managed to acquire lands and water for their establishments. By 1618 they were already in litigation with other Spaniards for this reason (Títulos, 4).

In the Marquesado the situation was less clear, and the many legal suits and countersuits succeeded in confusing it still more. The royal patent of 1529 gave the marquis domain over meadows, grasslands, mountains, and waters without limitation. In 1533 another royal decree specified that the territory of the communities could not be considered as property of the Marquesado but took no stance whatever on the uncultivated lands (García, p. 95). The Marquesado authorities appropriated them for their own benefit, granted them to others, and, above all, gave out lands in perpetual leases for the payment of a rent.

Between 1613 and 1623 alone they granted more than two hundred perpetual leases (García, p. 97). Thus, two *caballerías* of land and a cattle-ranch site within the limits of Chalcatzingo and Jonacatepec were delivered to Pedro de Aragón in 1617 (Títulos, 1). In 1618 the marquis authorized Aragón to plant sugar cane on one of the *caballerías* (Títulos, 1 : 12). In the same year, Aragón fought with the Indians and the Augustinians over the right to use the water, alleging that the watering rights had belonged to those lands from time immemorial. The deputy justice of the peace of the Marquesado government "came looking at the irrigation ditch . . . through which came a very great amount of water to irrigate a very large quantity of land . . . and ordered that he might enjoy use of it one natural day every week for the watering of his lands" (Títulos, 4 : 9–11). From this almost modest beginning would arise the hacienda of Santa Clara de Montefalco.

The original gifts of lands and waters grew almost uninterruptedly during the entire colonial epoch by means of the petition of *composición*. The royal finances, always on the verge of bankruptcy, favored this procedure, thanks to which it was possible by means of paying a sum of money to legalize in fact situations in which the boundaries and prerogatives of the original endowment had already been exceeded. These little arrangements were widely used. Even the Jesuit owners of the Chicomucelo and Cuauhtepec haciendas, in the temperate country, where they were already planting cane in 1619 (Sandoval, p. 129), had to pay thirty-five hundred pesos in 1643 for the *composición* of ten *surcos* of water* and seven hundred pesos for the adjustment on the land, even though they had alleged that their titles were extremely ancient (Chevalier, p. 215)—ignoring that the Company, having arrived in Mexico in 1572, had not yet completed a century of existence in the country (Chevalier, p. 188). All the owners of mills in what is today Morelos settled with the king by paying *composiciones* of between eight hundred and more than four thousand pesos (Chevalier, pp. 215–16). There must have been a great deal to settle.

In 1679 Domingo Arrigorrieta, possessor of the land given in perpetual lease to Aragón, paid the king for authorization to found a press for making sugar and *panocha* ("brown sugar"), despite the fact that cane had been planted on that land for almost sixty years and that the press had functioned all that time, since Aragón had received authorization for it from the marquis in 1618. Arrigorrieta's property was called Santa Clara Huexotla and had six slaves (Títulos, 10 : 1).

In cases of conflict the injunction was also used as a mechanism for land appropriation. In 1736 Pedro de Segura, new owner of Santa Clara, won an injunction that sanctioned the plunder of lands from the communities in a suit that the Indians had initiated.

Transformed into commodities and capital, the land and water were traded vigorously. The owners of Santa Clara changed frequently until the appearance at the end of the eighteenth century of Nicolás de Icazbalceta, who founded the empire of Santa Clara Montefalco and Santa Ana Tenango (Títulos, 1 : 27). The royal grant, *composición*, sale, and transfer were the mechanisms that favored the accumulation of land.

In the area, from the sixteenth century on, the conquerors exercised domain over the territory. The three types of dominance over the peasants noted by Eric Wolf (1971, pp. 70–78) were established simultaneously: the patrimonial type in the Marquesado, which "implies the right to collect tributes from the inhabitants of the place in exchange for letting them live and work there. This dominance became the inheritance

---

* A volume equaling 198.826 liters of irrigation water per minute.

of a lineage of men, their patrimony"; the prebendal, with *encomiendas* that "do not belong to select stock or lineage; rather, they represent guarantees of income—benefices—in return for the freedom of performing a certain kind of work . . . it is a payment that is made to the state, to the sovereign, on the part of the peasant"; and the mercantile, through grants and *composiciones,* "in which the land is considered the private property of the landholder, a material unit suitable for being bought and sold . . . and has a price like other commodities. Moreover, the land, beginning from the moment at which it is acquired, can be employed to produce other commodities for sale." The three forms of domination coexisted, and to a certain extent they supported one another. The Spanish crown, under whose protection the forms of subjugation were established, expected from its colonies the formation of capital that could be used in the mother country for, among other things, subsidizing the deficit in its balance of trade. Attentive to this interest, the crown put an end to the *encomienda,* withdrew the prebend, severely limited hereditary patrimony, and favored and urged on the mercantile mode, which was more efficient for converting the exploitation of the land and the natives into capital.

The Old Owners of the Land Refuse to Die. One of the formal steps necessary in order for the Spaniards to be able to exercise acquired ownership was taking physical possession of the land without any objection. The Indians were always there to object, to defend their old rights, although it did them little good. In doing so, they exercised a prerogative authorized by the Indian legislation that vaguely declared respect for the territorial patrimony of the indigenous peoples. The Spanish monarchs, troubled by the total disappearance of the native population in the first American colonies and publicly pressured by vigorous voices that denounced the genocide before the court of the mother country itself, produced protectionist legislation that included the recognition of indigenous ownership on its original terms. Often in contradiction with specific laws and applied in an environment in which the original population and its agriculture were deteriorating even as the new entrepreneurs' avidity for land grew, this principle never had much practical application; nevertheless, it created a precedent that the Indians would never forget.

The viceregal authorities, often caught between the sword of the entrepreneurs and the wall of the crown, felt it was necessary to fix clear boundaries for the Indian lands. In 1567 the marquis of Falces, viceroy of New Spain, created the village *fundo legal,* or common land, a square measuring one thousand *varas** on each side, with the village

* Or .838 meter.

church at its center; he prohibited making royal grants to Spaniards within a certain distance of its boundaries. In 1687 a royal order modified the *fundo legal* and granted the communities six hundred *varas* from the last house in the village in all four directions. The threat to Spanish ownership that this order implied obliged the crown to decree, scarcely eight years later, that the six hundred *varas* were to be measured from the village church (Florescano, pp. 57–58); this left barely some one hundred hectares for the communities' territory. Sometimes royal patents conceded lands to the natives. This occurred in Tepalcingo, where Felipe III made a grant of a cattle-ranch site and eleven and a half *caballerías* of land, that is, around 2,250 hectares, in 1609.

But all these measures did not hinder the plunder of the lands from the indigenous communities, although perhaps they checked its pace and gave the Indians the opportunity to fight back legally, to begin an extended agrarian struggle on the basis of legal titles that proclaimed them original owners of the land. The history of the struggle is the history of plunder. The royal ordinances are "obeyed but not acted on" by local functionaries, in obvious complicity with the landholders. The titles of the estate of Santa Clara serve as evidence. From 1617 the Indians of Temoac objected to the grant given to Gabriel Sánchez de Segura because they "had no uncultivated land." The grant conceded him more than 850 hectares (Títulos, 3 : 22).

In 1618 the Indians of Jantetelco complained about Pedro de Aragón because of the plunder of water "that is ours, and we possess it quietly and peacefully from the days of our grandfathers and ancestors, water with which we irrigate our seedbeds and vegetables with which we sustain ourselves . . . and we pay many tributes and personal services . . . every day said water is less due to the establishment or ongoing establishment every day of many wheat fields that are irrigated with the water that comes from the canal . . . which we opened with our sweat and which we clean various times every year because it is closed by the floods from the *barranca*. . . ." As previously mentioned, Aragón was given an injunction and a whole day's irrigation (Títulos, 4 : 14).

In 1699 the Indians of Chalcatzingo sought an injunction against Antonio de Arrigorrieta because "almost two years ago, the above-mentioned planted a strip of cane on said lands. . . . [Arrigorrieta] returned and said that they were just dogs and other reasons, for which I notified him of a fine of two hundred pesos, so that he would contain himself without abusing said Indians" (Títulos, 18*b* : 4). Just a little later on, Arrigorrieta, a native of Vizcaya, lost control, since "in that place the Indians had no hamlet, and it was a great disgrace that they should have claimed such a thing and that they could not bring, as they had brought, colored flags or trumpets, that they were just drunkards, to which some answered in the Castilian language that he should not abuse them, because it has been a custom among the natives when they took possession to bring flag and trumpet" (18*b* : 5). Not only was he not fined for contempt but the authorities also "were ordering and ordered that said Antonio de Arrigorrieta be protected in the possession of all the lands that he had planted and the spring" (18*b* : 11).

The usual story was repeated in 1736 when the Indians of Chalcatzingo requested an injunction because "the servants of Don Pedro Segura had kept them from planting a piece of land, as well as driven away their livestock and imprisoned the Indian mayor, Miguel Felipe, in the Jonacatepec jail for having come out to defend said land" (Títulos, 40 : 92). The lawsuit was long, since pressure on the land had increased. One witness said "that he also knew the little hawthorn woods and today it has already been prepared for sowing . . . in the same way he knew the road that went from the village of Jantetelco to that of Jonacatepec, because part of the lands had been readied for planting" (40 : 1). A careful measurement was carried out on the basis of which it was concluded that in accord with the dimensions of one thousand *varas* square for the *fundo legal,* "neither the village and seat of Jonacatepec nor that of Jantetelco lacks any of the lands that they ought to enjoy, because the ones they possess are plenteous, and Amayuca has more than eight *caballerías* left over in all four directions . . . and the village of Chalcatzingo has an excess of more than six *caballerías,* and these have thin and rocky soil, and even so, many of them are tilled . . . and the ones that it enjoys as a village and some others are of good soil; and, moreover, they enjoy a dale that the two mountains of Los Halcones form" (40 : 58) —thus reaching the conclusion that these excess lands ought to be surrendered to the sugar press at Santa Clara. The Indians appealed, claiming that "the measurer says that Amayuca will have eight *caballerías* and Chalcatzingo six, without considering that they are mountainous, rocky, gullied, and unfruitful, and with the measurement, the lands they were planting, using them because they are fruitful, were taken from them, so that today some of the lands are useless . . . [although], as is public knowledge, they paid tribute and have paid greater amounts in tribute than Segura" (40 : 59, 60). Somewhat superfluously, the authorities upheld the owner of Santa Clara, since the proof submitted by him "is superior and more relevant than that which said natives gave . . . for that man's consists of thirteen witnesses, all Spaniards and above reproach, without legal blemish . . . [against] eight witnesses, all Indians" (40 : 1).

The villages that were relying on a royal grant were also plundered. Tepalcingo lost more than 550 hectares at the hands of the Tenango hacienda. The procedure is not clear, but tradition says that the image of Christ of Tepalcingo was not content with the chapel that housed it.

By that time it was already famous and honored with a great fair, celebrated since 1681, on the third Friday of Lent. The priest proposed construction of a worthy shrine, begun in 1758 and finished in 1782. This was a large, costly project, and in order to finance it, in part, they applied to the hacienda of Tenango, surrendering in return the use of some lands, which quickly came to be the estate's absolute property.

Toward the end of the eighteenth century the villages had already been circumscribed more or less strictly to their *fundos legales*, just when they had to support a population in the process of recovery. In contrast, the grants bestowed on the Spaniards, eight times greater than the *fundos legales* to begin with, had grown regularly and systematically and had been concentrated in fewer hands. In all the cases, the limitation in area was accompanied by the partial or total plunder of the villages' water; in others, like Chalcatzingo and Amayuca, by expropriation of the best lands: those with deepest soil, the most level plots, and the areas nearest the irrigation system. Obtaining a harvest sufficient to satsify even the low levels of Indian subsistence became an impossibility in land so exiguous that in many cases it could only be used with prolonged fallow periods because of the poor quality of the soil. The land did not cease to be farmed, but its production was inadequate. In order to make up the deficit, the Indians had to sell their other resource, their labor.

This resource had been systematically extracted from the community from the very beginning of the colony through personal services for the benefit of the trustee or through the *repartimiento,* or distribution of lands, which obliged a percentage of the males to work for the Spanish entrepreneurs, a practice that continued at least through the course of the seventeenth century. The demographic crisis and the forced extraction of labor made work the critical, scarce resource in the community. This may explain the abandonment of intensive agriculture and the adoption of the extensive systems by the natives for their own crops for self-sufficiency, especially for the cornfield. Draft animals and the fallow period became advantageous, since they permitted increasing the yield per unit of work invested. When demographic pressure on the severely circumscribed holdings of the communities increased in the eighteenth century, it almost always proved impossible to increase the intensity of cultivation, because of the poor quality of the soil and the lack of water for irrigation. This encouraged the formation of a labor supply, since the native had to obtain a monetary income to complement his productive insufficiency as an autonomous *campesino.* This "voluntary" supply made the obligatory labor distribution less indispensable, and eventually it disappeared.

The Indian pressure on the land created not only a labor supply but also a demand for territory. In contrast, the Spanish entrepreneur had land in excess. Sharecropping increased, which meant a double benefit for the entrepreneur: an income from his idle land and the permanent settling, on his own land, of labor who also owed him gratitude and obedience. The areas handed over for sharecropping were adapted to the extensive system of cultivation and were fixed at one *yunta* of sown land. This area did not produce sufficiently for sustenance of the Indian sharecroppers, who had to work for the hacienda under the conditions that it established.

Despite everything, the Indians knew that the land belonged to them because of history, because of their rights, and also because of their labor, which, whether in their own community or on the hacienda, was what made the land produce.

Sugar and Capitalism. Sugar cane is an exotic plant. Columbus first brought it and planted it in the Antilles. From there, Cortés took it to plant in Mexico, in the region of the Tuxtlas of Veracruz, where it was grown from 1528 on. Antonio Serrano de Cardona was responsible for the second Mexican plantation, in Axomulco, very near Cuernavaca, around 1530. A few kilometers away, Cortés founded the Tlaltenango mill, the third in New Spain, on his own "estate," which quickly absorbed the one at Axomulco (Barrett, p. 11; Chevalier, p. 64).

From then on, the cultivation of cane and sugar production spread rapidly through the territory of the colony, but they were concentrated particularly in what is today the state of Morelos. The reasons for this rapid expansion were economic. The Spaniards had come to enrich themselves, and therefore they sought remunerative businesses. In agriculture, the best was sugar, which was considered a luxury item and had a high price per unit of weight. This permitted its export, and during the sixteenth century it was consigned to Seville and even to Peru. But above all it had a strong internal market composed of the Spaniards and perhaps even the Indians. At the end of the sixteenth century, the priest Acosta said, "It is a crazy thing, the way sugar is consumed" (Chevalier, p. 63). Between 1540 and 1560 the price of sugar doubled, and it continued to increase until 1590 (Barrett, p. 19). Growers who could do so replaced their wheat crop with cane. In order to offset this tendency, in 1599 the authorities suppressed the services of Indian forced labor in the mills, with the aim of reserving it for raising wheat and for other activities that were considered more important (Chevalier, p. 65). It seems clear that in the sixteenth century the most effective way to reproduce capital in agriculture was to plant cane and to make sugar.

The reasons for which sugar production was concentrated in the Morelos territory were numerous: the hot climate, which in Mexico is generally determined by altitude, and the presence of permanent streams that permitted irrigation. In many cases, complex hydraulic works had been built by the Indians before the conquest, and it was only a matter of expropriating and adapting them. The abundance of labor was the result of the high concentration of the indigenous population, due to those very irrigation works. Nearness to the largest major market, Mexico City, which was also the best center of distribution, gave the Morelos planters an additional advantage under conditions in which the transportation cost was extremely high.

At the beginning of the seventeenth century there were some twelve to fifteen hydraulically powered mills or animal-drawn presses in Morelos. The mill founded by Cortés was the largest (Barrett, p. 4). At least eight presses using water from the Amatzinac River were located in the *oriente:* the ones at Tlacotepec and Zacualpan, founded between 1580 and 1590 (Sandoval, p. 48); those of the Jesuits at Chicomucelo and Cuauhtepec, knowledge of which dates from 1619 (Sandoval, pp. 108, 114); Santa Clara, founded by Pedro Sáenz de la Rosa, about which we have information from 1650 (Sandoval, p. 98); San Carlos Borromeo in Jonacatepec, which had fourteen *caballerías* of land and six *surcos* of water in 1729 (Sandoval, p. 128); and from 1695 the San Nicolás Atotonilco sugar press of Don Bartolomé de Esquioz (Títulos, 15 : 22). The press at Zacualpan became perhaps the first hydraulic mill in the zone in 1619, when it was conceded a grant for that purpose (Sandoval, pp. 127–28). It is not known whether it was finally authorized to make use of the water that it wanted to draw off very near water outlets belonging to the Jesuits, to the hacienda of Carmona and Tamariz, and to the villages of Temoac and Huazulco—all of which opposed it (Sandoval, p. 144).

The luck of these enterprises was varied, and only two would survive until the nineteenth century, Santa Clara and Tenango, which belonged to the same owner. The sugar business was always large-scale and tough. It does not do to plant cane if the equipment for transforming its juice into sugar and molasses is not nearby, since approximately only a tenth of its weight is preserved as the final product; the cost of transportation between the field and the mill is still one of the critical factors for success today. The cane plantation is and was an agro-industrial complex implying high investments. According to Chevalier, establishment of a mill required around fifty thousand pesos in the sixteenth century (p. 65). The presses, more modest, also demanded high sums, and their operation was more costly. The totals of these investments were not amounts commonly found among the capitalists of New Spain in that century.

The stability of sugar prices during the greater part of the seventeenth century, along with the prohibition against the Indians' obligatory service in factory tasks, encouraged increased investment in slaves of African origin. Management and administration as well as financial capacity and entrepreneurial aspects became critical in the face of a harshly competitive market. Not all the owners held up, and the transfer of property through resale became characteristic of the industry. Despite the risk, the cultivation of cane continued to be the most profitable agricultural activity, and around 1680 the capital invested in sugar exceeded that for raising wheat (Chevalier, p. 68).

From then on, production began to be concentrated in a few large, efficient productive units. This trend was demonstrated in the area in 1732 when the Jesuits, considered the most efficient producers and the model cane-plantation administrators, demolished Chicomucelo and cut production at Cuauhtepec in half (Sandoval, p. 110), while spending ninety thousand pesos in another zone to buy a mill in which they would invest again as much to enlarge its capacity (Chevalier, pp. 67, 68).

Chevalier placed the average value of the mills in the mid-eighteenth century at around eighty thousand pesos. The Santa Clara hacienda fits these estimates. In his will written in 1695, Antonio de Arrigorrieta appears proud of "his principal dwellings, new, of stone and mortar . . . and his church and new chapel of said materials, with an arched roof and with his new altarpiece at the main altar, . . . and his building for presses, for cauldrons and stoves, copper utensils, livestock and implements, and twenty-three slaves of different ages . . . as well as a livestock ranch called Tlayca with bovine and equine livestock" (Títulos, 12 : 4). When the estate was liquidated in 1708, the body of the hacienda was valued at 55,140 pesos, even though the resplendent arched roof appeared cracked from side to side (Títulos, 22). Some years after the distribution of the inheritance and after unfortunate administration by the heirs, the sugar press was sold with an inventory value of 18,500 pesos (Títulos, 25 : 1). It was obviously a ruin that was going to be rebuilt soon.

Toward the end of the colonial period the tendency toward concentration in gigantic enterprises was made more evident as a natural result of the capitalist dynamic that clearly characterized the cane plantations and industries of New Spain. Consistent with this process, and despite the individual troubles of certain enterprises, the area planted in cane grew constantly until it became the dominant element of the Morelos *oriente* landscape.

The Structure of the Hacienda. From the time of the colonial era on, producing sugar for the market and earning money from it presupposed having many elements and combining them efficiently. The territory of the haciendas was made up of a group of units that had different purposes but whose areas were in a proportional relation.

The territorial heart of the hacienda was formed by the lands devoted to cultivation of sugar cane; these had to bring together a set of characteristics like those afforded by the area's hot country. But on these lands another of the obligatory requirements for development of cane, a plant that has a growth cycle of more than twelve months and a high demand for moisture, was scarce: water for irrigation. This originated and was abundant in the cold and temperate countries, where the climate and soil were hardly favorable for the growth of cane. For that reason, the first sugar plantations arose in the temperate country and on the border of the hot country. The landholders moved the plantations toward the south but held on to the northern property that gave them access to water, which was brought by trenches, pipes, and aqueducts to the plantation, embedded in the hot country. Later the haciendas extended their property further north in order to capture the sources or the most voluminous streams and to be able to expand the areas under cultivation for cane located several kilometers to the south. Control of water was one of the principal motivations for territorial expansion.

Water was not only indispensable for irrigation but also permitted control over the occasional frosts, fertilization of the soil with the sludge, and prevention of plagues and blights, factors that explain why irrigation was used even in the rainy season, when moisture was abundant (Barrett, p. 44). Water was also the source of power that moved the mill presses, which were much more economical and had greater capacity than those moved by beasts in the old sugar presses. The area controlled by irrigation works would need to be at least two times greater than the area harvested annually, in order to permit the recuperation of the soil by leaving it fallow (Barrett, p. 45). It is quite possible that in the area the cost of these works would have been similar to that recorded by Barrett for Cortés's mill at Tlaltenango, where the aqueducts represent a third of the total value of the enterprise (p. 42). But in the *oriente* that capital had been contributed by the Indians through the pre-Hispanic works and the maintenance in the colonial period, and the systems were kept almost intact on the haciendas. The powerful sugar enterprise appropriated what would have meant the most burdensome investment and implied technical problems that could be solved only with great difficulty—without any cost to itself at all.

Besides farmlands for cane, the estate needed and had great areas of land devoted to livestock. This livestock included various species, particularly oxen or mules, indispensable for sugar production. These beasts performed three types of tasks: transport of the cane to the mill or press, plowing and cultivation work, and traction to drive the presses in the plant. Apparently, animals trained to carry out one of these jobs were no good for any other. A mill like Tlaltenango had around 600 animals at the end of the seventeenth century (Barrett, pp. 66, 131–32), and one as modest as Santa Clara had 142 (Títulos, 15).

Often the grasslands and pastures for the animals that worked in cultivating cane were used for other species like cattle and sheep, destined for feeding the slaves and permanent resident workers. These lands did not require irrigation, although they did indeed imply some slight territorial investments, especially the handsome, even excessive fences, built of readily available stones and nearly two meters high and more than a half-meter thick, that still cross the fields. They served to separate the pastures and to keep in the livestock. In the colonial era these lands represent the largest area within the haciendas.

Corn was the principal element in the diet of the personnel attached to the hacienda. Some owners tried to raise it on their own to supply their slaves and domestic servants, devoting another area of land to this purpose. The brutal increase in the price of corn, which quadrupled between 1540 and 1620, determined the owners' elimination of the rations. However, the slaves and permanent workers were allowed to grow it themselves on hacienda lands during the entire colonial epoch (Barrett, pp. 19, 95). Sharecropping began—rental of the hacienda's land to its permanent laborers so that they themselves might cover the principal expense of their subsistence without any cost to the enterprise.

Sharecropping was already practiced in the area in 1617, when Solís stopped planting cornfields for the Indians on his lands, and it soon revealed its true potential for the landowners: by appropriating the land and giving it out for sharecropping, it was possible to tie down seasonal labor. Through sharecropping, the area for dry farming of corn on the haciendas began to grow rapidly.

Lastly, some haciendas sought their own territory for a supply of wood for heating the cauldrons in which the cane sap was boiled. The mill at Tlaltenango consumed between 10,000 and 20,000 loads of wood, of 250 pounds each (between 1,250 and 2,500 tons), a year for more than three centuries (Barrett, p. 72). In the area, the forests were concentrated in the north, in the cold country, and the estate properties were extended that way, killing two birds with one stone: obtaining both wood and control over the sources of the streams of water.

Thus, the complex territory of the sugar-cane haciendas, with all its resources, was acquired without any cost. By installing a capitalist enterprise that produced for the market, the Spaniards converted these indigenous goods into capital redeemable for money.

The technique of raising sugar cane was not very complex. The equipment was simple and underwent almost no modifications until the end of the nineteenth century. Very early on, when the native population was numerous, and animals scarce, the mattock was used to prepare and break the soil for planting. After this short stage, the equipment was reduced to the *criollo,* or Creole, plow, drawn by animals, and the *coa,* or "hoe," which the Indians carried to work for watering, cleaning, and weeding cultivated areas (Barrett, p. 44). The *criollo* cane, quite juicy and offering a good yield of sugar, never degenerated, nor was it replaced. The task that required the most attention was watering, making sure that the water flowed slowly and constantly. Fertilizers were not used, and if so, they simply added the sludge from the canals and the clay from the purgers; fertility was maintained with the fallow period (Barrett, p. 45).

Cane is a noble, safe crop that, with irrigation, can be planted—or cut—at almost any moment. Under the Morelos conditions, this plant had no natural calendar, and the estate owner could establish it freely. However, by analyzing Barrett's data (p. 46) it is possible to conclude that the calendar for cultivating cane was adapted to that of the subsistence crops of the Indians, on whose work the hacienda depended. Thus, in the eighteenth century, the cane planting was done in the months of October and November, when the corn had already been given the last weeding, the *despacho;* it was suspended in December when the corn harvest, or *pizca,* was done and begun again in January and February. It permitted the sugar-making season, which also depended on the work of the Indian villagers, to coincide with the dry months, from January to May, in which there was no dry-farming activity.

Once cut, the cane was brought to the plant on carts drawn by oxen. Here the technical operations were complex and specialized: first, presses squeezed the juice out of the cane; afterwards, in the cauldron house, the juice was put to boil until molasses was obtained, a more complex, delicate operation; finally, in the purging house, the molasses was put in molds to harden and to be refined in a complicated and highly specialized process. The sugar was moved by mules and oxcarts to the city, the principal center for its distribution and consumption.

Although the technology did not undergo important modifications during the entire colonial era, specialization and some refinements permitted increases in yields from the fields and increments in the production of the sugar extracted in such a way that between the sixteenth and nineteenth centuries, sugar production increased 50 percent per surface unit planted, even as production per unit of work invested quadrupled over the same period (Barrett, p. 104).

These schematic figures confirm a clear tendency (apparent in many other accounts) to maximize the yield of the scarcest and most critical resource for the sugar plantations: labor. The proportion of labor in the cost decreased from 75 percent between 1591 and 1600, to 70 percent in

1622–24, 67 percent in 1768–95, and 62 percent in 1811–31. Even so, it was always the most expensive item. Because of the character of the operations, the hacienda needed two types of labor: one for the mill, with more or less permanent employment and of a specialized nature; the other for the field, clearly seasonal and of an unspecialized character in an agrarian society. A 1529 viceregal command that prohibited employment of Indian village-tribute laborers in mill jobs made the division between the two types of jobs more clear-cut, for, as if by exception, the command seems to have been rigorously enforced in order to protect other activities to which the crown gave more importance, like mining and raising cereal crops (Barrett, pp. 74–92).

Mill workers were classified by race and by method of recruitment. On the large plantations, three groups can be identified. The first was made up of the Spaniards, who performed administrative duties like that of overseer; very specialized technical functions like those of sugar master, dispenser, and purger; and also took charge of overseeing and directing field work as cane masters, plowmen, and cane guards. The second group was composed of the black slaves who worked in the mill and at the cauldrons; in some cases, they attained such mastery of the task they performed as purgers and even as sugar masters that they brought very high prices. Finally, there were the *naboríos*, salaried Indians who lived on the estate and performed specialized duties outside the factory as carpenters, blacksmiths, and potters or in the fields as irrigators and who not uncommonly had been recruited because of debts. Slavery, begun in 1542 with Cortés's major importation of Africans for work on his plantations, was important as a method of recruitment of labor in the sixteenth and seventeenth centuries, when the Indian population reached its lowest levels. As this population recovered and the *mestizo* group grew, a supply of "free" labor arose, which made slavery more onerous and redundant. The work that the slaves had done before was taken over in the eighteenth century by the *naboríos*, who, to be sure, ceased to be called that and were renamed *criollos* (Barrett, pp. 78–92). The change of name reflected a clear ascent of the permanent employees over the *comuneros*, the Indian villagers.

On the more modest haciendas, like Santa Clara at the turn of the seventeenth century, the division was not so sharp. The only Spaniard was the owner, who busied himself in all the tasks. The sugar master was a slave valued at four hundred pesos. There were twenty-two more slaves and apparently not many *naboríos*. The slaves, valued at eight thousand pesos, represent almost one third of the worth of the hacienda, although it must be considered that neither the land nor the irrigation works was appraised, for they were not the property of the landholder but were taken on perpetual lease from the Marquesado del Valle. Even so, and taking into account that the entire factory was appraised at scarcely three thousand pesos, this proportion gives a clear idea of the great value that permanent labor attained.

The field work, especially clearing, weeding, and cutting of cane and, later, the irrigation, was performed by Indian villagers. The law of 1599 that declared that work in the cane fields would not be obligatory but voluntary was not complied with as rigorously as the prohibition against the natives' working in the mills, and the landowners were able to enter contracts for labor supply with the governors and heads of Indian villages. For this purpose, the large estates created a specialized post that a Spaniard assumed, the *recogedor de indios,* or "collector of Indians," entrusted with negotiating and enforcing compliance with the terms worked out.

For the simple Indian villager, the contribution of services to the haciendas continued as before 1599: forced labor for which he often received no remuneration, since it was paid directly to the governors. At the beginning of the eighteenth century this system deteriorated, and the estates had to negotiate with captains of squads of free laborers who were paid personally (Barrett, pp. 86–92). Despite these forms of recruitment, the most constant complaint of the owners and colonial administrators involved the irregularity and scarcity of field workers. This is explained in various ways, from physical lack of a work force in the communities because of the demographic decline in the face of hacienda expansion in the sixteenth and seventeenth centuries to the very nature of the peasant economy in the eighteenth century, when the labor supply was more abundant but only worked to meet its subsistence level and having attained this, suspended its activity (see Chayanov).

The irregularity and scarcity of the supply of indigenous labor was perhaps the most important motivation for the last and definitive territorial expansion of the Morelos *oriente* haciendas, which expropriated enormous areas that they could not and did not intend to work. With this, they met many goals, all aimed at guaranteeing a regular, sure supply of labor for cultivating sugar cane. First, they squeezed the *comuneros* into a territory incapable of producing sufficiently for the subsistence of its possessors, who worked it with extensive systems and had no possibility of replacing them with intensive ones. The compression required the villagers to make up their subsistence with the sale of their labor power for the benefit of the hacienda. Those who did not obtain space on the communal lands had to take hacienda lands for sharecropping or emigrate without a clear destination. Tying down the sharecroppers fundamentally sought to ensure the supply of seasonal labor. As part of payment for renting the land, the Indian was required to work for the hacienda without payment one or two weeks a year; more important than the free labor was the fact that the landholder could establish the calendar for its delivery. Sharecropping secured a work force that inevitably depressed the cost of salaries. As if this were not enough, the estate obtained an income in the form of corn and fodder as another part of the payment for the rental of land that it could not work and that was not in its interests to work directly.

The colonial sugar-cane hacienda was undoubtedly an attractive business. Its success was not derived from its internal characteristics nor from its technology, but from the appropriation of the native resources: the land and the irrigation works, acquired at no cost; and the permanent use of the Indian labor, the principal capital expense of the operation, for which it paid an amount much lower than the villagers needed for subsistence. The hacienda's rationale derived from its capacity to monetarize, to convert local, nonmercantile resources into capital. This was possible because of its introduction into a colonial system founded on the political and military power of the Spanish state.

II   PEACE, ORDER, AND PROGRESS

Progress

Lands With a Single Owner. In 1897 the engineer Manuel Pastor was given the responsibility of mapping the haciendas of Santa Clara de Montefalco and Santa Ana Tenango, which were located in the district of Jonacatepec and belonged to Luis García Pimentel, a powerful but rather eccentric entrepreneur. Those who knew him when he was already old recall that he did not talk much and that wrapped in a *sarape* "like a bullfighter," he liked to pass the time walking around and whistling. He was the owner of the largest landholding in the state of Morelos: 68,181 hectares—almost 68,182, by the meticulous cartography of the engineer Pastor—an area virtually identical with the geographical expanse of the entire Morelos *oriente*.

The borders of the estate and the physical region coincided fairly strictly, with the exception of some points: on the north the boundaries of the hacienda stopped at the contour line at two thousand meters, a little below the village of Hueyapan, while the area itself extends to the peak of Popocatépetl. The plantation made up for this loss by spreading further to the east, where it projected into the state of Puebla, and toward the southwest, where it reached the ridge of the Tetillas, deep in the Sierra de Huautla. The area that the estate lost in this comparison with the region was the high forest of pines and firs that was to be appropriated by another large enterprise, the San Rafael paper factory; the land it gained was pasture and rough, jagged mountains. Even so, all the level and irrigated lands of the region, with the exception of the miniscule pieces belonging to the villages, lay under the domain of the hacienda. It had reached its maximum size, which would remain unchanged for some fifteen years.

The hacienda lands totally surrounded twelve villages—Tlacotepec, Zacualpan, Temoac, Huazulco, Amayuca, Jantetelco, Amacuitlapilco, Chalcatzingo, Jonacatepec, Atotonilco, Tetelilla, and Telixtac—as well as two old settlements, Amilcingo and Popotlán, which were not recognized as villages. One ranch, or small property, the one at Amotzongo and Copalillo, also remained totally encircled. Three other

42

villages, Atlacahualoyan, Axochiapan, and Tepalcingo, all located toward the south of the area, had boundaries with the hacienda on three of their four sides, and the last one had the bad luck to have its fourth side adjacent to the Tenextepango hacienda, the property of Porfirio Díaz's son-in-law. Three new population centers had sprung up around the sugar works: the *reales,* or "compounds," of Tenango and Santa Clara, each with more than five hundred inhabitants, and San Ignacio, which was much smaller. The populations of the first two, comprising permanent estate workers and their families, were larger than those of some villages, like Atotonilco, Amacuitlapilco, or Chalcatzingo.

Almost the entire territory of five municipalities lay within the limits of the García Pimentel property: Zacualpan, Jantetelco, Jonacatepec, Tepalcingo, and Axochiapan. Since these formed a judicial and political district, with its seat at Jonacatepec, the hacienda coincided, not just accidentally, with a politico-administrative unit that included more than one tenth of the area and one fifth of the municipalities of the state of Morelos.

The maximum length of the hacienda was more than fifty kilometers, an expanse of land that gave the owner possession of two rocky peaks more than eighteen hundred meters high (and, as an added luxury, full of archeological relics), as well as four churches and many roads that came together at the *reales* of Tenango and Santa Clara. Here, in the hot country and near the center part of the estate, were the administrative headquarters of the enterprise. Some of these roads continued toward Puebla, Cuautla, and Yecapixtla, where the railroad from Mexico City to Cuautla crossed. A complex web of paths linked the area with neighboring villages and penetrated deep into the sierras that surrounded the region.

The estate bordered upon other, similar establishments, like Tenextepango and Coahuixtla on the west, Matlala and Atencingo on the east. The boundaries were scarcely indicated by the few markers, since at that time these borders were the result of gentlemen's agreements. The boundaries with small properties were posted more emphatically, and the boundary markers multiplied along the village limits. Obviously García Pimentel had no need to fear any intrusion on the part of these little towns; however, the villages seemed to have certain reservations concerning the opposite possibility.

The Morelos *oriente* had, then, a single owner. No one knows precisely the details of just how this ownership came to be so concentrated, given an area as extensive and as varied in its forms of possession during the colonial era as the one that became the haciendas of Santa Clara and Tenango at the end of the nineteenth century. Lands formerly property of the Church, like the haciendas of Cuauhtepec and Chicomucelo, which belonged to the Jesuits, had been added to the estates; other lands had once been part of the Marquesado del Valle, bestowed in perpetual leases like the original plantations of Santa Clara and Tenango. The properties of individuals, derived from royal grants and agreements, obviously lands that had once belonged to the villages, were also added in. This concentration resulted from the measures taken by liberal governments to market the real estate of secular and religious corporations for private acquisition. This is far from implying that this immense property would have been purchased in an open market and without resort to expropriation by violence, even though the land titles sought to hide these procedures behind complicated legal formulas. As the tiresome repetition of family names among the landowners from the era of independence on suggests, inheritance also contributed to the concentration through endogamous marriages and through establishment of undivided estates, the thinly disguised, true primogeniture of mercantile societies. The hacienda, whatever its solid roots in the colonial era, is above all a typical product of liberal capitalism. The estate of Tenango and Santa Clara was a very good example of it.

The Land and Its Products. Pastor's 1897 map shows us the territory of the estate divided according to six grades of soil and by uses of the land. The greatest area was devoted to dry farming and covered 28,870 hectares, 42 percent of the total. This land was not worked directly by the hacienda but was given out to the villagers for sharecropping for the planting of corn according to criteria that established that at least half the land would remain fallow. Even with only one third of the land tilled, the estate received in rents some 13,750 *cargas* of corn, a little more than 2,000 tons, with a value at that time of nearly 70,000 pesos. This corn was sold in Mexico City and easily represented the plantation's largest source of income after sugar cane, but with the difference that it represented almost no expense. Indeed, the greatest investment had been made with the colonial domination of the territory and the subjugation of its inhabitants.

Grassland occupied second place in area, with 20,653 hectares, 30 percent of the total expanse. The pastures of the area are poor and not very attractive to the introduction of specialized livestock raising; for this reason, the hacienda directly administered only some small ranches for breeding, like San Nicolás Atotonilco and Ixtlilco el Chico. With the exception of some fine horses, the plantation did not maintain livestock other than work animals, which were fed with the fodder paid in rent by the sharecroppers and with some by-products of cane, like the tips of the stalks; the limited grazing was done in the fallow cornfields near the compounds. A part of the pastures was rented out to the small livestock-breeders from the villages, an arrangement that produced a good income for the hacienda, and it is probable that another great portion of these lands remained unused.

The estate did not directly exploit its mountain lands either, but these 13,830 hectares, which covered about one fifth the total area, provided some income through payment of duties for use made by the villagers. As these fees were high, the mountains represented the space least used out of the whole area. The forest-covered land, scarcely 2,549 hectares, which represented less than 4 percent of the total, was rented as a concession to some rich villagers from Tlacotepec who were obligated to sell the estate their products, especially wood for fuel, at prices somewhat lower than those usually paid.

These four types of land occupied a bit more than 96 percent of the total surface area of this great property in 1897, and except for a minimal portion, they were not worked by hacienda employees. The hacienda did cultivate the remaining 3.4 percent of the territory directly. It was almost all devoted to raising sugar cane, which covered 2,238 hectares, or 3.3 percent. Two mills, at Tenango and Santa Clara, were chosen for making sugar. Atotonilco, Cuauhtepec, Jantetelco, San Ignacio, and the other sugar mills and presses absorbed by the hacienda were dismantled in the interest of economies of scale, and their buildings were given over to other uses, like storing corn. The lands irrigated for cultivating sugar cane were concentrated around these mills: 833 hectares at Santa Clara and 1,405 at Tenango.

Apparently, each plantation constituted not only a unit for growing, milling, and refining cane but also a relatively autonomous administrative unit that exercised control over dry-farming and grassland areas and to which some ranches and subsidiary establishments were attached. Both plantations had similar facilities on their grounds, including even a house and garden for the owners within the walled enclosure of the compound, in spite of the fact that they were only ten kilometers apart.

Of the total land devoted to sugar cane, only one third produced a crop for milling in a single annual cycle, as was the usual practice on Morelos haciendas. Another, equal part of the land was planted for harvest in the next cycle; and the other remained fallow. Given this method, production must have run between 1,850 and 2,250 tons of sugar, figured on a conservative yield of 2,500 to 3,000 kilos of sugar per hectare (Barrett, p. 119). This volume would have represented a gross income of around 200,000 pesos from the sales of sugar and by-products —a more than respectable sum at that time if one recalls that the Free and Sovereign State of Morelos had an annual budget of around 350,000 pesos (Magaña, 1 : 74).

A fifty-eight-hectare coffee plantation on the Cuauhtepec estate was the last remnant of the earlier stage in which greater diversification had been sought around the ever-predominant cultivation of sugar cane. In Cuauhtepec wheat had been raised with irrigation, and the landowners had installed an hydraulic mill in the compound to process this grain. When the water that irrigated the wheat was transferred to the cane fields, the Cuauhtepec hacienda and its settlement, then treated like dry-farming lands, were rented to an individual who was primarily concerned with livestock and buying wheat from the peasants. In 1905, upon the death of the tenant, Epitasio Mora, the hacienda named an administrator and dismantled the mill. San Diego, a part of the property that had also been a wheat farm, was sold to a private party as dry-farming land for corn when the water was diverted to lands readied for cane. Some ranches on which the hacienda had raised dairy cattle were handed over to tenant farmers. Despite the great ecological variety of the territory held by the planters, their exploitation of the land had only one purpose: to plant more cane, to produce more sugar, to earn more money.

The Conditions of Liberal Progress. Various conditions favored the increasing specialization and the expansion of the cultivation of sugar cane in the state of Morelos. At the turn of the nineteenth century the country was experiencing a period of unrestrained economic growth, and Porfirian progress encouraged capital investments, rewarding them with fantastic rates of earning.

The laws of disamortization were the prelude to the growth and modernization of the sugar industry. Under their protection, the hacienda consolidated its position as the dominant economic and social institution in the Mexican countryside and in the state of Morelos. These businesses turned into the sole "legitimate, progressive institutions. It seemed that other kinds of communities existed as resources for them, that all human beings in Morelos must surrender their personal destinies, superior or inferior, and become mere factors in the planters' cosmopolitan enterprise" (Womack, p. 44).

More than half the total territory in Morelos had passed into the hands of the Porfirian haciendas, while small property, including the urban house lots of the villages and cities, had use of less than one fifth of the surface area. The remaining quarter, consisting of communally held mountain land, could only be developed with federal concessions, which were always granted to the large paper-making firms. The haciendas' properties encompassed almost all the arable land and all the irrigated areas. Nevertheless, only 10 percent of these lands, around thirty thousand hectares, were devoted to growing sugar cane, and only ten thousand hectares produced each year (Diez, 1 : ccxxii). The phenomenon observed in Santa Clara and Tenango followed the general pattern in the state: 90 percent of estate lands were not cultivated by the owners, who were, however, still able to dominate the population by virtue of controlling the land.

The indisputable, protected ownership of the haciendas and the capital accumulated by means of expropriation made investment in expanding landholdings and in modernization of the refining process not merely possible but attractive and profitable. Making investment even more appealing, new industrial technology offered possibilities for using machinery to increase the yield of each unit of work invested and thereby to increase the entrepreneur's profits as well. The dubious splendor of the machine was introduced in 1880, when García Icazbalceta, owner of Tenango and Santa Clara, installed on the latter estate the first centrifuge machine to replace the old purge system for draining off molasses; the yield of sugar from a ton of cane almost doubled. From that point on, mechanization fever set in: Imported were cranes and scales, *decauville* systems—mule-drawn railway flatcars—for transport, centrifuges, mills, and boilers which enabled them to replace hydraulic power with steam. Proud of their progressivism, many planters boasted of investing more than half a million dollars at a time on importing machinery that was obviously not produced in the country.

Realizing the advantages offered by these mechanical innovations implied a larger scale of operations, which was translated into a need to increase the volume of cane that kept them going. The great haciendas were consolidated to form huge agro-industrial systems around the modern mills. Many of the thirty-four plantations and all of the smaller presses stopped milling in order to supply the twenty-four modern installations, which belonged to only seventeen owners by 1910. The estates of Tenango and Santa Clara were the largest land unit, at least three times bigger than the next largest, the Amor hacienda, with twenty thousand hectares. However, the García Pimentel plantation occupied only third place in terms of production volume, and the Amor property barely made tenth place (Womack, pp. 385–86; Magaña, 1 : 39; and Diez, 1 : xlix, l, li). Although the size of the property was an influential factor, the capital invested was the best index of the power of the enterprise.

Another technological innovation assisted modernization: the introduction of railroads, which afforded cheap and rapid access to centers of distribution and of consumption of sugar while simultaneously favoring further imports of machinery. The entry of the railroad into Morelos was spectacular although rather unfortunate. In 1881 the Mexico-Cuautla stretch of the interoceanic railroad was opened with a brilliant ceremony presided over by the president, General Porfirio Díaz, in the company of the very cream of hacienda society. The great landowners had an additional reason for celebrating: not only was the train coming to them but they themselves were the owners of the corporation that built the railway. Among the major stockholders were Mendoza Cortina, owner of Coahuixtla: García Icazbalceta, of Tenango and Santa Clara; Goríbar and Delfín Sánchez, the latter the son-in-law of Benito Juárez—all notable sugar producers who were simply diversifying their capital investments. All these illustrious names were not enough to prevent the escort train from falling into a gorge on the first return trip when a poorly constructed bridge collapsed, leaving a total of 149 dead and 112 critically injured among the private citizens and military personnel (Sotelo Inclán, p. 394). The price in blood exacted for progress was paid bravely, especially because it was the blood of unknown men, and in 1894 the railroad from Mexico to Cuernavaca was inaugurated (Diez, 1 : lii). In 1902, the branch that linked Cuautla with Puebla opened.

The railroad also implied the increase in the economic scale of the haciendas by requiring increases in the tonnage transported in order to keep its rates low; this demand was satisfied with real pleasure, since the market for sugar remained favorable for a period of almost twenty years, enabling the landowner's gross income to increase more than 100 percent per ton of cane cut. The increase in prices was the consequence of various factors, from increases in the international demand as a result of the gold fever in California to the greater urban concentration produced by economic growth. Although the Mexican economy as a whole was oriented more and more to the external market—in which raw materials were sold and everything else was bought, in a new form of colonial status—Morelos sugar was always destined for internal consumption and above all for Mexico City. The rise of new sugar zones in the western part of the country and on the Veracruz coast sometimes put that market in danger, but the landowners defended it vigorously with tactics like dumping, which obliged the newcomers to run the enormous risks of an international market speculative in nature. On the other hand, in order to avoid competition from foreign sugar, the plantation owners obtained from the government a protectionist tariff on imported sugar that was translated into a substantial increase in the domestic price (Womack, p. 48).

The double gamble of capitalist progress made growth and specialization not only attractive but imperative, a condition of survival. Faithful to its dictates, the landowners expanded: between 1880 and 1900 they doubled their sugar production, and they quadrupled it between 1880 and 1910 (Diez, 1 : clxxxvi), thanks to the technological innovations and to the socioeconomic conditions of the country during the Porfiriato. The spirit and the letter of disamortization and of liberal reform were realized, but the capitalist utopia of wealth that is reproduced only until the enterprising individuals are satiated and then spills over to the rest of society was still very far from being realized.

The Aquatic Limits to Growth. All the haciendas ran into more or less severe limits to their growth. For some it was land, for others capital. On the estate of the García Pimentel family the most serious obstacle was the inaccessibility of water. At the end of the nineteenth century every trickle in the area was channeled toward the cane fields, and no other irrigated crop remained within the boundaries of the property. Moreover, all the water of the Amatzinac villages, which had had irrigation since pre-Hispanic times, was expropriated for irrigating cane. Villages like Huazulco, Temoac, and Popotlán, which had been able to grow irrigated wheat until 1885, were totally deprived of water. In the area, it seems, a concession was made only to the village of Zacualpan: it was allowed water to irrigate its orchards from dawn Saturday until dawn Sunday. This weekly allotment was scarcely half the water that the village received daily before the plundering.

At the cost of the aridity of the entire region, the hacienda was able to create its two plantations. Santa Clara was irrigated by water from the Amatzinac by means of the Tenango irrigation ditch, or *apantle,* and by the streams from the Los Arcos Gorge by means of the San Pedro Mártir aqueducts. The Tenango plantation received the water from the Amatzinac *barranca,* which was christened the Tenango River at that point in order not to leave any doubts about ownership, and from the Atotonilco Spring through the Atotonilco and Telixtac *apantles,* constructed in 1885; furthermore, the deep *apantle* that carried water from Atotonilco to Tepalcingo was blocked up. Those thirty-seven kilometers of aqueducts, complemented by seven basins or dams, served only to transport the water from its sources to the headquarters of the plantations, from which *apantles* many more kilometers in length distributed it through the *suertes* or *tareas* of cane.* This impressive hydraulic network, which must have been worth a great deal but cost almost nothing, since it was basically an adaptation of the pre-Hispanic system, served to cover a total of only some twenty-two hundred hectares dedicated to cultivating sugar cane in its three phases: production, planting, and fallow.

In the first decade of the twentieth century, in order to respond to the attractive and irresistible demand for growth, the hacienda overcame the water problem, bringing it from the Aguahedionda Spring, quite near the city of Cuautla, through a system fifty-eight kilometers long

* Each equaling about 2,500 square meters.

that crossed through the dried-out lands of ten villages. This entire system functioned by means of gravity through *apantles,* bridges, tunnels, and dams, with such refinements as an iron bridge constructed and mounted in England so that the water could cross the Amatzinac River. Luis García Pimentel did not idly boast of his investment of $166,000 in this project (Womack, p. 48), and perhaps in making that calculation he would not have included the thousands of days' work supplied for free by sharecroppers as part of their rent for the land. Projects of much less magnitude had cost other landowners without that benefit, or those who had it in a smaller proportion, more than $200,000 (Womack, p. 48). With this project the hacienda's system of canals to the plantations totaled one hundred kilometers. The water drawn from Aguahedionda was destined for the larger plantation, Tenango, which also permitted the growth of Santa Clara by means of more intense water drainage from the Amatzinac. The obstacle had been smashed, and water flowed in abundance toward the hacienda. But none of the plundered communities recovered so much as a single drop.

Thus the hacienda managed to reach production of 6,193 tons of sugar in 1909. Taking as a base a conservative yield of twenty-five hundred to three thousand kilos of sugar per hectare cultivated (although the second figure would be more probable given improved techniques in the refining process), between two thousand and twenty-five hundred hectares must have been in production annually (based on Barrett, p. 130), an equal number planted for the following cycle, and as many more lying fallow—that is, from six thousand to seventy-five hundred hectares dedicated to cane, three times more than a decade before, or one tenth of the total property, a ratio similar to the average of the Morelos haciendas. The estate's net income for sugar production in 1909 would have been around one million pesos, while the budget for expenditures of the state of Morelos that year was set at around half that amount (Magaña, 1 : 75, citing Diez).

Modernization and Its Price. The García Pimentel estate had to make constant, substantial investments beginning with the introduction of centrifuges in 1880 in order to succeed in tripling its total sugar production in scarcely twelve years. Thanks to the son of a specialized mason, we have an incomplete inventory of projects carried out in Tenango that illustrates well the process of modernization. In 1886 the brick chimney, the *chacuaco,* was built, which implies that the centrifuge had already been installed. In 1895 the old press was replaced by the modern mill, perhaps powered by steam. Barrett holds that steam was not introduced into Morelos for motive power before the revolution, which was surely the case in Tlaltenango, but this and other information contradicts his generalization. In 1900 an iron chimney was installed that today is probably emitting smoke across Jalisco, where the machinery was moved after the revolution and where the heirs of the estate founded a sugar mill. In 1901 they finished an alcohol distillery to produce rum, as did all the Morelos mills. This project contrasted with the moralistic tone that the pious younger Luis García Pimentel used when lamenting that liberalism had taken away the strength of the Church, which served "as the only restraint and guide . . . [for] the natural inclinations toward banditry" of the Indians, a change that had forced the poor, unfortunate landowners to impose their own, much harsher rules (cited by Womack, p. 40).

In 1902 a branch of the interoceanic railroad that linked Cuautla with Puebla arrived as far as García Station, scarcely three and one half kilometers from the Tenango *real*. With it, the estates' production would have a direct outlet, and transport by wagons to the Yecapixtla station, where machinery had entered and sugar had done out since 1881, would become obsolete. The muleteers and the people linked to transport, almost all from the temperate country, through which the road passed, experienced a harsh blow. The *decauville* system, platform cars drawn on rails by animals, also known as *trenes de mulitas*, was installed in 1905. This innovation had a double purpose: first, making transportation of the cane from the field to the mill, one of the critical aspects of the gigantic modern refinery, more rapid and economic; and second, linking the Tenango and Santa Clara *reales* with the railroad stations for shipment of the product. These tracks were functioning for that purpose until 1946, when trucks and tractors replaced them in transporting rice.

Also in 1905, a scale-crane, similar to the one that astonished a visiting foreigner in another mill, was installed to weigh the platform cars and unload them mechanically. Since perhaps the last half of the nineteenth century the Havana variety of cane had been introduced, replacing the *criollo* strain after more than three hundred years of use. This variation in the seed, the possible introduction of the plow with wheels, and some experiments with the use of guano as a fertilizer were perhaps the only technological changes in cultivating the plant and in the labors in the field, contrasting with the profound metamorphosis in sugar production. Otherwise, the Creole plow, the machete, and the *coas*, these last tools belonging to the peasants themselves, continued making the cane grow.

Besides requiring an increase in the scale of the plantation, the technological developments had another consequence of enormous importance: they displaced labor in order to replace it with mechanical power. The best proof of this effect is that between 1895 and 1910, while production increased considerably, the population of the *reales*, all composed of hacienda employees, declined in absolute terms: from 894 to 666 at

Tenango, and from 650 to 488 at Santa Clara, that is, exactly one fourth (*Censos nacionales*).

Despite the clumsy and ingenuous intentions of the younger Luis García Pimentel to encourage the transfer of the people from the villages to the *real* in order to allow improved specialization and to free the administrators from dependence on the peasants, who hated them and who were capable, the ingrates, of leaving them for a better salary (cited by Womack, p. 46), the truth is that it was not labor that was in short supply, but work. In the importing of sophisticated and frequently unnecessary machinery, about which the landowners boasted as if they had invented it, one recognizes one of the acts of these people presided over, not by complete economic rationality, but by a blind adoration of the modern and foreign, almost as symbols of prestige. From their statements it becomes obvious that the estate owners of the generation of Luis García Pimentel the younger were absolutely incapable of recognizing the mechanisms that made their wealth and its reproduction possible.

Indeed, there was such an abundance of labor that the young García Pimentel was able to introduce the cultivation of rice on the lands that were left fallow for cultivation for cane, and in 1908 he built an area for sun-drying the recently cut grain. Clifford Geertz has shown the perfect compatibility and ecological complementariness between sugar cane and flooded rice (Geertz, pp. 57–58), the first extensive in its requirements for labor, and the second intensive. In Morelos, the process was the inverse of the one Geertz analyzed in Indonesia, since rice was apparently introduced at the middle of the nineteenth century, when cane had already been grown for three centuries. Rice fills at least two functions on the hacienda: it contributes to maintaining fertility and, above all, it permits economic use of resources that are available in excess, like labor and water. The two classic deficiencies of the Morelos cane plantations, work-force and water, were beginning to be in excess from the landowners' point of view.

In order for labor to become abundant to a point of excess, it had been necessary to alienate it from natural resources like land and water, even at the risk of leaving them unused, which often occurred. With this purpose, the liberal laws were reduced to tangible facts. Physical protection of hacienda property by means of fences, solid stone walls, and barbed wire increased every day. There are still those who recall with astonishment that the hacienda built a stone fence several kilometers long around the village of Tepalcingo for no apparent reason. The *apantle* from Aguahedionda was fenced in with barbed wire along its entire length "so that the poor people wouldn't grab any water." Armed vigilance was added to this physical protection. There were guards over the water because the people from the Amatzinac diverted it by digging under the fence and the canal. The gamekeepers and woodsmen who protected the least exploited lands were the most feared. Anyone whom they discovered on the property, even if only to take a shortcut, was at least compelled to show that he had stolen nothing and to retrace his route. The people of Hueyapan always believed that the woodsmen had orders to shoot to kill, as had already happened on occasion in Ahuehuepan (Meyer, 1973b, p. 249). Progress was assured, and the landowners enjoyed it at will.

The Owners of the Estate. The owners of the hacienda had kept their domain through inheritance at least since the appearance of Nicolás de Icazbalceta, toward the end of the colonial era. He was succeeded by another Icazbalceta, who left no male descendant and gave way to the García Icazbalceta line. Perhaps some of the eccentricities that are remembered even now are due to one of the Icazbalceta family. Robalo visited the estates around 1890 and tells that "on one of the rooftops of the hacienda, there is a monolith that represents a man of normal size, seated in a grotesque position: it is said to be a portrait of the Vizcayan. This man, like Richelieu, had a decided fondness for the feline race . . . 100 cats lived with him . . . they called him a sorcerer and said he had a pact with the devil . . . for on Saturdays or paydays, he was on all four of his estates simultaneously" (cited by Sotelo Inclán, p. 398).

The people of Hueyapan still said at the beginning of this century, and with good reason, that the money earned on the hacienda did not give a good return because it was the devil's; they had less reason for believing that the landowners had taken the money out of the *cerros* by concluding a secret pact with that very demon in person. The grotesque monolith, with its arms open as if to indicate a measurement, still existed at the start of the twentieth century. They called it *el muñeco,* "the manikin," and said that two bags of gold were hidden in its base. They also used to say that it indicated to the workers that they could take away a piece of cane no bigger than its open arms. During the sugar harvest, the laborers slept in the same building where the monolith was; at times there were several hundred, occupying even the corridors. They christened it *el hotel del muñeco.*

The succeeding generations, the García Icazbalceta clan, were distinguished, not by their peculiarities, but by their serious and professional though pompous cultivation of the positive science of history as well as by the deeply reactionary character of their multiple political interventions. Don Mariano even arranged things in order to leave an image of kindness by his defense of the peasants in front of the cruel captains, actually his trusty employees. An image that Luis García Pimentel the elder took charge of blotting out with his unsociable character and his extravagances. He had the reputation of being half-crazy, and he was somewhat misanthropic, which did not prevent him from being possibly the most able of the dynasty as a capitalist enterpreneur and introducer of the modern mill. Luis the younger and his brother, Joaquín García Pimentel, who both inherited the double surname, represented the last generation of the hacienda owners. They were the *señoritos,* the spoiled young gentlemen, *los juniors,* educated and cosmopolitan, capable of adding luster to the enormous fortunes accumulated by their ancestors, fortunes so large that they continued to grow despite this generation's stupidities and squandering. They were, as Womack calls them, the perfect sportsmen, who precipitated the uprising in Morelos with their total incomprehension of what was happening on their country places, with that enormous arrogance and sense of superiority toward the peasants—who, according to Joaquín García Pimentel, had "many defects to be day laborers, being as he is, lazy, drunken, and thieving" (cited by Womack, p. 40)—and with their infinite though pious and unconscious cruelty.

That generation was capable of furnishing the houses of the *reales* with such luxury that to one ingenuous Tepozotlán journalist they recalled the palaces on the banks of the Thames (Womack, p. 50), which he hardly could have known. Luis the younger always liked bullfighting. From the time he was little he would play at bullfighting with the children of the *real;* they received him with pleasure, and he brought sweets. When bigger, he left behind his intimacies with the *realeños,* devoted himself to being respected, and fought bulls alone or with people from the family in a ring that he ordered built. He never fought bulls during the festivals, but kept his distance as a spectator among his guests. Yet, the young Luis generously rewarded those who distinguished themselves by their bravery and skill in facing the animal, like Joaquín Varela, who played the picador's role while blindfolded and made *banderillas* that let doves escape at the moment they were placed. Luis the younger was such an ardent fan that he once brought Gaona, the most famous and expensive *torero* of his time, to fight bulls with him on the Ixtlilco ranch. They killed so many cattle that Don Luis, the father, came out of his customary distraction and had them told that they should stop if they did not intend to finish off the livestock. Luis and his brother Joaquín honored some parties with their presence, but they never danced or allowed intimacies. Although their presence excited the people, they always maintained their distance. It is not known that they ever agreed to become godparents for the people of the *real.* However, they arranged for many of their actions to appear to be the result of an immense Christian charity.

The landowners did not live on the hacienda, but they spent one season of the year there—that of the sugar harvest, from January to March—and returned occasionally for some fiestas. They had a good time and practiced a healthy life in the fresh air. When the young ladies wanted to go out horseback riding, they called the stable boy to make sure that everything would be ready. He recalls that although he always accompanied them on their long cavalcades, he never saw their faces: "They always went with their hats and their very heavy veils." When the owners arrived, they were fetched at the railroad station by a special, covered flatcar—called "the awning" by the people—to shield them from the sun. The *realeños* came out to receive them joyfully, for they came loaded down with gifts—shirts, pieces of fabric, and sweets. It was almost a fiesta.

The permanent residence of the landowners was in Mexico City, where they occupied a large house in which each had his own servant, as a still-astonished *realeño* recalls. Perhaps the *señoritos* resided in Mexico City not only for the comfort, the civilization, the culture, and the formal bullfights but also because of their economic interests in other enterprises, whose nature and worth would be interesting to know.

The Realeños or the People. The real, daily management of the estate was entrusted to administrators and trusted employees, who played the role of villain that the landowners set aside and so ably declined. The chief one was the administrator, the absolute representative of the proprietors. Between 1898 and 1914 there were five administrators at Santa Clara. They did not last long in their post, apparently because they developed private interests that subtracted from their efficiency and trustworthiness. Among them were all kinds of men, from Chavarría, who was owner or renter of the rum factory while he was administrator, to Fernando Segovia, nicknamed The Radish because of his red hair, who often attacked the workers by kicking them. The last administrator, José Paredes, held the position during the revolution between 1911 and 1914. Assisting the administrator, but also submitting reports directly to the owner, were the major-domo and his lieutenant, responsible for the cultivation of cane; the purger; the sugar foremen; the chief mechanic; and the head of the warehouse, in charge of the plant and the milling process. There was every kind of man among them, too, although especially recalled are the Cuban foremen, experts in the new machinery, who took turns working twelve-hour shifts during the milling and who went so far as to strike some workers with leather clubs studded with nails that opened the flesh. The technicians were quite sought after and were fought over by the different haciendas, so that turnover among them was frequent. They all lived in houses or apartments within the closed area of the compound, and they had the privilege of being with the landowner in fiestas. In a certain sense, too, the renters, or *achichincles*, who represented the hacienda in the villages where they lived, were trusted agents of the owner or the administrators.

Outside the compound, around the principal buildings, lived the other permanent employes, in houses that were the property of the estate and that formed, properly speaking, the *real*. They were the heirs of the *criollos* and the Indians, although toward the beginning of the twentieth century they were called simply *realeños* or, more aptly, children of the hacienda. They were all workers specialized in tasks of the fields or of the mill, and they were installed in a rigid hierarchy according to their seniority and ability. Only the captains and the officials lived in the *real;* the laborers were hired by the week from among the people of the villages. Among the refinery workers were sugar-boilers, centrifuge operators, pressmen, mechanics, smiths, carpenters, and bricklayers; those who worked in the fields as permanent employees of the estate and lived in the *real* filled only positions of direction and supervision, like irrigation captain or captain in charge of unpaid labor, cane guard, and cutting captain.

The *realeños* had work paid for by the hacienda during the entire year, although salaries were paid out weekly. They had no contracts and no form of organization apart from work, but on the other hand they did enjoy some fringe benefits. The differences in positions and individual specialties implied variations in salaries, but the posts in the mill paid better than those in the field. This established another line of hierarchization, expressed through the style of dress: almost all the factory people wore trousers, while many of those from the fields still dressed in the traditional white breeches of coarse cotton.

Aside from the rigorous professional division, another line was established, determined by closeness to the owners or to the administrators. The favorites, called *dedos chiquitos,* "little fingers," were the ones who took care of the landowners, even in their whims. The *dedos chiquitos* served at the table, cared for the horses of the landowner and his administrators; there were two horse breakers who tamed horses for the young Luis and taught him how to lasso, for which they enjoyed many privileges, since playing *charro,* or fancy-dress cowboy, was the fad. Another fashion brought in eight Japanese *dedos chiquitos* to care for the gardens of Tenango and Santa Clara. Generally, the *dedos chiquitos* slept and ate in the service quarters of the compound. They relied more upon the munificence of the landowners than upon their low salaries and in that sense formed a servile, unquestioning group.

It was never easy to become a *realeño,* and it grew more difficult once modern machinery arrived. Many *realeños* at the beginning of the twentieth century had been born in the *real* and were children of specialized workers. The high mobility of the administrative positions did not operate at the level of captain or official, where one ascended slowly toward a limit that was never passed except through some fortuitous deed that won the favor of the owners or administrators. In general, the positions in the hierarchy seem stationary, the specializations rigid, and both have a strong hereditary character. Stability and solidity may be the dominant qualities of the *realeños* a little before the revolution.

The stability does not seem a consequence of the amount of the salaries, generally so low that they were on the edge of insufficiency, but one of something perhaps more important as a mechanism for tying people down: the constant income throughout the year, which almost nobody else in the zone obtained and the lack of which resulted in frequent, severe cyclical crises. To this security was added a group of fringe benefits, all the more important since salaries were low. The *realeños* had the right to a dwelling, for which they paid no rent, although without a good recommendation, it was not easy to obtain one of the stone houses built by the estate; the unlucky ones, the majority, lived in houses of *tlazol,* Mexican for "garbage," made of mud-covered cornstalks with roofs of straw, but which, in the end, kept one covered and at times were even cooler. The *realeños* enjoyed a rudimentary medical service: a doctor paid by the hacienda made a weekly visit to the sick who were not mere laborers. Moreover, if the illness coincided with their stay, the owners sent some assistance—a voucher for buying things, some pieces of coarse cotton cloth or sweets for the children, and on occasion even a get-well visit from one of the women of the owner's family. The *realeños* even died in peace: the owner paid for the coffins and the mass at Jonacatepec and, with a little luck, let the family have the house and even hired one of the sons.

When the *realeño* was needy, and he always was, he could obtain an advance on his salary for the week but apparently never for larger sums that would keep him indebted. As they did not receive land for sharecropping, and since the house plots were too little for raising a *calmil,* a field on a house lot, their supply of corn depended exclusively on the market, and they suffered from the great fluctuations in prices. When the scarcity of corn was quite severe, it was possible that the estate would give them some rations of grain, for, ultimately, it had all the corn that the sharecroppers turned over as rent. Moreoever, one could count on the gifts that the *patrón* gave during his visits. The pious landowners also cared for the spirit: in the *real* there was a school run by nuns; masses and baptisms were free; and the hacienda even paid for religious weddings so that the people, its people, would not live in sin.

Thus the *realeños* compensated for their low salaries with fringe benefits that tradition had established as secure but that appeared disguised as charity by being delivered as a voluntary act of the landowners or, even worse, as a result of a personal, humiliating petition. This type of individualized, personal relationship with the owners and their representatives was extended to all activities and served as an efficient system of control and dominance that intervened in every possible confrontation.

The landowners systematically strengthened the unilateral appearance of the asymmetrical relations with their permanent workers. Work was "given" as an act of kindness by the hacienda, upon which it imposed no obligations, even while they were created for the *realeño*. The benefits were given graciously and aided in the establishment of relations of vague loyalty that extended to all the acts of living and even reached the families. The work obligations of the *realeño* remained confused and were modified at the pleasure or whim of superiors, who took unconditional, unlimited obedience in their subordinates for granted. In order to consolidate the paternalistic character of the relationship, it was complemented by a simple, harsh system of sanctions. Physical punishment was not practiced, except in the occasional outburst of evil temper from some administrator; moreover, there was no jail or fine for *realeños*. However, when, in the judgment of a superior, one of them failed to fulfill his explicit or implicit obligations, he was summarily dismissed and his house taken away from him, his possessions moved out into the street; his replacements were available in advance. To add the final exemplary, didactic touch, other workers were required to perform the eviction under the implicit threat of a similar punishment. Apparently, the entire process occurred tranquilly and silently. There was only one recourse against the penalty: to seek pardon from the owner or to obtain the favor of one of the members of his family.

The complex hierarchical and paternalistic system to which the *realeños* were subject functioned efficiently, not only because of its own nature but also because of a set of external factors that made it possible. One was the backing that the hacienda received from the State. This was translated into legal legitimacy and the support of an armed force capable of protecting the enterprise physically and of repressing those who stood up to it. Another, perhaps the most important, was the presence of an enormous contingent of reserves of labor prepared to supplant unconditionally the permanent employees, beneficiaries, in the end, of a higher standard of living and, above all, of a high degree of security. The *realeños* still recall how at times, in critical spells, the villagers appeared asking for work in the *real;* refused, they offered to carry water, to bring a load of wood, whatever it might be: "They were pitiful, they were in such poverty." Work in the *reales* was more and more limited, and those who performed it acquired an almost aristocratic consciousness of their privileged position; they were, in the end, the children of the hacienda.

The Laborers or the Indians. The hacienda relied on the labor that each sharecropper contributed as partial payment for the rent of the land. Six days' work for each *yunta* of land, which could mean between ten thousand and twenty thousand working days a year. But this work force scarcely met a fraction of the great enterprise's labor requirements, which had, moreover, a marked seasonal character. Under these conditions, occasional laborers, contracted by the week or by the task, performed almost all the work.

The demand for labor was clustered in two periods—the dry months, from January to June, and the rainy season. The greatest employment was concentrated in the first period, for that was the harvest season, and the mill worked at full capacity. Besides the cutting and transporting of cane, the critical and most intense tasks, other work was done in the fields: preparing and sowing some of the plants that would be cut after sixteen or eighteen months, watering and caring for the cane already growing. When cultivation of rice was introduced, other tasks were added: preparation of land, *aborde* (building up irrigation ridges), planting in seedbeds. Projects like constructing buildings and canals, which the hacienda undertook so vigorously in the first decade of the twentieth century, were by their nature carried out during the dry months, as was the maintenance of the hydraulic system. The variety of these tasks was translated into an irregular rhythm in the demand for labor.

During the rainy season the demand decreased perceptibly and had an even more irregular rhythm. The mill stopped, and the work in the fields was reduced to some plantings; irrigation; cleaning and weeding; fencing to prevent the invasion of livestock and, at times, of people. But even these jobs exceeded the capacity of the permanent work force: the *realeños* performed only the direction of the field work, and the sharecroppers, dispersed and with limited obligations, could not cover these tasks either, so peons, or laborers, were taken on. With the introduction of rice, which needs great amounts of labor, hiring increased, especially in the months of October and November, when this grain was cut.

The tasks of the laborers was quite varied. In the fields they served as plowmen in soil preparation, planting, and weeding. It was not easy work. At noon the animals had to be removed from the yoke in order to rest; the laborer to whom it fell to match up two lively oxen had to count on suffering for awhile, and some gave up their noon rest in order to be able to choose a good pair of oxen. They also planted, watered, and cleaned the cane fields and acted as both wagoneers and *macheteros* (clearing brush) during transporting. With rice, the chores became more complex, and some, like building up earth ridges to channel irrigation water, went to specialized laborers. Many of these tasks were paid by the day and were watched over by a foreman; others were paid by task completed.

The jobs in sugar production were also varied. The boys were water carriers inside the mill and looked after some other chores. Their elders served as *bagaceros,* who put the cane in the sun to dry so that it could be used for fuel; as *cadeneros,* who unloaded the carts before the introduction of the crane; or in the mill, where the work was more tedious and difficult. Others sun-dried the sugar, stamped the bags, and loaded. The occasional chores were called *polillas,* and people from all over got together to sweep the compound, to carry wood, or to haul away trash. Practically all the physical effort that made the great enterprise function was contributed by the peons, the dispossessed villagers.

Getting access to work was not easy. The best route was recommendation to one of the administrators or perhaps to one of the captains. Being known for returning year after year helped considerably in obtaining it; for this reason, some even brought their children so that they would begin to be recognized and, with a bit of luck, would be taken on as water carriers. In order to get field work, it was necessary to line up at the hacienda gate starting at dawn on Monday. When the captain came out, the peons were already waiting; the first ones got work for the whole week. People came from all over the Morelos *oriente*, especially from the villages near the *reales* but also from more distant villages and even from some outside the area, particularly from the pottery villages of the state of Puebla. The majority of the laborers worked only during the dry months, but others returned in the months of September, October, and November. In the last years before the revolution some laborers managed to work for the estate during the entire year, depending on being hired by the captain week after week.

The working day began at six in the morning, just as the whistle of the *chacuaco* sounded and the captains began to call the roll; at twelve, the whistle once again, for a meal and a brief rest. Before two, work began again, continuing until eight at night. Twelve hours, the same in the *real* as in the field. Those who came from far away could not return to their villages in the same day and stayed in the *real.* Those at Tenango had the *hotel del muñeco,* ill-suited and without facilities, but those at Santa Clara did not even have that and stayed where they could. The hacienda did not give them rations or food. The laborers, especially the field workers, received tortillas from their homes. The families paid a *tlacualero* to bring them tortillas, thoroughly dried out to weigh less, every two or three days. In the *reales* there was someone who sold tortillas, always a little swig of rum, and perhaps even *mole* for a hot meal from time to time. The laborers did not receive any type of fringe benefits. The sick ones had to return to their villages, frequently without collecting for a few days of work. As for the landowners, the peons never saw them, let alone speak of some gift on their part.

The laborers depended on the captains and were related to the enterprise through them. The captains hired them and supervised them, and wages or dismissal depended on them; they were all *realeños*. Physical punishment was neither frequent nor necessary; blows, always a result of the chief's temperament, are remembered as something exceptional, not as an institutionalized corrective. Nor was it likely that a laborer without ties to the estate would let himself be struck with impunity. Once the competition for getting work was overcome, strong ties of solidarity were established among the plantation laborers for the short time in which they remained together. In the fields the work squads were almost always formed of neighbors from the same village.

The laborers' salary was set per day and was paid on Saturdays; for some jobs in the fields compensation was established by the task. In 1910, the daily salary for the laborers hovered between three and four *reales*, 37.5 and 50 *centavos*, although the last figure seems to be the most common one for adults. Working by the task, it was possible to take away up to seventy-five *centavos* or a peso daily during the harvest season, but one had to sweat hard for it. On other haciendas the salary was a little higher, but the work was not convenient because of the distance. Some remember that when they worked on building the railroad the daily wage approached one peso. But it is said that at that time one managed even with half that: a *carga* of corn cost between five and ten pesos; a pound of dried meat cost eighteen *centavos*, and a pound of meat with the bone in, twelve; an ox cost fifteen pesos; and a house lot could be obtained for less than fifty pesos.

The hacienda had no company store nor any other method of tying people down through debts. Sometimes the laborers were paid with vouchers, but these functioned like money everywhere. The peon was after money: he was a free worker in the liberal sense of the word.

Peace

Those Years. When the old peasants of the villages of the Morelos *oriente* speak of the epoch of the Porfiriato and the hacienda, they refer to it rather frequently as the "time of peace." There is no shadow of irony when they say it, and at times one even perceives a little bit of nostalgia. The *centavos* were worth something, even though they were few; fiestas abounded; and one could breathe in the tranquility. In some peasant homes the first sewing machines had made their appearance— treated with care, shown with pride, almost as a symbol of the *centavos* put aside over many years of hard, uninterrupted work. They do not speak with rancor about the landowner, a distant figure haloed by paternalism, who gave splendor to rural life; however, they recall the administrators and servile employees with scorn. They have never forgotten the injustice under which they lived, and they speak lucidly about the dispossession and exploitation to which they were subjected. They venerate Zapata, destroyer of the haciendas, but they recognize that the system had, in the last years, its guarantees, its own tradition-sanctioned norms, which in the end were respected. But that crystallization of a centuries-old dominance that was expressed through rigid institutions and forms, that very peace, was only the final stage of a long process that was coming to a close and the clearest sign of its decadence.

The Expropriation of the Villages. In Morelos the territorial plunder of the villages was already quite advanced by the time the colonial epoch concluded. Some communities were rigorously limited to their *fundo legal;* others from the viewpoint of the landowners and functionaries, still retained excess areas that were nothing but badlands and rough mountains to the peasants; a few, the luckiest, possessed some land, severely reduced by the hacienda invasions. The limited land resources of the villages at that time were already insufficient to support their populations and would be even less able to absorb constant demographic growth like that registered in the nineteenth century. But plunder of land did not diminish during that century; indeed, it was accentuated under the protection of the liberal laws.

Some villages simply disappeared. In 1876, when Díaz ascended to power to inaugurate the "era of progress," there were 118 villages and 56 *ranchos,* or unincorporated rural settlements, in Morelos. Eleven years later only 105 villages and 36 ranches remained, and in 1909, not more than 100 villages survived. Communities like Tequesquitengo, intentionally flooded by an estate owner, Acatlipa, Sayula, Ahuehuepan, and Cuachichinola disappeared from the map, covered by cane fields (Womack, p. 44). Other villages and cities declined or languished under the haciendas' territorial siege, which obliged them to expel population for lack of space. The Porfiriato participated in this process with enthusiasm; public lands were sold to the haciendas, and after 1880 new titles were bestowed in their favor or their many, obscure titles were consolidated into a single, clear one (Womack, p. 42). Nevertheless, the population kept growing in Morelos as a whole: in 1850 there had been 113,841 inhabitants; in 1895 they came to 160,115, and by 1910, to 179,594 (Diez). This increase was absorbed by the municipalities, and no spectacular urban development was registered. The disappearance or paralysis of some villages, compensated by the growth of others, was the result of the reaccommodation of the labor force according to the requirements of the omnipotent sugar industry.

In the Morelos *oriente* none of the old villages disappeared; all survived the ferocity of the expropriation and the possibly more severe effects of the modernization of the industry. Between 1895 and 1910 the population declined in only four communities and in each case less than 10 percent. In the largest one, Tepalcingo, the demographic decline was not triggered by emigration, but by a smallpox epidemic that killed 523 children in 1903 (the only one who survived was paraded through the entire village with a band of musicians). All the other settlements grew at a rate similar to the state's, and one, Axochiapan, grew more than 50 percent without the hacienda's playing a determining role in the case. In the area, the nineteenth-century territorial plunder by the hacienda was less intense than in other regions of the state—perhaps because the villages had almost nothing left to expropriate and because the obstacle to the growth of the hacienda cane fields was never a lack of land but the scarcity of water and, possibly, of labor. Even so, there was plunder, especially in the villages that had lands contiguous to the plantations. Plunder by bits: a pasture, a field lying fallow, an almost isolated lot where a boundary line could be straightened out. It was a campaign of rapine against lands dismembered beforehand.

Many stories are told about the methods of plunder, some of them almost in the realm of legend. In Tepalcingo the village pledged lands to finance construction of a grandiose church worthy of its most famous image. In Hueyapan the landowner used to give an ox each year to help celebrate adequately the feast day of its patron saint, but one day he demanded payment for his pious contributions. As there was no money, it was decided to pay him back with land. A just method was agreed upon for determining the amount: The hacienda owner and the people of Hueyapan would go out the next day to meet one another and fix the boundaries at the site of the meeting. The folk from Hueyapan, confident that the *hacendado* already had a great deal of land and that he was not going to get up at dawn for a chunk of mountain, slept tranquilly and got up late. They were mistaken: they intercepted the landowner scarcely three kilometers from the village church, and there the boundary marker was planted. In other villages the story of the animals given by the landowner for the fiestas is repeated—as in Jonacatepec, where they tell that the hide of the donated bull was made into a thong whose length in land was the payment for the festival. In all these accounts there is a common element: the intrusion of the land-owner into the ceremonial life of the village as a mechanism for creating indebtedness.

Once in the realm of exact recall, other methods appear, like corralling, through which the owner of a piece of land surrounded by the hacienda was closed into it with a stone or wire fence. In Chalcatzingo, Chucho Tadeo, as purchasing agent for the *hacendado,* corralled the land and livestock of a stubborn landholder who refused to sell and spent several days carrying jars of water to his animals so that they would not die, until he saw the light. In Zacualpan a pasture that had belonged to the village was corralled, and if some peasant's animal entered, the hacienda kidnapped it. For its ransom, the peasant had to pay two pesos, almost one tenth the value of a cow. When the peasant got the money together, he found that his animal had died of thirst or that he had to pay up to five pesos for the forced lodging of his property.

Although territorial plunder on the part of the hacienda did not attain great proportions during the nineteenth century and in fact was suspended in the last decade, the effect that it had on the villages was devastating. This impact did not derive so much from the area lost, which was certainly important, as from the resources that were associated with those small areas. Given the extent to which the communities had shrunk, each piece of remaining land was the location of one more essential and irreplaceable resource out of the many involved in the complex process of cultivation. The final plundering definitively broke the precarious balance that made it possible to have available all the resources necessary for agriculture. The villages of the Amatzinac, orchard keepers from the very beginning, lost their water in the nine-teenth century. Almost all lost their pastures, whether through dispos-session or through having to incorporate them into farming; those lands had supported not only the animals but an entire technology based on animal traction.

The system of rotation of fields, which was the method for maintaining the fertility of the soil and, in part, for sustaining the draft animals, was affected by the expropriations that obliged the peasants to eliminate the fallow period or to reduce their crop areas. The gathering zones, which supplied fruits, fuel, and even products that could be sold, were also lost. In this case the hacienda was not the only plundering enterprise. In the cold country near Chalco the San Rafael paper factory, said to belong in great part to a son of Porfirio Díaz, appropriated the rights to exploit the mountains of Hueyapan. These losses took control over essential resources away from the community as a whole and forced it to resort to external sources to supply them: the peasants came to be dependents of the hacienda or its associates in their basic activity. But even in a dependent state they never ceased to practice an autonomous agriculture with regard to their own goals, and when this was in danger, the hacienda itself opened new alternatives to permit the planting of corn. There was neither goodness nor Machiavellianism in this, but an urgent need for cheap, seasonal labor, which could be provided only by peasants with a production of their own, however insufficient. The essential need of the enterprise contributed to the survival of the plundered peasant community.

The Appropriation of the Villages and the Rich Campesinos. Another effect of the liberal disamortization of community lands was the private appropriation of land that had belonged to the corporation. This measure sanctioned and favored the accumulation of the already scarce territorial resources of the group in a few hands and resulted in a polarization in the internal stratification of the communities.

From the colonial epoch on, a fixed portion, a parcel, was given over to each *comunero* for perpetual use, and its possession was transmitted by inheritance. The parcel could not be sold under any conditions, nor could it be transferred to another line of descent (Miranda, pp. 55–56). As land ran out in the face of a growing population, this mode of tenancy favored the preservation of the extended family as a domestic unit and perhaps encouraged the fragmentation of possession; that is, it encouraged the functioning of mechanisms for redistribution and slowed down accumulation but did not guarantee equal access. The new domestic units lacked territorial patrimony, and they had few possibilities of coming to acquire it.

The legal measure that ordered private titles for community lands did not create the unequal access to territory. However, the reform laws converted the land into a commodity that could be acquired with money, which favored accumulation, intrusion of owners from outside the community, and exclusion of long-term landholders. The liberal legislation permitted the final expansion of the hacienda and the penetration of the paper mill into the cold country. The entrepreneurs negotiated, threatened, and, when it came down to it, used violence to dispossess isolated individuals without community backing. It happened that way in Hueyapan, where only a few *comuneros* had declared the mountains their private property around 1880. Protected by their titles, they received loans from the factory that they could never repay and that they redeemed by yielding their right of exploitation. Not only did the community refuse to support them, but it criticized them harshly.

Disamortization also opened the way to outsiders who established themselves in the villages and bought urban plots and parcels of land for farming. Some were hacienda employees, administrators or chiefs who settled down in Jonacatepec, near their work. They acquired livestock in order to rent it to sharecroppers or to serve as transport contractors for the hacienda. Others established themselves as merchants or even as liberal professionals who often bought land or livestock and cornered the corn trade. They also depended to a great extent on the hacienda, which generated almost all the money that circulated in the area through the payment of salaries, since the *campesinos'* production, destined for their own self-sufficiency, did not enter the market. The merchants maintained very close ties with the hacienda and acted as its banking agencies in order to avoid the still-risky transporting of money. There are still those who recall having picked up the weekly wages of the enterprise from the merchants of Jonacatepec. The professionals, a pair of doctors and the inevitable lawyer, were also associated with the hacienda, from which they received salaries for providing their services. Even the famous rum factory of Zacualpan relied on it for the supply of its raw material, molasses, and even for its clientele.

The outsiders did not participate in the traditional organization of the communities. They did not take part in the fiestas, nor did they usually acquire such ties as co-parenthood. They remained apart and directed their social relations toward the hacienda and its employees. In the fiestas held in the *reales,* the professionals and merchants figured prominently, in a position similar to that of the administrators and most trusted chiefs.

But some of the rich were people from the community or closer to it than the outsiders. They were the ones who somehow had managed to get hold of a surplus of corn, whose value they reproduced by lending it *a la dobla,* that is, at 100 percent interest. Disamortization enabled them to take possession of various parcels and to increase the scale of their operations with the production from this land. In the last decades of the nineteenth century these earnings could not be reinvested with attractive yields in the reduced territory of the community, where there was little land to be accumulated and where resources that would have permitted intensifying its productivity were lacking. The hacienda blockade established a severe limit upon the process of village capitalization. The rich peasants and moneylenders, incapable of competing with the hacienda, ended up by associating themselves with it in a subordinate position that let them increase their earnings. The activity that permitted that association was livestock raising specialized in draft animals that grazed on lands leased from the hacienda and were rented to sharecroppers. Rent for the animals was paid in corn, and in the first decade of the twentieth century some livestock owners and moneylenders from the largest village sold the hoarded produce directly in

Mexico City during the months of scarcity and returned loaded down with as much as two bags of silver. Some bought land in the sierra, outside the hacienda boundaries, and became ranchers.

The hacienda, for its part, needed trustworthy people in the villages to represent its interests—to administer the land given out for share-cropping and to collect the rents; to buy land for it—people who had power and who would support local authority in order to control the peasants. The rich were the natural choice, and the hacienda gave them preferential use of land that it was not cultivating; it let them develop noncompetitive but complementary activities, livestock-raising and usury, and in return for that, it converted them into its local agents. Some of the rich villagers became *arrendatarios,* as the administrators of sharecropping were called, and others, livestock raisers and money-lenders or contractors for the hacienda. The majority did everything at once: the merchants had cattle, and the *arrendatarios* farmed and loaned out corn and money. Even the doctors and the lawyer were involved in usury and trade. They were, in the end, enterprising men. There were also very few of them.

The hacienda did not prevent the rise of a rural bourgeoisie but inhibited its development. The estate never gave it autonomy and kept it assimilated with the resources that it possessed or generated. The rural bourgeoisie prospered in the shadow of the hacienda and, in return for its protection, served it unconditionally.

The Sharecroppers or Patrones de la Milpa. The expropriation and private appropriation of the villages' lands practically finished off the average peasants—those who had the wherewithal, those who could plant on their own account, without dependence. At that time *tener como,* or "having the wherewithal," meant seven hectares of land and a team of oxen, a little money, and a lot of luck. Some had even more than that, almost no one had exactly that, and the great majority lacked it altogether. If they had a little good luck, they could obtain land as sharecroppers of the hacienda, or as they came to be called, "godchildren of the hacienda."

The unit for sharecropping was the *yunta de sembradura,* the amount of land that could be worked with a pair of oxen. The area of the *yunta* varied, according to the quality and location of the piece of land, between twenty and thirty-five *cuartillos'** worth of planted corn. One *cuartillo* of seed covered a *tarea,* 1,000 square meters, so that a *yunta* varied between 2 and 3.5 hectares, the latter more common in the hot country. For use of a *yunta* of land the hacienda was paid 5 *cargas* (each

* Each a value equaling 1.891 liters.

about 181.629 liters) of corn at the end of the harvest, between 100 and 200 fodder sheaves at the moment of harvest, and a week of free labor or its equivalent. People from Zacualpan, Chalcatzingo, and other nearby villages had to clean two *tareas* of cane, which each measured 2,500 square meters, or 25 *surcos*. The rest paid in unspecified jobs—like the opening of the Aguahedionda canal or the putting up of fences. The rent represented a bit less than 10 percent of the average harvest of corn, sometimes, when the year was good, only about 5 percent.

The rent for the land did not constitute a severe limitation on cultivation. However, few peasants could become sharecroppers, since the hacienda determined which fields would be let out according to a system of rotation that prevented a field from being farmed two years straight. Such management made access to the land difficult and transformed it into a scarce resource subject to unequal distribution, which implied a process of selection. The requisite materials for becoming a sharecropper—in fact merely the work tools—were within everyone's reach relatively easily because of their low cost. However, the personal relationship with the hacienda functionaries needed for a recommendation, or with the *arrendatario,* was much more difficult to attain. Access to the land was at stake within the framework of the social relations in a stratified rural community.

Under these conditions, two types of producers obtained land as sharecroppers. First were the rich, who could pay for their own crops and even lend corn and livestock to others. Tightly linked to the *arrendatarios* and land overseers of the hacienda, when they did not play these roles themselves, the rich had no difficulty in obtaining more than one *yunta* of land for sharecropping, often three and sometimes more, although that was not very usual, since beyond a certain limit they preferred to rent out the teams or to lend money instead of raising crops directly. The wealthy did not perform physical labor but took on servants to do it. Even for payment of obligatory tasks, or *faenas,* to the hacienda, they hired peons to do the work in their place.

Almost no one had available just one team and resources of his own to take on sharecropping independently. The perfect stability that such a position implied made it uncommon. Moreover, remaining too long a time in this situation of independence from the moneylenders did not make access to the land any easier. The average peasant could not represent anything but an exception in such an accentuated process of polarization. The sharecroppers of Hueyapan who had their own team were subject to other dependencies within the framework of their own community.

The majority of the sharecroppers were definitely second-class godchildren. They took a single *yunta* of land in sharecropping and needed to resort to loans of other resources to pay for the crop. However, they were people who had an elevated position in their community, which permitted them to have a personal relationship with the hacienda's representatives. The nature of the relation was asymmetrical but compensated with a strong dose of prestige. When the hacienda's *arrendatario* was a livestock owner or moneylender or was associated wth this group, it was preferable to be his debtor, but with a reputation for paying back in full and on time; if he was a merchant, it was useful to be his customer and occasional debtor. Tradition gave preference to those who had been sharecroppers for prolonged periods, a kind of right by seniority, and it was not, then, surprising that the godchildren were the villagers who were older and who had most standing within the group.

For these sharecroppers the first step was to agree by word of mouth on the rent of a team with one of the livestock owners and to request the land from the *arrendatario*. For a team of oxen one paid between eight and ten *cargas* of corn at the harvest, almost twice as much as for the land. The animals were picked up in the owner's pasture toward the middle of May in order to prepare the *calmiles,* and they were returned in the month of August after the last cultivation of the cornfields. During that time, they had to be fed fodder stored since the previous cycle, although after the start of the rainy season some grass sprouted and reduced the consumption of fodder. If an animal died or got sick, the peasant was in debt for a long while. If one of the sharecroppers, or *patrones de la milpa,* "patrons of the cornfields," as they were called, did not have a plow available, he could rent one for an additional charge, although almost all owned their farming implements.

After obtaining land and team, the *patrón* had to reach a bargain with the *sirvientes,* the servants—a *gañán,* "plowman," and a *peón,* "laborer" —so that they would work in the cornfield. Both received a salary in cash and a ration of corn, which became still further deprivation for the *patrón.* His reserves of corn were exhausted from July or August on, and especially in September—*septihambre** they called it—and then he resorted to the loan *a la doubla,* according to which the corn received had to be repaid twice at the moment of the harvest. The length of the term did not modify the interest, which remained fixed at a simple 100 percent. In order to get money, he had to make sales in advance: for each five pesos borrowed, he had to pay back two *cargas* of corn at the moment of the harvest, when they would be worth five pesos each in the market. Everything by halves.

In a normal year the yield was two hundred to one for the seed planted, some seventy *cargas* from one hundred fifty kilos per *yunta* of land,

---

* A pun on *septiembre,* the Spanish name for the month, and *hambre,* "hunger."

which meant more than two tons per hectare in the level, deep areas of the hot and temperate countries. In the good years this yield could increase up to 50 percent, and it could be reduced by the same proportion in the bad years, which were certainly more common. Out of the total production, two thirds, or some fifty *cargas,* belonged to the *patrón* of the cornfield; the other third was harvested by the servants. The costs of planting took away from twenty-six *cargas,* when no debts existed, to thirty-eight when all the corn and money necessary had been borrowed. In the best of cases, which does not seem the most frequent, after the harvest the *patrón* retained some twenty-five net *cargas* of corn, one or two of beans, and some seed for squash, which was planted along with the corn. All the beans and squash and at least eight *cargas* of corn were devoted to the family's ordinary consumption until the next harvest.

The *patrón*—he was not called that in vain—had ceremonial obligations to his servants and to his laborers: the fiestas of San Miguel and the *pizca* or *acabada* (harvest's end), for which he offered food and drink to his workers and during which more *cargas* of corn were consumed. The inadequacy of the harvest to cover the expenses of subsistence and position obliged the *patrón* or the members of his family to work for the estate in the dry months. Thus, the *patrón de la milpa* was dependent in two directions: on the hacienda in order to have work; on the local rich men for obtaining land, for use of the team, and for receiving loans— which placed him in a complex network of asymmetrical relations.

Payment for the dependence, the rent fund that the *patrón* transferred to others, represented between half and two thirds of his share in the harvest. Six *cargas* went to the hacienda, and eight, at the least, remained in the hands of the local bourgeoisie for loan of the ox team, which was the most expensive item in the cost of farming, and up to thirty-two if he had to ask for loans to cover all the other expenses. The great difference between the price of renting the land, the price of the team, and the payment of interest cannot be explained in terms of supply and demand, of abundance or scarcity of natural resources, but in terms of a social system of dominance with multiple, diversified objectives.

At the fairs a good pair of animals could be obtained for a little less than what one paid by the year to rent them. The high price of renting an ox team had, then, no relation to the supply of livestock but was regulated by the alienation of the villages' territorial resources. The production of fodder on a *yunta* of land, part of which was surrendered to the landowner, was not sufficient to maintain the animals for the whole year, and they had to be taken to pasture. When such pasture land existed, it was so far away that one of the members of the family had to leave work to devote himself to caring for the animals; moreover, the hacienda had to be paid a fee for the grazing. Under these conditions, determined by the landowner and his associates, it turned out to be anti-economical to own only one team, particularly because of the loss of income that its care implied. For the owner of a larger herd, who had to devote a cattle tender to its care anyway, the distance from the pastures was a lesser problem that did not significantly alter the cost. On the other hand, the livestock owners were the same ones who distributed hacienda land among the sharecroppers, and they could convert rental of a team into a condition for access. Thus they could maximize the extraction of surpluses in the only sector that the hacienda left free: the peasant's autonomous production.

The hacienda, for its part, was interested in increasing the appropriation of a surplus created in the work done in its service. For that purpose, sharecropping filled two functions: tying down the labor force and producing income. At the beginning of the twentieth century the first function had pre-eminence, and the second was marginal without ceasing to be profitable and attractive. The hacienda made the land into a scarce resource, withdrawing it from cultivation in an artificial way in terms of its requirements for labor and of the price of salaries. The relatively low rent for the land enabled the estate to have sharecroppers and to pay them little, increasing the appropriation of surpluses in the peonage for the cultivation of cane. With the same objective, the hacienda put a high price on use of the mountains—which was fifty *centavos* a day up to 1910, equal to a laborer's daily salary—for the purpose of discouraging the gathering tasks that could draw labor away from the cane or rice, even though the mountain territory was the least exploited within the enormous property.

Between the hacienda and the local bourgeoisie there was no critical contradiction, inasmuch as the areas of activity from which they drew the surplus differed. From the hacienda, the bourgeoisie received a warrant for plundering the sharecroppers of their own production, but they paid for it by extending the domain of the hacienda where the latter could not reach: to the base of the peasant social organization, the rural community. The *patrones de la milpa*, diluted reflections of the medium-scale farmer, paid both and remained tortured within a system of rigorous and efficient domination.

Cultivating a *yunta* of land required two men and an ox team for the labors of the first plowing, furrow plowing, planting, and the three *beneficios*, or weedings, from the beginning of June until the middle of August, and more people for the tasks of *zacateo* (stripping leaves from the cornstalks) and corn harvesting. For the permanent work the *patrón* took on two servants: the *gañán*, who drove the ox team, almost always an adult man and head of a nuclear family, and the *peón*, who helped him, generally a young bachelor. The *patrón* rarely took an active part in the physical labor, but devoted himself to supervision and direction. The relatively advanced age of the *patrones* did not influence this; having more to do with it was the tradition, apparently quite ancient, that gave them a position that implied behavior rewarded with something as ubiquitous but as real as prestige. In turn, the *patrón* had to redistribute the scarce goods to those who had access to him because of his position.

The *patrón* repaid his servants in three ways, established by a traditional code that governed all the relations for production and that had the value of the most rigid contract: a weekly salary of two pesos for the *gañán* and one peso for the *peón*, which equaled two thirds and one third, respectively, of the salary the hacienda was paying its day laborers at the beginning of this century; a weekly ration of twelve *maquilas** of corn for the *gañán* and six for the *peón*, which in those years were worth one peso and fifty *centavos*, respectively, so that the salary of the *gañán* equaled what the hacienda paid; finally, the *gañán* was allowed to plant six *cuartillos* of seed, and the *peón* four, which were worked along with the *patrón*'s cornfield and which represented almost one third of the *yunta* taken for sharecropping.

The rigorous, asymmetrical treatment that the *patrón* received from his superiors contrasts with the almost privileged treatment that he gave to his servants, whom he paid as well as the hacienda did and gave access to land besides. The servants were his people, his own relatives or co-parents and rather often his own sons; he was united to them by multiple egalitarian ties that only permitted a horizontal, symmetrical relationship. In regard to his servants, his position was governed by mutual service. The *patrón de la milpa* was one of the points of articulation between the two systems: the peasant community and the liberal, bourgeois world with its pretensions of modernity and progressiveness.

The Servants and Their Work. The majority of the dispossessed villagers could not become sharecroppers, godchildren of the hacienda. Not enough land was handed out by the hacienda for everyone to cultivate, and many could not bring together the few explicit but functional characteristics for receiving it. Thus, placing themselves as servants was the basic strategy for obtaining subsistence. In the ten weeks that they served the *patrón* and the one that they dedicated to the harvest of their share the *gañán* and *peón* received more than half their annual income. In cash, and calculating corn at its lowest price, that of the harvest period, the *gañán* obtained some eighty-six pesos from his salary, his corn ration, and his harvest of twelve *cargas;* the *peón* got

* Each about two liters.

got forty-three, the perfect symmetry of halves, in the same period. To earn the same amount working on the hacienda took the *gañán* twenty-nine weeks, more than half a year; it took the *peón,* who because of his age received a salary of only three *reales* daily on the estate, twenty weeks of work, in the hypothetical case that he was able to get it, to equal his income as a servant.

Moreover, during the rainy season the *gañán* and the *peón* could obtain other income in the fifteen weeks that remained free for them, although it was not easy to find work in that period. They earned sure money by working as day laborers in cutting fodder and in the harvest in the *patrón*'s cornfield. To be able to pay the costs of the fiestas for the Day of the Dead, at the beginning of November, the servants requested an advance from the *patrones,* called a loan *al desquite* ("until they get square"), which they returned working in the *pizca.* That loan did not carry interest, even though in order to make it the *patrón* had to sell some *cargas* of corn on time, for which he paid 100 percent interest.

But monetary values do not express the real difference in the income of the servants, who received corn or, better, access to land to produce it. This product constituted the basis of the diet and the most important item among the expenses of subsistence. In the area, its prices were subject to a very high seasonal variation that at its extremes reached 100 percent. In December and January a *carga* of corn was worth five pesos; six in February, March, and April; seven in May and June; eight in July; and ten in August and September. During October and November the price dropped a little, given that red corn harvested from the *calmiles* was available. The availability of storage represented a considerable saving that was forbidden to the estate's full-time laborers. In fact, this storage, although insufficient, was the key mechanism for the subsistence of the peasant family.

Access to the land also meant other advantages, like the availability of beans and squash for home consumption; of fodder for maintaining a burro or a calf; or of *elotes,* "ears of corn," which lessened the rigor of September, the hardest month. All these products represented real income, which in the peasant economy was frequently expressed as a withdrawal from the cash economy. But not all would be earnings: access to land through service also gave other so-called advantages, like being able to borrow, to a limited extent, money or corn from the moneylenders, that is, to become eligible for credit and a more intense exploitation.

Another device for obtaining access to land, apparently developed toward the end of the Porfiriato, was *medianía,* in which the *patrón* put up the land and the team, and the *mediero,* or "partner," the work; they divided the harvest in half. The *patrón* came out almost equal or perhaps received a little less, but without any direct responsibility; however, the partner, who worked as a *gañán* and brought a member of his family as *peón,* almost doubled his share. The *medianía* formula was not very common and was almost always related to the excessively advanced age of the *patrón* or to special cases like those of the Hueyapan share-croppers, who combined resources to be able to raise crops more than twenty kilometers away from their village.

The resources obtained by the servant and even by the *patrón* with access to land for cultivation did not manage to cover the subsistence of the nuclear families, much less that of those organized on extended bases, which seemed to be the most common domestic units. This inadequacy as producers obliged the peasants to intensify use of their only resource, labor power. The handiest method, almost universal for complementing income, was to work as peons for the haciendas during the dry season. The people of Hueyapan, who lived far from the cane fields of various haciendas, had the option of hiring themselves out where the pay was better, almost always on the Calderón and Casasano haciendas, where they earned up to sixty-five *centavos* a day and received better treatment; however, to ask for lands in sharecropping they resorted to Santa Clara, since the others did not have sufficient land available. This option was not present for the other villages of the area because of distance, and their people sought to get themselves places as laborers at Tenango and Santa Clara. The labor supply was intimately related to the harvest results and the price of corn. A disillusioned administrator commented in 1905 that after a bad year the laborers presented themselves in multitudes but that if, unfortunately, the price of corn kept rising, the crowds dissolved to go raise it in their own. (Barrett, p. 88).

From the villager's point of view, work on the hacienda was always insecure. Sometimes there was work, and sometimes not; it could last six months or one week or could end in a conflict. The insecurity and the meagerness of his earnings obligated him to multiply his effort in many tasks that helped in the difficult labor of continuing to live. Not only were the house lots in the villages home and property but they were cul-tivated as intensely as their nature permitted. In the *calmiles* the preco-cious red corn was sown some three or four weeks in advance of the planting of the fields so that there would be early *elotes* and corn in November. The timing was more important than the quantity, since it eased the most critical period of the year. A number of fruit trees also grew on the house lots, and some barnyard animals were raised there. The gathering of wild fruits and products had been considerably reduced in the expropriated villages by the high fees that the hacienda demanded for the rights of use. Even so, these products played an important role in self-sufficiency. The women and children, who found it easier to outwit the vigilance of the foresters or to avoid conflicts with them if they were discovered, collected firewood, gourds, and red cactus pears for home use or to sell in small quantities. This work managed, once again, to be subtracted from the cash economy, in which, by definition, the peasant was plundered of part of his surplus. Moreover, it permitted the women and children of the peasant family, who had no access to the paying jobs on the estate and in the village, to make a significant contribution in products and money; thus they acquired considerable importance in the family economy.

In the communities that still retained free land resources, exploiting them came to compete advantageously with the attractions of day labor. In Zacualpan, which had retained part of its share of water, the complex orchards were cultivated intensively in order to produce an almost continuous harvest: when the walnuts were not yielding, the banana, plum, or quince trees were ripening. The fruits were sold in the village market, which served as a regional distribution center for the temperate country and for the pottery villages of the state of Puebla. The orchard owners could not serve as peons, although they managed the impossible in arranging to be sharecroppers in order to have corn. The other villages of the temperate country, dispoiled of water, had converted their orchards into small plots, on which they planted corn and winter wheat in succession. In Hueyapan, the village with the most free territory, the exploitation of resources was quite varied and intense.

Some of those who rented land from the hacienda preferred to pass the dry months extracting oak charcoal that was sold in Cuautla at 3.50 pesos per *carga;* since they could produce up to two *cargas* a week by working without stopping, they earned almost twice what an hacienda laborer did. Others directed their efforts to cutting lumber, beams, and shingles, risking penalties from the San Rafael forest guards, or to scraping resin, from which they extracted wood tar and oil of turpentine, sold in the region for construction and for making soap and house paint. All of them, to some extent, extracted *pulque* from the maguey plants for consumption and for selling in the zone; some gave it all their time so that they could sell it in the state of Puebla. The *hacenderos,* as those who went down to the haciendas as sharecroppers or peons were called, began to buy livestock for cultivating the land, using the extensive though meager pasture lands of the volcano, since no one would rent to them in the hot zone. Toward the beginning of the twentieth century the most daring undertook cultivation of a new crop, marijuana—since then seriously harassed when practiced by *campesinos* without any influence. But even in these villages, the best, most intensely used of the area, the unequal appropriation of resources pushed toward peonage an increasing group that could not produce a sufficient amount.

To the extent that the hacienda grew and became specialized, the villagers of the entire area found themselves compelled to intensify their labor to pay the quota of surpluses, the surplus labor, which the hacienda and its associates claimed in order to accelerate their process of capitalization. The villages that lost most through expropriation, those nearest the sugar plantations, delivered almost the entire quota of work to the hacienda; in other villages the intensification was used on their own land, but the surpluses were captured by other agents of the liberal capitalist system. But the old formula continued to rule: the principal burden of subsistence, the cultivation of corn, had to remain the responsibility of the peasants themselves.

In the first decade of the twentieth century the situation in the Morelos *oriente* was rapidly changing. Many people could not obtain access to land even as servants. In Chalcatzingo, almost 40 percent of the adult males had to find places as year-round laborers on the hacienda. The *patrones* and *sirvientes* of the area resorted to the estate in search of work, no longer just in the dry season but also in the critical months from August to November, a fact that created conditions for the introduction of a crop as intensive as rice. Despite this development, people recall that the lines for getting work grew longer and longer before the gates of the hacienda. Villages located outside its borders, like Tepexco or Hueyapan, expropriated by other entrepreneurs, joined the peonage in the first decade of the twentieth century, making the competition for land and work more severe. The old, proven formulas were breaking down as fewer people had access to land to raise corn, and the hacienda, saturated by the labor supply, appeared less disposed than ever to the full proletarianization of labor, which would have meant much higher salaries. The precarious balance of peasant subsistence was endangered in the Morelos *oriente*. The hacienda did not see the danger, or submerged in the vital process of constant growth, it could not or did not want to open new alternatives.

Order

A Confused and Agitated History. In the first quarter of the nineteenth century what had been New Spain became, after eleven years of struggle, the brand-new Mexican Republic, which was inaugurated with a half-century of violence, internal strife, and plunder on the part of the industrial powers. What is today the state of Morelos, especially the Cuautla and *oriente* valleys, actively participated in the struggle for independence around the leader Morelos, who engaged in one of his most important battles in Cuautla in 1813. The Creole ranchers and their *mestizo* cow hands, the rural clergy, and the Indian villagers gave their support to Morelos, who carried out the most lucid, congruent effort to turn the political struggle into a social revolution with agrarian overtones. Two military chieftains of importance, Francisco Ayala of Mapastlán, which today is called Villa de Ayala, and Mariano Matamoros, parish priest of Jantetelco, arose in the zone, and there they formed contingents that fought along with Morelos's forces (Diez, 1:lxxvi–xc). At that time, the form of fighting in which the inhabitants of the South acquired mastery and even virtuosity appeared: guerrilla warfare.

The landowners also participated in the war of independence, but on the other side. In 1808 the owner of the Temixco and San Gabriel haciendas in the Cuernavaca Valley, Gabriel de Yermo, headed the coup that turned the viceroy Iturrigaray out of office because, confronted by the disappearance of royal power in Spain, he was disposed to recognize the popular sovereignty proclaimed by the town council of Mexico City. Yermo, an hacienda owner and great merchant, led his colleagues in a number of political interventions and military adventures in the first third of the nineteenth century (Sotelo Inclán, p. 223).

With the proclamation of Iturbide as emperor, one much closer to the landowners than to the guerrillas, political independence was obtained and the social revolution put to flight, but at the cost of a long stage of violence, bossism and military insurrections, banditry, and peasant uprisings, which were always put down but never annihilated. In Morelos, at that time part of the state of Mexico, this phase was begun with the uprising by Vicente Gómez in an 1823 countercoup to a landowners' insurrection led by a Yermo, one of Gabriel's descendants. This movement came to acquire strong racial and agrarian connotations that, manipulated by Creole politicians, were resolved in the expulsion of the Spaniards, decreed in 1827, first from the state of Mexico and later from the entire country. One third of those from the Spanish peninsula left the state of Mexico. The others remained, the Yermo family among them, making full but not very generous use of bribery (Sotelo Inclán, pp. 29–43); the liberal government of Gómez Farías had to expel the Yermo family explicitly in 1833. This government imposed radical measures, like the suspension of the tithe to the Church and the expropriation of the Marquesado del Valle. It was no accident that the Plan of Cuernavaca was promulgated in 1834 to depose the Gómez Farías government and to bestow power on Santa Ana, who retained it intermittently for twenty years (Sotelo Inclán, pp. 252–56).

Under the protection of this military leader with all his charisma and

picturesque gestures, himself an *hacendado* from Veracruz, the great
properties were expanded at the expense of the villages. Different and
successive state laws liquidated communal property in extensive regions
of the country (Meyer 1973*b*, p. 28). Supporting the state legislation,
federal decrees legalized and protected the expropriation. In 1853 a
decree from Santa Ana prevented communities embedded within
private properties from setting themselves up as politically organized
populations (Sotelo Inclán, pp. 273–74), although under colonial rule
they had been territorial units with political autonomy (Miranda, pp.
54–73). With the advent of the federal republic, their situation
remained confused, since they lost their political specificity and were
integrated into the national municipal system but continued to be
corporations with territorial domain. The 1853 decree liquidated many
of them as political entities and deprived them of naming their own
authorities, their representatives.

In the face of territorial expropriation and loss of political recognition,
agrarian uprisings broke out all over the country. Jean Meyer lists
twenty important ones between 1834 and 1857, among them the caste
wars of Sonora and Yucatán and the "communist" uprising of the Sierra
Gorda (Meyer 1973*b*, pp. 9–17). Many local rebellions that went
unrecorded developed around that time. In Morelos, too, things heated
up. In 1849 four hundred men met in Tlayecac to demand land and
better day wages on the haciendas, "since it is notorious that almost all
these villages do not even retain their *fundo legal,* as well as how for
several years now they have relied on the system of paying the day
wages of the haciendas' workers in *vales* ["coupons"], which lose half
their value on passing into the hands of these unfortunates" (cited by
Sotelo Inclán, p. 257). From that point on, the peasants' demands would
have the double mark of the bases of their existence: land for autonomous cultivation and better salaries for their work as laborers for the
sugar plantations. Also in 1849 a rebellion in Jantetelco, which seemed
quite extensive, was thwarted when the ringleaders were captured.

Arrizcorreta, then governor of the enormous state of Mexico, issued
a circular in which he denounced the situation in the hot country of
Morelos, where the haciendas "hold usurped all or the greater part of
the *repartimiento* lands, which they have acquired through frauds,
clandestinely or by force. . . . Of the short day wage that they pay their
workers, they give a part in paper that has value only on their property,
thus requiring that those unfortunates take articles that generally
are of poor quality and very expensive" (cited by Meyer 1973*b*, pp.
40–41). The sound intention of that circular was to ask the landowners
to make some concessions to the villages, because if some uprising like
the one at Jantetelco broke out, "its first victims would be the owners or

administrators" (cited by Meyer 1973*b*, p. 43). But the latter did not understand it that way, and furious, they protested to the governor that creating a "greater scandal . . . would give fuel to the blaze that threatens us" (cited by Sotelo Inclán, pp. 261–62). The rich landowners took measures to defend themselves with arms, the very same ones they used for plundering, and they exercised their enormous power as a pressure group to obtain the governor's resignation. They triumphed. In 1850 the prefect of Cuernavaca, named after Arrizcorreta's resignation, asked for the promulgation of an agrarian law "that would moralize the workers on the haciendas, granting the owners and administrators correctional powers over their dependents" (cited by Diez, 1:cxxviii).

The Morelos landowners' indignant manifesto of 1849 was signed by, among others, Marino Icazbalceta (owner of Tenango and Santa Clara), Antonio Icaza, Ignacio Cortina Chávez, Gómez de la Cortina, Mendoza de la Cortina, Francisco Iturbe, Santiago Goríbar, Luis Rovalo, Manuel Irazábal, and—of course, he is there—Gabriel de Yermo. Another adherent was Andrés Quintana Roo, the hero of the struggle for independence, to whom the revolution had done justice by turning him into a landowner in the area of the state of Hidalgo (Sotelo Inclán, pp. 261–62). The coincidence of these names with those on the society pages of our day, scarcely 125 years later, is not, then, accidental.

From then on, the landowners acted publicly in an organized fashion, although they had been mobilizing themselves clandestinely, in secret, for a long time. Their public actions were confined to two principal kinds: as a pressure group before the congress, the governor, and the president and as the patrons of private armed forces that contributed to the creation and maintenance of a climate of violence in Morelos that persisted until 1875. Occasionally, as it sometimes happens when violence is encouraged in the defense of specific individual interests, the landowners lost control, and their mercenaries stood up to them, coming dangerously close to the peasants' demands. In 1856, "in the two months preceding this date, [plantations] already sacked by gangs of malefactors, some formed on the haciendas themselves, have been those at Tenango, Atlihuayan, San Miguel, and El Treinta . . . and some with gangs of more than two hundred malefactors . . . and coaxing the Indian villages with offers to destroy the haciendas and to distribute their lands and water to them" (cited by Sotelo Inclán, pp. 291–93).

Even then, the government not only gave the landowners authorization to raise their mercenary armies once again but also sent the federal army to back them up. The landowners' organization was formalized as an association to keep away and persecute gangs; the central committee was formed by Payno, liberal minister of the interior; Joaquín García

Icazbalceta, owner of Tenango and Santa Clara; and other landowners (Sotelo Inclán, pp. 291—93). That same year, they used the second tactic, political pressure: When Olvera, Castillo, and Ponciano Arriaga, deputies to the Constitutional Convention, voted against the expropriation of the indigenous communities that the proposal for Article Twenty-seven implied, the landowners addressed themselves to the congress to pressure it in favor of the original proposal. The communiqué was signed by García Icazbalceta, Goríbar, Escandón, and Muñoz Ledo (Sotelo Inclán, p. 298)—once again, the society page.

The private armies turned out to be efficient for seizing land, for repression of peasant movements, and for the liquidation of villagers, but not for reestablishing peace. The violence that they generated culminated in an assault on the Chiconcuac hacienda in which some Spanish subjects died, which provoked an incredible scandal that eventually served as a pretext for the presence of Spain among the interventionist powers whose troops invaded Veracruz at the end of 1861— although the Spaniards did not disembark. The scandal was also used to discredit General Juan Álvarez, who had headed the Ayutla revolt that eliminated Santa Ana and opened the way for the liberals and whom they wanted to blame for the killings. Álvarez responded with his "Manifesto to the Civilized Peoples of Europe and America," in which he dramatically denounced the landowners' behavior and the complicity of the authorities in the expropriation of lands and work from the Indian communities (Diez, 1:cxxxii). General Álvarez had been discredited as agrarian candidate for the presidency superfluously; no one else would hold back the triumph of the pure, orthodox liberals.

The Liberals and Their Triumph. In 1856 the legalizing of the process of territorial expropriation and of the loss of political recognition of the indigenous community was finished with the promulgation of the Lerdo Law, which denied ownership of land to indigenous communities, the corporations, and the Church and its organizations. A year later this law was ratified as Article Twenty-seven of the liberal constitution. The peasants' reaction was added to the climate of general violence that broke out in the country with the wars of reform, in which the demands of an agrarian character were weakened, although the history that has been made of these wars has also contributed to diluting them.

In the history of Morelos the association of violence and agrarianism is more or less clear throughout the course of the nineteenth century. Armed groups proliferated in the confusion, and all of them were generically considered bandits. Among them, those who had been (and often formally still were) regular soldiers of the federal army stood out —like the band that attacked Cohuecan in 1858, with the happy result "that no one had perished, for only one horse came out of it wounded," according to an altarpiece that exists in the church of this village, located on the left side of the Amatzinac. The federal troops were also important in forming the bands of *plateados,* the "silver-plated"—called that because of the metal decorations they attached to their clothes—who operated on the Amilpas plain between 1861 and 1863. The group commanded by someone named Leyva, made up of about four hundred men, attacked the village and church of Tepalcingo in 1862; there were dead and wounded, and the priest calculated the losses at thirteen thousand pesos. In his report he said that the group was formed by bandits and *federales,* a name that in time came to be identified with all the violence exercised against the peasants. The *plateados* were annihilated by a private group of "vigilantes" who received support from the landowners and freedom from punishment by the government for carrying out the summary executions.

But this did not calm the violence, any more than could the short period of the Second Empire, despite its laws of a clearly agrarian character. In 1864 Maximilian ratified the reform laws, to the dismay of the conservatives, but in 1865 he returned juridical identity to the villages, though not to the Church, granting them leave to litigate on the issue of territorial ownership. In 1866 he issued a law on community and *repartimiento* lands and, in the same year, an agrarian law that conceded the *fundo legal* and communal lands to the villages, including by expropriation of private property when necessary. In 1867 the emperor was shot by the liberal forces after having lost his conservative base of power by ordering measures like the ones cited.

A State is Born. That same year a decree from President Benito Juárez created the Free and Sovereign State of Morelos. Part of it was formed by the Jonacatepec district, or the hacienda of Tenango and Santa Clara, established as a judicial seat since 1825, and in 1849 it acquired its definitive size upon losing the municipality of Yecapixtla and incorporating Zacualpan (Diez). The formation of the state of Morelos was obtained with the support of the military and liberal bureaucrats and, surprisingly, despite the opposition of the *hacendados.*

The reasons for their opposition do not appear to be very clear, although it has been suggested that they would have preferred dealing with a prefect named by the governor of the state of Mexico rather than with a governor produced by an election. It is more likely that the landowners, who definitively had been liberals on the agrarian question but quite near the conservatives and the empire on politics, feared some revenge from the new governing groups. When the Constitutional Convention was held in 1856, there was an attempt to incorporate

Morelos into the state of Guerrero in search of the protection of the agrarian general Álvarez. Ignacio Ramírez, "the necromancer," commented then that "the interests of a hundred feudal landowners prevail against your votes" (Sotelo Inclán, p. 256). Don Ignacio was exaggerating: there were at most some twenty-five hacienda owners, but they had uninterruptedly gained in strength and aggressiveness.

When the state of Morelos was formed and Leyva, a veteran liberal, was elected as its first governor, the landowners confronted him, perhaps with the support of Porfirio Díaz. A group of property owners, among them García Icazbalceta, sought protection from the federal judicial system against the state budget law and offered as evidence the constitutional weakness of the governor, who could not defeat them. They had very good reasons: the fiscal value of the 30 haciendas was 3.5 million pesos, while the state budget was less than 150 thousand pesos annually.

To Leyva falls the dubious honor of having extinguished the violence with a more extreme, inhuman violence, carried out by the head of the *rurales*, Manuel Alarcón. This enabled Leyva to survive the planters' opposition for several years, but in 1875 he found himself forced to resign. He had committed two unpardonable errors: in 1867 he had defeated Porfirio Díaz in the election for governor of the state, and in 1872 he had brutally extinguished the last outburst of widespread violence, an uprising in Jonacatepec against Benito Juárez and in favor of Díaz. At the head of the triumphant Tuxtepec Plan, Díaz was the most important national figure in 1875, and he would continue to be so during the following thirty-five years.

Peace and a Big Stick. The pacification of Morelos was the result, not of the elimination of violence, but of its concentration in a single actor: the State. The private mercenary bands were replaced by a single group: the *rurales,* the federal mounted police, under the command of Alarcón. He suppressed the banditry, rustling, and agrarianism in a simple, summary way: through execution of the suspect under the justification of the *ley fuga,* attempted escape cut short by bullets; speedy justice indeed. Violence came to be institutional patrimony, and all crimes that were not committed under the protection of an official position or mission ceased.

Under the cover of state violence it was possible to begin application in the villages of the disamortization laws promulgated fifteen years before. In 1871 Governor Leyva appeared pessimistic because the village "resistance is tenacious in its opposition to the redistribution that could be done" (cited by Sotelo Inclán, p. 348). "As late as 1872 the disamortization laws began to be carried out by the villages . . . the state of

Morelos has much to do in this matter; the Indian prejudices still subsist," said Ribera Cambas, *científico*, liberal writer (cited by Sotelo Inclán, pp. 356–58). Indeed, a great deal was done in this matter.

The communities did fight for their lands tenaciously. They chose their representatives, hired lawyers, and applied to the courts, only to lose again and again. They sought agents, connections, and influence and resorted in vain to General Díaz, only to receive vague promises and very explicit repression. They persisted. The *hacendados* and the government, blinded by liberal thought and the enjoyment of power, were surprised by the resistance and attributed it to the disruptive action of individuals, of agitators, and proceeded to liquidate the leaders. Jovito Serrano, representative of the community of Yautepec in a lawsuit with the hacienda of Pablo Escandón, who would later be governor of the state, was detained by the secret police and exiled to the forced-labor camps in the territory of Quintana Roo; along with Serrano went thirty-five Morelos villagers who had also resisted the advance of disamortization, and nothing more was ever heard of them (Womack, pp. 49–50; Magaña, 1 : 84–86).

The levy, forced recruitment for the federal army, carried off many agrarian leaders on the planters' direct recommendation to the local district prefects. Other communal leaders were threatened, beaten, or bought off by the owners or by their faithful servants who occupied positions as guardians of order in the municipalities. The most tenacious opponents were murdered. That was the fate of Antonio Francisco, a Tepalcingo village official, who, protected by the royal grant given to his ancestors and under the belief that he could rely on the support of Ignacio M. Altamirano, a liberal military man and *costumbrista* writer, fought in the courts against expropriation by the Tenango and Santa Clara hacienda. He was a stubborn, proud old man who never wanted to heed the polite invitation of the Jonacatepec district prefect to forget the lawsuit and to go to live as far as possible from the hacienda. In 1886 he was murdered by a party of *rurales* under the direct command of Mauel Alarcón, who is said to have told him before killing him, "Well, you're going to stay right there as a boundary marker" (Magaña, 1 : 79–82; Sotelo Inclán, pp. 401, 402). In fact, in 1891 the village of Tepalcingo was surrounded by a thick stone barrier that the hacienda ordered built.

The murderer, veteran of the liberal wars and recognized as the pacifier of Morelos, had a higher destiny: in 1894 he assumed the governorship of Morelos, which he retained until his death, certainly from natural causes, in 1908 and from which he served the planters, so much so that on a modest scale, he became one of them. He was a good example of the Porfirian politician—administrator of peace and the big stick—who knew how "to go through the motions of a compromise, pose, juggle, fake, do magic—at that, Alarcón was a home-grown genius" (Womack, p. 13). Under his government the complaint of liberals like Ribera Cambas that the benefits of disamortization "had not been exploited, although they would give individuals abundant, fixed resources" (cited by Sotelo Inclán, pp. 356–58) ceased to be true; those benefits were certainly exploited by the planters.

The Return of the Institutions. Sheltered by the Porfirian peace, the battered institutions of Morelos recovered their old state of repair, in decline since the end of the colonial era. Throughout the Morelos *oriente* pretentious public buildings sprang up: town halls, pavilions in the rejuvenated central plazas, markets named for liberal heroes, the first school buildings in the history of the zone. The citizens participated enthusiastically in this edifying fever. In Hueyapan the first school was built in 1888, making use of the free *faenas* of its population. To obtain the materials, they resorted to a rather unusual method: all the men who crossed the *barranca* to come down to the center of town had to bring an evenly shaped stone on their backs; the women who did laundry at the river had to bring a bucket of sand. Teachers appeared, some dedicated, others out for a good time; some collecting salaries from the municipality and others from the state and the federation. On the *reales*, the hacienda paid the teachers, who were soon replaced by nuns. Education flourished. Luis Cabrera, brilliant politician of the revolutionary era, who was a teacher in an hacienda school in Tlaxcala, found colonial teaching methods in use and received precise instructions from the administrator about "not teaching anything more than reading and writing and the catechism of Christian doctrine, with absolute prohibition of arithmetic and, above all, 'of those things about civic instruction that you people bring and that serve no use at all'" (cited by Silva Herzog, p. 204).

In fact, such civics lessons were not very useful. Periodically, like a boring, punctilious ritual, elections were held in accord with liberal precepts. When it was a matter of electing a president, there was only one candidate: General Porfirio Díaz. The same thing happened in elections for state governor and for federal deputies and senators, who were designated openly by General Díaz, who occasionally also named the Morelos state deputies. The first was an important political office, since the governor was, in practice, a personal representative of the president of the republic, to whom he was accountable. The others were sinecures of a different caliber, without any power except to raise their hands when they were told to. As sinecures, all were substantial, not so much for the salaries, but for their place in a ring of corruption recognized and encouraged from above. In return, they owed absolute fidelity and unconditional obedience to the president. The enormous power that Díaz exhibited had been appropriated at the cost of weakening all centers with independent power to make decisions. This was not only public knowledge and recognized as valid, but praised as well, even by many of the system's severest critics, like Andrés Molina Enríquez (Molina Enríquez, pp. 42–46).

Elections were also held to name the municipal presidents and trustees and other local authorities in the villages attached to the municipality. Frequently, especially at Jonacatepec, the municipal seat nearest the hacienda's *reales,* a figurehead from the enterprise had to be elected, although in other municipalities and villages authentic representatives of the community were often chosen. Antonio Francisco, the assassinated leader, had been a trustee and municipal president. It mattered little: the free *municipio,* fundamental cell of national political life according to the liberal constitution of 1857, had in practice been dispossessed of all power. It almost totally lacked economic resources, and the few that it collected were devoted to paying teachers and buying some materials for the pompous buildings that otherwise were built with the free labor of the residents, since for such purposes communal norms survived. With those resources the most that could happen was that the secretary, an appointed, unelected official, would be corrupted and devote himself to usury, as occured in Tepalcingo. The sphere of decision-making for the municipality was severely limited to acting as mayor's office for the village and to the routine, bureaucratic tasks of record-keeping. Important matters often were not even submitted to municipal authorities, and their decisions could be vetoed by the *jefe político.*

All the functions of executive power were concentrated under that title. Its official name was prefect, and the extent of its jurisdiction was the district; although named by the state governor, he was chosen by the president in a perfect pyramidal structure (Hansen, p. 195). The prefect's power was enormous, and the district force of *rurales,* under the command of a commissioner, was attached to him. In fact, the justice of the peace, judicial agent for the district, was also attached to the *jefe político.* Obviously, the municipalities that made up the district received orders from the prefect. As it happened (and often happens still), there was no relation between the degree of authority and the miserable pay of a prefect, who had to even out his salary on his own. Quite commonly he would offer his services to the planters for a stipend or some other sinecure, which transformed him, in the words of Luis Cabrera, into nothing "more than the hacienda owner's stableboy" (cited by Silva Herzog, p. 203). In the case of Jonacatepec, where the political and judicial district coincided with the hacienda's territory, the existence of such a relation is no far-fetched hypothesis.

The district prefect kept the peace by exercising repression in all spheres of human activity, and he punished past and present actions as well as future ones. A network of informers kept him up to date, and he acted to punish some poor unfortunate who had two women besides his wife living in the same house as readily as he did to oppress a possible conspirator seeking a copy of the documents on his village's land. When the hacienda fired someone, it notified the district prefect, who took charge of the dismissed person; it is said that many men were driven out for not tolerating the foremen's meddling with their women. The prefect's authority to impose punishments was quite broad. In cases of highway robbery, rustling, and rebellion he could hang the accused on the supposition that he was guilty. In common crimes he had two options: the levy or delivering the criminal to the justice of the peace in order to keep him busy. In political matters he could use the levy or imprisonment without trial or legal complications.

The punishment most frequently used was the levy—simple, speedy, and without red tape. In the first decade of the twentieth century this meant two things: recruitment without appeal for the federal army and banishment to the forced-labor camps—actually haciendas in Valle Nacional and the territory of Quintana Roo that enlisted their labor from among prisoners.

Forced recruitment threatened all the peasants. The district prefect handed some men over to the army because of some bit of gossip that he had heard, others for a drunken spree or a scandal and even for being proud and arrogant, so that they would serve as examples. There were ways to escape the levy. The best was a good recommendation, such as one from the hacienda owners. The levy never took workers from the *real*. If one of the *dedos chiquitos* was touched by scandal, his *patrón* put him on the train and sent him to another hacienda while he arranged things. If one were neither a "child of the hacienda" nor recommended, he had to use money to stop the levy; it cost 250 pesos, a year and a half of a laborer's salary, to ransom someone who had already been seized. It was a pity that few had the money, because the investment was worthwhile: one only returned from the army through a good recommendation or by deserting; on the other hand, no one ever returned from banishment by any means.

Thus, when someone knew that the levy threatened him, he *banished* himself alone and went to another region. Moreover, he suffered because he had no pass, the receipt for payment of a personal tax that devolved upon all citizens of the municipality. The tax was not high, but it was certainly frequent. Some recall that it was paid every three months, and others believe that it was monthly. This receipt, which was demanded everywhere, was a very efficient mechanism for control of the population and aided in tying it down.

The presence of bands of the regular professional army closed the circle. While those caught by the levy were taken to fight against the Yaquis or the Mayas, the troops in the center of the country were, apparently, a nucleus of volunteers to which recruits from the levies in other parts of the country were added. The officers were professionals trained in military schools who had replaced the veterans of the wars of reform and intervention. The character and composition of the soldiery continues to be a great unknown, a theme to be researched. But the army was there, in Tenango, to safeguard internal order and the liberal, democratic institutions.

Indians and Civilized People. In the first decade of the twentieth century all the institutions that wielded power, the ones in which resources were concentrated, acted in the Morelos *oriente* in a differentiated and discriminatory fashion upon a population divided into two large groups: the Indians and the *gente de razón*, or "civilized people"— the *macehualtin* and the *coyume*, "carriers" and "coyotes" in the Mexican language, according to the differentiations made by the Indians themselves. This held true not only for government institutions but also for the hacienda and business and, of course, for the Church. All of them distinguished between the citizens, the sirs and misters, and the others, who were simply the rest, the majority.

This separation, inherited from the colonial era, no longer had a strict racial content, nor did it operate only by skin coloration, although these features had great implicit importance. President Juárez, the glorified, nonpareil figure of liberalism, was decidedly a man of color, as was Porfirio Díaz, the father of peace and order, although he bleached out a little more each year that he exercised power, and after thirty-five years he seemed virtually blonde. That was sufficient for politicians, but to be a *señor* it was better to have a light tone, a pure, lengthy genealogy, preferably, at least in Morelos, with Vizcayan surnames.

Language had also lost rigor as a distinctive feature to the extent that the Indians were being Castilianized. At the beginning of this century many of them already spoke only Spanish, although the elderly still managed Mexican, but there were villages like Hueyapan that clung to their vernacular tongue. Also, the names of the *macehuales* were changing. Earlier they had used the names of two or three saints in order to be recognized, but no last names. The civil registration campaigns, relatively intense under the Porfiriato, required them to take a surname in order to be registered and to be able to deal with public matters. Sometimes the judges prescribed the names, but at other times the Indians chose them: they looked for a *coyume* name that they liked among the ones they knew, and they bought it from its owner, paying him for the right to use it in the registry, to show off a civilized last name from then on.

The two great colonial barriers, color and language, were still perceptible but were broken down, although without the implication that a profound social division of an ethnic character that placed people in one group or the other had ceased to function. Everyone knew it and acted accordingly. The new barriers were more ubiquitous, more numerous, and less rigid, but they were there and they were operating. One of them was activity: the planters, their administrators and chiefs, the merchants and professionals—all were *coyume* by definition; the *patrones de la milpa,* the *sirvientes,* and the peons were *macehuales.* Some people remained in the middle: the livestock ranchers and money-lenders; the rural bourgeoisie was made up of both groups, although civilized people predominated. The *realeños,* the children of the hacienda, uprooted from the Indian group but clearly subjugated, were distinguished with a category of their own, *criollitos,* which freed them from the stigma of *macehuales* but did not fully turn them into civilized people.

Place of residence also served as a barrier. In all the villages a modern plaza with new public buildings and businesses had sprung up next to the church. In its vicinity the *coyume* built their houses, which in some cases were even brick and, more than that, had furniture. The others lived in the *barrios,* the wards or neighborhoods that had formed the village from the colonial era on. Each one had the name of a saint, the *barrio*'s patron, whose cult served as a framework for organization of the *cargo* system of wardens, stewards, and marshals that still functioned at the beginning of this century through the participation of the *macehuales.* In the *barrios* the good houses were adobe with a straw roof, but the majority were *chinancalito,* mud-covered cornstalks with a palm roof. In them there were no furnishings, perhaps one or two chests or trunks and a sewing machine in the more prosperous ones; however, an altar with some lithographs of venerated images, lit by a wax candle, was never missing, and nearby, the first photographs of the young couple on their wedding day. Never missing either was a granary, the *cuexcomate,* which ruled the activity of the *macehuales* according to the volume of corn it stored: the less corn, the more work.

Costume also differentiated them. *Coyume* men wore trousers, and the women dresses; Indian males wore breeches and shirts of coarse cotton, and the women, *enredos* and *huipiles,* wrapped, woven skirts and long, woven sleeveless tops. The *coyume* items were bought, the

Indian homemade. More and more frequently factory-made cotton fabric was purchased, so that the country was not developing that vigorous textile industry, which required the Indians as customers, in vain. But in the hot country there were still those who gathered native cotton from the trees in order for the women to weave a few meters of cream-colored cotton cloth that had great strength and cost nothing more than the labor, which was, indeed, considerable. For those who could find paid employment it was much more reasonable in terms of time invested to buy the fabric with their daily wages; it was also reasonable for the hacienda owner and the textile industry to appropriate for themselves the surplus produced by the *macehual* in his work for the hacienda. For that reason, only the most elderly, who could no longer work as peons, used cotton woven locally. However, the women, who could not get paying jobs, wove their own clothes, not only because of tradition but to turn their labor into a saving on expenses. Only a few garments were bought—shawls or loud-colored blouses or clothing for children who were going to school, in part because of pressure from the priests, teachers, and public employees, unconscious sales agents for the textile industry but conscious promoters of "progress," so that the children would dress like "nice, decent people" or like "Christians," terms which were, after all, synonomous.

Customs distinguished the groups, too. Those of the *coyume* were touted as being dictated by rationality and common sense, like bringing Japanese gardeners for the *reales,* while the Indians were accused of being immersed in the irrationality and fanaticism of savage, ancestral traditions. The *coyume* practiced modernity and secularism, as they understood it. No fanaticism, like spending a year's income on making a saint's-day fiesta, but the pure, economic rationality of killing bulls, worth many years' income for several peasants, in no less company than that of Gaona; contributing to the Church, but as charity; marrying in white as God commands; and buying and saving for the future. As for relatives, few and only close ones; as for the others, the further away, the better. Among the *macehuales* everything was a ceremony with fire-works, feasts, rum, and music; enormous families that were made even larger through the innumerable co-parenthoods and that entertained one another at weddings and baptisms; stewardships and festivals for the saints and the dead, crosses that were decorated in the cornfield and that gave a pretext for a moderate spree when the harvest was being done; no savings because, among other reasons, there was nothing to save.

Those barriers separated two worlds that kept themselves isolated by the practice of endogamy. Weddings between *coyume* and Indians were not very common, although anything else was allowed, as long as the children were incorporated into the inferior group. Under these conditions it was very difficult to move from being *macehual* to being *coyume*. The only way to manage it was to accumulate a great deal of money or power, and neither of those was available in the Morelos *oriente,* where the hacienda monopolized both. However, it was common for a particular barrier to be crossed. Some Indian might become a livestock owner and moneylender, others could live in the center of town, and many more wore trousers, though not without suffering from the ridicule of their friends: "Now our *compadre* has become a dandy!" The ethnic barriers were continually changing, as they always had, but they did not cease to permeate the entire existence of the inhabitants of Morelos in the first years of the twentieth century just because of that.

Each group had its own ideology, its stereotypes, and its prejudices, but one group's dominated, and the other's were subjugated. The *Monitor Republicano,* an urban newspaper, said in 1878: "When dealing with similar rebellions without any kind of ideal, and advanced by a race of such limited intellectual grasp that it cannot understand reason and justice, when it is impossible to explain to it what prescription is, that it is the principal right that can be asserted against the usurpation that the Indians claim to have had done to them on what they have never possessed with the characteristics of ownership, there is nothing to do to avoid greater evils, but to appeal to the only resource that civilization has against barbarism: force. Let the Indians understand that we are the strongest, and their ignorant threats of communism will cease" (cited by Sotelo Inclán, p. 380). In turn, one who was *macehual* says, "I remember very well just that peaceful time of Don Porfirio Díaz . . . the supreme government was strong, it was like God the Father."

III   REVOLUTION

The Revolution of Emiliano Zapata

Revolution: Talking and Doing. In the "modern, civilized" world, to speak of revolution is to speak of ideology. Too often it is not even talking, but speech-making, loaded with slogans and watchwords, that separates the good from the bad according to their ideas and personal convictions. The official histories of revolutions are almost always the tiresome narration of a confrontation between ponderous oratories delivered by heroes, who barely pause for occasional battles. The history of defeated revolutions is almost never compiled, and their ideologies go on to fill up the warehouse of utopias and millenia. The triumphant revolutions, which are written about even in capital letters, have been sanctified to be adored or repudiated. Perhaps inevitably, in post-industrial capitalist society revolution has been turned into something abstract.

For this reason it is surprising and, in the beginning, irritating to speak with the veterans of the Zapatista movement, the people who attempted the most consistent revolution in Mexican history. Their narratives are simple and concrete. Names play a part in them, as do the little, every-day things. Of all the themes of the revolution, the veterans prefer to tell about the battles, seen with the eyes of the soldier in the trench. Their conversations are rich and prodigal in details that to the ears of the worshipful listener sound like heresy in their apparent insignificance. The battle of Cuautla, definitive in forming the rebel Liberating Army of the South, may be talked about as the confrontation between three pals crouched down in a stone corral and a federal soldier, who fired a shot every so often while entrenched in a house belonging to a rich man who used to lend corn and who had surely buried two big bags of gold, because he used to have three horses and once. . . . Or the general development of the battle is told through the orders of the chief and through talk of his cunning, "for little by little he filtered his troops into the *barranca* and, ever so quiet, they ambushed the federal troops, who did not even know where the shots rained down from."

Bravery and personal exploits have an important place in their memories which are never exempt from irony, "because everyone was afraid but that Felipe Neri"—the legendary Zapatista general—"he was deaf and did not hear the shots landing close by, so he was never scared." They do not hide defeat or the chases in open flight, when the federal troops, who had better horses, kept hanging back, even though the Zapatistas went dismounted; those who never ran are not veterans but dead men. There is always a memory for the grotesque and sometimes even for the macabre, but never an ideological pronouncement, an explicit reference to their principles and demands, nor a joke about those of their opponents. Speeches never spring from their lips, and the few clichés that dot their stories are the result of subsequent reading, public ceremonies, and speeches, which they adopt knowing that they are going to satisfy the solemn listener.

This listener, astonished, starts to wonder whether these combatants might equally have fought on the other side, on any side. For the veteran the answer is obvious and self-evident: the Zapatistas were volunteers; they never used forced recruitment, and desertion was never really punished. They fought for and among their own people against an enemy that was always clear: the federal soldiers, the mercenary or impressed troops who came from outside, the intruders who protected others who were also outsiders. To the extent to which the obvious things that the veteran does not mention become explicit, clear, and simple, oratory becomes unnecessary and redundant.

But one further step is still necessary to penetrate the ideology of the Zapatista movement. The almost infinite, prolix details, which at first seem to disrupt the logic of a coherent narrative, are full of significance; they assist the veteran in explaining the causes and in marking the boundaries between bands. In this there are neither esoteric mysteries nor unconscious hidden expressions. For him, each thing has a specific position, a precise framework of relations that clearly locates it in a context. This objective location, lacking the rhetoric of people who have proper names instead of a generic title, guided the action of Zapatismo. Its ideology was expressed in congruent actions that radically trans-formed reality; moreover, always expressed in the concrete, it was fluid and dynamic, directed according to the way the conditions were being modified—and, along with them, the positions and relations of things and people. The ideology of Zapatismo has a great similarity to the peasant's activity: directing the natural process of the growth of plants and acting in congruence with the phenomena that affect it. Certainly, there was little explicit abstraction: it was not necessary for the Morelos villagers, who, with their fidelity to their principles and their permanent struggle for the important things, were able to make Zapatismo the most ideologically consistent movement of the Mexican Revolution.

The Rebellion. The first stage, the birth of Zapatismo, was an armed defensive reaction of the peasants in the face of a set of external aggressions. It was a rebellion. Many specific causes provoked it, all of them more or less directly related to the breaking of the precarious equilibrium between the great capitalist enterprise and the peasant community. The balance between land and work had been broken by the disproportionate growth of the modernized hacienda, and the peasant's survival was severely compromised. The threat of action by the public authority, which functioned, simply and openly, as a committee of the hacienda owners for the solution of their problems, was becoming more ominous. The governor of the state of Morelos, Escandón, was a planter and certainly not an upstart like Alarcón, his predecessor; indeed, his haciendas occupied a resplendent sixth place for their sugar production (Womack, p. 385). The election of this inept politician had been accomplished fraudulently in the face of an opponent, the engineer Leyva, who, a little without planning to and a great deal without wanting to, had mobilized the Morelos villagers in his favor with unsuspected force. His defeat and the repression that followed it left the peasants without recourse to anything but their own efforts. It also left them with both clear lessons and vague remnants of organization for their future action (Womack, pp. 8–36).

In the summer of 1910 Zapata and the people of his village used arms to defend the lands on which they raised their autonomous crops. Surprisingly, not only did they manage to survive their action but they received support from General Díaz himself. He was trying to slow down the disillusioned reaction of the new aspirants to power in the face of his last, clearly unpopular reelection. Under those conditions, the appearance of agrarian conflicts was certainly not quite opportune. His tardy agrarianism was superfluous: the peasants did not calm down; on the contrary, they were emboldened, and in a disarticulated but violent fashion they launched the rebellion.

The new aspirants to power, led by an obscure northern *latifundista*, Francisco I. Madero, were no less surprised by this revolt that continued day after day in the countryside. Indeed, they had solemnly proclaimed armed rebellion against the dictatorship in November 1910, but they had been defeated almost immediately, their troops taken prisoner or decimated and their organization disintegrated. In the first months of 1911, while the blackest pessimism grew among these inexpert but grandiloquent revolutionaries, the peasant rebellions broke out autonomously. These were local, unarticulated reactions in which violence was turned to as a last resort for survival, but without the formulation of any longer-term program. The explicit revolutionaries had the Plan of San Luis, which, luckily for them, contained in one of its clauses demands of an agrarian nature, but they lacked the strength for rebellion and an organization capable of obtaining popular support. Under these conditions, a strange, spontaneous alliance arose over the march of events, which in less than four months finished off the dictatorship of General Porfirio Díaz, the only strong man in the country for over thirty-five years.

The rapid fall of the all-powerful government, of something that had been like God the Father, seemed to surprise its defenders and its enemies alike. The truth is that the giant had feet of clay. The Porfiriato, the brutal political dictatorship that had concentrated immense power in a single person, was in other aspects of its action, especially economic ones, a meek, authentic liberal lamb. The State never managed—nor sought—to establish an economic base of its own or under its direct control. All economic activities were developed by private parties. The activities central to enhancing its economic worth, like extractive industry, banks, and railroads, were in the hands of foreign investors, whom the Porfiriato so successfully indulged with concessions that their capital represented two thirds of the total investment in Mexico in the first decade of the twentieth century (Hansen, p. 26). This composition of capital was resolved into a clear colonial configuration for the Mexican economy: natural resources and cheap labor were intensively exploited in order to extract, basically, minerals and raw materials that were consumed in foreign markets, in the industrialized countries; almost all the manufactured articles that Mexico consumed were purchased in those countries—a classic model of dependency.

The enormous flow of foreign capital, more intense that that of European capital that arrived in the United States in the stage of its greatest growth (Hansen, p. 26), permitted sustained growth of the Mexican economy. Between 1900 and 1910 the gross national product grew at an annual rate of 3.3 percent, while the population grew at only 1.1 percent (Reynolds, p. 40). This growth was concentrated in the mining and petroleum industries, with an annual rate of 7.2 percent, and in agricultural production for export, with an annual rate of 5.6 percent (Reynolds, p. 39). Under the protection of this general expansion arose a small but aggressive industrial sector that produced for the domestic market. Its most important activity was the textile industry, which made cheap fabrics and not only managed to supply the national market totally but within ten years succeeded in raising by 25 percent the per capita consumption of cotton cloth (Hansen, p. 30)—out of which, surely, the peasants' breeches were made. The sugar producers, with their modern mills, outdid this feat and managed to increase per capita consumption of sugar by 50 percent in the same span of time (Hansen, p. 39).

The Porfiriato was proud of progress and let the private capitalists do what they liked. But it lost out on modernity, the goal it longed for. The mechanization of modern industries enabled them to increase production appreciably without increasing employment and even, in some cases, reducing it. The textile industry eliminated twenty thousand employees between 1875 and 1910, a period in which its production increased 68 percent (Reynolds, p. 43). Between 1900 and 1910 employment in services grew more slowly than the population (Hansen, p. 33). In the first decade of the twentieth century, to the degree that modernization was accelerating, destroying many crafts, there was not enough work for the population.

This inability of industry to offer employment built up the population in the countryside. In 1900 agriculture employed 66 percent of the population, a figure that increased to 68.5 percent in 1910 (Hansen, p. 33). Agriculture, systematically sacrificed in favor of more modern activities, had grown only 1 percent annually, more slowly than the population, between 1900 and 1910 (Reynolds, p. 39). But while the sector devoted to agriculture for export was growing constantly and spectacularly in the hands of the hacienda owners, the effect on production of traditional food crops was considerably more negative yet. Between 1877 and 1910 the per capita production of corn was reduced by half, and that of beans by three quarters; it was often necessary to import these grains, basic elements in the Mexican diet (Wolf 1968, p. 19).

Carefully examined, progress provoked disaster, particularly for the peasants, who, faced by the terrible harvests of 1910, launched a rebellion against the government of Porfirio Díaz and took it by surprise. The entrepreneurs offered the government all the support necessary to put down the barbarians' uprising, but when it persisted and they saw their most sacred interests endangered, they tearfully bade farewell to the dictator, who, solemn and sad, set off en route to France, and threw themselves behind the successor who offered the best possibilities of halting the peasant insurrection. They owed the dictator for favors and sinecures, but they owed loyalty only to their own interests.

The government of progress had only two groups of unconditional servants: a host of almost thirty thousand corrupt public employees, who were not going to hurl themselves into the struggle with anything more than inkwells, and a professional, mercenary army of almost forty thousand men, which, although it was never defeated nor severely disrupted, was not capable of putting down an almost generalized, multitudinous uprising. In Morelos, the federal army was conquered in Cuautla by the troops commanded by Zapata, which outnumbered it ten to one. This ratio gives an idea of the strength and extent of the peasant rebellion and of the inability of the repressive military force to confront a general uprising in the countryside.

The Revolution. The surprised victor inherited power with all its limitations, in accord with the bungled agreements of Ciudad Juárez, which ordered the discharge of the revolutionary troops, of the peasants, and left intact the government and, worse yet, the federal army (Magaña, 1 : 118–19), and he decided to turn his dreams into reality: a modest program of political reforms that would grant participation in the exercise of power to the modern, decent urban groups that had been formed or consolidated on the road toward the progress of Porfirian growth. Francisco I. Madero, called *el leader* by the press, did not understand the force that brought him to power—the peasant rebellion—and he did not show himself disposed to execute the agrarian program that had been offered as an enticement to the peasants to get them to adhere to his reform movement. Feeling powerful, an apostle of democracy, he threw himself completely into politicking and was easily captured by the entrepreneurs for the protection of their own interests.

The Morelos peasants, strengthened by the military triumph, did not remain satisfied. They did not want the vote in the first place; they wanted access to the land. On occupying Cuautla, while Don Porfirio was still president, Zapata had sent orders to the villages to occupy the usurped lands (Womack, p. 58), as a clear index of what the *campesinos* expected from their recently obtained power. The Zapatistas entered into direct conflict with the heirs of power from the interregnum of León de la Barra on. The provocation came from the federal government, which perhaps perceived with greater clarity than *el leader* the enormous risk that the southerners' radical agrarian demand implied for all the beneficiaries of progress. The cream of the federal army was sent under the command of the man assumed to be the most capable of its chiefs, Victoriano Huerta, on a punitive expedition to annihilate the "tribes," where, said Gregorio Ponce, panegyrist for León de la Barra, "Zapata's primitive socialism was sweet to the rudimentary intellects of the poor, ill-educated people of Morelos" (cited by Magaña, 2 : 58). *El leader* Madero, who was also an apostle of peace, tried to mediate in the conflict but withdrew from it as soon as he saw that neither his charisma nor offers of bribery were enough to silence Zapata's position.

In the face of the army's aggression, the peasants openly declared their *counterrevolution,* as Zapata unrestrainedly called it to distinguish it from the revolution that the Maderistas were grandiloquently proclaiming. In this stage the movement made evident its autonomy, derived from a set of particular, radical demands that a simple change of groups in power did not resolve. A few days after Madero assumed the presidency and ordered renewal of the campaign against the southerners, they made their objectives explicit and public by proclaiming the Plan of Ayala on 28 November 1911. In it, they disavowed Madero and those who participated with him in the government as traitors to the revolutionary goals of the Plan of San Luis and added a radical agrarian program that ordered the return of plundered lands to the villages; expropriation of one third of the large estates, or *latifundios,* to give to peasants who lacked land; and the nationalization of the goods of planters, *científicos,* or bosses who opposed the plan.

To leave no doubt, it ordered immediate possession of the plundered lands and their occupation by armed peasants, without the necessity of decisions from higher up. With this program, notable for its conciseness, the Zapatistas ceased being local rebels only to become revolutionaries seeking power with the aim of realizing structural changes in the whole society. The Plan of Ayala was never abandoned nor modified in its essence until 1918. No concession was ever accepted: it was a total, coherent program for its followers, who, convened in a revolutionary meeting, declared, "We are partisans of principles and not of men!" (Womack, pp. 387–97). President Madero replied with equal conciseness and named Juvencio Robles, who earned his nickname "the incendiary" by fire, as chief of the federal campaign in Morelos. For him, not without reason, the entire population was Zapatista and hostile, and to finish off the guerrillas, he burned the villages and forced their inhabitants to go to the cities. Evidently, Zapatismo revived with the fire.

Pressured by the urban press to eliminate the peasant uprisings, Madero replaced Robles with the civilized general Felipe Ángeles. He also made ambiguous declarations on the agrarian problem, which the press synthesized in their true essence: "The president assured not having offered lands," said *El Imparcial,* headlining the chief executive's confused statement. The delicate equilibrium satisfied the hacienda owners but not the peasants. Pascual Orozco, rising in the northern part of the country, threatened to extend the rebellion through the entire land and to break the precarious balance. The entrepreneurs, who had thought of Madero as a necessary evil to pacify the rebellion, withdrew their support from him, this time without shedding a tear, and sought another alternative: a military coup capable of using violence effectively. With the decided intervention of the United States ambassador, Henry Lane Wilson, although apparently without the enthusiastic consent of his government, the entrepreneurs gave General Huerta their approval of his military revolt at the beginning of 1913. Madero, the unsuccessful peacemaker, was shot.

The Zapatistas responded to the coup with bullets. They knew Huerta firsthand and rejected his offers of negotiation. Orozco, less consistent, settled with Huerta, but other forces in the North, headed by Venustiano Carranza, confronted the military dictator in the name of

Constitucionalismo. The Zapatistas always maintained that the first shots against the usurper came from their rifles, and they paid a high price for it. Juvencio Robles was named as chief of military operations in Morelos for a second time. Huerta, the strong man of many of the entrepreneurs, was the most effective agent for the destruction of the enterprises, at least of the sugar plantations, which shut down their mills in 1914. Worse yet, he managed things so that the Americans would land in the ports of Veracruz and Tampico in 1914 in a crude attempt to overthrow him in the name of protection of their afflicted citizens and their sacrosanct interests. Again, the Zapatistas refused to come to an agreement with the dictator, although they offered to fight the invaders on their own. Violence was the general keynote in the country, and the dreaded total rebellion was unleashed.

The military strength of Zapatismo attained its maximum power in this struggle. By the middle of 1914 its operations were directed at taking Mexico City. On 20 July Milpa Alta fell under its control. But one week before, Huerta had resigned and hurriedly left the country. While Zapata organized the final blow, Huerta's successor, Carbajal, the man who had negotiated the surrender of power to Madero for Porfirio Díaz in Ciudad Juárez, repeated his accomplishment: he surrendered the capital to the Constitutionalists in Teoloyucan without even consulting the Zapatistas. The southerners found that the federal troops who blocked the way to Mexico City were replaced by Constitutionalist forces, who were no less belligerent.

Seizure and Loss of the Government. The forces that had actually been allied to overthrow Huerta were polarized around two extremes: the reformists, who fought for changes of a political nature within a legalistic framework, and the agrarians who demanded the immediate restructuring of the country. This division did not merely separate Zapatismo from Constitucionalismo, the most powerful group as a military force; it was also sharply apparent within this latter group: the Carrancistas demanded pacification of the country as a prerequisite for beginning a weak reformist program, the same one Madero had followed, while Villa's followers somewhat disjointedly pushed for the imposition of radical measures. In the middle, the Obregonistas were wavering between these two positions, in which the personal ambitions of Carranza and other chiefs to take power were also at stake.

In an attempt to unify the factions, at the end of 1914 a revolutionary convention was called together, a meeting (to which the Zapatistas were not invited) that Carranza hoped to use to legitimize his leadership. The attempt failed: the convention proclaimed itself sovereign in Aguascalientes and invited the Liberating Army of the South. Suspicious,

Zapata did not want to send a delegation but agreed to send a group of observers, who in an evident alliance with the Villistas imposed a radical tone on the meeting, which approved "in principle" the agrarian postulates of the Plan of Ayala. The convention named a provisional president and formed a government that was housed in Mexico City, occupied by Villistas and Zapatistas, while Carranza, who had disavowed it, directed his government in Veracruz. The Army of the South was represented in the Convention government, and Manuel Palafox, Zapata's secretary, held the post of minister of agriculture. Agrarianism was in the government.

They did not have the pleasure for long. Scarcely two months after being named, the president and his cabinet, unable to resist the pressures of the peasant chieftains, although they were themselves Villista moderates, fled over to the Constitutionalist group. They were replaced by others no less moderate, who, with many changes, were to continue together until October 1915, when at last they broke up in a disorganized fashion. Thus from April of that year, when Obregón, finally leaning toward the Constitutionalist group, inflicted two severe defeats on the Villistas at Celaya, the Convention was militarily the weakest group and controlled the least territory. In October 1915 Constitucionalismo received the definitive pat on the back when the United States government actually recognized Carranza and declared an embargo on arms destined for other groups. With this measure, the military inferiority of Villismo, which was the most important force in the Convention, became irreversible. In fact, the Convention government never managed to impose its authority nationally, although it is true that it never took the steps that could have extended its hegemony.

The two groups allied to form the Convention government, the Villistas and the Zapatistas, could not overcome their differences nor their mutual distrust, and the government never overcame its internal tensions. The Villistas who dominated the cabinet, certainly the blandest and most polished from that band, systematically held back the taking of radical measures. It does not cease to be ironic that the agrarian government was unable to proclaim an agrarian law that would substantially improve on the one Carranza promulgated in a masterful demagogic maneuver on 6 January 1915. The Convention's agrarian law, which never was approved and which Palafox finally promulgated in Morelos under Zapata's protection, might perhaps have changed some things. Not only were the laws held back but, what is worse, concrete actions and demands were never backed up, and Palafox, the highest ranking Zapatista in the government, was forced to resign. For their part, Zapata and his troops did little to avoid Villa's military defeat; in fact, after the Convention government denied them ammunition, they went into seclusion in Morelos and maintained a unilateral truce during the whole first half of 1915.

It is not easy to explain the agrarians' obvious failure to become rulers or to establish an efficient, durable alliance among themselves. Profound differences emanating from the framework in which the movements had arisen made the immediate alliance between Villistas and Zapatistas difficult, for until only recently they had been separated by thousands of kilometers and had had no previous contacts. Besides, some profound similarities blocked the action of the agrarians' government. The Zapatistas, like the Villistas, saw the government as an entity differentiated and distanced from the revolutionary process. This process was carried forward by the troops and the armed villages. Meeting with Zapata on 4 December 1914, Villa said, "I understand very well that we ignorant men make the war and that the cabinets have to take advantage of it, but, then, for them not to give us anything to do!" (Gilly, p. 147).

This vision corresponded to the real experience of what had taken place in Morelos and Chihuahua, where the *hacendados* and their domain were wiped out in four years of struggle. The hacienda owners and the wealthy who had taken refuge in the cities, the bureaucrats and politicians, were the ones who needed the government; in the villages it was not needed: they governed themselves. For that reason, Villa and Zapata sent the Convention government their secretaries and pen pushers, the ones who made speeches, but did not fight. In the same meeting, referring to the city dwellers' government, Zapata said, "Well, I believe we will not be deceived. We have been limiting ourselves to herding them on, carefully, carefully, on one side, and on the other, to continuing to let them graze" (Gilly, p. 147). None of the generals with effective command of troops held an important post in the government; there was still a great deal to fight ahead. The revolution still had not triumphed as either a social process or a military force. Villa said, "As soon as we get things arranged, we can go on to the northern campaign. I have a great deal to do there. Up there they are still going to fight hard" (Gilly, p. 147).

Neither Zapata nor Villa watched over the actions of their governing agents; they let them make do while they concentrated on continuing the revolution. Perhaps this negligence was a grave error with irremediable consequences, but it was the result, not—as it is frequently presented—of the fear of power on the part of the two picturesque local leaders, but of their congruence with a revolution that was being made from below and that still had not triumphed. The capture of the State, ever the enemy of the peasants, was not the Zapatistas' revolutionary objective; it was the consequence of a revolution at the base, in the free and sovereign villages.

The Utopia. In 1915 peace returned to Morelos. During that time Zapatismo made the revolution in its territory. The distribution of land, ordered by Zapata since 1911, could finally be carried out during that brief interval in the midst of constant warfare. The old colonial documents, jealously guarded by village authorities, came out again, and on the basis of them, brigades of agronomists and engineers, recruited even from the old federal army, began the distribution. The process, which was not exempt from problems arising from the old conflicts between villages, was completed with great speed. In less than six months, by March 1915 and in time for planting for the rainy season, some one hundred villages had received their share and began to work their land, recovered with such difficulty. The subjects of this radical agrarian reform were the villages, the plundered communities, which, along with the land, received the authority to manage it freely, without interference from the State, which lacked jurisdiction in that matter, in accord with the Zapatista decree of 1914 (Womack, pp. 207–8). The village could choose between communal management and its modalities or definitive shares on a lot-by-lot basis with only one restriction: the possession of land would be transmitted by inheritance, and it could not be sold or alienated. In October of that year, the measures adopted were summarized in an agrarian law that confirmed the aspirations of the Plan of Ayala and whose third article said: "The Nation recognizes the traditional and historic right which the villages, ranches, and communities of the Republic have of possessing and administering their fields of communal distribution and communal use in the form which they judge proper" (Womack, p. 406).

The Morelos mills were nationalized, and despite the almost total destruction of the machinery, four of them were working at the beginning of March 1915, and four more, among them the one at Santa Clara, would function before the year's end. The great factories were managed as a public service to mill the cane planted by the peasants and were administered by the combat generals. Their profits, which obviously were modest when not altogether nonexistent, were handed over to the general headquarters to defray the expenses of the army. Zapata himself tried to encourage some *campesinos* to plant cane for the market and in an indirect way to finance the struggle, with very little success to be sure (Womack, pp. 236–37).

After four years of living threatened by hunger, the peasants planted cornfields and used the water, confusingly distributed among the villages, to obtain harvests of chiles, tomatoes, and onions. The Zapatista government of the state of Morelos distributed among the municipalities a half-million pesos as credit for the purchase of seeds and tools. The villages threw themselves into work with enthusiasm and obtained abundant harvests from the burned-out fields. A surprising imitation of prosperity reached the peasants, who, perhaps for the first time, were living better than the inhabitants of the cities.

Along with this modest economic well-being arose what Womack calls a rural, rustic democracy with egalitarian nuances. The village authorities, the civilians, recovered the power entrusted to the military chiefs with relatively little friction. The Army of the South, "far from an autonomous military corporation. . . , was simply an armed league of the state's municipalities" (Womack, pp. 236, 237). Zapatismo always understood that its survival depended on this quality and worried about maintaining this character. The villages were given not only land but political autonomy, and the exercise of it was guaranteed in the face of the military chieftains.

Local democracy operated upon its old mechanisms, linked with family relationships and co-parenthood, more than on formal schemes of parliamentary democracy. The most common of those mechanisms was consensus, preceded by broad negotiations; seeking that consensus, they turned to general headquarters at Tlaltizapán for Zapata's intervention in obtaining it. This permitted broad, at times even exhausting, participation, which made authority flow from the base toward the chiefs. Zapatismo's other characteristic mechanism, one intimately linked with consensus, was decentralization of authority. Zapata was more a coordinator and a leader than a chief who concentrated political and military power. Policies, not orders, emanated from his headquarters, and neither verdicts nor documents were accumulated there— to the sadness of historians. The personal relationship, the dealing between acquaintances with an authority of their own and an objectively defined position, never ceased to be practiced. In 1915, while the most intense political and administrative reforms were being carried out, Zapata and his colleagues could give themselves the luxury of long, pleasurable talks, washed down with a drink, without fearing that Morelos would disintegrate. This little miracle, an anticipation of the peasant millenium and an experiment in the realm of utopia, came to pass in an area militarily besieged and without sources of supply.

In the second half of 1915, while the cornfields were growing, the Army of the South returned to combat. In April 1916, almost at the time for preparing the lands for a new crop, the Constitutionalists entered the state as conquerors who made the memory of Juvencio Robles pale. The Zapatistas lost their territory and took refuge in the mountains, at times hurriedly. Along with the Tlatizapán headquarters, all of the rebels' strategic reserves fell into Constitutionalist hands, and 283 persons, 154 of them women and children, were killed. The new commander, Pablo González, who never won a battle, emptily proclaimed his triumph (Womack, p. 250).

The Carrancista invasion depopulated the rural settlements of Morelos. Civilians fled from a soldiery that killed in hot blood and cold blood alike: in one village more than two hundred peasants accused of being Zapatistas were shot in a single day (Womack, p. 250). Those who did not escape rapidly enough risked being deported to forced-labor camps in the Yucatán peninsula to be turned into *gente de bien*, "decent people"; possibly more than five thousand people in Morelos were captured for that purpose in scarcely four months. After the invasion came plundering that was meticulous to the point of being grotesque: whatever lacked value or served no use for the invaders was destroyed lest the guerrillas find some purpose for it. The recently distributed fields could not be planted, and starvation threatened once again. In mid-September 1916 Pablo González attempted the final solution: he ordered that all civilians be concentrated in the cities for deportation. The peasants and their villages were facing physical extinction.

From the mountains, Zapata responded to the threat by decreeing a "General Law on Municipal Liberties," which had a strong communalist tone and guaranteed the political autonomy of the villages (Womack, p. 260). This decree, which obviously could not be applied at that time, was a concrete political declaration that reaffirmed Zapatismo as an armed league of independent villages that were fighting to survive. The civilians remained loyal to Zapatismo, and it continued pressing forward toward the utopia. The guerrillas kept on acting. Their military activities were moved outside Morelos to alleviate the pressure on the villages; their targets were chosen more for political reasons than for military ones. Mexico City again smelled gunpowder and dreaded Zapata. The tenacity was worth it: in December 1916 the thirty thousand men commanded by González, who had not found anyone to fight nor even anything to plunder, abandoned Morelos without triumph and without defeat. The Zapatistas occupied their territory again.

The Struggle Was Not Only for the Land. In February 1917 the agrarian principles of the Plan of Ayala, softened in some of their more radical points, were incorporated into Article Twenty-seven of the new constitution that the Constitutionalist band promulgated. One of the old demands of the Zapatistas was fulfilled, but those who swore allegiance to the new law were still shooting at them to kill. The delegates who represented Morelos before the Constitutional Convention had been named by Pablo González, the plunderer; only one of them was from the region, and he was an enemy of Zapata. The new constitution looked to the southerners like a demagogic maneuver on Carranza's part, so they did not give up their own project, the Plan of Ayala, and remained on a battle footing.

Moreover, the new constitution did not satisfy all the demands of the rebels from the South, although it gave considerable weight to the agrarian problem. The Zapatistas had fought not only for land but also to exercise domain over the territory through the free community. In the course of the struggle, the Zapatista principles had become a radical political program that sought the transformation of the nature of the State. Zapata and his chiefs were fully aware of this aim and rejected all alliances with other rebel groups, which, like Carrancismo, offered land but not power. Despite their military inferiority, derived from the lack of the supplies that would permit them to undertake major battles, the Morelos peasants stubbornly maintained their autonomy.

With Morelos barely recovered, Zapatista action focused on politics, on their unsatisfied demands. From November 1916, at Zapata's suggestion, a Consultation Center for Revolutionary Propaganda and Unification had been formed to guide the villages and direct their actions (Womack, pp. 271, 280). In fact, it was an attempt to form a mass political party capable of taking control over the forces unleashed in the revolutionary process through the participation of the villagers. The mechanisms of this peasant democracy moved decidedly away from those of parliamentary democracy and were based on the small autonomous village corporation, capable of acting through assemblies and by seeking consensus and total participation. In March 1917, scarcely a month after the constitution was promulgated, three laws issued by Zapata posed clearly and concretely the demands that the new Magna Carta did not satisfy: autonomy and freedom for the villages. These laws, which sought to regulate the relations between the villages and the army in order to guarantee once again the civilian character of the movement and to normalize the functioning of the municipalities and town councils on communal bases, emerged from a lively meeting of chieftains, who legislated about the future with enthusiasm even while, with the obstinacy of victors, they put off their decisions on alliances with other revolutionary groups (Womack, pp. 274, 275). The positions of Zapatismo in 1917 were clearly focused on the "refoundation of the state, as a commonwealth of villages" (Womack, p. 269).

The Zapatista laws of 1917 were issued atop the ruins. In Morelos there was famine. The population had been decimated, and the communal structures were in fact broken down because of death and flight. There were neither crops nor livestock. In 1918 epidemics and starvation annihilated or drove out a fourth of the meager population that had survived seven years of brutal repression. The laws did not seek to order but to guide, to reformulate a program, to give hope a rebirth and to create the instruments to realize it. They were, as Womack says, crude but essential acts in the political struggle of an isolated, mutilated band that refused to die or to back down.

The other groups, those seeking to form a powerful State capable of starting anew on the path toward progress and modernity, had been strengthening themselves in the meantime. A slow and agonizing process of mutual concessions guaranteed with shared sinecures and positions managed to attenuate the differences. The constitution, painfully ambiguous between radicalism and worn-out, classic liberalism, allowed the resurrection of the central State as a monopoly of power. Strong external support gave them the legitimacy of military power. Carranza had available a greater force than his predecessors since 1910 had had, and he hurled it against Zapata and the Army of the South. Again, he conferred the command upon Pablo González, who in exchange for his ineptitude offered unconditional loyalty and who, at the end of 1918, before the poor harvests could be got in, began a new campaign against the Morelos villages, which did not offer resistance (Womack, p. 308). But he did not succeed in triumphing this time either, and the Zapatistas, dispersed in small, autonomous bands, could still demonstrate that the struggle was going on. The Army of the South, without weapons, slowly dissolved, without surrendering. The soldiers returned to their villages and continued to offer support to the few combatants (Womack, pp. 213, 314). In April 1919 Zapata was assassinated in an ambush, without ever having come to an agreement.

Without their chief, the Zapatistas performed their last miracle. Although defeat was apparent, they did not disintegrate. They remained together to struggle, to negotiate, and to save the little that remained. To a great extent, they accomplished it. When Obregón overthrew Carranza in 1920, the Zapatistas were with the victorious band, but in order to survive they had to renounce utopia.

The Collapse of the Old Order

The Revolution Arrives in the Oriente. In the Morelos *oriente* the rains bear a sign according to the direction from which they come: the waters from the north are stormy and bearers of hail; those from the south come loaded with heat and plagues; those from the east are cool and gentle, and the crops grow with them. But to the west it never rains; the revolution came from there, and at first it appeared like an uncontrolled, external phenomenon. The survivors say that the struggle came to them from the outside and that they were simply added to it.

Apparently, the worst effects of the hacienda expansion were cushioned to a certain extent by the great territorial expanse of Tenango and Santa Clara and by the relatively low demographic density of the area. Despite the growth of the cane fields, this combination allowed the area to supply itself with corn and even to export it, a privilege that no other zone of Morelos shared. This cushion of corn, which eased the threat that hovered over the peasant subsistence, contributed to delaying the appearance of the agitation. The relative isolation of the zone and its subjugation to a single, monolithic, undisputed authority had the same effect. The electoral campaign of 1908, which mobilized the peasants in the political arena, is scarcely remembered in the *oriente,* and it left fewer traces there than in the dense valleys of Las Amilpas and Jojutla; it also left less resentment, no active group, and no lesson about organization. The 1910 corn harvest was apparently not as bad as in the rest of the country, and 1911 appeared less threatening for the peasants. When Madero proclaimed his revolution everything was going along with apparent tranquility in the domain of the García Pimentel family.

But news and rumors of what had happened in Villa de Ayala filtered toward the zone, where they sowed a mute anxiety and a vague hope. Already the name of Emiliano Zapata was not unknown to them, nor was his battle to recover the land alien to them. Although the threat that had driven Zapata to armed defense was attenuated in the *oriente,* it did not cease to be felt because of that. Moreover, the accumulated rage was similar. Thus, when shots sounded in Jonacatepec and Jantetelco in the spring of 1911 the revolution erupted definitively, mature like a natural phenomenon, and everyone became involved in it with a different sign and direction.

The Hacienda Collapses. The revolution took the planters by surprise. The majority of them did not even know to recognize it and thought that the bandits would promptly be exterminated by General Díaz's powerful federal army. They did not react even when the revolutionaries took Jojutla in the face of the powerlessness of Governor Escandón, a career soldier, who undertook a not very gracious flight. Cuautla had fallen under the control of Zapata, and the all-powerful General Díaz had been exiled. Then the planters flung themselves into counterrevolution.

They acted on various levels. As a political pressure group they tried to win over Madero, ultimately an *hacendado,* and the meek, surprised heirs of power. To a great extent they succeeded, and Ruíz de Velasco, one of their own, accompanied Madero on his swings through Morelos and could influence him in part. They also published manifestos and organized meetings. They used the press to create an image of Zapata that would fill the city dwellers with terror; the figure of the "Attila of the South," with his barbarous tracks emerging from a dark past, became familiar and commonplace. Their propaganda sought to unify all the defenders of progress to "destroy Zapatismo, which is threatening to destroy what we hold highest: our nationality" (cited by Womack, p. 132).

Through another route, they gave their political and even economic support to the representatives of the old Porfirian regime, the bureaucrats and the federal army, so that they would destroy Zapata. In 1911 the planters organized themselves to subsidize the government of the state of Morelos in its persecution of the Zapatistas. The García Pimentel family, the most skeptical, organized their private police with fifty mercenaries under the command of an old district prefect and stayed to defend their property (Womack, p. 119). Few followed their example, and filled with terror or healthy precaution, they went to Mexico City to do battle in the politics of the government office waiting rooms. The majority of the estates remained in the hands of the administrators.

On another level the haciendas and the Zapatistas coexisted for almost three years. Save for occasional sackings of the owners' houses, the revolutionaries took care of and respected the hacienda as a productive enterprise capable of turning plants into money. In December 1911, with the same vigor with which he had ordered the recovery of lands usurped by the haciendas, Zapata prohibited anyone from "destroying or burning the property of the haciendas, because these will be the patrimony and source of work for the villages" (Womack, p. 128). This order reflects concisely the real situation of the peasants of Morelos, who in 1910 did not have the capacity to attain their subsistence as autonomous cultivators with their own resources. It also reflected another situation: the haciendas were the only institutions with access to the markets and with the possibility of transforming the peasant surplus into a commodity, into money. This was vital for sustaining the rebel army, which lacked any kind of external financing. Zapata put taxes on the haciendas to defray the cost of purchasing ammunition, and betting on both God and the devil, they paid him. The haciendas also concentrated under their power all the accumulated wealth that was kept in Morelos; they had machines, workshops capable of producing almost anything, energy, communications—all the important resources for a war fought with industrial weapons. The Zapatistas needed those elements, and they got them.

Paredes, the administrator of Tenango, maintained relations with the Zapatistas. The people remember that many revolutionary generals, among them Emiliano and Eufemio Zapata, came to Tenango and negotiated with its administrator. One *realeño* recalls that he made rubber capes for the rebels on Paredes's orders and with the knowledge and approval of the García Pimentels.

Three sugar harvests were milled in that ambiguous situation in a territory in which there was combat. At times the federal army protected the mill while the rebels took care of the cane fields and even served as laborers in the field, only then to go off and fire a few shots. Obviously, the equilibrium was precarious, and the planters were not satisfied. They continued to give all their support to the most reactionary currents. They gave it to Huerta in his military coup, and when he named Juvencio Robles as military chief for the second time, they rejoiced. Only the young García Pimentel brothers, the only ones who had been witnesses of the results of Robles's first campaign, were opposed. They realized that generalized repression increased the civilians' support of Zapatismo. Worse yet, the "reconcentration" that Robles sought left them without labor; his methods were "not only stupid but completely counterproductive and odious," said Luis the younger (cited by Womack, pp. 159, 160). They wanted to negotiate with Zapata, and Joaquín sent a plea for peace to Eufemio (Womack, p. 170). But the other *hacendados,* among them Luis García Pimentel the elder, feted Robles as a savior in Cuernavaca (Womack, p. 172).

However, this time they were mistaken. Robles's campaign, by blood and fire, fragmented the resources that the haciendas manipulated. The army burned not only the villages where the laborers came from but also the cane fields, to keep the guerrillas from lying in them in ambush. Despite the protests of the owners, the liberating action of the federal army ruined the great enterprises. Moreover, the Zapatistas' patience ran out; convinced that the equilibrium was neither possible nor desirable, they turned the hacienda *reales* into military objectives. In April 1914, at what would have been the height of the sugar harvest, all the Morelos haciendas had fallen into the hands of the rebels, and not a few were burning.

The last to fall was Tenango and Santa Clara. Joaquín and Luis García Pimentel the younger were the only *hacendados* who remained to defend their property with the aid of a mercenary force, which had been reduced from the fifty members that it had at the beginning to ten Japanese soldiers and a French officer, the last extravagant act of a desperate aristocracy. The young men cried a little, listened to phonograph records, buried things of value, and after the United States invasion that destroyed their last hopes regarding the Huerta dictatorship, they fled without fighting on 24 April (Womack, pp. 180–81). One of the *realeños* recalls that the García Pimentels said to them on leaving: "Look, boys, ask the men to be careful. Get them to give you permission, and you work the machines so that you can earn a few pesos."

The empire of the haciendas was liquidated. When Huerta fell the great owners fled or hid; some exiled themselves voluntarily, and one of them was even imprisoned by the Convention government. They had lost their great landholdings and almost all their political influence; they were, in the end, on the defeated side. Despite this, they were all alive and still rich, ambitious men.

The Hacienda Survives. In Morelos the peasants divided the land. For Zapatismo, the haciendas continued to be very important as the sole means of exchanging work, their only resource, for military supplies for their army; and the rebels decided to get the factories going. The planters, believing that the mills would not move without them, were emboldened. One tried to negotiate the return of his properties by offering to give work to the wretched *campesinos* in exchange. He did not even receive a reply.

The Zapatistas expropriated the mills and, performing miracles, succeeded in reconstructing some of them. Administration of the mills was handed over to the rebel chiefs, and somehow sugar was produced. Santa Clara, in the hands of the sullen General Mendoza, one of the first to rebel, milled cane toward the end of 1915. But the Zapatistas never tried to rebuild the hacienda as a great territorial enterprise. It was a question, not of changing owners, but of transforming the relations of production. The land, the water, and the cane belonged to the peasants; the refinery became a service institution for growers and had neither lands nor peons. The earnings of the mills were supposed to serve a social purpose: Zapata thought of paying pensions to the families of the fallen. In practice there was very little profit, and it was devoted to military expenses. Apparently, the system functioned in a relatively disorganized way, but not without efficacy, and none of the chiefs was accused of profiting personally from his assignment. Measures were considered for passing from a military to a civil administration under technicians from the credit bank founded by the revolutionaries.

The experiment of the Zapatista haciendas lasted only briefly. Before the conclusion of the 1916 sugar harvest the *reales* were occupied by the Constitutionalist army, and the haciendas were placed under their military administration. The Carrancista chiefs who took over the management, with the complicity of their superiors and even in cooperation with Pablo González, devoted themselves to plundering on an industrial scale everything that the Zapatistas had managed to save. Railroad cars loaded with machinery left Morelos for unknown destinations, and the ruin of the haciendas became more grave. Later the haciendas were leased to Carrancista army officers for their personal benefit. The sinecure included not only the factory but also the territory, and the conquerors charged the vanquished for the rental of the land.

In the realm of corruption and politicking that Carrancismo had established, the *hacendados* moved at will and better than anyone else. They skillfully maneuvered among the different factions of constitutionalism, and by the end of 1919, barely a few months after the death of Zapata, they obtained the unconditional restoration of their properties and their personal immunity, guaranteed by Carranza. They performed miracles of political coordination and were reborn as a pressure group. Little by little, the old names rang out again in the fields of Morelos. The planters also worked financial and technical marvels, the basis of which was the renewal of the peonage and of sharecropping, and they managed to obtain modest production, which opened the hope of reestablishing the modern, flourishing enterprises. Luis García Pimentel the younger summarized the achievement in these terms: "The combination of prehistoric methods with the railroad is one of the most curious things. But out of it are coming some green stalks of cane" (cited by Womack, p. 348). He also synthesized the climate in which this occurred. After complaining about the ingratitude of the *campesinos,* who received him not with affection but with demands, he warned: "Today militant Zapatismo is entirely dead, and the bands that remain are few and without importance . . . [but] the Zapatismo that has not died, nor will die, is pacific Zapatismo, for these people have thievery in their blood, and nothing nor nobody will be able to take it out of them" (cited by Womack, p. 349). Surprisingly, for once young Luis was right.

The Children of the Hacienda. "When the hacienda was finished off, we were left like orphans," recalls one of the *realeños.* "The government left, and then it didn't come back. Huerta and Cartón went, and then the disorder came."

The children of the hacienda, the proletarian aristocrats, did not rebel with Zapata. One of the old *realeños* says that only three from Tenango went with the revolutionaries—two laborers from the cane crop and one who transported lumber for the sugar cauldrons—the rest remained loyal to the hacienda. Because they were uprooted from the land and the communities, all their immediate interests were bound up with the hacienda's survival. The alternative that Zapatismo offered them in its first phase, a portion of land, was not attractive to them, and the revolutionaries, who gave priority to the recovery of the plundered communities, had no concrete program to implement it. The *realeños* took shelter under the hacienda and, worse luck, shared its destiny.

Some *realeños* definitively took the side of the government. Allied with the rich from Jonacatepec, they formed squads of volunteers to guide the federal troops in pursuit of the rebel guerrillas, apparently with very little success. Others volunteered to fight at the side of the García Pimentels and their Japanese against the Zapatistas; perhaps the fact that their wish went unfulfilled saved their lives. There were not many who behaved that way, but they were significantly more numerous than those who clearly joined the revolutionaries or cooperated with them.

The majority of the *realeños* opted for passivity, for doing their work and not interfering. It was impossible. Many surprised and dismayed *realeños* found themselves enlisted by force in the squads of volunteers. But such services did not make them immune to the repression of the federal troops. The army hung two of them, apparently the victims of some intrigue, under the accusation of receiving Zapatistas in their houses at Tenango. The levy grabbed others, and the intervention of Paredes, the administrator, or even of the García Pimentels was necessary to rescue them. But at times not even such influence was enough to exempt them, and several were lost forever. One, caught by the levy, deserted to join the rebels. Soon afterwards he abandoned the revolution for the peripatetic but dangerous task of transporting out of Morelos the money of the García Pimentel family, who guaranteed him immunity against the federal troops.

The Zapatistas did not like the children of the hacienda very well either, but in the end they respected them, except for the *dedos chiquitos*, the favorites. They gave them the same treatment they gave the wealthy from the villages: they took them prisoners and forced them to pay their ransom in cash. That happened to the master bricklayer who built the Tenango guardhouses in which the federal army was entrenched. Paredes, the administrator and intermediary with the Zapatistas and the federal forces, also intervened in this rescue.

Amid so much distress, the *realeños* took refuge more emphatically in the protection of the hacienda. When it closed down, the majority dispersed and abandoned the *reales* of Tenango and Santa Clara. Only the most trusted, like the administrators, followed the *patrones* to Mexico City. Other specialized technicians and workers obtained positions in the cane-growing zone of the neighboring state of Puebla. Of many, nothing was ever heard again, but others, especially the artisans, joined the peasant communities and ran the risks of the civilians. Some returned to the *reales*, and when the factories were set going by the Zapatistas, the Constitutionalists, or the planters, they worked in them. When the mills stopped, they cultivated the land and fled from the troops in their effort to survive. Little by little, and forcibly, they became *campesinos*.

The proletarians of Morelos in the strictest sense, the children of the hacienda played a meager role in the revolution of the South, and its sign was predominantly reactionary. Their position as affiliates of the capitalist mode of production, lacking autonomous resources, turned them into natural allies of the planters; both faced an external threat, the peasant rebellion. Their position of real privilege and their immersion in a paternalistic, authoritarian system of dominance halted the rise of a revolutionary consciousness that would have opened for them an alternative of their own. Their numerical weakness, one of the consequences of technological modernization, reduced their weight in the process that modified the social and economic structure of Morelos.

The Rural Bourgeoisie. The local wealthy people did not join the revolution either; instead, the revolutionaries went looking for them. The wealth this group had accumulated in money became the primary source of financing for the rebels. They did not produce or transform anything; they simply prospered at the expense of the villagers, who had many grievances for which to collect. From the first, the rich were partisans of the government, and they lived under protection of the federal forces; some cooperated with them as volunteers.

The first to fall were those who had more autonomy with respect to the hacienda—and enjoyed its protection less—and more social distance with respect to the communities; they were very few, scarcely a handful. José Solís, to whom the García Pimentels had sold an hacienda of two hundred hectares and who was also a merchant and usurer, was killed by Gabriel Tepepa's people. The owner of some sawmills was attacked by the people of Hueyapan, who took everything he had. Others paid their own ransoms. The greater part of them fled after a scare; they were too vulnerable.

Those who were more closely associated with the haciendas and in direct contact with the villagers could defend themselves a little better, since they could resort to protection from one side and to negotiation with the other. Their capital, almost entirely invested in livestock, was more vulnerable still, and it was slaughtered for the supply of the troops, whether federals or revolutionaries. In the year 1913 the rebels even prescribed an order of priorities for slaughter: the livestock of the planters and of the enemies of the cause would be taken first; then that of supporters, "but always taking into account that they should be persons who would not be harmed much"; and it was forbidden to take animals from poor people, as well as oxen or cows giving birth that would make cultivation or reproduction possible (cited by Gilly, pp. 71–73). The livestock of the wealthy always remained in first place, even if the owners expressed sympathy for the rebels. The federal troops drove off all cattle alike.

Many of the wealthy or the well-off, those closest to the estate, went away—some with their livestock, others with some savings, and still others with nothing at all. Those closest to the communities, who were also the least rich, left or returned to integrate themselves into the communities and became *pacíficos,* or "noncombatants." The local bourgeoisie, which performed the roles of intermediation between the great capitalist hacienda and the peasant community, was dissolved in the revolutionary process. The *coyume,* or the civilized people, more linked with the hacienda, disappeared in the years of struggle, while the Indian livestock owners survived, lost within the framework of the community. The ethnic barrier was demolished. To be *catrín,* a "dandy," or to seem to be, ceased to be a privilege only to become a risk. Some city dwellers were killed by the revolutionaries because of their appearance and attitude. Color, costume, and attitude had been instruments of oppression that to a certain extent served as a boundary between the opposing bands. Indeed, some dandies did go off to the revolution, but upon doing so they stopped being dandies.

The Rebels

The Formation of the Army. The bulk of the Zapatista troops came from the rural communities of Morelos. To fight wherever the battle was, the youngest "still just boys, sixteen or seventeen years old," who did not yet have families, went off, openly joining the revolutionary band. That generation was also the one most threatened by the levy, the forced recruitment that the federal army used to fill up its ranks and to impede the growth of the rebel groups, and by lack of access to land and work. Many of the veterans explain their entry into the revolutionary army as a response to the levy: "If it was between their taking me to fight far away, God knows where, and staying here, it was better for me to fight here." "I didn't want to be a revolutionary, but the government wanted me for a dead man; better that I went to shoot a few bullets."

In fact, many people seized by the levy joined the Zapatistas after escaping the federal troops: "They took me to fight against Villa, but I did not give them the pleasure very long because then I ran off from them and joined up with the revolutionaries." Others explain their course as a defensive reaction in the face of a total threat: "If the government was going to kill us, better that they killed us fighting"; "Among us boys, we encouraged one another: 'Let's go to the revolution because things are going to get ugly. If they are going to kill us, better that it be fighting.'" Indeed, the relatives of the last speaker, who was fifteen years old when he joined the forces of General Mendoza, believed that a wild bull had thrown him down the gorge, and they looked for him anxiously. Others gave much more specific reasons. The Zapatistas asked one man for his horse for their troops: "The horse goes, but he doesn't go alone," he said, and he joined the rebels. Another was detained by a federal *guacho,* or draftee, from whom he escaped by running off. "Then I stopped, all scared, and I thought: there was nothing left to do but to go all the way."

Men who were forty or fifty years old did not join the almost-regular forces of Zapata unless by exception. "Some snot-nosed kids took away Don Perfecto's pants for no other reason than that they were rebels. To avenge himself, he got involved as a rebel and was a commander in 1918." That generation had family obligations, at times even grand-children, the children of the young men who had gone off to *la bola,* the brawl. They also fought occasionally; when the battle came close, they joined the rebels and fired off some shots. Afterwards they returned to their homes or to the mountains in which they were hiding and continued to work the fields. Zapata and his chiefs always insisted that the villagers should be armed for their own defense as the exercise of a natural right. They believed that an armed base was the best guarantee for keeping the revolution within its ideals, without deviations or betrayals. Thus, each villager became an irregular militia man who fought against the federal forces in his own territory without giving them any respite. Moreover, they ended up confronting bands who called themselves Zapatistas, and perhaps they were, who threatened the villages with sacking and disaster. More than a few shots were fired from militia rifles. Chiefs who entered the fight with two hundred soldiers finished with five hundred if they won, with thirty if they lost, only to get back to two hundred a few days later.

All those who went off to the brawl with Zapata or joined his forces in some battles did so voluntarily. Zapatismo did not recruit by force. There are those who tell of having heard Zapata say to his soldiers: "You can follow me, but understand that I don't want to take you by force. Let whoever wants to follow come along, but if I'm left with just one soldier, I will resist with that one." The lack of external coercion was counterbalanced with a strong pressure within the communities in favor of Zapatismo and by a severe repression against government supporters. The villager was given a choice of fighting or not, but not of choosing sides.

All the veterans' explanations give the definite impression that the Zapatista uprising was a defensive reaction by the peasants to a set of threats. They describe the revolution as a response in the face of succes-sive aggressions. The communities reacted adapting to the armed struggle the old strategies for survival that they had been applying from the beginning. The preservation of the family as a basic unit had priority.

To attain it, just as the young men were once sent out as laborers to get a money income, during the war they were sent to fight. The preservation of the community as an efficient unit of cooperation to permit the subsistence of families with insufficient resources was consolidated; it was the community that took sides and prevented the rise of factions. It was also the community that fought, and when the time came, administered the recovered territory. Zapatismo was the action of the communities to defend their survival through armed struggle.

But the rural communities were located at the base of a complex system bound in interdependence to the national entity. Their pure defensive reaction necessarily broke with the arrangement of the whole. Zapatismo assumed the part destructive of the old balances that its defensive reaction objectively implied, and when it proposed its own plan for the reorganization of the whole, it became clearly revolutionary. The Zapatistas, as Womack says, knew that to go on being peasants, they had to transform the rest of society, and stubbornly they tried it by the path of armed struggle.

The Zapatista Forces. A man who went off to battle joined the forces of some chief and fought along with them. He would strive to join people from the same village under the command of some acquaintance: "Three of us went; one was the colonel's godson." But none of the veterans remained under the command of a single chief. They stayed at his side for a time and then changed units or returned home. They looked for another chief "because I didn't like his style anymore" or "because I got wounded, and afterwards I joined up with others." In the most difficult period, when the rebels broke up, many changed chiefs "because I suspected that he was going to betray us by becoming a Carrancista."

Many of those who returned home wounded did not rejoin the struggle again; healing was long and painful. Others returned to respond to urgent appeals: many young men became the heads of extended families and returned to their villages to take charge of their new responsibility. The man who went to the revolution to follow his horse came back when they killed it; while he fought he was distinguished by his almost suicidal bravery. Some speak of "becoming tired of fighting after several years." Many, however, returned for only a few days to share in agricultural chores, to rest a little, and then to rejoin the fight. After the death of Zapata the army dissolved with the same mechanisms. "The chief said: 'Whoever wants to follow should follow me, but whoever wants to go should go, should get back to his home and his work.' By then nothing was left of the revolution. I went back, rejoined my *patrón*, and went on working." The combatants returned home with their arms, which they jealously hid, and some even with their horses. Thus, when the chiefs called them again in 1920, they formed an army in a few days: "We did not fight; we just backed up General Obregón."

This mobility of the combatants, which made the Zapatista irregular forces waver between forty thousand and barely two thousand or three thousand men, constituted a severe limitation on the rebels' ability to undertake major battles. Little was done by the staff to halt it. The only effective possibility for containing that constant flow, the availability of supplies to maintain a regular army, was beyond the reach of the Zapatistas. The dispersion had to be managed in the tactics and strategy of the revolutionaries. In December 1911 Zapata ordered his chiefs to give their men a furlough to return to their villages to harvest corn (Womack, p. 128), the only guarantee for the feeding of the troops. The war, like agriculture, became a seasonal phenomenon, recurrent, almost indefinite. Perhaps one of the factors that delayed Zapata's assault on Mexico City in August 1914 was that in the first two weeks of that month the cornfields were given the last weeding, the *despacho*.

On the other hand, this fluidity prevented a militarist structure from appearing within Zapatismo. Chiefs were named and supported by consensus among their men. There was an implicit code that could not be violated without risk of being left alone or being disavowed. The real impossibility of halting desertion turned the authority of the chiefs into a delegation of support from their people. The pattern was repeated even at the highest levels, and Zapata himself was more like a delegate who coordinated the action of many autonomous units than an authoritarian chief with his own source of power. The big battles, just like the political decisions, were the result of long conferences in which they took the pulse of things at the same time that they argued and encouraged one another. Indeed, once obtained, the consensus was firm to the point of exasperation.

Military prerogatives and privileges were systematically avoided by opposing and sacrificing the authority of the chiefs to the village authorities. With this, again, military efficiency, understood as the centralized accumulation of strength, was lost, but the revolutionary base was extended. The Zapatistas were not out to capture the centralized power of the State; rather, they sought its refoundation.

The Leadership. The Army of the South was formed by bands, by commands with a high degree of autonomy in their action. This was a consequence not only of the impossibility of maintaining a regular army because of lack of supplies but also of the fluidity in recruitment and in length of service. The functioning of each band was only possible because of the existence of a direct, personal relationship among all its members, or at least among a central nucleus that gave articulation to the group. One joined up with Mendoza, with Neri, or with Camacho, whom he came to know and to deal with personally, but he did not join the Eighteenth Battalion. "It's that the general appreciated me, had confidence in me because he knew that I wasn't one of those that backed down"; or "General Mendoza told me, 'Look boy, your dad doesn't want you to go with us. Better stay here.' But then he even made me a colonel"; "Although I didn't know them, I went to fight with them. When they saw that I was sincere, they presented me to the leader, who told me: 'If you're here to fight, just stick around and stay ready.'" Behind that apparent informality operated a multiple network of ties established beforehand: kinship and co-parenthood, friends in common, mutual references, the intangible proofs of an identity among acquaintances. The Zapatista soldier had to establish his standing as a member of some community or to pass a long series of tests before being admitted as an unconditional comrade of the rebels. In Morelos Zapatismo there were surely adventurers; what is surprising is that there were so few.

Surprising, too, is that given the importance that the leaders had as permanent nuclei of the rebel units, a personal, individualist *caudillismo,* "chieftainship," did not arise. All the principal chiefs remained together and loyal until the end; even after the murder of Emiliano Zapata they were capable of naming a successor, Gildardo Magaña, by unanimous consensus, although the process was slow and tortuous, as the election of Zapata himself once had been. None of the central chiefs fought personally at the expense of their troops or of the civilian population. Very few are known to have exceeded and abused their authority in order to impose a regime of terror among the troops. This is explained in part by the transfer of a mechanism that operated in the communities even before the rebellion. There the chief's position was conferred not only for personal qualities but as a consequence of services offered to the group. Communal chiefs named by consensus had to have an objective history of service in order to be delegated authority. Moreover, the office itself was understood as service, never as a sinecure. The military chief, just like the earlier figure of the *patrón de la milpa,* who had to redistribute his access to the land, had a set of obligations that he had to fulfill, and two sources of pressure, his troops and the other chiefs, above all Zapata, ensured that he generally did it.

For the leadership, the confidence of the people was not enough; personal bravery in every test, ability to command, craftiness, and even a way with people were demanded. The Zapatista chiefs were strongly individualized personalities, endowed with a great charisma that made them subjects of legend. This individualization, necessary for serving as an organizing nucleus of the troops, was never exempt from problems. The careful battle plan for taking Chilpancingo broke down when General Encarnacíon Díaz dared General Heliodoro Castillo with these words: "I have offered to eat dinner tonight in Chilpancingo, and if you'd like to accompany me, I invite you," and they began combat before the planned time; luckily, they won the battle, and during it the federal general Cartón, one of the hangmen of Morelos, fell prisoner (Magaña, 3 : 313–14). Amador Salazar and Felipe Neri, both important Zapatista chiefs, once played cards and decided to bet something for the cause: that night Salazar entered Yautepec alone and killed the federal commander of the stronghold in a personal duel; with that, he paid off the bet that he had lost (Magaña, 2 : 118–19). Eufemio Zapata died shot by Sidronio Camacho, another Zapatista chief, when Camacho found out that Eufemio had struck his father. Few veterans reproached Camacho's action, nor did they even consider him a traitor when he went over to the Carranza side after killing Emiliano's brother; he did the right thing, and he had no other alternative. The chiefs enjoyed privileges: they had the best horses, they dressed with rustic elegance, sometimes they had money and drank the best liquor, and they all had many children. No one complained about these things: they were the symbols and prizes of their status, of position won through hard service. But none of them was a *caudillo* who would put his personal ambition ahead of the cause. "Emiliano would not have let them."

Almost without exception the generals in command of troops were natives of the Morelos villages. However, almost none was a typical villager, for, on the contrary, they were located in an almost marginal position in respect to the community in terms of their principal activity. Francisco Mendoza was a rancher and rustler, Salazar a cowboy, Neri a kiln operator on the Chinameca hacienda, Gabriel Tepepa captain on the one at Temilpa, Morales a saloon keeper from Ayutla, and José Trinidad Ruiz was a Protestant preacher from Tlaltizapán (Womack, pp. 73–79). The exception was Fortino Ayaquica, a first-generation textile worker at Atlixco.

The Zapatas were merchants at times and horse breakers at others. Almost all the chiefs had a touch of the adventurous and enterprising that set them apart. But all participated in the community as a framework of social relations; Zapata, de la O, and Salazar had been elected community authorities. Like the Zapatas, almost all had been renters of land from the hacienda, *patrones de la milpa*, or came from families that were. Their relatives, their acquaintances, their families, and their loyalties were with the plundered communities. In them they formed almost an elite because of their more comfortable, or less painful, economic position and their knowledge and contacts with a wider world.

Almost all were around thirty years old at the beginning of the movement, and some, like Emiliano Zapata, were still bachelors. They had a
reputation as wild, as unbroken, and as rebels; the local district prefect
had kept an eye on more than a few of them because sometime they
were going to have to pay up for their pasts. Nobody had doubts about
their affiliation with village interests. They were, then, a natural choice
for directing an armed adventure. They responded with loyalty, and the
enormous respect that even Emiliano himself showed for the old
communal leaders is still remembered with pleasure.

The local chiefs began their own movement alone, and they retained
military and political direction of it until the end with an almost fanatical
zeal and with an enormous distrust toward the dandies from the city.
Some of these joined the Zapatista movement for ideological or romantic
reasons, and they played an important role in it: they took charge of
expressing it, of editing its proclamations and laws, of preparing the
speeches of its chiefs. But the fundamental document of the rebels of
the South, the Plan of Ayala, was derived from an exchange of ideas
among the local chiefs, which was elaborated by Zapata himself and
Otilio Montaño, a rural schoolteacher from Villa de Ayala and the only
"intellectual" who participated in the uprising from its beginnings. The
intellectuals who joined later—the Magañas, the Soto y Gamas, Manuel
Palafox, Miguel Mendoza—did many important things. They legislated
and negotiated, even went to the government to represent Zapatismo.
They served as secretaries and founded organizations and commissions,
which they then made function. Above all, they gave ideas that the
combat chiefs worked out slowly in order to offer a daring, original plan
for the reorganization of society. Some even directed combat troops;
and Gildardo Magaña inherited the chieftainship from Zapata to save
whatever was possible. This group's part was definitive in structuring
the revolutionary movement of the South, but it never came to control
or direct it. The very character of Zapatismo made that impossible; it
was a collective movement that never allowed direction or manipulation
from outside.

None of the principal chiefs rose out of the Morelos *oriente*. Again,
the combination of its isolation and self-sufficiency in cultivation of corn
that delayed its mobilization was important. When the García Pimentel
domains were added to the brawl, three outstanding chiefs were already
operating in them and had established themselves on their periphery:
Ayaquica in Tochimilco, to the northeast of the area; Mendoza, the
most important, in the mountains of the east; and Neri, in the southeast
of the great plain. For long periods Zapata himself had his general
headquarters in Huautla, sheltered by the rough, hostile sierra. The
peasants of the *oriente* joined this force and fought at its side. But

their land remained in the center of the battle and of the revolution.

The Popular Army. One of the mechanisms that governed the size of the military units of the Zapatista rebels was the supply they could have available. The chiefs had as many soldiers as they could get rifles, bullets, and even tortillas. There was usually very little of everything, and it lasted only for a few days. When the guerrillas were near, the villages, as they had done with the laborers who worked for the hacienda, sent the *tlacualeros* with their load of tortillas and at times even fresh foods of the day. They did this even when they were occupied by federal forces. At night the *tlacualeros* went out, or the rebels came in surreptitiously; they always found time to eat something hot and even to have a little drink in the homes of their providers.

When the troops were far from their villages the population fed them in some way. The Zapatistas asked for help "with goodwill," without threats, and at times they even paid for their foods, even though it was with the money they printed in Chilpancingo. "The gesture was appreciated," although one had to hide or burn the bills, for if the federal troops found them, they could hang people for possessing them. At times they also took food against people's will, by force; again, it is surprising that these occasions were so few. Even in 1918, in full military defeat, Zapata ordered his troops, "When asking for food, you will do so with kind words; ask for everything you want politely, always showing your gratitude" (cited by Womack, p. 314). Since 1916 Zapata himself had officials who extorted from the villages expelled dishonorably from his ranks to guarantee that his forces would not become groups of bandits who only fought for their own survival (Womack, p. 218). To the same end, it was urged that the villages maintain armed militias for their own protection.

In 1917 and 1918 the villages, which managed to sustain themselves only with difficulty, could not keep up their provisioning of the Zapatistas. The army and the population had to depend to a great extent on the import of food from the zones controlled by the enemy. The civilians became muleteers, bringing corn from Puebla and Toluca. Bribery enabled them to pass enemy checkpoints—for one peso per person or per animal, the federals looked the other way. But money was needed, even for that, and the Zapatistas did not have it, nor could they get it in a devastated territory without production and almost without population. The army was reduced to a few bands with a handful of permanent guerrillas. Even these few had to eat tortillas made not just of the kernels of corn but out of the cobs and the flowers too. The military strength of Zapatismo was practically destroyed.

The villages could never provide the arms and the ammunition; they had to be obtained by fighting, by taking them away from the enemy. The Zapatistas never had an external supply of armaments, and this was denied them even when they were in the Convention government. Martín Luis Guzmán, who formed part of the government in the Ministry of War, received instructions regarding the Zapatistas: "If they ask you for arms, or ammunition, or trains, don't give them so much as water." He complied faithfully: "I exhausted all imaginable resources in order not to supply them with arms, cartridges, or locomotives" (cited by Gilly, p. 162). Moreover, the Zapatistas, isolated in the center of the country, had no access to the international market, particularly the United States, any more than they had the necessary capital. Thus, they contrived to set up a factory that reloaded spent cartridges with pieces of steel cable (Womack, p. 243), to buy arms from the national factory through corrupt military men, to make hand bombs—but always in quantities that were insufficient when not simply ridiculous. Its enemies armed the Zapatista force, although certainly not willingly. The result was the extremely heterogeneous armament: the 30-30 carbine dominated, but there were Mausers and Savages and even fowling pieces suited for hunting rabbits at most—all of a different caliber; occasionally a French machine gun or some cannon from an obscure source appeared. As a rule, there was no more ammunition for this complex arsenal, which sometimes seemed more like a museum, than what the guerrillas carried on their backs, in their cartridge belts. To obtain it they often had to assault some enemy garrison, on occasion only with muzzle loaders, called *coachcleras,* and dynamite cartridges.

The rebel army, like the peasant society from which it emerged, was always kept at a strict subsistence level, without external supply, almost without warehouses and without capital. Thus it had to wage war with forces emerging from the capitalist sector, organized around the centralized accumulation of troops, arms, and ammunition, that is, of capital.

Again, as they had always done, the peasants confronted accumulated power with the coordination of a collective effort: they joined thousands of small individual or corporate efforts so that, synchronized, they might generate strength. To make this possible they extended solidarity, the mechanisms of redistribution that previously existed in order to attain survival. To a certain extent, within Zapatismo everyone became *compadres* and relatives in order to carry out a popular struggle.

The Guerrilla Warfare in the South. The nature of the peasant society and of its military force, like that of the enemy bands, shaped the strategy and tactics of the contestants. The successive factions that confronted the Zapatistas, although representing different tendencies and offering different programs, were in the end forces arising out of post-industrial capitalism. Their military objective was the capture of political and administrative centers, of the primary cities. To obtain it they accumulated troops and supplies and deployed them in large, decisive battles. According to the rules of their game, triumph or defeat meant the gaining or loss of power, understood as a storehouse of centralized means of control and dominance. They were civilized people, and they fought a modern war.

The Zapatistas, on the other hand, had to avoid the great battles, in which they had everything to lose. Without artillery, without more ammunition than they carried in their cartridge belts, they could not accept a war of strongholds. They did not want control over the cities, where, away from their sources of supply, their troops were weakened. When the fearsome Attila of the South took Mexico City, his troops, out of the reach of the *tlacualeros,* went through the streets begging for food with their best manners. The conquerors of the capital of the country, the dreaded "tribes" and "hordes" who terrified the soft, flabby city dwellers, the rustic socialists with their limited intellects, behaved like polite beggars, perhaps to their own disgrace. In the cities Zapatismo had no allies nor even sympathizers. Occupying cities turned the rebel army into police of a hostile territory. The power that the cities stored in their administrative institutions was what had been expropriated, alienated, from the defeated groups. The Zapatistas did not want to hold on to it, but to dissolve it: they fought for the decentralization of power, to make it ubiquitous, like the guerrilla warfare.

The Zapatistas controlled the countryside, and their enemies, the cities. The tactics of both were congruent. The federal troops fought in formation with platoons under the command of officers who directed the action of each soldier; however, "we rebels fought in a gang." When the chief had given the general directions, each Zapatista acted almost on his own accord, with a great deal of personal initiative, to carry them out. If they were lucky, they hunted the federal formations like ducks in a shooting gallery; if not, they disbanded more or less chaotically. The federal troops, with greater fire power and with longer-range arms, tried to fight from afar, on the plain, in the open field. The rebels sought to avoid these clashes at all costs. Their 30-30's reached scarcely half as far as the federal Mausers, and their bullets could not be wasted. However, they knew the terrain like their own homes; some rocks and trees even had their own names. For this reason, they fought up close and sought ambushes in the complex web of gorges on the mountainous slopes, where they could blend in with the enemy without offering him any defined front. They say that once Zapata and his people were on a mountain when they realized that the federal troops had them surrounded;

they let them climb up, and then they slipped away through a gully. When the federal force reached the top, the Zapatistas set the mountain on fire and hunted them down in the confusion.

The federal troops learned quickly and ended up locking themselves into strongholds, especially haciendas on which there was no civilian population and which turned out to be almost impregnable for the guerrillas. A good part of the war in the South passed in that way: the federal forces in their forts, barricaded, and the Zapatistas in the fields. The federal soldiers could occupy the villages and remain in them, but they never knew if they had taken them. The Zapatistas entered the village by night to eat supper, while the invaders locked themselves into the principal building with the thickest walls, where they could not be attacked.

The federal troops went about in uniform to distinguish themselves from the civilian population; the Zapatistas, on the contrary, sought to be confused with them and not to be identified. Often the federal forces arrived in a village in pursuit of the guerrillas with whom they had fought a few hours before and found only civilians, earnestly occupied in cultivating the land or resting after their work; they looked for arms without finding them, and exhausted horses did not appear either; they interrogated the villagers, sometimes violently, but almost never obtained an accusation. The guerrillas dissolved among their people; they continued to be villagers. At times, as Zapatista soldiers they acquired a little of the money that the chiefs or the general staff obtained; at others, they produced as *campesinos;* there was no clear distinction, and no one seemed to look for one. Fluidity was the strength of Zapatismo. As peasants they obtained supplies, found refuge and rest, and regained strength to return to the attack.

However, the federal, or Constitutionalist, armies formed an autonomous social corporation, separated from other social groups by its own function: to impose the dominance of a central power by force. It was a professional corporation, without any productive function and sustained by expropriating the surpluses of other groups. To be separated from those groups in order to make the existence and the strength of the external power evident and to repeat in their internal organization a rigid, centralist scheme were and are essential conditions of the army that serves the capitalist State, in which the mechanisms of power, like the capacity for repression, are accumulated and stored like commodities.

The Zapatista Battles. The Zapatistas wanted to win the war, and they had to stage major battles, of all kinds, to attempt it. Since the people carried their whole arsenal on their backs, it was necessary to gather together considerable personnel to equal the fire power of a wellmunitioned army. Numerical superiority was indispensable for confrontation. In Cuautla there were almost ten rebels per federal soldier; at Jantetelco there might have been more. But even with this numerical advantage, the Zapatistas could not sustain trench warfare against forces with artillery and machine guns. Thus they surrounded their enemies, and with the circle scarcely closed, they launched a general, definitive attack that only ended with a victory or a defeat. Although the combat might last several days, the Zapatistas' attack was continuous. Once the troops were located on the most advantageous terrain, there was no longer an opportunity to carry out elaborate tactical maneuvers, only a single great effort from thousands of combatants.

At that moment the cavalry had the central role. The power to cross the barricade of gunfire from the besieged federals depended upon the cavalry's thrust and speed in order to succeed in penetrating their positions and to fight from within. The Zapatista horsemen were skilled, trained in the game of riding the bulls, the most popular one at fiestas in the state of Morelos. They handled the lariat masterfully, and it is often told how they lassoed the enemy machine guns to open the way for the massive, though irregular, infantry—often armed with little more than muzzle-charged shot guns that could only be loaded with the necessary parsimony. The more or less regular army was mounted. That gave it great mobility and also, frankly, that noteworthy speed in retreat. But in the big battles there were not enough horses for all the volunteers involved in the assault, who ran behind the animals like madmen, whether during the attack or when they happened to give chase. The cavalry, like the number of more or less permanent soldiers, continued to be reduced little by little on the fields devastated by years of war. The losses could never be replaced, and the gains became less and less frequent.

When the federal troops were fortified within walls or trenches, not even a cavalry charge was enough to break their dense lines. Then ingenuity came forth, personal initiative accompanied by almost suicidal bravery, but always protected in the profound knowledge of the territory in which they were fighting. The first time the Zapatistas took the hacienda of El Treinta, they broke down the inner door of the compound where the federal troops were entrenched with a locomotive going full speed. The second or third time, there was no longer a locomotive, and the hacienda fell when the Zapatistas entered the enclosure by climbing a mango tree that grew outside and jumping from its branches. Near Hueyapan they ambushed the Carrancistas in a gorge to which they had lured them by making them follow some volunteers, to whom the chief had said: "Just keep within gunshot range. Don't let them get discouraged." In Cuautla, one of the hardest battles because the city was defended by the *quinto de oro,* one of the elite corps of the Porfirista army, which left a bullet wherever it cast a glance, the Zapatistas used volunteers who went close to the enemy lines to hurl dynamite shells at them. One of the unsuccessful throws cost Felipe Neri, who was directing the dynamiters, his hearing and almost his life. But not even this was enough to break the *quinto de oro.* Then it occurred to someone that the federal soldiers were entrenched in aqueducts and canals: The Zapatistas ran gasoline through the canals and set it afire. The members of the *quinto* emerged and came within gunshot. A rebel who was a very good hunter knocked down several; then he explained that if "not even a stag had ever escaped him despite running a lot, with less reason would a federal soldier, who ran less and who was bulkier besides." They tell that Zapata sent Don Porfirio the uniforms of the *quinto de oro* with a note that said, "Here are the wrappers so that you can send me more *tamales.*"

But the big battles, which had an enormous political importance for the Zapatistas aside from their strict military value and from serving as a source of provisions, implied an enormous price, especially in lives lost. There is, of course, no list of Zapatista casualties, but these were great, apparently much higher than those of the federal forces. If the battle ended in disaster, the loss of arms, ammunition, and horses had to be added to the loss of life. Zapata and his chiefs had to measure each encounter with care, taking into account all their limitations.

The rebel Army of the South, in contrast with Pancho Villa's Division of the North, could not move freely throughout the whole country. It was tied to its bases, the civilians, who supplied it; its great mobility was reduced to the limited sphere where the communities were to a lesser or greater extent also Zapatistas. When they took Mexico City, the rebels had to leave their horses outside: in Milpa Alta, Coyoacán, or Xochimilco, on lands and pastures of the *campesinos.* Pedro Martínez and his companions had to flee the Carrancistas on nothing less than a trolley car (Lewis 1966, p. 87). The cavalry, the knowledge of the terrain, the possibility of being assimilated into the population, the food supply—all the resources that gave strength to the Army of the South—were profoundly rooted in the rural environment, and outside it they turned against the guerrillas. "In Mexico City, just by seeing one another, we knew who was a rebel, as if we were uniformed."

The resources that gave mobility to the other armies that were independent of geography, from trains and arms to the modern field hospitals that Villa's forces used, were external not only to peasant society and economy but to the country. They were made in the industrial nations, and their acquisition was negotiated with merchants, particularly from the United States. The Zapatistas could never acquire them directly, and whenever they used them, it was because they had taken them from the enemy. Perhaps the military efficacy of Zapatismo would have been increased with their use, just as its enemies' was increased, but its political program would have been modified in that process, almost imperceptibly but possibly as profoundly as its adversaries' program was changed. Military technology has never been a neutral product. Perhaps it is worth the trouble to emphasize that.

The Federal War. While Zapatista guerrilla warfare could not obtain a military triumph over the well-supplied professional armies, it could not be overcome militarily, either. Porfirio Díaz was the first to prove it: his army, almost intact, had lost the war. The peasant guerrilla fighting could only be annihilated along with the population from which it emerged and into which it dissolved. Juvencio Robles, a career soldier, was the first to act accordingly. His attacks were directed not only, nor even basically, against the Zapatista troops, but against the entirety of the population and its resources, whether houses, crops, or domestic or work animals. His favorite weapon was fire. Wherever his troops passed, villages and planted fields were burned and livestock shot. Generalized terrorism was added to this destruction: murders of isolated individuals or the systematic shooting of people who seemed to be Zapatista—and everyone in Morelos did. Colonel Cartón, one of his fiercest subordinates, carried a coffin and some chains with his column, because he was going to capture Zapata dead or alive. His luck failed: He fell prisoner to the Zapatistas in Chilpancingo, and after his trial, he was shot.

When the federal incendiary campaign failed, it was necessary to go even further. Again, Robles acted in that direction, and he designed the policy of *reconcentration,* as the peasants called it—*recolonization,* as the federal forces and the press said. This consisted of moving the people to the cities or larger villages, where they were in fact installed in concentration camps (Womack, pp. 155–56).

Robles failed, although he had two opportunities, as military chief of Morelos under Madero and under Huerta, but he left behind disciples. Pablo González followed him faithfully and even added to the recolonization in strategic hamlets the consequent final step: mass deportation. He carried out reconcentration several times between 1916 and 1918, and the deportation of several thousands in 1916. To these steps were added the plunder of anything—no matter how worthless—that might have some value and the systematic destruction of the little that some peasants still retained. The indiscriminate terror, murders, forced recruitment, and deportation continued. The population fled, the fields remained unplanted, there was starvation, and epidemics appeared. In 1918 one of them sowed death in Morelos, and even Cuautla remained, in effect, deserted: "The Spanish influenza continues its pacifying work in Morelos," proclaimed the daily *Excelsior* in November that year (cited by Womack, p. 306).

Morelos territory was offered to colonizers, and bringing in thirty thousand Japanese to repopulate it was even seriously discussed. Zapatismo as a military force had disappeared, along with almost half the population (including both the dead and the emigrated), all the wealth, the agricultural production, and even many of the villages of the state of Morelos. The society that had given life to Zapatismo was disarticulated and threatened with death. In 1919, when they murdered Zapata, the federal forces declared their final victory.

A little in vain. The people still remained, and they continued to be Zapatista; loyal chiefs remained; hidden old firearms that could still shoot remained; even plants remained. It is said that a federal soldier who grabbed a *chichicaztle,* a tree that produces skin irritations, made the famous remark, "Even the sticks are Zapatistas." He was right. In 1920 the Morelos communities rebelled again, no longer with strength to radicalize a revolution, but still with sufficient energy to obtain their own survival.

The Civilians. Many people who survived the revolution do not have exploits to tell about. They are the *pacíficos,* the peasants and their families who remained in their villages and gave permanence to the process. Although they do not say so, they, too, were Zapatistas, some perhaps without even wanting to be, and they played a central part in the southern revolution.

Their tales are quite different from the combatants'. In their stories the beginning of the revolution appears confused, even distant. They heard talk of some fellow Madero who had risen against the government, but only when they speak of Zapata do they use the word *revolution.* Many were skeptics. Things were not good, but surely *they* were not going to be the people who would change them. When the young men of their villages left to fight, some saw it as a boys' affair that could not alter peasant destiny. They kept on working, paying rent for their lands, and offering their services as laborers on the haciendas.

But even without admitting it, they were linked by affinity, almost by kinship, to Zapatismo. They were not going to deny a tortilla to those from the village, nor could they refuse to aid someone wounded if he was one of their people. These were things that were simply done, without even thinking. When Zapata put forth the Plan of Ayala, even the most skeptical changed their opinions a little. What was asked for in the plan was obviously just and necessary, and a great deal of thought was not needed here, either: these were things that everyone had always known. It was no longer like when they were fighting for Madero and his political plan. The sense of affinity was extended, although in varying degrees, to all those who went under the banner of Zapata.

But not everyone wanted to be committed. With the war, too many colonels and generals had sprung up, men who said they were revolutionaries and who, followed by a few armed men, committed robberies and assaults and claimed personal vengeance. Security was lacking, and injustices were committed that led the civilians to enclose themselves in expectation. The groups proliferated, and Zapatismo had not obtained either the strength or the consistency to check and to regroup these bands. Zapata had a passive sympathy among the civilians of the Morelos *oriente*. But it was the federal army, through its action, that made obvious the affinity between the villagers and the rebels and turned that passive sympathy into clear collaboration.

The Suspension of Guarantees. On 9 February 1912 the federal army burned the village of Santa María and set fire to its forests, the principal resource exploited by its inhabitants. Days before, Juvencio Robles had declared: "All Morelos, as I understand it, is Zapatista, and there's not a single inhabitant who doesn't believe in the false doctrines of the bandit" (Womack, pp. 133–34).

The civilians saw themselves aligned with, and treated as, Zapatistas. "They seized my father as a prisoner, a man who was a peaceful person, but for the government forces he was Zapatista, and they strung him up; they did not kill him, but he was very scared, and shortly after, he died from the fright." They forced the people to abandon the villages before setting them afire. "Some *pacíficos* wanted to stay, for they had not taken sides, and the federals killed several of them." Everything that the families owned and treasured remained in the villages. Some managed to flee with a sewing machine, their most precious possession, on their backs. The women were raped, and the corn reserves thrown out. In Zacualpan they carried the first corpses, killed by the federal troops, to a new cemetery that had not even been dedicated. In the first flight some did not stop running until they left the state of Morelos; generally, they were the most well-to-do. Others had nowhere to go or did not want to leave; these returned to their villages or to others nearby.

Meanwhile, Zapatismo, by then organized, had managed to absorb the dispersed bands. It had established a tolerable discipline in order to defend civilian interests, and orders that strove to guarantee respect for the peasants went out from its general headquarters. "Where there were Zapatistas, there were guarantees." They took measures to make examples: Zapata dismissed municipal presidents who abused the *campesinos*. General Ayaquica executed a soldier who had raped a village girl. Some other young women thought: "If the government may carry me off, it's better for me to go with you," and they went with the Zapatistas.

The *pacíficos,* without many options to be sure, became Zapatistas openly and even enthusiastically. Many even joined in the shooting when the war passed near their homes. Others entered the haciendas, which they had previously feared and respected, and sacked them. Defense groups were formed, and even village authorities were chosen for their Zapatista convictions. Robles's prophecy had been fulfilled in good part through his own active participation.

Persistence. The civilians devoted almost all their time and energies to surviving. It was certainly not an easy task: conditions changed day after day, and strategies had to be adjusted at the same pace. The gradual disappearance of the sugar plantations, which provided the resources that complemented the cultivation of the cornfields, thrust the peasants into old, almost forgotten activities. Along with the hacienda, its territorial control disappeared, and previously forbidden resources were opened for the *pacíficos.* The mountains became important, and the gathering of their products—wood, wild produce, or zacatón root— as well as their rustic production by weaving rope or burning charcoal absorbed the time of the *campesinos* and provided vital resources. Moreover, they were able to have limited access to water and managed to begin vegetable crops on miniscule plots. Besides, beginning in 1912, some ceased paying rent for lands taken in sharecropping just to see who was the brave soul that was going to collect them, although others, fearful of future reprisals by the hacienda owners, kept on paying until 1914—by that year there was no longer anyone to pay.

Level land, once a scarce resource, had turned into an abundant one. Anyone who could planted the area that he fancied. But while many wanted to, those who actually farmed were few. There was a shortage of draft livestock. The federal troops shot it, sometimes to eat and other times only to strip off the hide; "even with the starvation there was, the buzzards were eating good meat." The Zapatistas also got to the oxen and ate them. In the precipitous flights or in the forced concentrations, the livestock was lost. Those who had rented out animals before had lost them or had taken them out of Morelos. It was livestock, not land, that became the key resource for planting the plains in the Morelos *oriente.*

On those lands enormous risks were run in planting. If some had had the luck to be able to plant within the suitable dates, they might not have it for harvesting. The federal troops finished off the planted fields— sometimes they burned them; at other times for a greater affront, they gave them over to their droves of horses for green forage. For obvious reasons, the Zapatistas cared about the harvests. Thus, many decided to plant *tlacololes* well hidden in the mountains and at a great distance from the villages or camps. These little cornfields, planted on the slopes after the mountainside had been cleared and burned off, were worked by sheer human effort, with machetes and *coas,* without the aid of animals or plows. It was devilish work, but many remember the abundant yields of the *tlacololes,* which enabled them to survive those years, with a certain gratitude.

Yet not only did they have to obtain production but they had to keep it. When the federal troops burned the villages, they burned the corn reserves for the entire year with them; if they did not burn, they plundered or forced the *pacíficos* to feed the troops and the horses, and even the dough for tortillas had to be ground by their women. At night, when the Zapatistas came in, the villagers had to give them something, too; "at times, between the two we were left without eating." The one group snatched it away, and the other asked for it, although if they were not from the zone, they did so with a carbine at their sides. The people recall that they received friendly, almost familial treatment from the Zapatistas, and that is always appreciated, all the more when opposed to the insults and ridicule from the federal forces. But between the one side and the other, they sometimes carried off the whole corn supply.

In those first years, some *pacíficos* went away for good to live in the mountains "like animals," but others stayed in the villages even though they had already been burned. Those who had burros or pack animals left to seek corn outside the state; out of what they obtained, they had to sell a portion to the Zapatistas. They could trick or buy off the federal soldiers, but not the rebels, "who knew us." Some even became muleteers. Even so, they lacked corn and the money to buy it. There was almost nothing to sell: what had been gathered, some little animal, or old, treasured possessions. But few people could pay cash. By 1914 there were already various issuers of bills, "pure cardboard," which were not worth anything or were worth less in other areas.

There was scarcity and starvation. The *pacíficos* protected themselves by reorganizing the use of the territory, setting themselves up on the mountains and slopes and abandoning the rich plain of the cane fields to the point of leaving it almost a desert. They concentrated on the agriculture of self-sufficiency and on the exploitation of mountain resources. Without even planning to, they had broken their dependence in regard to the hacienda. They had become more autonomous, although at a high cost, and they had remained.

The mere perseverence of the *pacíficos* was Zapatismo. The rebels continued to have a base and a program of demands that all shared. Zapata was the undisputed chief of those who faced a common enemy.

The Survivors. The peace of 1915 gave the *pacíficos* a respite. In that year lands were distributed to the villages of Morelos. Land was left over; missing were the wherewithal and the people for cultivating it. Each one worked what he could. Conflicts between neighbors or with people from other villages were not rare, but the authorities, many recently elected to replace those lost in that constant fleeing, could mediate and calm matters. Even the military chiefs intervened to settle spirits down or to clarify obscure boundaries. In Zacualpan, they remember above all else about agrarian reform that Emiliano Zapata himself established that a parcel with irrigation was for the Virgin of the Rosary, so that her feast day would be celebrated with its harvest. This plot still retains that purpose. People from Tepalcingo remember that when they were asked which land they wanted, they chose the plain, while those from Ixtlilco, cattlemen on the *cerros,* preferred the mountain.

Although everything was in short supply because of the war—in Zacualpan even single women—the *pacíficos* threw themselves into work. They formed partnerships and took on new servants to replace those who went away; ox teams were loaned and rented; streams and irrigation ditches were diverted for planting. Not everyone got an equal foothold—some who had animals even took advantage—but all of them managed, and they were satisfied. That year no one stole the harvest from them, and for the corn they gave to the Zapatistas, they received slips of paper that were worth something in the market. It was a year of abundance. The land, rested and fresh, much of it previously planted with cane, yielded good crops. The villages recovered even in the political sphere: they chose officials, had meetings and assemblies; "they even taught themselves to express their ideas." Some of the fugitives returned from afar, and others came down from the mountains. Almost nobody wanted to abandon his *tlacololes,* "since they might be of use again."

The Carrancista attack outdid all the previous ones. "They killed people any place. They cut ripened wheat and threw it out to their horses. The Carrancistas said, 'These raggedy folks don't know to put up a fight,' and kept on shooting them down, and they carried them off as a bunch. They killed my father in the door of his house. . . . During 1916 and 1917 the rich were poor, and the poor, crazy. There was a frightful scarcity, and everyone went around dressed in Villista jackets. . . . They killed even the dogs or cats—they shot everything that moved. . . . In Cuautla it was hell; it stank from so many dead. . . . They gathered us together with the cattle—there were about four hundred head—and Guajardo took them away; we could only get back twenty-five. Then we went away to the *cerros* to live like animals." In the mountains the winter of 1918/19 was severe. Then they got sick from starvation and exhaustion. It was a miracle that the epidemic did not finish them all off, but it did take many. The federal forces no longer found anyone to fight with, but the persecution did not cease. Then they killed Zapata. Little by little, the *pacíficos* came down from the mountains, and others returned from far away; also, some who had gone off as rebels returned well into the night. Yet these were not villages that were reunited, but only a handful of survivors.

Tenaciously they began to reorganize themselves. Some requested lands for sharecropping from the haciendas reestablished by their old owners. The majority could not even attempt it because of the lack of animals; some did not want to out of pure pride, and they returned to their *tlacololes* and the back-breaking labor there. Many worked alone, for they had been left without relatives. All the families were incomplete, and by joining together, they went about forming new units capable of producing. They named authorities to replace the missing ones, many of them put to death for being Zapatistas. The new ones were Zapatistas too.

Some remnants of military groups—Zapatistas and even Carrancistas—became bandits and preyed on the *pacíficos*. The victorious army folded its arms, as if hoping that there would be more deaths. The peaceful people ceased being peaceful. They dug out their buried weapons and formed militia, *defensas sociales,* to protect themselves. These organizations brought together veteran Zapatistas, who knew about fighting if they knew about anything. They won the respect of the people and influenced the restructuring of the communities a great deal. "At the eleventh hour, we, the Zapatistas, were the ones who imposed order."

IV DISTRIBUTION

Reconstruction

Who Won the Revolution? Many Morelos Zapatistas were asking themselves this question in the year 1920, when Carranza was the first Constitutionalist chief of state and Zapata had already been murdered. The answer was painful: for them, everything had been lost. Their experience indicated to them that the new regime was a ferocious reincarnation of the Porfiriato. The Constitutionalist army had made the worst memories of the federal army's brutality pale with its actions. The haciendas had been unconditionally returned to the old owners. Peace was being imposed through repression and vengeance. The failure to fulfill the agrarian law of 1915 and the Constitution of 1917 confirmed the judgment of Zapata, who had considered them cheap demagogic maneuvers that served merely as a pretext for isolating and discrediting the agrarian movements.

Carranza was not going to distribute the land, but return it. He maneuvered to consolidate the power of the liberal State and to halt the social movement unleashed by the revolution, and his actions set out to restore the political order. His obsessive dedication to the formation of a strong government protected by a formal legitimacy left ample margin for action by the forces that wanted to restore Porfirismo without Don Porfirio—in effect, the forces of order and good government. Supported by these weak but pretentious ghosts, he proposed an obscure civilian, the engineer Bonilla, to succeed him in the presidency. Worse yet, he tried to impose him, and that was his downfall. After being assassinated, Carranza moved on to swell the pantheon of the martyrs of the revolution.

The *caudillos* and their followers were the victors, and their weapons represented in the first and last instance the only effective power in the country after ten years of struggle. Their position was curious, almost unheard of. The *caudillos* and their troops did not form a pyramidal army, subject to a centralized leadership, but a set of corps grouped around relatively independent chiefs among whom unstable alliances were being established and dissolved. The mobility of modern warfare had turned the Constitutionalist forces into professional troops with a

133

considerable number of mercenaries, who continued to be uprooted to the point of forming an independent social body. Many had been peasants, but there were also laborers, cowhands, artisans, businessmen, and even some workers from the Red battalions. The leaders, among whom northerners dominated, also had quite varied backgrounds, although the majority had come out of that vague group of the provincial middle class circumscribed by the power of the hacienda owners.

But in the course of that fighting where there had been real gunfire, chiefs and soldiers had lost their local or regional affiliations, and they had few ties with their countrymen or with the social groups from which at some point they had come; they lived off the army, and within it they had created a new network of social relations. The long years of struggle had brought together a heterogeneous force that formed a plundering, adventurers' legion. In the Constitutionalist army there was no ideological identity, but a coincidence of specific interests over a short term, all licitly sheltered by the imprecise, occasionally contradictory pact of the 1917 constitution. Radical leaders like Múgica and Alvarado fought under the same flag as Pablo González, a reactionary and inept besides. Some of the leaders directly served the interests of the powerful, but the army as a group, with its many internal contradictions, and perhaps because of them, was free of an external institutional or class-based servitude.

The old dominant classes, above all the narrow group in which the Porfirian hacienda owners dominated, had not been liquidated, but they had lost their strength, and in many parts of the country, their interests and properties. Despite the encouragement and capacity for maneuvering that Carranza gave them, they were a defeated group. A liberal government endowed with its own strength and legitimacy, as opposed to that which rifles gave, had not crystallized either. Under those conditions, the rootless military host, that species of caste created in the long process of the armed struggle, had the effective power in a severely disorganized country. In an almost unanimous alliance they rejected the Carrancista plan for transferring power to a government of civil administrators and bureaucrats; they also rejected its attempt to halt social change in the name of formal legality.

The Constitutionalist army was revolutionary in its way. Alvaro Obregón, the military chief with the most prestige, was elected to fill the presidency of the country. A large set of alternatives opened before him, all derived from the unusual position of freedom of the group that brought him to power. Obviously, the possibilities of choice were not infinite. A group of external limitations and another one, no less considerable, of contradictions within constitutionalism reduced the number of actions possible; but even so, few governments have faced a period with so many possibilities open. Obregón chose national reconstruction as his path.

Zapatismo had not won the war, much less the revolution. For many, the death of Zapata was the epitaph of the Army of the South. Without surrendering weapons to the enemy, the combatants returned little by little to their demolished villages. Only the most persistent, scarcely a handful, continued in rebellion after Zapata's death. Like the Constitutionalists, they were also the most rootless, the ones who had nowhere to return to or who did not want to go back; some were not even from Morelos. Their links with the villages were perhaps cordial but increasingly distant. Moreover, although they were only a few in number, they had devoted themselves completely to the struggle, even forming a small independent group. They radically maintained the old ideal, but living among the *cerros* was difficult, and sometimes acts were committed that contradicted that ideal. Almost without realizing it, the rebels ceased to be an armed league of the villages.

Magaña, Zapata's successor, negotiated feverishly to avoid the annihilation of the movement. Carranza demanded the unconditional surrender of Zapatismo. To win time, some of the chiefs agreed, but none turned himself in physically: "Indians, but not blockheads." Pablo González, fearful of a new failure in trying to capture them, let time pass. Rituals of peace were performed, but in fact it did not exist, although there was no fighting either. The saving offer came to Genovevo de la O. They say that Obregón arrived and said to him, "Now I am a Zapatista," and that Genovevo answered him, "And what do you bring to show it?" The old warrior's question was heeded, and weapons began to arrive. They were used for parading in triumph as part of the Obregón forces that took Mexico City. Observing the parade together from the National Palace were Genevevo de la O and Pablo González, the ever so faithful Carrancista who opportunely changed sides, both of them converted into Obregonistas (Womack, pp. 353–59). The war in Morelos had ended.

The rebel Army of the South was incorporated into the national army as its Division of the South. Magaña and Genevevo de la O were named division generals, and de la O was given leadership of the Morelos troops. In 1920, Soto y Gama was called on by Obregón to form for his support the National Agrarian Party, which obtained seven seats in Congress. Villareal, a Zapatista sympathizer, was named minister of agriculture, and Miguel Mendoza, one of the Zapatista ministers of the Convention government, was given the direction of the National Agrarian Commission (Womack, pp. 359–62)—the organizations in charge of the distribution of land and from which emerged the first laws and administrative measures to make it effective. With them, institutional agrarian reform began its tortuous history. Obregón also gave the Zapatistas charge of the government of the state of Morelos. The governor, Parres, let the villages know that he was expecting their territorial claims and promised that any request would be judged within twenty-four hours.

It Doesn't Cost to Ask. The call from the government of Morelos was not unheeded, and claims began to arrive. At the end of 1923, 115 villages had received provisional grants (Womack, p. 368); among them were some military camps and new settlements. Almost all the villages of the Morelos *oriente* received their provisional *ejidos* in those years. But behind the notable statistical success were concealed complex, confusing processes. The Obregonista distribution was a new beginning that made no mention of the Zapatista distribution. Zapatismo had not left a record of its agrarian actions, taken on the march, with weapons in hand, often with verbal settlements between honorable, trustworthy men. Many of them had died, and others did not return; the few documents were lost or discreetly rejected as useless papers by the local agrarian commission of the state of Morelos. The disavowal of Zapatista agrarian reform was not only a problem of mechanics, of implementation; it was essentially a political decision. Without any sharp or violent declaration, the Zapatistas' delivery of land was declared illegitimate by reason of principle: it was done outside of the State. In effect, it was an act of banditry that on being recognized would leave a dangerous precedent: that the land could be taken without the intervention of the central government.

But the new beginning of governmental agrarian reform went even further. The villages that retained the colonial documentation or a clear memory of their boundaries, like Anenecuilco or Tepalcingo, answered Governor Parres's call with petitions for the restitution of their historic ownership. They were discouraged in their attempt. Practical reasons were brought forth: the difficulties of reconstructing boundaries out of use for centuries, the lack of personnel, the unnecessary complications. Moreover, to facilitate matters, they were permitted to present a double application: one for restitution and the other for the grant. The villages accepted reluctantly, and in some cases they had to face internal divisions with long-term consequences. Again, behind the practical justification breathed the political reason of state. Agrarian reform was not going to legitimize the historic right of the villages to the land nor strengthen their autonomy; it was not going to carry out acts of justice, although the legislation authorized the government to do so. On the contrary, it was going to distribute the land as a unilateral concession from the State, like a favor from a powerful figure who retains for himself the right to watch over the fulfillment of his supreme edict and to intervene overtly in its administration to create a political clientele. When the agrarian distribution in Morelos was considered finished in 1929, out of the two hundred thousand hectares (in round numbers) distributed, less than two thousand, scarcely 1 percent, had been restored to their owners; the rest had been granted in accord with the system of *ejidal* possession (Diez, 1 : ccxxi).

On the other hand, the property of the haciendas was partially preserved.

In 1929 the hacienda of Tenango and Santa Clara still retained thousands of hectares, although its owners could not work them. The García Pimentel family had been exiled outside the country when Obregón took power and the distribution in Morelos began. They turned their enormous power over to lessees, rich villagers who paid a rent that was barely symbolic if indeed they paid anything at all. The lessees planted corn and wheat. Those were not the times to attempt rebuilding the irrigation system or the cane plantation. The remnants of the Tenango mill were dismantled and moved to a safe, peaceful zone. The planters, exiled and fearful, continued to be the owners of the largest land expanse in the Morelos *oriente* and maneuvered for the advent of better times for themselves.

The remainder of the old communal property not expropriated by the haciendas, the *fundos legales* that were appropriated privately as a consequence of the laws of disamortization between 1880 and 1890, were neither restored to communal ownership nor incorporated into the new *ejido;* on the contrary, with the approval of some of their owners, especially those who were not residents of the villages, they were preserved by the agrarian authorities as small properties. All property owners were excluded from those qualified to receive *ejido* in the first distribution, without consideration of the area of land that they possessed, which was often less than four hectares. In Temoac and Zacualpan the orchards that comprised only five *tareas,* or a half-hectare, were excluded from the distribution. In Zacualpan this separation meant that the census of eligible persons was quite limited, so that the village was given only 567 hectares of *ejido,* while neighboring villages that had a similar population but had lost more orchards were given between 1,000 and 2,000 hectares. The people of Zacualpan did not view this favorably, and they felt plundered by their neighbors who received lands situated within the traditional boundaries of the village "through the fault of the government." Even today, the people of Temoac and of Zacualpan are not characterized by the cordiality of their relations.

The recognition of ownership and the granting of the *ejido* were complicated by the distribution of water. Zacualpan was assigned a volume that should have been divided equally between the orchards and the *ejido*'s irrigated lands. The water never arrived in the stipulated quantities, and its distribution has been the source of recurrent conflicts between the *ejidatarios* and the orchardists from the San Nicolás *barrio.* This decision marked the political life of the village, and only the multiple interweaving of family and of economic interests between the two groups has halted the outbreak of violent conflicts. In San Gabriel Amacuitlapilco the minimal water from a meager spring was left for the exclusive benefit of the small-property holders, while the *ejidal* lands remained without irrigation; in Chalcatzingo the same thing happened. The conflict in San Gabriel was solved with somewhat macabre poetic justice when the spring was stopped up by highway construction work.

In Jaloxtoc, 74 property owners possessed 1,406 hectares in 1921, but only 18 of them had more than four hectares, among them some with more than 50 hectares. On the other hand, more than fifty growers had no land. The distribution in this case was quite complicated: the largest landholders were not affected; those who had less than four hectares retained their property and were included in the *ejidal* distribution but were granted parcels for dry farming; while those who had no land were granted irrigated lands. This vain attempt at Solomonic justice led to unequal ownership, which got worse when, at the end of the twenties, there appeared a second generation of peasants, who had been children at the time of the distribution. Access to the land was unequal from the beginning.

Those who fared best in the long run were, after all, the people of Hueyapan. They considered themselves satisfied when the forest seized by the paper factory was returned to them. Surrounded by rough, steeply sloping land, they did not even want to bother requesting an *ejido*. But an active resident did not agree, and by force of stubbornness he made them sign a petition for a grant. The result was the predictable one: they were granted some rough mountains, considered non-arable lands, which were handed over for the collective use of the village. The communal grant turned out to be the most adequate one, and the agrarian conflicts within Hueyapan were less intense and bitter than those from which other villages have suffered.

In those other villages, the residents found themselves divided into groups according to form of land tenancy. A legal and institutional framework put them into competition for the resources. Worse yet, it designated different channels for their management. Neighbors who had collaborated up to that point, sometimes members of the same family or even brothers, were manipulated in opposite directions and occasionally to their own surprise, found themselves, in turn, facing a common problem. Like two people who cover themselves with a single blanket and have to say to each other, "Don't pull lest you uncover me."

National Reconstruction. The generosity of Obregón toward Zapatismo was a political measure with multiple motives and objectives. His regime had chosen short-term national reconstruction. To obtain it, he tried, not to suspend social reforms, but to channel them, under the State's direction, in a conciliatory, populist project.

The cost of the revolution had been great. The population of the country, which was 15.2 million in 1910, had been reduced to 14.3 million according to the census, 14.5 million according to later calculations (Hansen, p. 42). Physically, there were a million fewer Mexicans, and possibly more than a million died in the decade. The economy was no less affected. Agricultural production had diminished, mining lost 40 percent of its production, and manufactures 9 percent; the railroads, the pride of Porfirian development, were particularly damaged (Hansen, pp. 42–43). There was no money circulating, and the banking system had practically closed its doors. In turn, the petroleum industry, wholly concessioned to foreign companies on very favorable terms, had grown spectacularly to the point of doubling its production under the protection of private armies. The petroleum firms and other enclaves of external economies constituted the only flourishing sector, untouched and organized, in the Mexican economy. This intrusive sector with diplomatic protection commanded great strength of uncertain limits. Unlike Carranza, who had entered into direct confrontation, Obregón cautiously avoided all conflictive inquiry into the real power of the foreign entrepreneurs. The presence of a powerful, organized foreign entrepreneurial sector constituted one of the real limits on the alternatives open to the Mexican revolution.

To complicate the situation even more, the central government was profoundly disorganized. More than half of the governments of the federal states were occupied by revolutionary chiefs, half of whom had never even carried out the rite of an election (Hansen, p. 206). The majority of them governed for their own personal benefit, and they disliked and distrusted intrusion of the federal government in their territories. The fiscal collection was poor, done by burdening consumption with excise taxes; taxes on foreign trade provided more than one fourth of the federal income. Of that, almost half was devoted to maintaining the army. Perhaps for that reason, Obregón is credited with the remark of profound strategic value that "there is no general who could resist cannonades of fifty thousand pesos." The authority of the central government did not flow toward local governments. At times not even simple communication flowed. The danger of praetorian uprisings was not in any way remote.

Under these conditions, the government was defining prioritary goals: the reestablishment of the central power of the president capable of restoring order, the reactivation of economic activity, the maintenance of coexistence with the imperialist presence. To attain these objectives, conciliation among the groups mobilized by the revolution was essential and urgent. Behind these tactical, immediate proposals a long-term objective, an idealized vision of a future society, was gaining force. Obregón and many military *caudillos* shared a positivist education. They believed in immutable laws, rooted outside society, that directed peoples along a predetermined path. In them one perceives, half-hidden by radical language, an almost Spencerian vision of evolution, a social Darwinism in which the classes were natural phenomena derived from the differing abilities among men. Private property was equally natural and immanent in society; wealth was the fruit of effort and dedication within the framework of enterprises as productive units for a market of unlimited exchange.

Accordingly, the national State was a natural and inevitable organism that, distanced from the contradictions between the classes, could arbitrate between these same classes, protecting the weak and watching over the legitimate rights of the powerful. But arbitration was not enough to balance the forces in a country inherently backward and devastated by the war, so the government had to intervene rigorously to halt the avarice of the wealthy in the face of the ignorance and degradation of the poor. Moreover, it had to take a directive role in the fulfillment of the laws of history; the power of the State was the domain of natural justice (cf. Córdova 1974a). The coarse *caudillos* also had their own utopia and pursued their millenium: that of capitalist development, neither more feasible nor less arduous than that of the Zapatistas. Even today the first is exalted for its pragmatic realism, while the second is considered unrealizable. Paradoxes of history.

The agrarian problem was the central one for beginning the national reconstruction. In practice, the *caudillos* divided it into two parts: one political and the other economic. The economic problem was to produce a great deal, preferably for the export market. The pressure of the external debt, which Obregón was negotiating at the time, was intense; the government's poverty was also great. Agricultural export was conceived of not only as a short-term palliative but also as a permanent alternative of development in a country lacking capital and, according to Obregón, efficient entrepreneurs. The intensification of the sale of raw materials abroad was even proposed as a way to break external dependence (Córdova 1974a, p. 293). Ideally, Obregón, himself an entrepreneurial agriculturist, saw the daring and modernized small-property owner as the supplier for the external market, but in practice he protected the great *latifundista* enterprises, at the time the only ones that were producing for the international market, "to avoid an economic imbalance that could bring us to a period of starvation" (Silva Herzog, p. 275).

The entire Obregonista agrarian scheme almost never mentioned the distribution or the *ejido,* and it mentioned restitution even less. However, in his four years of government Obregón distributed 1,170,000 hectares in definitive resolutions and 3,250,000 in provisional possession, according to what he himself reported to the country (cited by Bassols, p. 51). It became apparent after the fall of Carranza that reconciliation and national reconstruction could not be obtained without silencing the agrarian demand, the most consistent and persistent one not only in Morelos but in the entire country since the promulgation of the Plan of Ayala. Laws and speeches were not enough to quiet this demand: the distribution of land had to be initiated with sufficient intensity to calm the most active centers of the agitation. The state of Morelos was among the first selected for distribution on a large scale, and the rest of the agrarian action was concentrated in other regions where the Zapatista ideal had caught on, like Tlaxcala, Guerrero, Michoacán, Puebla, and Mexico.

But the distribution had many more political possibilities than simply calming agitation. It permitted transferring toward the State the loyalties of the peasants benefitted by the grant, converting them into subordinates. In order for this to be possible, it was necessary for the peasant masses to lose the initiative for the distribution and for that initiative to pass into the hands of the State through the formalization, the institutionalization, of the process of territorial redistribution as a government monopoly. The Constitution of 1917 provided the legal framework to permit the transfer by affirming that "the ownership of lands and waters included within the limits of the national territory corresponds originally to the Nation, which has had and has the right of transferring domain over them to individuals, constituting private property. . . . The Nation shall have for all time the right to impose on private property the modalities that the public interest may dictate. . . . It will be the right of the villages, ranches, and communities that may lack land and waters or that may not have them in sufficient quantity for the necessities of their population to be granted them" (taken from Silva Herzog, p. 250). The statutory procedures of the constitution and the institutions charged with performing the distribution turned the peasant into a direct subordinate of the government, which centralized all the decisions, all the resources, all the tricks.

For greater political gain, Obregón let all his agrarian measures be taken or carried out by the Zapatistas participating in the government, notably Soto y Gama, Villarreal, and Miguel Mendoza. All had been secretaries of the general staff of the Army of the South, people of words and the pen, outsiders who on being uprooted from the specific context in which the revolution was made, and without the control of the combat chiefs and their bases, returned to the realm of verbal illusions, of concepts and metaphysical morality, to the revolution as a word at the service of the State. But their old affiliation and their lost fidelity were capitalized upon in the realm in which the distribution had meaning: politics.

The two meanings of institutional agrarian reform, the economic and the political, could be reconciled by reasons that were almost natural. The agrarian agitation had implied war and destruction. Where combat was most intense, the haciendas were destroyed before the distribution. In Morelos, for example, the cost of rebuilding the mills was estimated at around $25 million (Womack, p. 361); the indemnification of the property holders affected by the distribution would not exceed, in the worst of cases, two million pesos, payable in installments with bonds on the agrarian debt. Also distributed was dry-farming land devoted to subsistence crops in the most densely populated zones, which the government regarded with disinterest and a certain commiseration. The plantations that produced for export — in Yucatán, Laguna, the hot country of Michoacán—were preserved until the arrival of the utopia of *los farmers mexicanos*. This not only had economic advantages for the government but also produced political gains. The preservation of those emporia was the result of a benevolent action of the State, a concession. The old landholding group, quite bruised by the years of struggle and permanently threatened by new distributions, never recovered its arrogance. The Morelos planters addressed themselves to Obregón to complain about the distribution, but "the tone of both letters was courteous and respectful . . . and motivated by eagerness to stimulate the economy of Mexico" (Silva Herzog, p. 288). The landholders never recovered their power, and little by little they negotiated their subordination to the State in return for economic gains and sinecures. They, too, were covered by the national reconciliation. By 1924 the economy was recovering slowly, and the State was being strengthened. The revolution seemed to have entered its constructive stage.

Birth of the Bosses. In Morelos the distribution progressed as rapidly as the changing procedures of the twenties allowed. These, ultimately, were not so expeditious. It took the *oriente* villages between five and eight years to change their provisional grants into definitive ones. To slowness was added the nature of the process, eminently bureaucratic. The official letters, the reports, censuses, questionnaires—all in writing —became the normal vehicle of communication and agrarian transactions. The direct, verbal relation that had influenced the Zapatista distribution so much was also invalidated, declared illegitimate. The new distribution was an esoteric procedure for initiates, a species of priests who served as intermediaries between the remote State and the people of the community.

The villages had to seek and anoint intermediaries who would represent them. These people needed special characteristics, principally literacy and a certain degree of urbanity that would facilitate dealing with the functionaries, who consciously or unconsciously imposed a language, a tone, almost a protocol, although as part of it they frequently used the words *compañero*, "friend," and *camarada*, "comrade." After thirty-five years of oppression tinged with racism and ten years of war, these "virtues" imposed from outside were not abundant in the rural, semidestroyed villages of the Morelos *oriente*. The villages had to resort to those who had spent the revolution outside or to their children, well-to-do people who had fled to protect their modest fortunes. Later they returned with those fortunes or with what was left of them, always quite enough when compared with the poverty of those who had stayed to fight or to survive. Those returning took in their hands the intermediation of the claims for territorial grants in many villages in an almost natural manner in order to conform to the procedure imposed from outside.

They fought loyally; they defended a legitimate interest on their part. Before the revolution they had managed to accumulate links with the hacienda, forming a species of dependent court that undertook the tasks that the hacienda could not or did not want to cover with its own activity but that had no independent access to the land. Once the hacienda disappeared, new fields for their entrepreneurial activity were opened beginning with the land distribution. So genuine was their interest that in some villages, like Zacualpan and Tepalcingo, they were the true promoters of the distribution and initiators of the proceedings, in accord with the way they perceived the winds to be blowing at governmental heights.

At times these enterprising promoters stumbled against some resistance from the people who had neither land nor capital nor even much confidence or hope. Moreover, they were a little afraid, and many adduced, with a knowing though extemporaneous vision, that the hacienda would return, and they did not want to fall out with it. But beyond fear, justified by the defeat, there was distrust in the face of a process that they could not control or even know. This feeling was accentuated by the character of the intermediaries, whom they knew from long before. The orchardists of Zacualpan saw the distribution that the well-to-do promoted as a danger to their miniscule properties and withdrew from the process; the same thing happened in Temoac. In other villages, people who shared this fear were almost obliged to participate in petitioning for lands because they owed money or used ox teams belonging to the enthusiastic promoters.

Some of the veteran Zapatistas who had distinguished themselves in the struggle and attained military ranks also participated in the distribution. They had the contacts. They could get to Magaña, Parres, and Soto y Gama, or at least to chiefs like Mendoza or Genovevo de la O, who could give a push where needed. They had influence above, as well as prestige among their people. They also had a little money—Obregón had been generous in licensing the Zapatistas—and they had their horses and their weapons. But they did not have the education, the manners, nor perhaps either the character or the desire to go around dancing attendance in government waiting rooms and paying homage to the dandies. Few of them represented their villages in the distribution procedures, and the majority looked upon the appearance of the new managers with relief.

In some places the veteran officers and those who returned were united by their common interests. The first group provided legitimacy and influence, the other, resources and manners; both had somewhat more money than the rest, and nobody had too much—yet. Along with the land, the power to administer the new ownership, to distribute it among those who had requested it, came to the managers and their supporters, and in some way they took advantage of it to their own benefit. In some places they took more land than the others, registering their children and relatives in the agrarian census—even, it is said, children who were not yet born—or they simply occupied larger parcels; in other cases they appropriated the best lands, or, along with their relatives and friends, they used *ejidal* land as pasture for their livestock. The revolution was doing justice to its favorites everywhere; it could do it in the *ejidos*, too.

In many villages the people saw the plunder and did nothing: there was still land left over, and it went uncultivated; they were not going to fight for it. But they retained a clear memory and created a reserve of precaution and distance with respect to the new local bosses. Others complained to the government, from which they did not even receive an answer, and, in turn, they made themselves some enemies besides. Starting with the distribution, from the time of the new beginning, a new record of pending accounts, accumulated malices, and postponed vengeances was begun.

They complained to the government because they had no one to complain to in the village. The *ejidal* authorities, called the governing committee at that time, were the perpetrators of the offense. Between the relatives and friends to whom they had given land, along with those who owed them favors and money and those helped because they convened the assembly of *ejido* members, the top authority, when and how it suited them, but above all using its real or invented influences on the government as a system of pressure, the governing committee was to a certain point invulnerable. The municipal authorities were usually the same people who were on the governing committee or else their friends; moreover, they had no jurisdiction in land issues, although at times they did not respect that limitation. In Tepalcingo the people offended were numerous, and they organized to destroy the governing committee; they managed it, but it was not time to elect the municipal officials. While the authorities had not intervened to take care of the complaints, they did indeed do so to fight the new committee, discrediting it before the Morelos state authorities. They were successful, and at the year's end the "rich" won control over the committee again. The Zapatista veterans, who had served as judges during the rebellion, had died or were far away, and some were involved with the committee or the municipality. Little by little a local power group was being shaped with the support of the State, which they served as intermediaries in the realization of its policies.

Soon they took possession even of the *defensas sociales,* the villages' armed militias, which had arisen for self-defense when Zapatismo declined. This group, with police functions, exercised real, effective power in the villages. They had become bosses. To legitimize their history, many of the recent arrivals made themselves into old Zapatistas and even veterans. Those who had really fought remember with anger and bitterness how colonels and captains of the Liberating Army of the South who spent the revolution in Atlixco, in Mexico City, or even outside the country began to appear, with service records issued by mysterious offices using Zapata's name and signed by chiefs whom nobody knew. To top it off, some of these phony veterans with sufficient influence with the government were even given a pension. Bit by bit, even the history of the Zapatista rebellion was changing ownership.

The Triumph of the Institutions. In 1924 Adolfo de la Huerta, an aspirant to the presidency of the country, rebelled against the government when Obregón named Plutarco Elías Calles his successor. Two thirds of the Mexican Army followed him in this insurrection, according to official sources. Although antiagrarian and pro-U.S. tinges were perceived in their ambiguous uprising, de la Huerta and his followers did not formulate a clearly defined program, except that they were against Obregón and his group and wanted the power that these others enjoyed. The great military force that the de la Huerta movement brought together was not sufficient to overthrow Obregón and the forces that supported him. With the defeat, the army as an independent body, as a social group, lost the power that the destruction of Carranza had given it and never regained it again. Its successor in the monopoly of power was the government.

This was one of the results of the complex policy of national reconstruction. The most powerful pressure groups were represented in the government or negotiated with it on almost friendly terms, so that they offered it their support or they abstained; even the foreign firms, and with them the United States, satisfied by the 1923 Treaties of Bucareli, demonstrated reservations toward the military uprising. Some groups, like the agrarians and the unions—which did not automatically imply all peasants and workers—gave more than support. The agrarians even fought at Obregón's side, despite the fact that scarcely a year before, in 1923, the Chamber of Deputies had passed a law to disarm the *defensas sociales* and peasant militias because they implied a threat to public order.

Calles did not modify the program outlined by Obregón—reconstruction and development of the country on a capitalist model—but transformed the forms for implementing it. During his regime the efficient system of negotiation, of granting contradicting concessions, of incorporating pressure groups within the government, was institutionalized; permanent organizations capable of meeting these objectives were created with relative independence with regard to those persons occupying the positions.

Between 1924 and 1928, while Calles occupied the presidency, and during the six subsequent years, in which he acted as *jefe máximo,* "supreme chief," of the revolution, many of the State's dependencies were founded or reorganized. Among these institutions one must be singled out: the National Revolutionary Party (PNR), venerable grandfather of the present Institutional Revolutionary Party (PRI), founded in 1929 to solve peacefully the problem of succession posed by the assassination of Obregón, who was elected president for the second time for the period 1928–32 and never took office. The party became the only legitimate political arena in the country, and it permitted the problems of succession to be solved in a civilized manner. Within it, the military leaders met and reconciled their interests instead of fighting (Hansen, p. 126). In the same year as the founding of the party the last military uprising of importance, the Escobarista, took place and was rapidly stifled. Calles managed at least to make centralization of political power in the government almost complete, so that no social group would threaten it from the outside with sufficient strength to put its hegemony in danger. A system of almost-rotating alliances resisted any pressure group that acquired too much strength, and the army, the agrarians, and the unions were successively tested to maintain their discipline and subordination.

Economic reconstruction was also moving along, although not as spectacularly as its political basis—the reconciliation. Calles took the first two steps to increase the State's intervention in the economy, both in 1925: the foundation of the Bank of Mexico and the weak, erratic introduction of the income tax, which taxed income and not consumption (Córdova, 1974a, p. 352). In the long run, these measures would be vital for giving the State an autonomous economic base, but in

1925 reconstruction continued to depend basically on agriculture for export.

Calles took the measures that he believed would best serve the growth of agriculture, all in favor of private enterprise. Even more intensely than Obregón, Calles favored the rise of the small agricultural entrepreneurs, whom he christened a "rural middle class." In the realm of legislation and of the institutions he took measures to favor this process. In 1926 he promulgated the irrigation law, according to which the government took into its hands the development of hydraulic works; the lands incorporated into irrigation as a result of these works would be expropriated to be turned over to small property owners, who acquired the obligation to pay, on credit and on very advantageous terms, the cost of the irrigation system. In fact, the possibility of *ejidal* distributions in the new watering system was excluded. In the same year, the National Bank for Agricultural Credit was founded with the aim of financing agricultural activity in order to increase its productivity.

In practice, the rural middle class neither grew nor prospered; on the other hand, the *latifundios* were strengthened. New haciendas even arose during this period, like the one at Atencingo belonging to the former United States consul Jenkins, who between 1920 and 1930 cornered 123,000 hectares and turned them into the most productive sugar plantation in the country (Ronfelt, pp. 10–11). The people of the Morelos *oriente* neighboring the Atencingo region had, then, abundant reasons for fearing the reestablishment of the hacienda. The new irrigation works and the official banking credits also gave rise to new *latifundios,* notably those of the Calles and Obregón families, the children and relatives of the *caudillos,* who appropriated the lands recently opened for cultivation for themselves and seized the scanty resources of the bank for their private benefit. Caught in a vicious circle of conceding to reconciliate and of growing to survive, the State was in no condition to implement its own utopia.

The agrarian distribution was conceived of as a transition step for forming small properties, and to encourage the process the statutory law on the distribution of *ejidal* lands and the constitution of family patrimony was issued in 1925. This ordinance commanded that the *ejidal* lands would be divided into lots and that each lot would be assigned to a holder for indefinite use. The object of this law, according to its author, Luis León, was to grant guarantees to the *ejido* members: "No man will invest his work, his effort, his savings, if he does not have the absolute security of obtaining the whole product of his work, for himself and his own . . . this is a new form of communal ownership, having the advantage that the small property that the *ejidatario* enjoys cannot be encumbered, sold, or mortgaged" (cited by González Ramírez, p. 266).

Thus, a small property was established in which the land was subtracted from the market, deprived of its characteristic as a commodity so that its product could participate in a market of commodities. In another area, the political, it sought to nullify the community by taking away from it all autonomy in the management of the territory that was granted to it. The individual administrative committee was replaced by an *ejidal* commissariat, directly dependent upon the Ministry of Agriculture. The State, protective and benevolent, claimed for itself the right to intervene in the direction of peasant activity.

Agrarian reform during the Calles period had fundamentally political objectives. It sought to halt possible subversive action by the peasantry and extend the direct dominance of the State over the most numerous group in the population. No hope was placed in the economic results of the distribution, and the *ejido* members were not considered a factor in the reconstruction, which was left in the hands of the dynamic enterprises. Again, the poor dry-farming land, the rough mountains, and even badlands and rocky volcanic ground were distributed. Indeed, they were widely distributed: between 1924 and 1928, Calles distributed 3,045,802 hectares to 301,587 peasants, a little more than 10 hectares to each one (Córdova 1974*a*, p. 345), an area that more than doubled what Obregón had given out. The intensity of the distribution was doubtless related to the great Cristero uprising. Once this political pressure ceased, during Calles's *maximato,* the rate of handing out land of poor quality diminished, so that scarcely 3,444,982 hectares were given out in 6 years (cited by Hansen, p. 46). In the thirties Calles spoke openly of ending the distribution, of fixing a limit in order to guarantee fully the development of the capitalist enterprises in the countryside. The agrarian fervor of the *caudillos* lasted very briefly indeed.

*"A place for lizards and archeologists."** War damages were more severe in Morelos than in the rest of the country. Nothing was left of the flourishing sugar industry; none of the mills was in working condition in 1920, and many of the irrigation systems had been destroyed or were useless because of lack of maintenance. The houses of the *reales* had been sacked and burned, and their blackened walls at last acquired the aristocratic patina that their owners had wanted in vain to impart to them. The flourishing cities were almost abandoned, and the active commerce broken down. The peasants bought and sold outside the state of Morelos and at times, when the militia was not escorting them, were even preyed on by bandits.

The most serious and painful loss was that of human lives. Death and

* Womack, p. 270.

emigration had brought a reduction of the population to half of what it was in 1910. In 1921 quite a few of the emigrants had already returned. Even so, the population of Morelos was 42.5 percent less than 11 years earlier; in 1910 Morelos had 180,000 inhabitants, while in 1921 only 103,500 were recorded. The true loss was even greater than the absolute numbers reflect, since if growth had continued at the same rate as in Don Porfirio's time of peace, Morelos ought to have reached very nearly 200,000 inhabitants in 1921.

In the *oriente* the depopulation was severe, reaching on the average the same proportion as in the state of Morelos. In the hot country, where the haciendas were and where the fighting and repression were harsher, death and exile were more intense and produced absolute declines near half the population; in the temperate and cold countries, areas more for refuge than for battle, there was almost no absolute loss, although growth was inhibited. But, beyond that, the composition of the population was unsettled. A survivor from Zacualpan remembered with a certain melancholy that no marriageable girls were left in the village. He enumerated them all, and his fingers were more than sufficient for the count. The rest had fled, or by choice or violence they had ceased to be marriageable. Widows and unmarried mothers abounded, and the elderly were missing. The people reorganized themselves, and by joining together among relatives, sometimes quite distant ones, they established more or less complete domestic units to carry out production and consumption, although in general they had an excess of people who ate but were without clear productive functions, although they always contributed something. It is quite probable that the number of domestic units able to undertake production was reduced even more drastically than the absolute numbers suggest.

Under these conditions land was not lacking, particularly because the barriers posed by the hacienda to the use of the territory had been torn down. The people planted where they wanted. In Zacualpan, before the distribution, they simply notified the municipal president where they were going to plant; in other villages they did not even bother to do that: they chose land, sure that nobody would dispute them for it. In fact, the agrarian problem had not ceased to exist, but it had indeed ceased to operate. The most worrisome problem was what to produce with, not where to do it. The most troublesome need was the lack of work animals, of ox teams, especially when there was more than enough land and not enough hands, which made extensive farming attractive, for it improves yields per unit of work. The ox teams had been almost annihilated in the years of war. In Zacualpan in 1921 the census for the *ejidal* distribution recorded eleven teams and some other equipment; in 1919 in Tepalcingo, Guajardo, Zapata's murderer, confiscated four hundred cattle, out of which twenty-five were recovered, with a great deal of effort. Thus, many people kept on breaking their backs on their *tlacololes,* hillside crops that were worked without animals, which scarcely produced enough for the family's annual consumption. Others tried to get jobs as servants of those who had a team, through which they almost satisfied their consumption, although perhaps they worked a little less rigorously. Some misguided people hitched themselves to the plow and pulled until they obtained a harvest. The most fortunate got one of the returnees to rent them a team. The work was hard—it was necessary to break lands that had not been cultivated for many years and were overgrown with brush—but gratifying; for each seed cast on the earth, almost two hundred were gathered in the fresh, rested fields.

Those who had spent the revolution on the outside were again at an advantage. Their domestic units were complete, and they had a sufficient labor force. Moreover, they had livestock or some savings for acquiring a team and some calves to devote to breeding. With the team, they could obtain a sizeable surplus of corn. At that time there was not much to spend money on, and almost nothing to buy; money was scarce. The bills issued by the different governments during the revolution were worthless, even those from the Constitutionalists themselves; some fortunate people hoarded gold and silver coins, which did not come back into circulation. Prices were low, but few could pay them. Direct exchange, barter, gained importance in the communities again; the standard of exchange was corn. Those who had one or two teams were cornering this grain. From their surpluses, they loaned corn to those who had not been lucky enough to cover the year with their production. With the lending of corn, the old form of interest, *la dobla,* returned: for each unit received, two were paid back at the moment of harvest, four if it was necessary to wait an additional cycle. Moreover, they also charged in corn for the teams they loaned out: eight *cargas* for the use of the team. At the end of some years there were people who, between oxen and loans, surrendered half their crop to the livestock owner.

The livestock dealers invested their earnings in more work animals, which they bought at the Tepalcingo fair, but also in breeding and transport stock. With the latter, they reactivated muleteering and the trade between villages. They hauled and carried their own and other people's cargo, which was exchanged for other products. Some of the livestock owners and muleteers put little shops in the villages to supply basic articles to their countrymen. They were active and determined people, and despite the slow rate of the animals' biological reproduction, they got production underway. In Tepalcingo in 1926 almost two hundred *yuntas* of land were cultivated. The business also had its risks, and one especially severe one: rustling, the cattle theft that even the militia found itself paralyzed to suppress. Livestock was a highly quoted commodity.

The livestock owners were the same ones who used to represent the communities before the government and then occupied the positions of political and agrarian authority. At times they exceeded their grasp and went too far. When they filled the places on the individual administrative committee of the *ejido* responsible for annually distributing crop lands, they assigned themselves the open areas, the easiest to work, and compelled the poorest people—the very people to whom they rented the teams, people who had to perform the arduous task of clearing and plowing year after year—to break new lands.

This type of abuse served the president as a pretext for ordering the parceling of land in 1925. The bosses were scarcely affected; when the *ejidal* commissariat was installed, they took it in their hands too and assigned themselves, now in perpetuity, various parcels of the best lands. Again, the poor broke new land, some quite bad, and they were stuck with it forever. They produced less on it and had to borrow *a la dobla* even more. The bosses' group went on consolidating its position, and it was established as a new dominant stratum within the community, supported by the enormous power of the State, which established its dominance and control through them. The system proved its efficiency in the de la Huerta rebellion. In Morelos, the indomitable, rebellious territory, no one backed the rebels, and the population was solidly aligned on the government's side. The government distributed arms among the peasants so that they would guard the border of Morelos against the threat from the rebels in Guerrero. The new village bosses were, without the least shadow of a doubt, convinced agrarians. Their business was in the *ejido* and depended on the peasants' being able to carry out autonomous farming with livestock and on loans from them. The more land opened, the more earnings. Before them, perspectives were opening that were much broader than with the hacienda. They could grow, reproduce their earnings, and also—why not?—dominate, have command and authority. They would do it better than the hacienda owners because they were, in the end, people from the village, beneficiaries of the revolution. Through them, Morelos was incorporated, perhaps before any other state in the country, into the new, revolutionary Mexico.

The Freebooters. The national *caudillos* were sincere revolutionaries too. They were against the old, against what they often classified as feudal. They were enemies of the traditional hacienda, which they fancied was self-sufficient and not very efficient; they energetically declared themselves against the system of masters and serfs and opposed it to the free worker, owner of a modest patrimony. They were against the obscurantist Church, which promoted the backwardness of the people and kept them submerged in a primitive, pre-logical world dominated by superstition and resignation; they fought against it with diplomacy, with legislation, and even with weapons. They encouraged public education so that it would provide an objective, positive knowledge of reality that would be capable of founding a uniform nationality. They tried to *integrate* the Indians, survivors of a *primitive* historical stage, into the modern, rational world. They were in favor of *the people,* an abstract concept never precisely defined, sought their well-being, and introduced a program to obtain it.

The corruption that the *caudillos* practiced widely, splendidly, almost limitlessly, was not essentially counterrevolutionary, no more than the corrupt action of the bosses of the rural villages was anti-agrarian—both were simply congruent with the modernization project. There are many factors that come together to make capitalist development, if not viable, then at least desirable, and one of them is, almost by definition, the presence of a capitalist class that guides and promotes the process for its own benefit. In Mexico in the twenties that group did not exist.

The old Porfirian oligarchy tied to *latifundista* property had certainly not disappeared physically, but a good part of its capital had been lost or taken outside the country; as a group, it was divided and disarticulated by its political defeat and lack of power. Industrial capital was principally foreign, and its central activities—mining and the extraction of petroleum —were passing through a severe crisis, which, added to lack of confidence toward a host country that had turned bolshevik, discouraged investment. But even without this contraction, the foreign firms were appendages of foreign economies that functioned in terms of the nature and behavior of their metropolitan system and contributed to the expansion of native capitalism only in a derivative way and to the extent that it was congruent with their interest and central function. This coincidence did not occur between post-revolutionary Mexico and pre—world-crisis imperialism, which was interested in extracting raw materials and in selling finished products. The big businessman, perhaps the least damaged by the revolution, did not seem to have available either the capital or the initiative to set the growth process in motion. The financial sector did not exist at that time.

This is not to suggest that capitalism did not exist in post-revolutionary Mexico. It not only existed but was dominant, imposing its rules on the whole of society; but a complex of coinciding interests took part in this domination—those of foreign enterprises with their great economic and political weight, those of thousands of entrepreneurs in land or in manufacturing and commerce, those of the small local bosses, those of the generals, and, of course, with enormous specific weight, those of the government. But this coalition, to give a name to the coinciding interests, did not constitute a class either in its relation to the means of production or in its consciousness and internal articulation, but a complex of forces frequently in a contradictory and conflictive relation. Of course, there were rich men with flourishing businesses and others who wanted to be like them; there were heirs of haciendas and foreign *hacendados* who were getting rich, merchants who controlled a market, industrialists who profited, and small bosses who prospered; but it is also certain that although they concurred on the preservation of capitalism and were capable of alliances against total external threats like Zapatismo, their specific interests were in contradiction, and no one of them could obtain hegemony.

From the distance of history, it would seem that the military *caudillos* decided to start the process of capitalist development by creating a capitalist class beginning with themselves. They allotted enormous fortunes to themselves through the most unheard of ways—as, for example, the general who pocketed the budget for feeding his troops and horses, sold his weapons to the enemy, or had fewer people in his battalions to be able to collect their salaries, so that it was almost a miracle that the rebellions did not triumph. Others more subtly asked for credit from the National Agricultural Bank without the ingenuous intention of paying it back. Others accepted *mordidas,* bribes from individuals, which were as valid for freeing a murderer as for tracing the borders of an *ejidal* grant over the countryside in reduced scale. Others appropriated lands for themselves and then ordered the construction of irrigation works; or they simply bought at laughable prices ranches threatened by apparent agrarian action that was suspended after the deal. Many became contractors once a policy of constructing public works was reinstated during the Calles years. One of the most important was the highway from Mexico City to Cuernavaca, which was chosen because of its privileged climate as a site for the summer homes of Calles and his closest collaborators—all built on a single street that the people named the street of "Ali Baba and the Forty Thieves." The *caudillos* and their favorites amassed enormous fortunes (Córdova 1974a, pp. 276–79; Hansen, p. 207).

But real or potential enemies also received abundant benefits from the corruption. The management of corruption for political aims was one of the most effective instruments for attaining reconciliation. The distribution of sinecures attempted, and often managed, to transform political ambition into greediness for wealth. It also served to console those conquered in the struggle for political existence, who whiled away their frustrations in business, in the slightly vulgar luxury of the twenties, or in the epic carousing that was epoch-making and favored the massive importation of cognac, fashionable at the time. The coarse revolutionary generals and officers went soft and began to show extravagant tastes for showy houses, for blonde lovers (all the better if they were foreigners), for diamonds and jewels. Politics became a career and, as it has often happened, one of the quickest routes for individual social mobility and, moreover, one of the few open at that time.

But not everything was conspicuous and sumptuary spending. The wealth amassed in politics was also invested to reproduce itself according to the rules of capitalism. The *caudillos* and their collaborators were not going to begin buying corn on time or loaning it *a la dobla*. "They were freebooters, entrepreneurs *par excellence,* prepared to run risks" (cited by Hansen, p. 52), who undertook an enormous range of businesses, from pandering to aviation companies. But two branches of activity were the favorites: One was the acquisition of real estate, livestock ranches and irrigated properties devoted to export crops, which were going to contribute to shaping the model of agricultural development to a large extent and agrarian reform policy in a decisive way. The other favorite enterprise was the contracting companies that worked for the government and also contributed in a powerful way to forming the public-works policy, one of the decisive ones in the establishment of the nature of the country's economic growth.

The bourgeoisie having left the government, the freebooters were without a doubt a group dependent on the State, for they lacked autonomy and were always at the mercy of the political decisions of the *caudillo* or president in turn, unable to undertake competitive productive activities in an international market, except in export agriculture. But if analytically this might have been a group subordinate to the State, in practice, as specific people, they were the ones who dominated the government. This duality, this mortised connection between entrepreneurs and government, was one of the most important factors in the configuration of the Mexican State and of the model of growth of the country.

Rebellion and Obedience. In the twenties the revolutionary government had not resolved the demands of the peasants who had made the revolution, and it threatened the existence of peasants who had not participated. The political distribution, manipulative, did not make up to the *campesinos* for the intervention of the State in the life of the villages and for the proliferation at all levels of petty politicians who, like a plague of locusts, laid waste to the villages in search of patronage and profits. The rise of the local bosses, the agrarian leaders in a good part of the country, sowed divisiveness and discord in many villages.

Obeying instructions from above, they made the object of their agrarian claims, not the large, flourishing haciendas, but the peasants' small properties and, at times, even the communal lands. The *guardias blancas*, mercenary bands in the service of the hacienda owners, proliferated, forestalling agrarian action with murders. Besides, there was an abundance of bandits and rustlers, who were able to nullify the outrageous efforts necessary to obtain production. There was not enough livestock, but there were politicians, bureaucrats, and soldiers to spare; seventy thousand men were in the army, or at least they appeared on its payrolls (Meyer 1973*a*, 1 : 148). They all plundered the peasants through forced tributes, deceptions, and promises, to which they added scorn, abuse, and stupid arrogance.

A great part of the benefits of the corruption of the minor bureaucrats, less spectacular but perhaps more substantial than that the *caudillos* received, weighed down on the peasants. The local military bands charged duties for right of way to a market, asked bribes for allowing the celebration of a fiesta, dominated the gambling dens and saloons, requisitioned fodder or put horses to pasture in cultivated fields; but above all they committed murders, by chance or with premeditation, heeding orders from above. The bureaucrats joined in the plundering and repression enthusiastically—they collected real or fictitious taxes for their own benefit, granted licenses to the highest bidder, appropriated houses and lots, fined and imprisoned or, even worse, did not do so in order to protect the influential. The politicians, always placed in the bureaucracy, sold promises and illusions, almost indulgences for an afterlife in the kingdom of progress.

All the peasants' frustration was turned against the government, against the federal soldier and the bureaucratic pen pusher, against the *caudillos'* insolent display of wealth. The revolutionary government and army were likened to the Porfiriato as if they were the same thing, a fact even sadder because so many had struggled to change it. This climate favored the government's purposes. Internal division took strength away from peasant action and demands; while they fought among themselves, the *campesinos* were pacified and even reconciled with other groups in the society. The conflicts were weakening them as a pressure group; the distribution and the expectations it aroused created a group that was supportive even though it was not enthusiastic. Internal conflict and the manipulation of it also allowed the preservation of the productive haciendas, particularly those of friends of the regime, and the destruction of the feudal power of the old *latifundistas* who refused to cooperate with the institutions.

Control based on conflict and extreme tension was inevitably risky, and it had grave consequences. In 1926 the peasants of the west and center of the country rebelled, and there were weaker ramifications in other zones. The uprising exploded around the conflict between the Church and the government and became an armed rebellion of large proportions, the Cristero rebellion, which, despite the silence of official history, represented a severe military threat to the Calles government. The Cristiada was "a movement of reaction against the 'Mexican revolution,' a revolution that carried on the modernizing enterprise of the Porfiriato" (Meyer 1973*a*, 1 : 387). The Cristeros failed in formulating an autonomous plan and in creating their own leadership and were manipulated and betrayed by the sectors that were most conservative, in the nineteenth-century sense of the word: the ecclesiastical institution and the urban middle class, which sought, at the least, the restoration of the Porfiriato or, even better, the return of Santa Ana's *caudillismo*. These groups used the enormous strength of the peasant uprising to negotiate on favorable terms their insertion into the system of reconciliation and national reconstruction. They succeeded, and they permitted and even supported the sacrifice of the combat chiefs.

On the other hand, many agrarians were radicalized to the left. In 1926 the National Agrarian League, founded by Úrsulo Galván, a leader from Veracruz, and participated in by Soto y Gama, among others, formulated a program that established as a goal the socialization of the land within the framework of world revolution (Silva Herzog, pp. 343–44). The league, in which many local bosses looking for a career took part, did not manage to take root deeply among the peasants, other than by exception. In 1929, the year of the Cristeros' surrender, the league, penetrated by official corruption and by the sectarian influence of the Communist party, broke up and lost almost all its influence. A year later, Úrsulo Galván, one of the most promising leaders of the period, suddenly died of natural causes (Centro de Investigaciones Agrarias, 2 : 369 [hereinafter CDIA]).

In 1929 the peasants, who had constituted the principal contingent of the armed revolution that brought the *caudillos* to power, were relegated to last place in the national organization, since they had ceased to represent an external threat to the regime. From then on, they were the poor relations of the revolutionary family.

In Morelos these events were echoed weakly, as though with a mute. The Cristero uprising was backed by small bands that did not get the support of the population and at times were persecuted by it. Pedro Martínez recalls that once five or six Cristeros entered Tepoztlán and that the village militia killed one of them (Lewis 1966, p. 124). Of the three miniscule bands that operated in the territory between 1926 and 1928 one was annihilated by Adrián Castrejón, a Zapatista chief who served in the national army, and the others were disbanded without punishment or glory (Womack, p. 371). The failure of the Cristero rebellion in Morelos had to do, above all, with the radical advance of agrarian reform, certainly exceptional in the national framework. It also had to do with the absence of a significant group of small property owners, of independent peasants, as well as with the part the clergy had played as unconditional servants and even as direct employees of the planters. The majority of the priests of Morelos had fled along with their patrons and had taken refuge with them in the cities to let the stormy period pass; two exceptions prove the rule, and they sided with the Zapatistas. Moreover, in the revolutionary struggle the people of Morelos rescued their religiosity from the hands of the clergy: the Virgin of Guadalupe became a symbol of the rebels, and Zapata, the ferocious Attila anathematized by the clerics, granted lands to the village churches so that they could defray the costs of religious festivals with their harvests. To a certain extent, Zapatismo practiced a revolutionary Christianity in spite of the Church and the dignitaries.

With the peace, the priests returned to the villages to face the distrust of the people. They kept discreetly quiet, and some even boasted of being agrarians. None dared to call peasants who received land thieves, as they did in other parts of the country, and the only priest who risked calling those who fought for distribution "goats" was immediately transferred by his bishop (Meyer 1973a, 2 : 226). The Morelos clergy and even their bishop recognized the obvious: the distribution of Morelos could not be halted. The government held the same opinion. Between 1920 and 1929 several governors of the state of Morelos were dismissed, and the first election held since 1912 was won by three candidates at once. Despite this confused political situation, the distribution never stopped, and in September 1929 the local agrarian commission was dissolved because it had fulfilled its function. Officially, the agrarian problem in Morelos had ceased to exist; the agrarian reform had been carried out to its ultimate consequences (Womack, p. 372). In that period more than two hundred thousand hectares, almost 40 percent of the geographical area of the territory, had been granted to the *ejidos.* Eighty-six thousand hectares were arable, and of those, twenty-one thousand were considered irrigated; the rest were classified as pastures, mountain, and rough. Almost twenty-five thousand peasants received lands: on the average, a little more than four arable hectares and as many more of rough land or grasslands for each one (Diez, 1 : ccxxi). More than 120 villages had received *ejidos,* which occupied almost three fourths of the land that could be tilled. But perhaps the most radical aspect of the distribution was its consequences for the dominant enterprise, the hacienda, which had been destroyed completely.

The government, supported but also pressured by the Zapatistas entrenched in national politics, conceded in Morelos what it was not surrendering in other sections: It had to nullify the most radical and dangerous peasant movement; it had to incorporate it in order to give legitimacy to its own agrarian program. It had, moreover, to take possession of the figure of Zapata for itself. For that, it handed over the land, with true magnificence, it may be said, but demanded and obtained political support in the beginning, and later submission. The Zapatistas who supported Obregón lost their influence on being moved away from Morelos by Calles. De la O was transferred, and a northern general took over his post as military chief of the South. Magaña was kept far away, charged with organizing military colonies throughout the whole country. Soto y Gama and his agrarian party lost presidential support, and little by little, they were led into sterile, verbal opposition. All the vacancies were filled by people devoted to the regime, which established a pact with the local bosses. Even minor positions were bestowed in exchange for fidelity and were rewarded with corruption.

The state of Morelos, the land of Zapata, had a great deal that was exceptional, that anticipated the future. The revolution turned government incorporated it early. The peasants were not satisfied. They did not like the new bosses, but, after all, they were their own people. Nor did they like the government, which, little by little, became an oppressor, an alien, as it had always been in the past. But they had been given the land. Their utopia had not triumphed, but they could survive. They had guarantees. Not everything had been lost in vain, and they could keep on being peasants. With infinite stubbornness, the *campesinos* of Zacualpan expressed their attitude when, on receiving the *ejido*, they noted on the certificate: "They signed for the sake of obedience, but not in agreement."

The Crisis

Winds from the North. On 29 October 1929 the monster suffered a breakdown. A great financial catastrophe took place on seemingly remote and distant Wall Street. The crisis of liberal and colonialist capitalism had exploded—an enormously complex phenomenon that reverberated throughout the world, brutally in the dependent countries. The United States reduced the volume of its international trade to one third of what it had been; other colonial powers did the same, and even more severely. The countries that directed their economic activity toward exportation, as did Mexico, found themselves deluged with raw materials that they themselves could neither process nor consume. The largest firms in those countries were devoted precisely to the production of exportable raw materials, and soon they were left, in fact, without business. The saying, "When the United States sneezes, Mexico gets pneumonia," was confirmed.

The crisis of 1929 brought to conclusion tendencies apparent for some time. Between 1926 and 1929 the absolute value of Mexican exports had declined because of the drop in petroleum production; between 1929 and 1932 exports would be reduced by a third again. Imports, too, were reduced to levels lower than those at the beginning of the century (Solís, p. 97). The 1930 gross national product was one eighth lower than that for 1925 (Reynolds, p. 51). The effects of the crisis became more acute between 1931 and 1933, and in 1932 the gross national product declined 19 percent more than that in 1929 (CDIA, 1 : 59). Indeed, the whole decade of the thirties would be marked by recovery, and the effects of the crisis would be totally overcome only in 1940, when the per capita product in Mexico reached its 1925 level.

The most severe damage was to the export sector, whose total volume was reduced by half between 1929 and 1932 (CDIA, 1 : 59). Mining and petroleum, transport, and commercial agriculture for export were particularly affected (Reynolds, p. 51; Solís, p. 98). The drop in commercial agriculture was so severe that between 1929 and 1932 the gross agricultural product declined by one third (CDIA, 1 : 59); the product that suffered most from the closing of the international market was cotton, and sisal hemp and coffee fluctuated erratically (Solís, p. 98). Livestock, commerce, and electricity were affected less, although traditional agriculture, the subsistence crops, best resisted the collapse of prices in the civilized world, for obvious reasons (Solís, p. 98). Manufacturing and the sectors that served agriculture (presumably, traditional agriculture) were able to recover more or less rapidly (Reynolds, p. 51); in 1934 they exceeded 1929 levels (Solís, p. 99), while the traditional exports would need a decade and a world war to recover. Reynolds (p. 53) holds that proof exists that the Mexican economy reacted more strongly to the depression at the end of the twenties than other Latin American countries, from the point of view of individual sectors.

The State, the promoter of national reconstruction, was taken by surprise by the events, which, moreover, hit where it hurt most. At a single blow, the country had been left without a short-term plan. All the efforts of the *caudillos'* government to rebuild by starting with the export sectors were wiped out by the gust of wind from the North. The spoiled children, the haciendas that produced for export, faced bankruptcy and sank into inefficiency; the golden calves, the foreign enterprises, which had been cared for with exquisite precautions, collapsed without any consideration for their host country; the rural middle class lost its objectives and was turned from an illusion into an irony. As the economic growth of the twenties was halted, the plan of national reconstruction faded away like a mirage. A country that exported raw materials like the one that the northern *caudillos* had tried to develop made no sense in 1930.

The blow from the Depression was not limited to the export sector but was absorbed throughout the whole country, and its harshest effects were transmitted to the poorest people. The devaluation of the peso and the abandonment of the gold standard in reserves, which were the responses to the crisis (Solís, p. 98), provoked a severe rise in prices in which agricultural products rose less than industrial or imported products. To a great extent, inflation transferred the cost of the collapse of the international markets to the entire population, almost three quarters of whom were peasants. Even the government suffered a setback. More than a fourth of treasury income, which came from taxes on foreign trade, was lost as a result of the Depression. Federal investment and public expenditures were reduced by one fourth between 1930 and 1933, and only in 1935 did they equal the figures for 1929 (Solís, p. 98), although in pesos that were worth considerably less. The reduction affected public works, principally communications and transportation, that is, the contractors, the freebooters, and their personal as well as business interests.

The economic and programmatic bankruptcy of the reconstruction were not translated into the taking of corrective measures until 1933, and, in fact, they were applied only in 1934, starting with the inauguration of General Lázaro Cárdenas as president of the republic. This delay, this inaction that was expressed as total indignation against the outside world, cannot be attributed solely to a lack of understanding and information about what was happening; it was a result of the political struggle taking place within the State in order to establish the new model without losing the primacy only recently consolidated by the government. Among the more or less obvious factors that delayed the decision-making were the interests acquired by the *caudillos* by way of personal enterprises, all in keeping with the general policy of reconstruction. This was worked out in many ways: some *caudillos* redirected their enterprises, others left them the same and were respected, and still others even had to lose some of theirs in return for other more or less substantial concessions. This inaction at the time of the Depression enabled the State to maintain its hegemony, expressed in this case as the right to direct national policy on its own initiative.

In that process the party ceased to be the confederation of political organizations and the elector of candidates in a relatively civilized fashion and tried to become an organism of the State in which all the social groups would be represented and would negotiate the possible solutions to their requests without interfering with the hegemonic character of the State. In 1930 Portes Gil, perhaps with more clairvoyance than conviction, expressed it thus: "The PNR is a Party of the State . . . the revolution made government needs an organ of agitation and defense . . . we are not a party of class, nor do we claim to be one. We will openly support, as does the Government of the Revolution, the interests of the proletariat classes of Mexico, workers and peasants; but we invite the other collectivities to unite, always on the basis that the radical Program will be recognized by those collectivities. . ." (cited by González Navarro, pp. 96–97). Later, in 1933, the party formulated a specific design: the government's six-year plan, which settled the basis for founding capitalist development on industrialization. A new utopia was being generated—a country of workers and conscientious, efficient bosses who transformed natural riches in enormous factories, who mass-produced unlimited consumer goods with the proud seal "Hecho en México"—"Made in Mexico." In 1934 the first measures in accord with the newly manifest, revealed path were taken. It is not surprising that the great majority of them were agrarian measures.

Everybody in One Sack of Corn. When the peasants of the Morelos *oriente* received land, they thought without any doubt about planting corn. For one thing, there were not many reasonable alternatives: with the haciendas destroyed, communications suspended and damaged, markets disarticulated, and deflation or lack of circulating money, producing for the market made no sense. Nor did the dry-farming lands favor the multiplication of alternatives; the crop best suited to these conditions, almost the only one, was corn and the plantings associated with it, all susceptible to direct consumption by the producer without entering the market of monetary exchange. Moreover, the land and corn, conceived of as a single unit, were capable of serving as support of the autonomous persistence of the peasant family unit: the land absorbs work, and its fruit feed the producers. This cycle generated a surplus beyond the necessities of direct consumption that served for obtaining access to the means of production absent in the productive unit, like work animals or complementary work, as well as other goods for consumption. The cultivation of corn was the best response to real conditions, and to a certain degree, it permitted the partial and modest realization of the ideal for which the peasants had fought so much: the possibility of producing and surviving independently, without servitude toward the outside, with their own resources. Land and the possibility of raising corn on it were sufficient "guarantees" for continuing to be *campesinos.*

In the twenties the surface area devoted to the cultivation of corn, of the cornpatch, was growing slowly, but with surprising constancy. Each year, new land was broken as soon as new ox teams joined in the work. Also in that decade, they abandoned the *tlacololes*, the farming of cleared lands in the mountains that served as a refuge in the worst moments, which lost their attraction when compared with the extensive-fallow system made possible by the abundance of land. The hot country, where lands suitable and productive for this sytem of farming abounded, became the area's center of gravity. The Hueyapan peasants, fortunate in saving some livestock in their almost inaccessible volcano grasslands but lacking level, warm land for planting corn, rented *ejidal* parcels in the hot country, where the *ejidal* grants had been more ample and the human and livestock depopulation more drastic. The people of the temperate country also rented land down below and turned their *ejidos* into cornfields cultivated extensively. Through this exchange of resources among the families and communities—at times asymmetrical and at other times egalitarian, but always carried out among acquaintances who mutually identified with one another—scarce resources were concentrated in the most rational and productive activity, namely, planting corn for dry farming. Little by little, the cornfields multiplied, and at the end of a decade the Morelos *oriente* had become a gentle homeland with a surface of corn.*

In appearance little, almost nothing, had changed. The ox team and human labor, aided by rustic implements, continued to be the only energy resources used to manage the growth process of the plants. Nor had the calendar of local activity, governed by the rains, changed: planting by the feast of San Juan and harvest with the first full moon of December, almost always coinciding with the festivals of the Virgin of Guadalupe. The territorial unit of work, the *yunta* of land, was not changed either, and the necessity and the law of maintaining an equal area fallow for the recovery of the soil and the maintenance of fertility remained in effect. Even agrarian reform took this territorial norm into account and distributed, in theory, two *yuntas* of land for each beneficiary.

With the dissolution of the hacienda, the land had lost the character of a scarce good that had been imposed upon it to guarantee the supply of labor, but another resource, the ox teams, acquired this trait and limited the possibility of undertaking independent crops, making it selective and differentiated. Mechanisms were reestablished for distributing the scarce resource, the rental of the teams, and for increasing the number of family units that had access to production through servitude with the right to a share in the harvest. The *gañán* received 3 pesos a week and harvested 6 *maquilas'* worth of sown land; the *peón* earned 2

---

* A reference to the well-known poem of Ramón López Velarde, "Suave patria."

pesos and harvested land planted with 4 *maquilas*. Day laborers for the *zacateo* and the harvest were hired for a peso a day, but quite frequently the *patrón* who paid a *peón* collected the same amount from him a few days later—today for me, tomorrow for you.

As a consequence of the haciendas' disappearance, economic relations had necessarily turned toward the interior of the community; the latter had ceased to be a complementary unit in the great enterprise. After the revolution new sources of work outside the communities did not arise to replace peonage on the haciendas, and survival depended upon access to local resources. Social relations that established the channels for obtaining access to scarce resources were widened to encompass practically the entire community. The sense of belonging was strengthened, and the boundaries of the local community were marked more emphatically. Within these social boundaries all the basic economic relations were carried out: society and economy were identified in the unique framework of the rural community.

In the majority of the communities of the area the strengthening of the local corporations was translated into energetic attempts to revitalize the system of *cargos*, the stewardships associated with the celebration of church festivals. These organizations, which never entirely disappeared, had been weakened during the dominance of the hacienda, when they had been repudiated by the *gente de razón*, the civilized people, the elite, and remained in the hands of the Indians, the people of the *calzón*. In the twenties the religious organization acquired another specific, urgent objective: reconstruction of the churches, favorite fortifications and targets for sacking during the war. Even today the Jonacatepec church shows the scars of thousands of rifle shots and some from weapons of larger caliber; in Jantetelco the heavy dome was blown up by a well-aimed cannonade, whose paternity is still argued and whose damages are not yet repaired, while those in Jonacatepec are not only unrepaired but preserved with pride.

Committees enrolled in the traditional system of *mayordomías* were formed for the purpose of collecting from among the entire community the funds necessary for rebuilding the churches. The *faenas*, free labor compulsory for all members of the community, also became more frequent and harsher, to repair not only the churches but also the villages themselves, veritable ruins blackened by smoke, While the committees gathered the alms, the *faenas*, including those designated for the church, were administered by the municipal authorities. Both committed excesses. The people of Tepalcingo attribute the origin of the fortunes of many livestock-owning bosses to their modestly doing themselves the justice the revolution owed them with the *centavos* given as alms for the church. In other villages they recall how the streets that were repaired led to the houses of the rich and how many other public works were used only to benefit the bosses.

The communal strengthening was not, then, only an egalitarian process that distributed scarce goods, for it also concentrated them in a few hands. It had strengthened not only the relationships for redistribution and cooperation but also those of an asymmetrical character. In these, too, the appearance was one of continuity in methods: Rental of the ox team, the loan *a la dobla* and sales on time, and the local shop that charged more than the regional markets were the ways through which the production of the *patrón* and his *sirvientes* were appropriated by others. Rental of the team fluctuated between eight and ten *cargas* for the cycle, although in some places it could even be obtained for five, and the loans *a la dobla* and sales on time implied 100 percent interest; actually, the methods had not been modified, but their frequency and extent were greater. The disappearance of the haciendas had quite profoundly affected the vertical relations of exploitation. Even the object of the relationship had been transferred, from peonage—principal or strategic in the era of the hacienda—to the autonomous production, to appropriation of the harvest obtained by the peasant as the only way to capture the surplus. Obviously, the subject of the exploitation, peasant labor, continued to be the same, but it acted under different conditions. Laboring as a cultivator was encouraged, compelled in a certain sense, in place of being circumscribed artificially to an insufficient or prohibited territory.

The exploiters were not the same either. The distant hacienda owners surrounded by legends, the lazy *señoritos* full of pride, and their administrators had vanished. The new, rustic bosses, fighters, cunning and cruel, were *compadres,* cousins, and neighbors. Many had been legally elected to their offices or committees by the vote of a majority. Their power was not remote but concrete. They owed favors, blood loyalty, or recognition, but no gifts or charity were received in return. They were acquaintances who participated in and even promoted relations of a traditional kind; they were *compadres* to many and relatives of even more; they were, without question, people of the village. The direct exploiter, the one who appropriated the surplus in the first place, participated in the same social framework as the plundered; there was no social barrier or technological abyss between them. They were stuck in the same sack.

External conditions were also changing. At the beginning almost imperceptibly, but starting in 1930, when the effects of the international Depression became more acute, everything rushed headlong. To make the change more notable, 1930 was quite a bad year for the countryside: it rained very little, and the harvests were poor in the whole country.

Prices rose abruptly and would not cease to do so thereafter. Corn also rose from five pesos per *carga* in 1929 to ten in 1935 and 1937, but it rose in a lesser proportion and later than did necessary products. The inflationary process was parallel to the restructuring of the cash economies.

The rise of local bosses as monopolists, *acaparadores,* was weakening direct exchange, barter between complementary producers. The local bosses were decisive, not only in the monetarization of the exchange between villages but also in the timid introduction of industrial products to replace local products for consumption. The rustic shelves of the villages' little shops were filled with beers, matches, candles; even some canned food appeared. Some village businesses were even illuminated with oil lamps, and the first tortilla-dough mills with internal-combustion engines appeared, to change, some swear, forever and for the worse the flavor of the tortillas. The scarce new products were also urged on by the new evangelists of progress, the rural schoolteachers, who introduced the urban revolutionary norms as ideal models in the schools. During the years of religious conflict many of them were left without students after being denounced as "communists" by the priests. But with the support of the bosses and merchants, who in other aspects fought the schoolteachers and their "socialist" ideas, little by little the local cult of progress, of civilization, was gathering respect.

It was necessary to purchase more things with cash, and corn was worth a little less every day. The physical yields of corn had not been altered: in the Morelos *oriente* two *cargas* were obtained per *tarea,* a little more than two tons per hectare, a yield almost three times higher than the national average of the period; even in the bad years more than a ton was harvested per hectare, while the direct consumption of a family never exceeded eight *cargas* per year, some one thousand kilos at most. But the exchange value of the corn surplus was shrinking. It was reduced even more when it was necessary, in order to make purchases or to have money, to take a loan or to sell the harvest in advance to the monopolist boss, which occurred almost universally. In this case the loss of the corn's purchasing power was doubled by the interest. Before 1930 the salary paid in cash by the *patrón* to his servants was equivalent to ten *cargas* of corn; but if he had borrowed it, it rose to twenty *cargas*. In 1935 the *patrón* had to deliver thirty *cargas* to the moneylender for the same purpose. On adding up all the year's debts, for the team, money, and corn, it was not unusual for the moneylender to appropriate more than half the harvest of the *patrón* and his laborers, leaving them with a supply less than their needs for direct consumption, that is, obliged to go further into debt without any possible recourse. Toward 1935 the corn harvested on one *yunta* of land had "ceased to give" for the complete sustenance of a peasant family.

Changing to Remain the Same. In the report that President Ortiz Rubio presented to congress in 1931 he summarized the development of the agrarian policy of the military *caudillos:* they distributed 6,805,000 hectares among 3,800 *ejidos,* of which 1,701,000 were arable for dry farming and scarcely 245,000 others were irrigated, of which one tenth were in Morelos; on average, less than 3 arable hectares, of which only one-third hectare was irrigated, fell to each *ejido* member. Ten thousand applications for grants had been submitted, less than half had been attended to, and more than five thousand communities were yet to submit territorial claims. Despite this, the distribution was considered finished in five of the country's states, Morelos among them, and a deadline had been set for two more (cited by Silva Herzog, pp. 378–89). Scarcely 13 percent of the arable surface of the country was in the hands of the *ejidatarios* (Hansen, p. 47).

Presidents Ortiz Rubio and Abelardo Rodríguez distributed the land even more slowly: in the four years of their term, between 1930 and 1934, not quite 2 million hectares were distributed to 133,000 *ejido* members. The peasant uprisings had been overcome, and those who incited them were apparently peaceful. To guarantee the tranquility, the government proceeded between 1932 and 1934 to disarm the loyal peasants who had upheld it; they had disarmed the enemies after their defeat. The militias and *defensas sociales* did not like the idea, much less the procedure, but they had to yield in the face of the obvious superiority of the federal forces. In Veracruz the people from the leagues founded by Úrsulo Galván threatened armed resistance; the government withdrew the subsidy from the leaders, and they mediated to carry out the disarmament (González Ramírez, pp. 325–26). The government's infiltration of peasant organizations and corruption of their leaders were by then already an institutionalized procedure.

During the Calles *maximato* the rulers did not change either their goals or their methods, and they followed the revolutionary path of reconstruction loyally and determinedly. But if the *jefe máximo* and his straw men remained faithful to his program, reality had ceased to behave congruently with it starting with the world Depression, and the reformist spirit arose in other groups of the State. The first sexennial plan of the National Revolutionary Party was a program for readjusting the project for capitalist development to conditions emanating from the world crisis. Its recommendation on the agrarian issue was radical: to intensify the distribution and to reorganize its institutional apparatus (González Navarro, pp. 101–3).

President Abelardo Rodríguez converted the recommendations into laws and into government organizations. In January 1934 he decreed a reform of Article Twenty-seven of the constitution to free the *ejido* from the transitory character foreseen in earlier legislation. In the same month, he founded the Agrarian Department, the independent government organism in charge of the agrarian issue, which was previously the responsibility of the Ministry of Agriculture, which at that time was rightly accused of being reactionary. The new department reported directly to the president of the republic, who could name and remove its chief. In March of the same year, the Agrarian Code was issued, which made the permanent resident workers eligible for land grants, a right that had been systematically denied them to protect the haciendas that produced for the foreign market. It fixed the ways for working the *ejido:* individual parcels of four irrigated hectares or eight hectares of dry-farming land for cultivation, and communal control for grasslands and mountain areas. Moreover, the 1934 code bestowed on the president extraordinary powers in agrarian matters, and it granted him authority to intervene directly in the internal organization of the *ejido;* in fact, it made him into the born leader of the peasants, just as he was for the army (González Ramírez, pp. 327–40). In the legislative avalanche, despite the 1934 approval of a reform of the third article of the constitution so that education would be socialist, the legitimacy of private ownership of land was not put in doubt, and the protection of it was as revolutionary as its distribution (Partido Nacional Revolucionario).

With so much lawmaking, Abelardo Rodríguez had neither the time nor the energy left to carry forward the agrarian program, and he left the task to his successor. Starting with his presidential campaign, General Cárdenas outlined the new plan for development, sketched a new utopia: industrialization. Agrarian reform ceased to be a palliative with political purposes and became a program that sought "to create new wealth capable of being used in the acquisition of manufactured articles. . . . In the future the *ejido* would not only enable the subsistence of the *ejidatario* but also increase agricultural production. . . . The agriculturalist only produced 207 pesos annually, the manufacturing worker 1,211, and the miner 4,248; that is, 70 percent of the economically active population of the country received an average income of scarcely $56^{1}/_{2}$ *centavos* a day" (González Navarro, pp. 113–14).

The program, which affected vested interests, ran into veiled but determined resistance on the part of the *caudillos* and freebooters associated with land ownership. Cárdenas confronted it without evasion; he took the bull by the horns: he expropriated the hacienda of Calles's son-in-law, liquidated Abelardo Rodríguez's business, and when he had the power necessary, he exiled Calles—all without ever resorting to murder. Another line of resistance was offered by the hacienda owners involved with export products, the foreigners and the progressives, who were protected by the freebooters, if not actually their partners, and who were arrogant enough to organize *guardias blancas.* The Cárdenas regime expropriated some: those of La Laguna, Yucatán, and the Cusis in the hot country of Michoacán. Many learned from the lesson—Jenkins, the owner of Atencingo, surrendered the lands without asking indemnization on the condition that cane would continue to be planted on them; in return, he retained the mill as his property.

These measures occurred and were possible in an ambience of open political mobilization, in which the peasants took a decisive part. The agrarians were armed again, perhaps with older weapons, to serve as support for the government in the face of the affected interests and to avoid military uprisings. In turn, the army controlled the agrarians, and Cárdenas himself controlled both the troops and the agrarians. He warned them about the rules of the game: "The *campesinos* must cooperate with the army and view it as a brother. . . . Whenever divisions exist among the peasants, they will not be given arms" (Cárdenas, p. 115).

To obtain the peasant's submission, it was necessary to give him land. Cárdenas distributed 18 million hectares, more than double what his predecessors had given out, to 812,000 *ejidatarios,* a number equal to all the earlier beneficiaries. Each *ejido* member received an average of twenty-two hectares, not all arable, while those given grants previously had received an average of ten hectares, which were not all arable either (Hansen, pp. 46–47). Nearly half of the arable land area of the country and more than one third of the irrigated land passed into the system of *ejido* domain. In 1936 the National Bank for Ejidal Credit, devoted to financing production by *ejido* members, was founded. In its first year of operation it applied 31 million pesos to financing the La Laguna collective *ejido* and only 20 million pesos to the *ejido* members in the rest of the country (Silva Herzog, pp. 415–16).

All these measures sought to increase the participation of the peasant, the *ejidatario,* in development directed toward the interior and dominated by national industry, protected from the caprices of the international economy by a certain degree of autonomy. In that project it fell to the peasant to play many roles: to produce food for the cities at low prices and to consume industrial articles. The relations of exchange between producing cheap and buying dear implicitly involved a transfer of resources from the countryside to the cities, an enormous flow of capital to finance industrialization. The asymmetrical relations of exchange and their gradual and constant deterioration prompted the failure of traditional corn-based agriculture. In many zones, the ones most densely populated and with low production yields, the new generations emigrated toward the cities. There they became not only a source of cheap labor but also a source of pressure for keeping urban salaries low, while those who remained in the countryside went on to form a second army of reserve labor, ready for emigration.

The coupling of these roles converted agrarian reform into the central policy of the new plan for capitalist development in its economic aspects. The countryside's creating capital was dropped, but industry was chosen to reproduce it. From among the various types, the transformation industry, capable of delivering products ready for internal consumption, was selected as apparently the most suitable for being protected with regard to international markets; in fact, it was chosen for substitution of imports of manufactured products. In the Cárdenas sexennial, the number of firms, the capital invested, and the production in that sector were doubled, but like an obscure omen that nobody wanted to notice or, worse yet, that they interpreted optimistically as progress, the number of workers barely increased by 20 percent (Medin, pp. 118–19). Fundamental deeds like the petroleum expropriation made it manifest that the government not only was going to favor the industrialization process but would intervene directly in the realization of it.

The program of industrial development upon agrarian bases superficially gathered together the harsh lessons of the world crisis. It made growth rely on the activities that had best resisted the impact of the collapse of the foreign market—agriculture for internal consumption and the transformation industry for the national market. But the lag in correcting the course of growth meant that adjustments that particularly affected agrarian policy had to be made within a short time. The industrialized countries also took corrective measures to overcome the effects of the crisis, from the New Deal in the United States to the installation of fascism in Germany and Italy. The paths of the world powers were on a collision course over the reaccommodation of the zones of hegemony and the control of essential resources. These and other complex phenomena reactivated the international market, which toward the end of the thirties had already regained pre-Depression levels. Moreover, unusual junctures were created in the international political field; one of them facilitated, if it did not indeed permit, the expropriation of English and American oil firms by Mexico.

Mexican exports of raw materials began to regain importance in the national economy. In 1934 exports had recovered their 1929 levels in Mexican pesos; in 1937 they had increased 40 percent above 1929 and 1934, although in devaluated pesos (González Casanova, p. 12). The country and the government, which had not regained the fiscal income level of 1929, could gratefully, and even urgently, use the resources derived from exports, generated in the greatest part by entrepreneurial *latifundista* agriculture. But it was too late to go back on the agrarian promises of the six-year plan. The collective *ejido* was an attempt to reconcile the agricultural enterprises that supplied the foreign market with a radical program of land distribution. The complexity of collective organization, the great financial resources necessary, along with the resistance of the freebooters and foreign hacienda owners, who were down but not out and allied with the voices that decried "communism," slowed down the spread of the collective *ejido,* and production for export was regained by the private entrepreneurs. Starting in 1937 there was a change in the Cárdenas agrarian policy. Distribution was slowed down in order not to affect the productive enterprises, which were granted political guarantees in order to increase their activity. That year Cárdenas created *inafectabilidades ganaderas,* which under the pretext of accelerating growth in livestock-raising for export withdrew from distribution ranches with areas greater than those authorized by the constitution. That date has been considered the peak of agrarian reform (CDIA, 1 : 66).

The State emerged triumphant in the reorientation of the plan for Mexican capitalist development. It had come out strengthened and had even given itself the luxury of being civilized by banishing murder as a valid means for coping with opposition. General Cárdenas, referring to agrarian reform, synthesized his primary, undisputed role thus: "The state's involvement in the overall direction of the national economy is on both counts a function of public order: in social matters by guaranteeing economic autonomy to the endowed villages, and in economic matters by taking care that the total volume of agricultural production is not reduced, to the detriment of consumption and of foreign trade" (Cárdenas, p. 112).

When the Corn Ceased to Give. When the corn ceased to give, the peasants of the *oriente* began to try to find the wherewithal to keep making a living. The crisis was not the result of a diminishing physical yield of corn nor of a decline in the efficiency of agriculture nor even of demographic growth, since Morelos had not regained the population figures of 1910, but of the imposition of a higher rate of exploitation, which implied the capture of a greater proportion of the product by external sectors. The same harvest that only five years before managed to cover a family's needs ceased to do so around 1930. The crisis in the traditional crop was expressed in the lack of money, in the deterioration of the price of corn in relation to that of products that were needed and that had to be purchased with cash. Foods that completed the diet, clothing, fuel, and even beer or liquor cost more. Upon acquiring them, the peasant found himself left without the corn that he needed in order to eat. In sum, it was a matter of obtaining money to make purchases in a cash economy in order to leave the reserves of corn, which had always been the principal food, free and untouched for direct consumption.

In the Morelos *oriente* nobody stopped planting corn. On the one hand, there was no other dry-farming crop that could replace it advantageously, either in physical yield or with better economic results per hectare sown; on the other hand, no one wanted to give up the security of autonomously producing the most important element of his diet. The lands planted in corn not only were maintained but kept expanding at an ever-increasing rate consistent with the way family units were growing. In some *ejidos* the corn crop covered all the arable land received, half cultivated and half fallow, while in others new land, sometimes even thin and rocky soil, low in yield and always far from the village, was still being broken. The people of Hueyapan, who at that time suffered an epidemic that wasted the population, began to encounter difficulties in getting hot-country *ejidatarios* to lease them lands for raising corn, and they passed through one of the most difficult periods that they remember.

To a greater or lesser extent, all the peasants had a hard time. It was not easy to find activities that complemented growing corn and produced cash income. Many went back to gathering wild fruits and plants. Carving wood, making charcoal, and producing tar and turpentine from pine resin —all formidably strenuous activities—were intensified in the cold country; from below "you couldn't see anything but the clouds of the charcoal-makers' smoke." Also, on the Hueyapan lands peasants gathered the root of the zacatón, a tall fodder grass that was used in making brooms and pulque. All these tasks were burdened by a high cost of intermediation, which reduced the price of the product in the village by half in comparison with what could be fetched in the markets of Atlixco or Ozumba. The difficulties of transport by pack animals made it reasonable for the small producer, who had to lose three days of work to make a tiny delivery, to pay this cost; moreover, the local monopolists who operated as moneylenders compelled the producers to pay them in kind.

In the hot country, products for gathering were still more scarce; these included firewood from the mountains, zacatón root, and copal in the southern mountains, among things that could be sold; and gourds, edible insects, red-cactus pears, and some pigeons, among those that could be eaten and sold in small quantities and that contributed to reducing expenditures. However, in the hot country, gathering wild products did not represent a valid option for confronting the corn-devaluation crisis and was never developed in a regular way by men, but was left in the hands of women and children.

During their prolonged dependence upon the hacienda, the inhabitants of the area had lost all their handicraft traditions. They had occupations: they were good bricklayers, smiths, bakers, draymen, and, above all, workmen splendidly qualified for growing cane and for its transformation into syrups and sugar. Only the people of Hueyapan wove woolen coats and skirts for their own wear and not for sale. A short way outside the area, in San Marcos Acteopan and the neighboring villages, all in the state of Puebla, lacking irrigation water (and perhaps for that very reason left outside the hacienda's domain), the people had preserved an active pottery craft that was intensified with the beginning of the corn crisis, which was more severe for them because they had been granted only land of poor quality.

In the temperate-country villages what was to be the most widespread solution to the corn crisis arose: development of commercial agriculture devoted exclusively to the market. For one thing, the old orchards preserved in spite of the hacienda and even during the armed struggle still produced nuts, plums, thorn apples, quinces, and even coffee, products that were sold in the regional markets and that yielded cash income, while the dry-farming lands of the *ejidos* guaranteed the corn supply. But even more than in the orchards, it was on the irrigated lands granted to the *ejidos* that the intensive cultivation of short-cycle plants dedicated to exchange in the cash economy sprang up. The lands irrigated with water that previously went to the cane fields were given over to wheat, which was sown in October and threshed in April; then corn was planted from June to December, to be followed by chile or irrigated beans, which occupied the land from January to May.

In this or in other combinations that permitted rather efficient conservation of the fertility of the soil, wheat, chiles, and peanuts were introduced or grown again in the temperate country. These products, unlike those from the traditional orchards, bypassed the regional markets and totally entered the national market. The wheat was sold to the millers at Atlixco or was ground in Tlacotepec, where an old but efficient hydraulic mill was operating; in any case, the flour was lost in the intricate network of "modern" exchange. The peanuts were shipped out to Mexico City from the Yecapixtla railroad station, where they arrived from the temperate country on the backs of pack animals. The agriculture of the Morelos *oriente* was again linked to Mexico City as a center of consumption or distribution.

The intensification of agriculture with the introduction of commercial crops was tied to irrigation. The complex irrigation system built by the hacienda on a base of works of pre-Hispanic origin had remained unrepaired since the armed conflict. To a great extent, these works were destroyed during the fighting, since the irrigation ditches were natural fortifications. The open canals on the land had been obstructed and filled by vegetation and could scarcely carry a thin stream of water when they carried anything at all. Water from Aguahedionda had stopped flowing toward the *oriente*. Reconstruction of the irrigation system was not only a question of engineering but also involved complex institutional problems. With the distribution of the hacienda, central control over the hydraulic works was lost. Its volume of water, the only one available to the area, had to be distributed among more than twenty villages, which could irrigate only a small portion of their *ejidal* grant with it.

The *ejido* members benefitted, along with some small property owners who retained their right to the water, should have taken charge of the physical reconstruction of the work, an obligation that was specified in the grants, under the inefficient coordination of the Ministry of Agriculture. The incomplete reconstruction took almost fifteen years. The temperate-country villages, which received only a little dry-farming land of poor quality and which were located near the sources of the watering system, rapidly repaired the works, which, of course, were less damaged in that zone. Other villages, like Atotonilco, which recovered the use of its spring, which had been expropriated by the hacienda, put the works in condition for their own use before 1925. Others, like Jaloxtoc, granted poor dry-farming lands, began rebuilding the Aguahedionda canal in 1919, and after six years of hard labor, they received water for their lands in 1925; on that day there was a full-scale fiesta, and they say that the flow of rum could have been measured as the water was—in liters per second. In these villages water was a vital necessity for attaining a production capable of providing for survival, and their people participated jointly and equally in the reconstruction, despite the indifference of the authorities.

But in the villages that received abundant, good dry-farming land capable of producing enough corn, the reconstruction process was delayed; and it was only reactivated when the crisis of the corn devaluation appeared. Then the authorities were pressured to formalize the distribution of the water, and reconstruction projects were undertaken. In 1938 irrigation from the Aguahedionda canal arrived at Tepalcingo, southernmost point of the rebuilt system. In these villages participation in the works was much more selective. The people who had not obtained the wherewithal to cultivate a *yunta* on the abundant dry-farming lands were not going to invest their labor in something as remote as irrigation. In Tepalcingo not even a tenth of the *ejido* members worked on the reconstruction. It was an exceptionally hard task: they had to work on their knees to clean out totally blocked-up tunnels. Only those who worked or cooperated would have a right to the use of the irrigation water.

In the irrigated lands of the hot country various crops were tried, and two of them eventually predominated—rice cultivated with flooding and *el picante,* the Creole chile. In the predominance of rice, introduced by the haciendas, the presence of a government organization had a great influence. The recently founded National Bank of Ejidal Credit offered cash-advance credit for financing cultivation of this plant, while it denied support to other crops, especially dry-farming corn, where its action might perhaps have contributed to alleviating the heavy burden of usury. The initial relations with *el banco,* as it was called from then on, were not happy ones. A solidarity clause through which all were committed to paying the total debt acquired by the group, even though each one worked his parcel individually, was the apple of discord not only with the bank but also among the *ejido* members themselves. The local bosses also sowed distrust and rumors against the bank, for on one hand they were the bank's debtors in their own crops, while on the other, as moneylenders, they saw it as competition for their clientele. The bank's inefficiency and corruption came to complicate the confused situation even further, and the possible romance ended in a quarrel: the *ejido* members remained in debt and for many reasons refused to pay; the bank withdrew from the Morelos *oriente* for some years. Despite this, the nobility of the cultivation of rice was confirmed; capable of resisting the bank, the bosses, and the *ejidatarios,* it became the principal commercial crop of the area. The bank had fulfilled its objective after all.

Some attempts were made to reestablish the cultivation of sugar cane. Again, the pioneers were the people of the temperate country, where the rum factories were. These had a guaranteed and thirsty market that encouraged the people to plant their raw material and to buy what others sowed. Thus, modest cane fields that satisfied a local market were cultivated. In the hot country, too, some cane was planted to supply the crude sugar presses that prepared brown sugar or molasses for rum-making. The first mills reconstructed in the Cuautla region remained too far away to grind the *oriente* cane, and this factor limited the area covered by cane cultivation. The Santa Clara and Tenango mills were never rebuilt. The brand-new mill established by the State in Zacatepec and inaugurated in 1938—in spite of the fact that the peasants repudiated the cultivation of cane "because the bitter memory of the plantations was alive in their minds" (Jaramillo and Manjarrez, p. 32)—did not reach the area either, because of the lack of an efficient connection for transport from the field to the mill. Cane, the dominant crop in the landscape and in the life of the people scarcely twenty years back, was relegated to a secondary position, in a faithful reflection of the changes that were occurring.

The arduous rebuilding of the hydraulic system added only small portions of the *ejidal* lands to the irrigated areas; scarcely one tenth of the lands received this benefit. Irrigated land had again become a scarce, poorly distributed resource. In the *ejidos* that first made use of irrigation only the first generation of *ejido* members had access to water, while the new generations had to resign themselves, if they were lucky, to the dry-farming lands that nobody else wanted. In the *ejidos* that rebuilt later, access to water was more selective yet, and it remained reserved for those who had the wherewithal: the local bosses, obviously; the peasants who had managed to get a team; even the *patrones de la milpa* who rented work animals; but never the servants, who were, of course, the majority. But even the privileged who had a right to the water could irrigate very little land well with the slight volume they received. The irrigated parcels were five *tareas* in area, a half-hectare, sometimes even less, and only exceptionally—and for that one had to have a great deal of influence and power—reached one hectare. With these sizes, the irrigated lands were used as and considered a complement to the dry-farming lands, and they had a specific aim: to provide monetary income in order to leave free and give "guarantees" to the corn dedicated to self-sufficiency. The commercial irrigated agriculture did not replace the traditional but was combined with it. For the peasant, the important crop continued to be corn, and commercial crops barely served to free the principal crop from the debts that reduced it to the point of making it insufficient. The introduction of "modern" crops made the growing of corn more important— paradoxes of modernization.

Some villages did not obtain water, or so little fell to them that it scarcely supplied a handful of *ejido* members, but the lack of corn struck all equally, and they, too, had to seek the wherewithal. They tried to introduce commercial crops on the dry-farming lands. There were not many possible alternatives, without even mentioning rice or wheat, which needed either more water or planting on a calendar different from that for dry farming. The chile was either stained or rotted by late rains, or the frosts caught it: it could be planted only in tiny plots in some mountain *tlacololes* that received the *sereno,* the October dew. Only peanuts and rain-fed beans withstood the test, but cultivation of them spread very little because both yields and prices were low.

Everything was in short supply but imagination. The people of Hueyapan, the hardest hit at that time, found the ideal crop for overcoming the crisis. It had a great resistance to the climate and adapted easily, acceptable yields were obtained, and the prices were the highest in the agricultural market, but the serious problem was that neither the army nor the police sympathized with the planting of marijuana.

All the crops introduced to surmount the corn crisis were controlled by more or less closed monopolies. Wheat was ground and distributed by the millers—no more than two dozen in the entire country—who were the undisputed owners of the market. The same thing occurred with rice, for which the millers scarcely totaled a dozen, including those from Morelos and Veracruz. The chile remained in the hands of the tiny circle of wholesalers at La Merced, the great supply market for Mexico City, which at that time would have been controlled by no more than two dozen merchants. All were private businesses, and the government followed a hands-off policy or else did very little. These closed groups, able to speculate in unison, took advantage of the juncture in which the commercial crops were planted in search of a monetary complement, but not of subsistence, to impose prices so low that it no longer paid the capitalist enterprises to plant them. The peasants, who only sought to free their principal product, resigned themselves to the low incomes derived from their secondary crops.

The low prices imposed by the groups that controlled the markets were accentuated more severely for the producer by the great costs of inter-mediation. Many of the new commercial crops were purchased in the producing locality for half the price they received at their destination. This was justified by the difficulty of transportation that had to be carried out with beasts over frightful paths and even at the risk of falling into the hands of some gang of bandits. The producing *campesinos,* the majority of whom did not have even a team to work their land, were even less likely to have beasts of burden to transport their crops. Providentially, the local bosses happened to have droves and even some carts, which enabled them to remedy the scarcity. The cost of intermediation was 100 percent, as if to maintain the old norms established in traditional agriculture: everything by half. The local purchase was interwoven with the financing of the new crops or of the subsistence crop, which obliged the producer to deliver his harvest to the moneylender. The profit was good, so that some bosses became promoters of the "modern" crops without abandoning their old dealings with corn.

Around 1940 the peasants, somewhat perplexed, found themselves obliged to work twice as hard to obtain barely the same things as ten years earlier: to keep on living, just barely, with debts, commitments, harvests that faded away in bills. They had intensified their only resource, work, in order to pay a new and brutal rate of exploitation for the benefit of people from outside and of some—very few—from within, from among old acquaintances and perhaps even *compadres.* But they were fulfilling a larger design: feeding the Mexican people at low cost, although they themselves continued to eat the same as before—or worse.

Industry Made of Corn. In the second half of the thirties Mexico set out decidedly on the road of capitalist development through industrialization under the regime presided over by General Cárdenas. The option was chosen, to a certain extent, in the face of an open historical perspective. The effects of the Depression had, after all, weakened the rigor of the bonds of dependence, although the dominated countries had to pay a high price for it. Later, the readjustment of areas of hegemony among the opposing, belligerent powers created a conjunctural framework that in certain cases expanded the margin of action for the dependent countries. Moreover, within the country, a set of circumstances favored the juncture of aperture, of choice. The *caudillos* and their economic enterprises had been hit by the crisis or by the political succession. A mobilization of workers and peasants—particularly the latter, who had weapons avail-able—in support of the government neutralized a possible reactionary coalition or military uprising. The government had acquired virtual autonomy with respect to any pressure group that acted alone; in fact, it had obtained more than that: it had assimilated within itself, and in a subordinate way, all the political pressure groups. Since Obregón the government had not enjoyed so much freedom of action, which really permitted it to choose the alternative to follow, if not unlimitedly, then certainly from among several possibilities.

The choice of the model of capitalist industrial development was not as natural and obvious as it has since been made to appear. Certainly conjunctural conditions that favored it existed, but there were also others in the very structure of the society that contradicted it. Mexico lacked capital, a technological base, and an economic infrastructure appropriate to the industrialist plan. Put another way, because of their structure, the development of the productive forces did not naturally lead toward the rise of industry. It was necessary to pressure the whole society, and to do so brutally, to make up for the structural deficiencies in what industry required.

It is appropriate from this point on to establish a distinction: in this essay, industrialism is conceived of and is analyzed as a particular mode of production that is based on the availability and use of stored energy, which is only possible with a high degree of centralization in the manufacturing process. Thus, the industrial nature of an object will be determined by how it is produced and not by its characteristics or intrinsic functions. A radio, a bicycle, or a highway can be made in various ways, and only some of these, but certainly not all, will be industrial. Thus, when it is said that the development of productive forces by nature dispersed, ubiquitous, does not lead to industrialization, this does not imply an inability to produce complex manufactured things, but, on the contrary, the possibility of doing it another way.

The Cárdenas government intensified the task undertaken by its predecessors in order to create an infrastructure suited to industrialism through public works initiated directly by the State. Communications and transportation, imperative conditions for the functioning of industry and the articulation of the market, continued to be the principal items of federal investment. During the Cárdenas sexennial, roads absorbed 26.6 percent of the government's total investment, a percentage that was only exceeded by its successor (Hansen, p. 83). Moreover, the expropriation of the oil companies and the establishment of the Federal Electricity Commission in 1939 gave the government direct control over the energy sources vital for industry and had indirect effects that also favored industrial growth.

On the other hand, little—almost nothing—could be done to create a technological base. Without heavy industry, without scientific research, without the possibility of manufacturing machines for reproducing human effort, Mexican industry had to import factories from abroad. With the machinery came many implicit and obligatory complex consequences, like the organization of the enterprises, their magnitude, the character of labor, its training, and even the salaries that allowed its economic functioning. Worse yet, the nature of the product that could be obtained also came along implicitly. Clearly, Mexican industry was going to lack originality and would be limited to reproducing a foreign model of organization in order to produce objects identical to those manufactured abroad. But the technological base did not come included in the machines that it enabled to function. That base continued to be rooted abroad and had to continue being imported. The machines, uprooted from their technological base, could become what is, strictly speaking, their material nature: a heap of iron. In fact, Mexican industry was a geographic extension of the metropolitan industries that was fastened, by force and from above, into an environment that could not generate its own autonomous development; the evolution of industry would be, and has been, a derivative process, a reflection of external changes.

Much could be done, however, to create the capital necessary for funding the derivative industrialist plan. Foreign capital, frightened by the expropriations, the radical verbal pronouncements that proclaimed the advent of socialism, and the workers' demands for better salaries, not only suspended its new investments but withdrew many of those it had; in the Cárdenas period there was a net flight of foreign capital. Not only did the government not have money but it owed a great deal, despite which it threw itself into realizing substantial investments by operating on deficit budgets. The traditional private entrepreneurs, hardly more than a few, did not have sufficient money nor much desire to stake it on Cardenismo. It was necessary, then, to force the creation of internal savings so that the new investors would have to invest; that is, it was necessary to compel the population to transfer resources to the capitalists.

Not all groups were equally affected: industrial workers, located in a splendid tactical position with the arrival of the industrialist project, obtained on the average an increase in their real salaries (Medin, p. 128). In practice, the workers for the big enterprises, especially those that belonged to the government, received more-than-proportional increases, which consolidated their position as an aristocracy; the rest, humbly, had to contribute their tiny savings to development. The bureaucrats, the employees in the service of the State, raised to a special position by the government's predominance, also received net benefits during the Cárdenas sexennial, especially through long-term economic fringe benefits that consolidated their loyalty. The important function of widening the market for the products manufactured by the transformation industry fell upon these groups. Thus it was that the weight of the formation of capital basically fell back upon the *campesinos*. The decision was reasonable: they were the majority group, at least two thirds of the population.

The principal mechanism for extracting the surpluses and obliging the peasants to create new surpluses, which would also be transferred, was the unequal inflationary process. The official data, not very trustworthy and full of optimism, indicate a 60-percent rise in the cost of living between 1935 and 1940; other sources estimate it at 96 percent (Medin, pp. 127–28). A calculation of 100 percent in the increase in prices for the decade from 1930 to 1940 seems more than conservative. These statistical figures, compiled in the cities, are scarcely a pale reflection of the impact that these rates had in the rural environment. The average of 100 percent in the rise of the cost of living includes increases that double or triple that figure for some products, as well as others that were less than the average; these last are the ones the peasants produce. When the Mexican peso was devalued again in 1938 (Solís, p. 115), prices climbed rapidly, but those of the foods that the *ejido* members and *minifundistas* produced dropped in absolute numbers in 1939 and 1940. This decline was encouraged by the State through the creation in 1938 of the Regulatory Committee for Subsistence Markets (Medin, p. 128), which went so far as to import food products in order to knock down internal prices, striking with full force at the beneficiaries of agrarian reform in support of the unswerving intention to save for the formation of public and private capital destined for industry.

Corn, the sustenance of the peasant economy, which covered more than two thirds of the country's cultivated land area, was obviously the crop most effected by the inflation. Between 1930 and 1940 the average rural price of corn, according to official statistics, rose from 77 to 95 pesos per ton (Reynolds, app. F), scarcely 25 percent, compared with an increase of at least 100 percent in the general index. In the state of Morelos the real prices obtained by the peasants for corn not encumbered by loans were from 35 pesos for a ton of corn in 1930 and between 60 and 70 in 1940, and half that for the mortgaged portion of the crop. The peasant population of the country grew during the decade by some 2 million persons at most, less than a 20-percent increase over the 1930 figure, but their production of corn grew by almost 50 percent (Reynolds, app. F). To attain this, the *campesinos* had to open 1.25 million hectares for the annual cultivation of corn—in fact, 2.5 million hectares, since half of the land remained fallow. The cultivation of corn, which covered 64 percent of the land in 1930, advanced to 67 percent in 1940 (CDIA, 1 : 131–32) and occupied poorer-quality, less suitable land, which meant that the yield per hectare remained unaltered or perhaps declined a little. The peasant worked more strenuously but received less and less for his effort. When the labor reached its minimum valuation, the corn *ceased to give*.

Seen from the other side, from that of the government and the investors, the industrial project was full of short-term advantages, and it was the most rapid and intense system for forming and accumulating capital. Sheltered within a protectionist system, industry was isolated from international competition. This divorce, artificial inasmuch as their production was identical, made the industrial enterprises virtual monopolies, with a captive market in which they could impose their prices, lower standards of quality, or sell obsolete articles. Besides this central advantage, the industrial investors enjoyed additional protection: import licenses, cheap official financing, legal tax exemptions in addition to those permitted by double accounting, support from a policy of public works in their direct benefit, and even prestige and good conscience derived from participating in a patriotic task. The industrialists like to classify themselves as the progressive national bourgeoisie, although they had turned industrial investment into the most remunerative field for speculation and rapine. Such was the climate that those who were novice industrialists at the time recall that a factory that did not leave free and clear 50 percent of pure profit was not even taken into account and that the good ones left from 100 percent on up.

The advantages to the government were no less important, although perhaps they were less evident. In creating industry as a vertebral column for the articulation of the national economy, it was consolidating its own strength. The centralist nature of the State as a monopoly of power was becoming congruent with an activity that concentrated the entire monetary flow of the country, over which control could be exercised. Moreover, industry, which needed to be isolated from the international market by government policies in order to exist, was born under direct dependence on the State. Also, the *national bourgeoisie* arose as a product of the government's action and remained subordinate to its authority. The plan similarly permitted the enrichment of the revolutionaries and maintained that curious ambiguity between the functionaries and the investors. Clearly, the government was interested in the forced concentration of capital as the motor for a growth economy but also as a measure for improving the well-being of the urban population, from which the State emanated and whose modernizing interests it represented. Besides, it was interested in its own income, gathered to a great extent from totally monetarized urban activity. Finally, it should not be discounted that industry was inseparable from the conception of progress, of modernization, and even of national independence—far from it: National industry and capitalism were considered by the revolutionary leaders as an obligatory step in an inevitable evolution, and their advent was a sincere, progressive ideal. The State was the vehicle for a manifest destiny, the instrument of history with a *happy end.*

Reestablishment of the Peonage. If corn had ceased to give to the *patrones de la milpa* in the *oriente,* it was worse for the servants, whose share in the crop scarcely covered their direct consumption, in the unlikely case that they had kept it free of debt. Obviously, the servants did not have access to irrigated lands, although many of them worked regularly on rebuilding the hydraulic system, but they had done so for a day wage paid by some of the wealthier people, who had received title over the new irrigated land. More severely than their *patrones,* the servants felt the effects of the depreciation of corn as a lack of money for spending and for allowing them to leave their meager share of the harvest free for direct consumption. Although they had succeeded between 1930 and 1938 in getting the *patrones* to double the share paid in cash, this covered only ten weeks out of a year of fifty-two, in all of which money was spent. For those who were heads of families and trying to get together some money to undertake cultivation of a *yunta* of corn on their own, the urgent need for money became more worrisome. The more they delayed in obtaining it, the more risk they had of losing their right to *ejidal* land. For this group, the most numerous within the communities, there was no other alternative except to get paid work, to reestablish the peonage.

The introduction of commercial crops offered a possibility of employment. Since nobody could stop planting corn, the crops introduced on the irrigated lands were chosen in part because they had a calendar complementary with the cornfields. Wheat, but even more so chile, and especially rice, which was planted in seedbeds, involved tasks that required more labor than family units could provide, although it might be only for very short periods. This permitted giving employment to the servants and even to the *patrones* who had not managed to obtain grants of irrigated lands. In a certain sense, not only were the holders of the irrigated parcels able to give employment but they were forced to do it, even if it meant that they remained inactive themselves, because of social pressure to help a relative or even a son or because of being unable to say no to a *compadre.*

A group of *ejido* members was withdrawing from physical labor and took charge of watching over and directing the work of salaried laborers. In 1937 the engineer Alanís Patiño summarized the situation in these terms: "An *ejidal* group formed principally by the *ejido* members who had irrigated land, who enjoyed a relatively prosperous situation . . . where there are some people from other federative entities, moderately educated, and perhaps with tendencies toward being bosses . . . left their hardest work for other peasants to perform . . . and already in 1935 in Morelos there were 7,700 *ejido* members who devoted a considerable part of their time to working as day laborers in the fields, in many cases in the service of other *ejidatarios.*" The same writer observes that this situation occurred even though the dry-farming lands were not totally occupied or worked sufficiently, despite which he concluded that "the *ejido* economy of Morelos has not failed, and instead it is on the eve of exceeding the old levels . . . the agrarians of Morelos are not disappointed with the benefits of agrarian reform; they increased the benefits that they receive through their work, and other peasants will share in their gains" (Silva Herzog, pp. 439–40).

In the commercial crops introduced into the communities, one worked for a daily salary. On one hand, what the people wanted for their work was ready, hard cash, which could be spent immediately. On the other, sharing in the harvest did not work because of the very nature of the product, which could not be stored locally or consumed directly by the producers but was absorbed by an external, speculative market. Nobody had illusions about having two *cargas* of rice to try to sell to the Cuautla millers, who might not pay any attention to him, or finding that his chile had no buyers or that the buyers paid so little that it was not even worth the work of packing up the bundles. The diminutive size of the parcels did not favor a redistribution of production either.

The commercial crops made a new type of risk appear: the market, in which the poorest people could not give themselves the luxury of participating. For the *patrones,* the assumption of the risk socially legitimized the right to personal enjoyment of the profits. The salary relation, two pesos per day by 1936, became more and more frequent among the peasants, and it acquired its own rules of circulation and conduct. To contrast the difference between the forms of work, the service relations were formalized in religious ceremonies, the festivals of the cornfield like that of the Cross of San Miguel or those at the end of the harvest, in which the families of the *patrón* and of the *gañanes* and *peones* shared, while salaries were agreed on and formalized in the saloon, between drinks and in a personal, direct fashion, through which they created an additional benefit for industry—the consumption of beer. Even so, the idea of reciprocity, of mutual obligations that transcended the payment of wages, was implicit in the salary relations, and the hiring of laborers was determined by social relations established beforehand that extended into the future. Little by little, the *ejido* members who undertook commercial crops on irrigated lands became leaders of a work team linked by relations that neither began nor finished with the payment of wages.

The appearance of salary relations did not replace or even weaken the previous relations of cooperation but remained confined to a specific activity: commercial crops. In cultivating corn, servitude persisted, and in a sense, it was even strengthened with the introduction of commercial crops. For one thing, the fortunate people who possessed an irrigated parcel needed a supply of corn, and they could not neglect their crop, so they needed a trustworthy *gañán* more than ever. The *patrones de la milpa* who did not obtain access to irrigation tried to place themselves as peons in the commercial crops in order to get the money for the cash payment to their servants, to whom they were often tied by a kinship relation to which it was necessary to respond. For the *peones* and *gañanes,* servitude continued to be the central activity that gave them access to the basic product of consumption, around which the family economy was articulated, and enabled them to remove themselves from, or at least to palliate, the seasonal changes in the price of corn. Given the relative importance of corn, its specific weight within the peasant economy, service remained the best paid activity in the community, despite inflation. Although the devaluation of corn dragged down the price of peasant work, which was governed by the price of the grain, the seasonal changes in the corn price —100 percent in one year, 400 percent if it was encumbered with debts— amply exceeded the most severe rate of inflation.

Moreover, the introduction of commercial crops created new forms of cooperation to reduce or distribute the cost of the investment, but especially to share the risk and, in the event, to share the loss. Often, many of the irrigated parcels were worked *a medias,* "half-and-half." Some holders of irrigated plots who did not in fact have the wherewithal and could not assume the risk of failure rented their plots for money in order to continue raising corn. The communities created specific forms of association for redistributing access to irrigated land and the money that was obtained from its produce—salaries, going half-and-half, and land rental—while they conserved old forms of redistribution for corn—servitude, rental of teams, and the loan—some symmetrical, others clearly asymmetrical. But however much they were distributed, the resources that the communities had were quite meager for all the affected peasants to overcome the devaluation of corn with them. This created a supply of low-priced labor, and it was not going to be allowed to go to waste.

The first to take advantage of this resource was the hacienda, or what was left of it, which was more than a little, to be sure. After the scare that Luis García Pimentel the younger suffered when Zapatismo revived almost miraculously in support of General Obregón in 1920, his hopes of recovering the entire property vanished. In the first years of distribution the hacienda of Tenango and Santa Clara lost at least half of its area. The owners also lost some of their pride, and a few days before the time for claiming indemnization ran out, they presented a request for the government to pay them, even if it had to be with agrarian-debt bonds. They had luck or influence and managed to be indemnified with almost a quarter-million pesos. When the agrarian distribution in Morelos was declared finished in 1929, the hacienda still retained part of the original property, more than the most extensive *ejido* in the Morelos *oriente*. Moreover, they had kept the right and the actual grant for three hundred liters of water per second from the flow of the Amatzinac River.

The hacienda owners began to work their property again in the thirties. Although they had good lands available, the reduced volume of water and the agrarian claims made the costly repair of the large-capacity sugar mill inconceivable. They opted for cultivation of rice, which had been a secondary crop alongside cane, something that they knew and that did not need transformation works, since the grain could be transported without risk to the mills at Cuautla or Puebla. These were not good times for installing factories. Land that could not be planted in rice because of lack of water they leased for five *cargas* so that the old *realeños,* the children of the hacienda, excluded by law from the agrarian distribution in order to protect the big plantations, could plant corn on it. Again, this guaranteed the stability of labor for their rice fields.

The peonage was, then, reestablished. But the *realeños* could not attend to all the tasks associated with the crop by themselves, and teams of occasional laborers were hired for a daily salary from nearby villages. For some tasks, like the *aborde* in the month of April, up to fifty peons were needed; transplanting from the seedbeds to the fields in June or July required two hundred peons, and as it coincided with corn planting, these laborers had to be recruited in many villages; for the August and September weedings, one hundred laborers were needed, also from various villages; during the rest of the year, thirty laborers were enough, and these came from Tenango, from among the *realeños.* Moreover, land was also left over and rented for five *cargas* of corn to people from Hueyapan and other villages without arable land. The business flourished again, and the profits grew, but not so much as a *centavo* was reinvested in the country-side, where the security that the transformation industry offered was lacking.

In 1938 the heirs of the hacienda endured another scare. The reform of the 1924 Agrarian Code had made the peons subject to agrarian reform, and the *realeños* went after the hacienda. Not all of them; only a group labeled the *agraristas,* who had to call on outsiders to meet the minimum census for requesting a grant. Another group, the *latifundistas,* maintained, not without reason, that there was land left over for planting corn and that what they wanted was work in order to obtain money. The strife was intense; there were invasions of land and even deaths among the opposing peasant bands. In the end, the *agraristas* won and received *ejido* in Tenango. Other villages also obtained lands from the hacienda to expand their *ejidos.* But the hacienda survived. It retained 420 hectares of the best land and more than 200 liters per second of water from the

Amatzinac, which were soon augmented by a complementary flow from the rebuilt Aguahedionda Canal. Around 1940 the hacienda began to work its irrigated lands again and to make use of that labor force that, from its point of view, was struggling in forced leisure, in lack of work, and certainly in poverty.

The story of the hacienda of Tenango and Santa Clara was repeated throughout Morelos, and little by little a number of agricultural enterprises reared their heads, some in the hands of new, enterprising owners without aristocratic names but with political influence and a tremendous desire to make money. But not only the remnants of the large haciendas and the enterprises with irrigation and economic resources were making use of the abundance of low price of the *campesino* labor "freed" by the corn crisis, for some of the local bosses also set themselves up as commercial producers, starting with their own parcels in the *ejido* and some irrigated small property. Commercial agriculture again assumed a growing importance in the landscape of the *oriente* and the irrigated valleys of Morelos, which extensive cornfields still dominated in 1940.

Even the State resolved to contribute decidedly to preventing the idleness of the peasants by establishing the large Zacatepec cane mill, which made use not only of the work force of *ejidatarios* but also of their irrigated lands for planting cane. The mill was formally organized as an *ejidal* cooperative in which the peasants owned everything, but administration remained the responsibility of State functionaries, people from the Ejidal Bank, and the president named the manager directly (Jaramillo and Manjarrez, p. 33).

From the first harvest in 1938, when cane was left standing in the fields because of failures in the factory, things did not go well between the owners and the administrators. In 1939 federal soldiers had to intervene to impose order on the peasants and their leaders (Jaramillo and Manjarrez, p. 37). In 1942 Jaramillo, the *campesino* leader who promoted establishment of the mill and was the first president of the administrative council, took up arms against the government, which had created a new form of *latifundismo*. Luis Cabrera, author of the Carrancista agrarian law of 1915, said in 1937: "[This *latifundismo* is] under the control of the Ejidal Bank, which not only finances but directs the agricultural labors and administers *ejidal* agriculture. The peasant is treated like a peon, not allowed any initiative, and the Ejidal Bank is the new *patrón*. The land nominally belongs to the villages; but the Bank exploits it with the sweat of the *ejidatarios*. This control by the Bank, which I have called 'the modern version of *repartimiento* and *encomienda,*' will have sorrowful results" (Silva Herzog, pp. 436–37). In 1962 Rubén Jaramillo and his family were murdered by government agents.

The advance of commercial agriculture in the thirties, considerably more intense in Morelos than in other parts of the country, attracted laborers from other regions in which there were no local resources for overcoming the corn crisis, and they contributed, in effect, to keeping rural salaries low. Some came for a season and moved on, but others stayed, and many of them placed themselves on the agrarian census rolls, also bringing pressure on the land. In 1940 Morelos listed 182,711 inhabitants, with which it had regained the population level of 1910. Between 1930 and 1940 the population increased by fifty thousand persons, a little more than 40 percent in a decade. Almost forty thousand of the one hundred eighty thousand inhabitants of 1940 were not natives of the state, a bit more than 20 percent, while in 1930 there were scarcely seventeen thousand (Solís, pp. 206–8). Commercial agriculture produced this miracle, or more precisely, the corn crisis and the water produced it. The temporary respite that they gave the idle land had ended.

Anticipation of the Industrial Millenium. In Morelos the agrarian work of Cardenismo was minor and consisted principally of enlarging the original grants; of establishing new centers of population, many of them formed with outsiders, which certainly was not very popular among the natives; and of affecting some of the old haciendas in order to benefit those who were their permanent resident workers, their *criollos*. In all, the Cárdenas government gave out seventy thousand hectares to five thousand peasants, while the *caudillos* had distributed two hundred thousand hectares among twenty-five thousand *ejido* members. In 1934 Zapatismo as a threat or as a pressure group was extinct and did not merit any privileged treatment; it was already a thing of the past, the domain of history and official speeches.

But the people of the Morelos *oriente* gave their support to General Cárdenas's government, although at times they did not like it and at others were not even aware of what they had surrendered to it. The government got along with the politicians, with the bosses, whether they were *ejidal* commissioners, municipal presidents, local or federal deputies, and the peasants dealt with them in order to arrange matters that had to do with the government. These were more and more numerous: requesting land and water and keeping it free from seizure and invasions by individuals or neighboring *ejidos;* requesting construction of a school or road; avoiding livestock theft; arranging the transfer of the parcels of the dead or their descendants; and above all getting papers, documents, credentials for legitimizing any action or even the obvious fact of being alive and being a person. Many of the affairs that were previously handled by speaking to neighbors became problems with the government; for that reason, it was better to get on well with those who made themselves heard. Enlarging the area of State influence and reducing the number of persons with the possibility of intervening created a more and more effective system of control that guaranteed even the peasants' enthusiasm.

One of the most important mechanisms for consolidating State control over the peasants was the formation of an organization to group together all the beneficiaries of agrarian reform, even those who were still asking for land. There had been an effort to found such an organization since 1933, when some military chieftains and agrarian leaders established the Mexican Peasant Confederation. Involved in an all-out electoral contest, this organization had no success in its unifying purpose; however, it decisively influenced Calles's acceptance of Lázaro Cárdenas's candidacy for the presidency of the republic. Once the latter took office, he did not beat around the bush, and in 1935, as president of the country, he decreed the formation of the League of Agrarian Communities as the *ejido* members' sole organization. His decision was applauded, since, as the press said, "there will be, of course, the advantage of an order, a discipline, and a system with which it will be possible to put an end to the anarchy" (González Navarro, pp. 134–38).

The decree that gave rise to the League of Agrarian Communities and the organization that was derived from it was a marvel of ambiguity (Confederación Nacional Campesina, pp. 7–9 [hereinafter CNC]). The league was born as a political organization charged with representing the interests of the *ejidatarios;* in that sense, its establishment remained the responsibility of the National Revolutionary Party, in theory an organization independent of the government and not subject to presidential authority. All *ejido* members, by the mere fact of being so, became members of the league by virtue of the decree. The *ejidal* authorities, also by decree, would politically represent the *ejidatarios* and would form in each state a single organization that would be integrated into a Central National Confederation. This confederation was recognized as the only valid agent before the State for carrying out the administrative and bureaucratic transactions of agrarian reform; in that sense, the Agrarian Department, a government dependency, was allowed to meddle in the peasants' political organization. The hybrid character of the organization as a political institution and as an administrative extension of the government was the best guarantee of State control, since any agrarian transaction not channeled through the state league or the national confederation was ignored (see Medin, pp. 95–96).

In the same year that the presidential decree was issued, a good number of state leagues were created, among them the one for Morelos, and in less than a year, the organization had almost seventy thousand members (González Navarro, pp. 140–41). In 1938 the National Peasant Confederation (CNC) was established, absorbing the League of Agrarian Communities, which arose out of the 1935 decree. During the constituent assembly of the new organization some representatives from the state leagues complained before General Cárdenas about the party function-aries who occupied the leading positions and asked to be represented by *ejido* members who possessed a parcel of land. The president replied that they should not attack their own organization. The same day, he told the assembly that "the committee that hurls the organization that it repre-sents against the authorities is not meeting its responsibilities, since it has an expeditious way to make itself heard and even to insist on the guaran-tees of its rights within an intelligent, peaceful procedure" (Medin, p. 98). Since that time, ambiguity has become the normal form of existence of the CNC.

The National Peasant Confederation never formulated a program capable of gathering the peasants to its breast, and from its beginning it used coercion as a means of recruitment. Agrarian transaction was formalized in the extreme and became bureaucratic to the point of the absurd; it became so slow that generations replaced years in measuring it. Worse yet, it became infinite: when an arduous procedure came to an end, a change in administration or in the legislation required starting a new one of unpredictable duration. In fact, all the peasants of Morelos and in the country occupy their lands under provisional title and in hope of some document, of a confirmation that has already expired by the time it is received or new proceedings have already been begun. As the sole legitimate intermediary before the agrarian authorities, the CNC had guaranteed under those conditions the recognition and the adhesion of the peasants, whether voluntary or forced, a subtle distinction that did not matter much to anyone.

The political nature of the CNC permitted charging for the administra-tive intermediation in giving out land. The price was high: the transfer of the actual or potential power of the *campesinos,* the majority group in the population, to State control. During the Cárdenas years the treatment seemed fair and, to some, even generous. Fulfilling the pact required an apparatus, a bureaucracy capable of controlling and mobilizing the peasant according to the government's needs. The national functionaries of the CNC have been named by the president of the country ever since the foundation of the organization. The first secretary-general of the confederation, Graciano Sánchez, was the first of a long succession of rural schoolteachers who would occupy the same post; one or two *ejido* members, who certainly were not to distinguish themselves in their performance, would be chosen only by exception (see CNC). Starting with the secretary-general, all the organization's functionaries were designated from above, even obtaining control over the election of *ejidal* commissioners, who almost always came from among the group of local bosses or their followers. In this type of apparatus the requests arising at the base flow slowly and have to follow a long and tortuous path; however, instructions and political directives surge forth above and flow rapidly and easily toward the bottom. All the CNC functionaries above the local level were professional politicians or wanted to be, and they based their careers on docility toward those above and control of those below.

But the peasants were not the only ones affected by the ambiguity, by political alienation. In 1938 the National Revolutionary Party founded by Calles was transformed into the Mexican Revolutionary Party (PRM). Along with the name change, a serious attempt was made to turn the organization from an electoral arena into an efficient instrument of control and of centralization of political activity. The PRM adopted a formal, corporate-style organization and comprised four sectors: the peasant sector formed by the CNC; the worker sector, represented by the Confederation of Mexican Workers (CTM); the military sector, formed by the army "in their character as private citizens"; and the popular sector, whose nucleus was the Federation of Unions of Workers in the Service of the State (FSTSE).

It remained quite clear that each one of the sectors retained autonomy to fight for its specific goals and was committed not to interfere in or to recruit among the other sectors. The party adopted the indirect form and was organized with grass-roots organizations as units for affiliation— *ejidos,* unions, and army corps. Only in the popular sector was individual enrollment accepted, after many doubts, as an experiment (González Navarro, pp. 145–58; Medin, pp. 98–113). Each one of the sectors proclaimed the defense of its own individual interests, which sometimes contradicted one another. Moreover, the sectors were internally stratified and included groups that, objectively, were in contradictory positions. All the differences and divergences within the party were considered valid and even desirable to the extent that they were subordinated to the supreme interest of the revolution—the reconciliation of classes. With a nationalistic, populist tone, all sectors were asked to renounce or postpone their strategic demands in return for immediate concessions, which were multiplied as substantial sinecures for the leaders, the negotiators and manipulators. Many of them made personal fortunes and political careers for themselves. In exchange for the freezing of the positions of the sectors and their internal groups, the PRM opened the way to rapid, almost vertiginous personal mobility through politics.

Not only the peasant organization but all those that formed the party were acquiring government administrative functions, were incorporated into the State. The PRM began as a government organization, a position from which it derived its power with regard to the masses, with a specific goal—the political control of the population. The party was not at that time, nor has it been since, the source of autonomous power. It lacked authority of its own and a sphere of independent action. It never pursued the attainment of power but was created on the basis of it, with the aim of preserving it. Even the organizations that formed the nucleus of the party —the CNC, the CTM, and the FSTSE—emerged from presidential actions or decisions. The party's corporate organization was never a reflection of the composition and functioning of the State, structured hegemonically around the complex of industrial-development interests, but a design for obtaining the massive participation of the population, not in decision-making, but in the execution of policies emanating from the government.

The peasants' demands entered the State apparatus and had varied luck. Sometimes they were simply ignored, since negative replies were never used in the CNC. At other times the demands were transformed, lost their sharpness, their radicalism, and were adapted to the political orientations of the moment; even so, they might not be resolved or even dealt with. Some were settled partially or in a sense different from the original claim. If an expansion that affected a hacienda was sought, someone else's land was obtained; if one thousand hectares were requested, two hundred were received; if credit for corn was sought, credit for rice was offered. No claim was entirely resolved. All the petitions or demands were lost from sight. They passed from hand to hand and climbed the hierarchical ladder until they were lost in the heights and descended again, not infrequently in some other direction; the apparatus swallowed them. It was necessary to wait, to apply again and go on waiting, to get support and influence, to seek out circuitous routes, and, again, to wait.

Those who did not resign themselves to participating in the apparatus or to following its rules did not have many alternatives. No other peasant organization capable of exercising pressure or acquiring political influence within the system existed. There was not even an organ of expression, apart from the spoken word, that was not controlled. The national press, which gathered the complaints and demands of other groups, judged the government as radical and dangerous in regard to rural affairs; obviously, it was not going to collect the voices that complained about the State because of its timidity and conservatism. The local press, as corrupt as the national, loyally served the highest bidder, the *latifundista*. The peasant dissidence found only some occasional echo among the most conservative groups, the resentful who opposed Cardenismo from the right. The left was involved in the apparatus, determined to change the system from within and to bring the country to socialism. The other alternatives were silence or rebellion, always dangerously close to the most reactionary interests.

In Morelos some threw themselves into rebellion during the Cárdenas government. The most outstanding was *El Tallarín,* "The Noodle," who operated in the Morelos *oriente.* This episode involved Enrique Rodríguez, a Zapatista veteran who rebelled between 1935 and 1938 with "the second" Cristiada, the resurrection of the peasant movement defeated and betrayed by the Church without having any of its demands satisfied. *El Tallarín* Rodríguez used Zapatismo to legitimize his uprising. In his manifesto, he said: "The ideals of the villages [are revealed in] the Glorious Plan of Allala [sic]. Among ourselves, we the humble villages feel the cruelties of the government[.] And since filthy politics, much less ambition, are not found among us, they bring us their yearnings for rescuing the the true right of the villages[.] And although it might be a little late, we struggle as much for religion as for all the rights of the fatherland in order to defend the true reason of the villages. Water, Land, Progress, Justice, and Liberty, Long Live Christ the King, Long Live the Virgin of Guadalupe" (cited by Meyer 1973*a,* 1 : 378).

Perhaps before Rodríguez there were other *tallarines,* a name applied generally to all the rebels between 1920 and 1942, but memory of them and their demands has been lost. The rebels from the temperate country who went off with the *bola chiquita,* or "little brawl," of 1942 to defend their "guarantees," the right to continue being peasants, were also called *tallarines.* The *bola chiquita* exploded when compulsory military service was imposed because of Mexico's entry into the Second World War. The draft, the new levy, directly threatened the young men, but it affected the whole family, which increasingly depended on the salary income that the young men provided. But the *bola chiquita* was the expression of something more profound; it was a reaction against the threat of modernization, against the intrusion of the State, against dependence and subordination.

About the same time, other peasants with varying ideological positions rebelled—among them, Rubén Jaramillo, close to the left; while those of the *oriente,* on the other hand, did so on the right, quite close to Sinarquism. The *oriente* and the Jaramillo rebels, motivated by the same conditions, met and could not understand one another; neither of the two had a viable program with spirit, although they shared anger and disillusionment because of a revolution that had betrayed them.

The uprisings of 1942 dissolved in the face of the threat of the army and the conciliatory offers of the politicians. They say that General Cárdenas, who at that time was minister of war for the Ávila Camacho government, ordered the troops to get near the rebels without fighting them and only to do so in case they killed more than ten soldiers; the rebels never got close to that figure. Finally, there was a compromise: only a few young men were recruited, and the temperate country villages received the "benefit" of a highway that tied them together more closely.

Other rebels did not even express their frustration with an agrarian reform that turned against the peasants or with political alienation at the hands of the government; they simply unleashed their fury. The people of Huazulco, en masse, stoned to death a police chief and a band of soldiers who suspended the great Lent fair on the pretext that there was a smallpox epidemic, but really because they did not receive a payoff, an adequate bribe. In this brutal, spontaneous fashion, peasant opposition was also expressed toward the growing intervention of the State, which little by little was developing an image more radical than that of the worst enemy, namely, that of the *only* enemy.

But during the Cárdenas period rebellion or rioting was uncommon in Morelos. The majority joined the political apparatus or kept quiet. There was agrarian action, and the apparatus expressed itself with radicalism; there was movement and hope. The dream of the Mexican Revolution was not totally exhausted among the peasants. The president spoke of them frequently, always defending them. He also visited them and talked with them; he told them to wait or immediately resolved for them some demand lost in the apparatus. The government needed them and called on them; in some places it even gave them arms so that they would defend it. All this contributed to forging the illusion that the peasant had great political strength, and many believed it. But, above all, there was no repression, no systematic terror practiced by the government. The "guarantees" of the *campesino*—land, crops, the family's subsistence and its autonomy—were severely threatened, but government intervention still had not become intolerable, or almost never did.

Even *El Tallarín* himself, after three years of rebellion, lived to tell of his deeds: once when federal soldiers cornered him, he escaped on horseback at a gallop across a railroad bridge that had no flooring, only open railway ties separated from one another by seventy-five centimeters of emptiness. Well after he surrendered to the government, they offered *El Tallarín* a great deal of money to cross the bridge at a gallop again in order to film a movie. He refused. Back then he had done it because "I was up to no good." Times certainly had changed.

V   RECENT YEARS

Increase and Multiply

Twenty Years of Growth. By 1940 the Morelos peasants had received practically all the land that the revolution was going to give them, on which, as in the biblical curse, they had to increase and reproduce themselves by the sweat of their brows. They did so efficiently. In 1940 the state of Morelos had barely regained the population that it had had in 1910; twenty years later it had doubled the number and had 386,264 inhabitants, compared with 182,711 in 1940. The people of Morelos had not only preserved their own lineage but had also assimilated outsiders, whose numbers had gone from 37,000 in 1940 to 101,702 in 1960, when one out of every four inhabitants of the state had been born in another part of the country (Solís, pp. 206– 16). The majority of the people lived directly off agriculture, and an additional number gave it their services at high prices, despite the fact that between 1940 and 1960 Morelos *ejidatarios* were only granted fourteen thousand hectares, scarcely 5 percent beyond the amount of land given out between 1922 and 1940. Agrarian reform had shown results at last.

In the Morelos *oriente* growth was not so spectacular. In almost all the villages of the hot and temperate countries the population increased 50 percent and 60 percent, respectively, in those twenty years. Hueyapan did not grow more than 10 percent in the two decades, and between 1950 and 1960 it lost population. The area absorbed almost no outsiders and even forced out a few members of the native population who did not find employment. There was an absence of the conditions that would permit large-scale introduction of labor- or capital-intensive crops, like the rice and the cane that had enabled the valleys of the South and the neighboring valley of Las Amilpas to grow at a greater rate than the rest of the state. Also lacking were cities that grew, as did Cuautla, more rapidly than the state average thanks to the increase of service employment: business, transportation, and, to no small extent, the bureaucracy.

The most severe limit on the growth of agriculture in the area was the shortage of water. From the time the reconstruction of the Aguahedionda Canal was finished around 1940, and until 1970, no hydraulic project was carried out, apart from the drilling of a few deep wells and basins for private use. The water supply never regained the volumes that the hacienda used, in part because the water from Aguahedionda was distributed among the villages that lay along its course outside the area and in part because the distribution and maintenance projects, which were completed with the participation of more than twenty villages, lost effectiveness. In Tepalcingo, between 1956 and 1963 irrigation was halted because of the low yields that were obtained in the poor soil, unsuitable for maintaining fertility under intense and constant use; this motivated the suspension of credit from the Ejidal Bank, which had accumulated a debt that the peasants could not and did not want to pay. Although miracles of efficiency were performed in the management of water in some villages, the system as a whole had broken down.

Even so, all the irrigated land was covered by commercial crops that were not consumed in the area but produced money. The peasants planted wheat and rice in the temperate country and mainly rice in the hot country. These were safe crops, with predictable yields, firm markets, and more or less stable prices. The *ejido* members fulfilled the task of producing basic foods for the nation. In both the hot and temperate zones, they tried their luck with the cane that they knew so well and that also had a stable market, but the area's distance from the mills meant that acquisition of the sugar did not pay, so that after a couple of years it was abandoned. Only the fruits from the orchards and some irrigated crops that were inserted between the rice and wheat cycles, like beans, chile, or winter corn, were consumed and sold in the area and neighboring ones. To the degree that roads were reaching the *oriente* villages, the fruits and vegetables were expanding their market, even reaching Mexico City.

In turn, what was left of the old hacienda, the largest property in the area and the best endowed with water, embarked on the venture of speculative crops for the national market, just as the other enterprising landowners did. They tried their luck with tomatoes, squash, onions, and melons—the hacienda's most important crop for several years—but especially with cotton. In the fifties the fiber reached attractive prices and became, by a wide margin, the principal crop for Mexican export (Solís, p. 127). In the area, the cultivation of cotton failed roundly and was on the verge of causing the bankruptcy of the hacienda. Worse yet, it left a sequel of plagues that spread through the peasants' crops with unheard-of ferocity.

The old hacienda and some rich landowners, desiring still higher earnings, introduced important technical innovations, like the use of chemical fertilizers and the first tractor, during the forties. However, they suspended all investments in territorial improvements, and when a water pipe that supplied the ex-hacienda with water fell in 1960, accelerating the catastrophe of the second cotton crop, it remained inactive, since it was outside the estate's boundaries.

The participation of the hacienda and the entrepreneurs in the speculative markets for vegetables created conditions in which some peasants rather timidly repeated the experience. In 1950, in Zacualpan a few planted tomatoes and onions; in Xalostoc they also tried their luck; and a little later they would do so in Tlacotepec and Temoac. The experimenters had something by way of resources, plenty of family labor, and considerable audacity. Along with the new crops, the use of fertilizers was incorporated on irrigated lands, and a little before 1960 some of the rich *ejidatarios* bought their first tractor. In Zacualpan they still remember how the fertilizer was applied: they measured the exact dose for each plant with a soda-bottle cap; they also recall that the chemical powder was quite strong, that one's hands sweat on touching it, and that its odor was intensely penetrating.

But the greatest burden of the growth that enabled almost total absorption of the new native population of the area fell upon the extensive dry-farming lands of the hot country. Production had to increase more rapidly than the population, since a growing share of the harvest was appropriated by other sectors through local middlemen. The inability of the production of a *yunta* sown with corn to cover the subsistence costs of growing families was becoming more acute during the twenty years between 1940 and 1960. Little by little, but constantly, it forced the cultivation of commercial plants and the selling of labor, as well as expansion of lands planted as cornfields.

At the time, not many commercial plants could be grown on the dry-farming land on the plain. Although various crops were experimented with on a small scale, only the peanut withstood the test. Its cultivation spread from Zacualpan and Huazulco, where it was processed in the form of candy, to Axochiapan. Peanuts were planted in order to obtain cash loans, which were repaid with the harvest. That, of course, was paid for at prices lower than those on the national market and had to be handed over entirely to the moneylender. In the end, many peasants scarcely received enough money to pay for the altar and the food for the Day of the Dead, and at times not even that; the important thing was the initial loan, which was received exactly when one could not take outside work without neglecting the cultivation of the cornfield.

The peanut is a low-risk crop that tolerates drought well, and since its fruit grows underground, it is protected from many pests and even from hail. At times, on very few occasions, it is even complementary with corn, given that it grows in excessively sandy soils, where corn does not develop well; it is also complementary in its calendar, since by pushing oneself and working swiftly, it is possible to tend it without neglecting the cornfield.

At the beginning of the forties the peanut was planted only when sandy soil no good for corn was available, but around 1960 it was planted on corn land that was in its fallow year, so that the fertility and yields of both crops were affected. But labor had to be used more intensively, and the complementary calendars of the two crops made that possible.

Meanwhile, the cornfields grew and occupied all the land that was possible and some that did not seem to be. The land furthest from the villages, the poorest and rockiest, the very worst, was incorporated into cultivation. Scarcely a few years earlier it would not have occurred to anyone to plant this land, since the effort required was not repaid by the yield. But even these lands were not enough, and the pastures had to be planted. Livestock-raising was displaced to more distant locations, with severe consequences: the price of renting a pair of animals rose from eight to ten *cargas* of corn. Some peasants found themselves faced with the paradox that it did not make sense to pay such a high price for the team, given the low yields of the marginal land, while, on the other hand, they were also unable to give up cultivating that land without being left without the corn and loans they needed to continue living.

Livestock was also affected by various epidemics that reduced their numbers. The aphthous fever, around 1950, was met with a remedy as severe as the illness: the *sanitary rifle*, the slaughter of sick cattle and those suspected of being so. The killing, combined with corruption of health officials, was used by moneylenders to eliminate competition, especially the animals of peasants who through many sacrifices had raised one or two teams. In 1960 another illness, *rengue* or *derriengue*, severely reduced the number of cattle; the beasts simply fell, were crippled, and died. This epidemic almost served as an epitaph for the traditional live-stock-breeder and moneylender, for the *cacique*. But during the entire twenty years, the plague feared most was rustling, cattle theft, which increased beginning with the opening of the highways, which allowed the "gathered" livestock to be transported great distances to be slaughtered. Rustling reached such a magnitude in the fifties that a decree by the governor of the state of Morelos established the death penalty for cattle theft associated with homicide. That decree was interpreted by the villages' livestock guards as a right to kill rustlers, and many suspects were hung or shot under the *ley fuga*.

Rustling and its sequel of violence and murder were unleashed by the livestock owners themselves—who also formed the livestock guards in charge of curbing it—to eliminate competition, to avenge old affronts, to gain new positions of power, and, again, to ensure that their clientele did not buy or breed their own teams and escape dependency. The cultivation of the pastures and the epidemics made it more difficult for the peasant to acquire a team, so that livestock retained and even increased its characteristic as a scarce good, strictly monopolized by a few. Among these people, some were able to rent out as many as fifty teams in a farming cycle, for which they received some thirty-five tons of corn in payment.

Until 1950 the centuries-old system of leaving fallow an amount of dry-farming land equal to that which was planted had remained unaltered, although the marginal land and pastures had been incorporated into it. But since then, the urgent, undeferrable needs of the indebted peasants with growing families have obliged them to break the equilibrium that maintained fertility and to intensify use of the soil. First they planted peanuts and chile on the fallow land, which permitted a more intensive use of labor. Later the villages with less territory had to plant corn on these lands. The results went beyond the worst predictions, and the land submitted to such an energy-intensive extraction yielded less and less, until it took two years to get the same amount from a *yunta* cultivated year after year as a *yunta* rested with a fallow cycle gave in a single year. They were back where they had started, but with double the work—or more. The intensification in the expropriation of surpluses and the demographic growth that exercised pressure on a limited territory acquired the proportions of a grave crisis around 1960.

During all those years, the Morelos *oriente* was becoming "civilized" through closer contact with the wide world of capitalism. Markets grew, and money circulated more; schools appeared or grew in size and importance; some of the larger villages were even illuminated, thanks to electricity, which would reach even the smallest villages in the sixties. The government's civilizing efforts were devoted primarily to road construction, to the articulation of a wider market. While land was not being distributed nor even irrigated, at least not in Morelos, where it was urgently needed—on the other hand, the country's northeast, where there were few peasants, was being irrigated—and while the introduction of medical or health services was even rarer, road construction was a high priority, an obvious requirement of progress, the contractors, and the automotive industry.

In 1937 the government built the highway between Cuautla and Izúcar de Matamoros, which crosses almost through the middle of the Morelos *oriente*. Since then, trucks loaded with goods cross the area, either to take away the agricultural production or to bring in articles from outside. Before 1940 buses came (quite infrequently and somewhat hazardously) as far as Tepalcingo to bring people to the great Lenten fair. In 1942, when the temperate-country peasants took up arms against the government and started the *bola chiquita,* the formal road that connected with that zone was hurriedly built. Only Hueyapan, perched on the volcano, remained beyond the reach of modern means of transportation. In 1947 the passes that penetrated south of the principal highway were turned into the road that goes as far as Atencingo in the state of Puebla, passing through Axochiapan.

In 1949 the path between Tlacotepec and Hueyapan was opened, but the bridge over the gorge, which enabled trucks to reach the village, was built only in 1956. This road, unlike the others, was opened because of the stubborn initiative of the people of Hueyapan and thanks to the contribution of their free labor; the government, after considerable prodding, only gave the materials, including an abandoned bridge that had to be refitted.

Today one can get to all the villages of the area by bus. The old roads have been improved, and some other new ones have been opened. The highway to Tlacotepec has been asphalted at least twice, as a consequence of murky, poorly fulfilled contracts, which were, however, transparent to the critical inhabitants of the temperate zone. Today, the *mano de obra*, or "labor," roads, as they are officially called, constitute a source of employment during the dry season—rather feeble, of course, since not very many people are employed and the machinery of the private contractors who take charge of the construction has not been displaced. A healthy custom that also has not been lost is that a great deal of labor on the roads, especially maintenance, is contributed for free by the peasants as extra work for the benefit of the community. More recently, food rations were introduced to repay the communal labor, but they are worth only about a fourth the amount established as the legal minimum wage. To top it off, the government considers the rations a subsidy that aids the peasant.

The railroads were never fully rebuilt. They traveled along the branch that already linked the city of Puebla to Cuautla in the thirties, and since that time, no more money has been put into them. A new track that will cross the area on the route to Acapulco has taken so long in construction that it is already confused with the old one. The railroads seem like dinosaurs in their death throes in the face of a new species, trucks and cars, which are imposing their speedy ecological dominance.

The people of Morelos looked on the progress in communications with pleasure, although without much hope. Many things became easier—buying, for example, although obtaining the money to do it was becoming very difficult indeed.

The Last Decade and a Few Extra Years to Boot. Since 1960, the combination of a group of factors permitted the intensification of the use of the soil and of the exploitation of those who work it, while at the same time it prevented the explosion of the crisis. The Morelos *oriente* peasants managed to survive once more and to keep growing, the first thanks to the second. The population of the majority of the villages increased in a greater proportion than in the previous twenty years. Between 1960 and 1970 the villages of the hot and cold countries grew between 50 and 70 percent, and those of the temperate country more slowly. By 1970 Tepalcingo doubled its 1940 population; the Jonacatepec municipality registered an equal increase; and Atotonilco almost tripled its population, although the establishment of a tourist hotel and spa that are the property of the *ejido* influenced that case. Hueyapan recovered from its earlier stagnation and reached three thousand inhabitants. Zacualpan, however, grew scarcely 15 percent in the last decade.* Although according to census criteria rather more than half the area's population is urban, because they live in villages with more than twenty-five hundred inhabitants, not only did new industries fail to arise, but one of the rum factories even closed, so that all growth depended on agriculture. Even so, in the last decade, the *oriente* grew at the same rate as the entire state of Morelos, which registered more than six hundred thousand inhabitants in 1970.

The widespread use of chemical fertilizers on dry-farming lands, begun in the first years of the sixties, permitted elimination of the fallow period on a great deal of land and was perhaps the most important factor, although not the determining one, in the growth of agricultural production. Before that time, the use of chemical fertilizers had been limited to irrigated lands, on which the risks of losing an investment were, if not eliminated, certainly quite reduced. The dry-farming peasants had resisted adopting the fertilizer, not because they were conservatives or stubborn about progress, but because using it lacked economic advantages for them—that is, because they were rational. They argued that it was absurd to invest money in crops that could be lost for want of rainfall or because of other uncontrollable phenomena. Even if the crop were produced without problems, once converted into cash, the increase in the corn yields did not fully exceed the cost of the fertilizers or of the work in applying them. The potential profit was too low to compensate for the risks, even on the supposition that the peasants could buy the fertilizers. But since they did not have money for purchasing fertilizer and had to borrow it at 100 percent interest, their hypothetical earnings turned into a loss from the very beginning. All these reasons became secondary when the use of fertilizers ceased to be considered an optional investment and became an indispensable condition for obtaining a crop on lands exhausted by annual cultivation. By adopting chemical fertilizers, the peasant earned less, or to put it in its real terms, he lost more on cultivating corn, but at least he could continue eating.

The use of chemical fertilizers and the expansion of the area planted

* That is, 1960–70.

had other complex consequences. Apparently, the chemical products accelerated the growth of the corn in such a way that flowering moved ahead two or three weeks. Planting still starts around the feast of San Juan, when the rains become regular, but now ears of corn can be cut after 13 or 15 September, whereas previously they were not ready before the feast of San Miguel, 29 September. This precocity probably brought about an imbalance with the reproductive cycles of corn pests, which now attack more severely. To these pests have been added the ones resulting from the introduction of the speculative crops, especially cotton, which also rage in the cornfields. The people assert that pests able to finish off a crop entirely, without leaving anything behind, appeared for the first time barely fifteen years ago. For that reason, the use of chemical insecticides followed the use of fertilizers. These are also purchased with money, which must be borrowed at the customary interest rate. Cultivation of the cornfields can no longer be undertaken without realizing a cash expenditure, without consuming industrial products.

Two entrepreneurs had brought in the tractors for their own crops in order to increase their scale of operation and to reduce the costs for those who were not livestock owners. Since the tractors were large (because there were no others on the market) they were sometimes able to work the peasants' land for a price, almost as a favor. The business turned out to be so attractive that some entrepreneurs bought machinery to devote it almost exclusively to rental to the peasants. Basic tasks were done with this machinery: the first plowing or breaking new ground; at times, furrowing; and to a lesser extent, the weedings, or *beneficios*. In 1965 the entrepreneurs charged between twelve and fifteen pesos for each *tarea* of one thousand square meters, according to the type of work and the soil conditions; in 1972 they charged between eighteen and twenty pesos for the same area. In the larger villages, like Zacualpan or Tepalcingo, there were between six and twelve tractors of different sizes in 1972. However, there were none at all in the smallest villages, like Chalcatzingo or San Gabriel.

For the peasant, the appearance of the tractors signified an alternative to renting ox teams, which were scarce throughout the sixties. Moreover, the tractors showed more flexibility, since they could be rented to work half a hectare, four, or fifteen. The ox teams, on the other hand, were always cheaper when they could be used to plant one *yunta* of land. For anyone planting less, the rent was excessive, while for anyone who wanted to plant more, the strength and speed were insufficient. Fewer and fewer peasants had access to a whole *yunta* of land, but the few tractors could not even remotely manage to cover all the cultivated land. Thus, a new mode arose for renting teams: they began to be rented by the day—in the beginning for twenty pesos a day and now for as much as fifty, the services of the *gañán* included in the price. In fact, the teams began to compete with the tractors again: They equaled the machines' flexibility in working small areas, and they offered lower prices to make up for their slowness. But renting a tractor or team by the day has an obvious disadvantage compared with renting a team for the whole cycle: It has to be paid for in cash at the moment of use, and it will almost always be necessary to borrow in order to do so. Unlike the teams, the tractors remain not only beyond the peasants' reach but even beyond their hopes, and they imply an irremediable dependence. The price of a used tractor in 1970 was around forty thousand pesos, which equals several years' total income for an *ejido* member, and certainly not one of the poorest ones.

The fertilizers and machines broke the more or less fixed patterns or norms of traditional agriculture, and even the crops and their conditions were modified in a very brief span of time. Some traditional crops disappeared, as did wheat, which ceased being planted in the temperate country in the first years of the sixties because of the appearance of a pest that could not be fought and because of the need to give irrigated land over to an economically more intensive use. For this latter reason, cultivation of peanuts on irrigated parcels in the temperate country was also abandoned. Wheat and peanuts, which needed only two waterings a cycle, were replaced by vegetables that demanded much higher humidity. The competition for water and the appearance of pests, which totally finished off the production of avocados, made the yields of complex temperate-country orchards decline. Walnut trees, whose fruits attained a high price per kilo, lost more than half their yield. Some of the richer orchardists tore down the complex orchards and turned them into specialized ones, which in Zacualpan they preferred to devote to growing quinces. Others cleared away the old orchards in order to plant vegetables, for which they calculate more than double the economic yield—if the markets turn out favorable. Starting in 1965, vegetables became the favorite crops for the irrigated land in the temperate country.

At that time, raising vegetables on irrigated land also spread into the hot country: chile, onions, tomatoes, and squash, which alternated with the ever secure rice crop. The increase of external and demographic pressures in the face of the insufficient amount of irrigated land favored the spread of speculative vegetable crops throughout the dry-farming lands by 1965. They tried their luck first with tomatoes, then with green beans, and, later on, with onions.

With these plants, the peasants assume enormous risks because of the irregularity of the rains and the uncertainty of the market. Moreover, the risks do not only affect the work invested, since sizable quantities of money can be lost, too. The rain-fed tomato plant needs to be propped up on stakes and wire, so that the fruit does not remain in contact with the humid soil. The cost of cultivation exceeds that of the same plant grown with irrigation; moreover, the risks are even higher yet. These risks are compensated for by the possibility of attaining very high prices in a market with a small supply, since not many people are disposed to undertake the venture, and fewer still come through it successfully.

The peasants also operate with another relative "advantage," much less illusory than the market: the great amount of work these crops require, which constitutes the most expensive item in the cost, is contributed in great part by the peasant and his family, who do not ultimately calculate it as an expense, but as an investment. In the area, the dry-farming peasants who plant vegetables and do not include labor within the cost have to spend less than half, sometimes only a quarter, what an entrepreneur would spend on a similar crop. This "saving" in the investment enables the peasants to sell their produce at very low prices, so low that for the entrepreneurs they represent a net loss. This margin of exploitation is taken advantage of by middlemen, who turn it into greater earnings and who have become the enthusiastic promoters and timid financiers of these crops. This fact also helps to keep food prices in the cities relatively low.

For the peasants who plant speculative crops on dry-farming land the risk is similar to that of playing the lottery, and for the first time some of them can reckon their gross income in thousands of pesos. But unlike the lottery, planting tomatoes or onions requires a sizable investment in seeds, fertilizers and insecticides, and, especially, labor—all of which can easily be lost. Not everyone can cover such sums—only the least poor among the peasants, especially those who have a large work force available in the family. The women and children are a very important part of this work force; they are actually the most important resource for launching the venture. Even so, this venture is rather modest: between five and twenty *tareas* are planted, according to the land and the labor available, as well as the capacity for indebtedness. With this, they have to compete against the large agricultural enterprises, which rarely plant on dry-farming lands, but are situated throughout the entire country in order to gain a permanent supply, and against the active village entrepreneurs who do indeed risk planting without irrigation.

Not all the peasants held out, and after accumulating debts for two or three consecutive cycles, they abandoned the venture; some even had to leave to work outside in order to repay loans or to disappear discreetly. Others—almost none—stopped work, accumulated capital, and launched themselves totally into commercial agriculture as modest entrepreneurs. The majority break even, replacing in a good year the losses of the bad ones in such a way that their average income of a couple thousand pesos a year turns out to be scarcely any higher than what they obtained with the traditional crops, and lower than what they would take home by working outside at the going salary—if there were someone to hire them. The enormous effort that the peasant families expend to harvest speculative crops is the worst remunerated, the marginal one. They could console themselves by thinking that the same venture ruined the heirs of the hacienda, who had to sell lands in order to pay for the failures of their own speculative crops.

From the beginning of the seventies a growing number of peasants tried their luck with speculative crops on dry-farming land under the pressure of growing needs and with the dream of exceptional earnings that might enable them to get out of being poor (*salir de pobres*). This possibility becomes more and more remote because of the notable increase in the supply. In 1973 several hundred dry-farmers from the area battled with the onion, and in 1974 many more considered taking the risk in the hot and temperate countries. Not everyone had the means to cover the debts, and for many it was to be their last venture, but they all felt the pressure to make the attempt.

Competition with peasants frightened away some vegetable-growing enterprises by impinging upon prices through multiplication of supply. The oldest enterprises with the most capital, the most solid ones, which had considerable fixed investments that they had to protect, devote themselves to primary-necessity crops protected by official guarantee prices that offered secure, adequate earnings. Curiously, the establishment of official price supports was proclaimed and justified as protection for the poor *campesinos,* as a subsidy for the neediest. The enterprises that took refuge in the official prices, among them the ever more fragmented remnants of the hacienda, generally had available a supply of irrigation water that the primary-necessity cereals like sorghum, which was the favorite crop, could not use and that was simply lost. Again, the paradoxes of the system.

But another type of entrepreneurs, who have their capital invested in machinery that they rent to the peasants—and not in land, since they rent it from the peasants—not only persisted in speculative crops but expanded their scale. Some of them plant more than a hundred hectares of irrigated onions and have other crops simultaneously, so that they capture a considerable part of the peasants' irrigated land area. These new, daring entrepreneurs, many of them members of the new local bourgeoisie, establish multiple ties with the peasants, on whom they base their success and survival, and they are the principal promoters of the speculative vegetable crops.

Some of the earlier crops were continued during that decade of profound, accelerated changes. Rice, which previously was the most profitable crop on irrigated land, lost this appeal in the face of the substantial though risky income available from growing tomatoes or onions. However, the security of growing rice, which was supported by official credit and by guarantee prices, was noteworthy. Planting rice has come to represent a breathing spell, for it means a modest but secure monetary income that temporarily enables one to loosen the grip of indebtedness. The rice yields in the state of Morelos are by far the highest in the country and are obtainable thanks to the true virtuosity of the growers, who are nationally considered masters of their occupation. The virtues of the flooded rice crop in cleansing the soil, in order to break the reproductive cycle of the pests that threaten other crops and to restore the fertility of the earth, also gained importance. This crop's great demand for humidity, which exceeds that for other plants, severely limits its spread. The water necessary for planting rice could only be delivered to a part of the land each year. The peasants have established a rotation system that allows each one to plant rice once every three or four years. Everyone is grateful when his turn arrives.

The dry-farming peanut also continued to be planted, especially in the most arid villages and by the poorest peasants. Nobody expects a cash income from raising it. The market for this seed is dominated by a few *acaparadores,* and their monopoly has been strengthened by a disproportionate tax of five hundred pesos on each ton that leaves the state of Morelos, where, coincidentally, a large industry for processing this product just happens to be located. It turns out, when expenditures are rigorously accounted for, that the crop does not pay. But since the monopolists also finance the planting, the peasants can use a large part of the fertilizers received on credit for the peanuts in cultivating the cornfields, which frees them from acquiring a second debt. With a little luck, the peanut harvest pays the entire debt and perhaps even the cost of the altar for the Day of the Dead. This seed is harvested in October and permits use of the labor of family and neighbors when they have no other employment. Thus, no one expects to earn anything on peanuts but simply to lose less on corn.

Planting of vegetables destined for the local or regional market, including chile (the most important one), sesame, and irrigated beans, was also continued. Some new crops of this type spread in the last decade, including watermelon and honeydew melon, which are planted in the southern part of the area and are rain-fed, unlike those mentioned above. These plants are sown on very small areas, and no one grows them exclusively, for they are always combined with other principal crops. They are secondary activities that permit intensifying and monetarizing the family labor immobilized by care of the principal crops. They do not require high investments, and the expenditures made on them are frequently not even counted as such, since they use the same resources that are acquired for the central activity. The crops are sold as they ripen and on a very small scale: a couple of boxes or bags that are taken to the nearest market, where they are sometimes exchanged for other products necessary for family consumption or for sulfur or some insecticide that can save the principal crop. The importance of these crops is enormous but not readily perceived, since their results only appear when peasant activity is viewed as an integrated whole, which is how the peasants themselves analyze it.

In the sixties the cultivation of grain sorghum appeared and spread, and in 1972 it occupied more than the cornfields. In 1955 one of the heirs of the old hacienda was the first to sow this plant, partly as an experiment, but also because it attracted pigeons and he liked to hunt. The experiment with *milo maíz,* as sorghum was called then, did not continue. Ten years later sorghum reappeared in Tenango, and by 1971 it had been spread all across the hot country by the action of the Ejidal Bank, which finances its cultivation but not that of corn or peanuts. In 1974 more than fifty-five hundred hectares were receiving official financing for cultivation of sorghum. Only some villages like San Gabriel, Chalcatzingo, Huazulco, and Temoac, considered the most conservative, had, according to the bank, "shut themselves off" and refused to grow sorghum.

Sorghum is a dry-farming crop quite similar to corn. It has almost the same calendar and thrives on similar lands with comparable yields. They are plants that compete with one another. Sorghum has perhaps a greater resistance to drought and lends itself more to mechanization; indeed, it seems that harvesting it turns out to be uneconomical when done by hand. Yet, sorghum cannot be consumed directly; instead, it it used for preparation of balanced foods for animals. It is a commercial product that is processed and consumed outside the area, that requires total monetarization and the use of industrial inputs. The preference the bank shows for this plant is not, then, surprising, since it can replace corn ecologically and requires the total integration of the peasant into the market, with money, with development. It is an anti-peasant crop.

The *campesinos* risked planting sorghum not so much because of its commercial character—if it comes to that, corn can be commercial too—as because it came supported by official credit. They could plant it without spending so much as a *centavo,* since the bank handed out the seed, fertilizers, and money for the tasks of cultivation; it provided or contracted for the necessary machinery and took charge of machine harvesting and sales. The peasant merely provided the land. In exchange for it, he had the possibility of diverting resources received for the sorghum toward his own subsistence by using money intended for the labor in order to pay for family expenses. The peasants use the credit for the competitive crop as a complementary resource for subsistence.

In the cold country new crops have also made their appearance, especially pears and high-grade peaches, which attain good prices in the Mexico City market because they are harvested very early. The adoption of these crops is the result of a long process of experimentation, of trial and error. Between 1940 and 1960 the people of Hueyapan lost access to the lowlands that they used to rent for planting corn as their owners began using them. The lack of an autonomous supply of corn threatened the community's existence and was expressed in the halt of demographic growth. The rough, mountainous territory of Hueyapan was not apt for planting dry-farming corn. The peasants had to transform the land and create agricultural soil by means of constructing terraces in order to plant corn. To protect the terraces from erosion and to obtain fruits for consumption, they planted trees. At that time Hueyapan was far from the markets because of the lack of roads.

However, the Hueyapan peasants needed increasing quantities of money in order to acquire what they could not produce. They did not have many alternatives for getting it. They exploited the forest and its resources, planted maguey and sold *pulque,* and even wove wool more intensively. Some dedicated themselves to expanding commercial culti-vation of marijuana, which was not consumed locally, but the army and the legal authorities stepped up the repression and corruption. There was money in the crop, but it soon disappeared; however, the fear it left behind was permanent. Nobody likes to talk much about that time, but the "plant of evil," as some call it, helped them to survive.

Meanwhile the fruit trees produced, and, for better or worse, their fruits began to be sold in the area. The practices of grafting and fertiliza-tion with animal manure, which certainly are not due to the sort of government agricultural extension devoted to crops like sorghum, were improving the fruit and the yields. Moreover, the roads kept getting better, thanks to the effort of the people and in spite of the obstacles of the bureaucracy. In the sixties Hueyapan fruit began to arrive directly in Mexico City, where the enterprising producers took it, since not even the middlemen were interested in them. Today the Hueyapan villagers have seven trucks—no tractor, to be sure—and others come up to seek the paradise pears and peaches. Hueyapan has become a rich village by beginning with the intensification of local resources, without machinery and external capital, but above all with the physical labor of its people, efficiently mobilized by the social organization of a vigorous community some would call conservative.

The diversification of crops in the last decade did not displace corn and the crops associated with it. The cornfields are still present from the highest terraces won from the volcano to the extreme south of the plain. All the peasants with access to agricultural land raise corn on a portion of it.

Yet, corn has not only "ceased to give" but has "ceased to be a business," as its cultivators say, always eager to demonstrate with figures that the cost of the crop is not recovered with the value of the harvest. Raising corn now requires a cash investment to buy fertilizers and to pay rent on the tractors. These expenditures must be made in advance, and one runs the risk of never recovering them. Before, none of the costs of the crop, except the servants' pay, required expenditures in advance: no capital was necessary, only access to the land.

Despite the introduction of fertilizers, corn yields have declined between 25 and 40 percent: from two *cargas* per *tarea* to one and a half or one and a quarter in good years and even a half in the bad years. Investment in fertilizers takes between two hundred and four hundred pesos per hectare, and the rental of machinery requires between four hundred and nine hundred per hectare, depending on the strategy followed. These two cash expenditures take away from a third of the value of the harvest, as a minimum, up to more than half, without even considering the payment of interest. If the days of work, valued according to going wages, are added to this, the result is invariably negative. There is something new in this, as well: Earlier, tending the cornfield was considered a customary, uncompensated task, but today it is considered a cost that counts even though it is never actually spent. The previous monetary investment has brought about a change in the handling of the corn.

Despite the fact that every time corn enters the cash economy its producer loses money, nobody has stopped planting it. The rationale for this apparent absurdity is derived from a group of conditions. As the basic element of the diet, corn represents the greatest proportion of the total cost of the peasants' consumption; in very rough terms, it can be suggested that expenditure on corn is almost never less than half the total expenses, a proportion that increases the poorer the *campesino* is. Moreover, the local price of corn shows enormous fluctuations during the year. In the area, the variation between the extreme prices, taking the lowest price as a base, is at least 50 percent in years of abundance; less than twenty years ago it was 100 percent. Thus, the peasant who buys corn for consumption at the current price during the whole year spends a third more than if he bought at the lowest price. In purely quantitative terms, that means a minimum difference of 15 percent in real income, which is definitive for people strictly located at subsistence level. In other terms, closer to those the peasant uses, when there is not enough corn, life itself— the family, social relations—is in danger. The corn supply is a "guarantee" for the peasants' survival. Access to an independent supply that eliminates or diminishes the necessity of acquiring it in the market and at high prices continues to be the basic strategy for obtaining subsistence.

Independent cultivation of the cornfield is the most viable tactic for obtaining a supply, since the costs of family labor, which are calculated but not spent, enable the peasant to obtain a gross income from the corn crop; put another way, family labor receives a considerably lower compensation, but it leaves something, and that something is corn. As some people say, "As long as the loss stays at home." But when the grain must be sold, and every year a portion of the harvest *is* sold, the peasant feels the expropriation like an open wound; he can see how his loss is turned into profit for others two or three months later. Thus, in order to lose as little as possible, he has reduced the area of cultivation of corn-fields to adjust it to his requirements for direct consumption and has transferred his activities to other crops, which also represent expropria-tion but have a slightly more favorable relation between cost and income— or even without that, they contribute to freeing corn for consumption. The cornfield continues to regulate the strategies for survival. The peasants fashion a sophisticated economy on the basis of corn; at times it is a political economy.

In spite of the diversification of crops and the sale of labor, few *oriente* peasants manage to retain their entire production of corn. They normally have to devote a good part to paying debts and another to meeting obligatory expenses. They are caught up in a circle that accumulates debts from the past and obliges people to acquire more of them in the future in order to keep on cultivating. They lack capital and must necessarily live on credit. In rough terms, the majority of the area's peasants cover between four and six months' consumption with the corn harvest, which is used up at the point when new dry-farming crops are started. Then they have to borrow in order to eat and to plant, and at harvest time they have to pay back the loans, so that little remains for the next cycle. It is not that the peasant produces less of what he needs but that as a result of subjuga-tion, of a transfer to other sectors, he cannot keep it. In the area, only the peasants plant corn, and they not only manage to supply the region but also enable it to export. The inadequacy is due to the fact that they deliver at low prices and have to buy at high ones. Thus, all the peasants plant various crops at the same time, take risks, and work harder and harder. They develop multiple strategies and complex activities, all based on the most intensive use of their labor.

There is nothing new in all this; it is the old story repeated again. But to keep the tale going, important, perhaps definitive things have happened in the decade. The Morelos *campesino* has lost the capacity to produce with his own resources and depends upon the incorporation of energy from outside his system in order to continue producing. Over these external resources—the machinery, fertilizers, and insecticides—the peasant has no form of control, and he is barely acquiring the techniques for managing them. The lack of control reinforces the subordination, the dependence. The peasant, as a free organizer of energy-flows, is losing autonomy, only to become himself yet another resource for production as defined from the outside.

An inevitable effect of modernization? An obligatory response to the fateful march of history? Ask the people of Hueyapan, who have attained the same miracle of efficiency and growth in a different fashion, organizing their own resources autonomously and audaciously. They were lucky. Modernization was not very interested in them—they were Indians, and they were on top of a volcano.

Two Ears of Corn for Five Centavos, Three for Ten. As is well known, starting in 1940 the economic growth of Mexico was begun, and with some occasional stumbling it has continued uninterrupted up to our time. Also starting from that date one can reckon with a statistical register, which if not trustworthy is at least systematic and one of the essential instruments for orienting the development process and reflecting its triumph.

For many peasants, growth consists more than anything of a constant race with the increase in prices, one which they have always come out losing, although for varied reasons. The price of corn, which strictly regulates peasant life, rose tenfold between 1940 and 1970: from ten pesos per *carga* to one hundred at harvest time and from twenty pesos to one hundred sixty in times of scarcity. The increase in prices was neither constant nor regular but was concentrated in great part in a period of only five years. Between 1940 and 1945 corn quintupled its price, from ten pesos per *carga* to fifty, while in the following twenty-five years it would scarcely double the 1945 price. The increase in the area in the five years from 1940 to 1945 was higher than that of the average national rural price for corn that the statistics show—which was 300 percent (Reynolds, app. E)—which implies that the going prices in the area approximated the average national price. Before 1940 the regional price was half the average national rural price.

The more than proportional increase can be explained in two ways: first, the middlemen reduced their unit earnings; second, they reduced their volume of operation, that is, a smaller proportion of the harvests was commercialized. Knowing the middlemen, the second sounds more viable and means that the high prices caused the peasants to withdraw part of their production from the market. An observation: the profit from intermediation, what is obtained by buying and reselling at the going prices in different seasons, is different from, and in addition to, the moneylenders' profit, even though the people who obtained it turned out to be the very same *caciques*. The moneylender's profit remained unchanged at exactly 100 percent, since the price of mortgaged corn was half the one in effect for unencumbered corn.

Even so, it seems that between 1940 and 1945 the *oriente* corn growers saw the price of the crop that they sold increase in real terms, if it is compared with prices of industrial articles. Besides, at that time barter, direct exchange between producers in regional markets, was still normally practiced, although it was no longer the dominant form; monetary dealings had taken over in that role. Even through this mode, exchange between producers from the region was very important and satisfied the majority of needs for consumption. Industrial articles were indispensable but somewhat unvaried: hardware, including farming equipment; textiles, but not ready-made clothing; oil, sugar, a limited amount of pasta, and for special occasions, soaps, candles, and matches; the first cans of food, bottled soft drinks and, of course, beers, all considered rather extravagant luxuries.

The increase in corn prices at the beginning of the forties, when the area was almost totally specialized in this grain, softened the harshness of the end of the thirties, when the price of corn had dropped. The opening of new alternatives outside the region also contributed to this relief. The principal causes of the alleviation were outside the country: these were years of war among the civilized nations, and the unexpected but welcome air of prosperity was being breathed in a climate that hid the decline in real salaries and the increase in the profits and incomes of the entrepreneurs (Reynolds, p. 57).

When the world war ended, the Mexican government wanted to take advantage of the capital reserves put away by the entrepreneurs during the conflict and of the relative bonanza of the postwar years in order to consolidate the recently initiated industrial development and to accelerate the accumulation of capital. Agricultural production for the national market, especially the peasants', was the most affected by this policy of creating internal saving to finance development. While national price indices rose 7.4 percent annually, the prices of agricultural products for the internal market only grew 2.9 percent annually between 1946 and 1949 (CDIA, 1 : 195). In order to emphasize this tendency and to avoid an increase in industrial wages, massive corn imports were made (CDIA, 1 : 249). The average rural price of corn stabilized and even declined in 1948 and 1949 (Reynolds, app. F). The going price in the Morelos *oriente* was maintained without change, but it deteriorated severely in its exchange relation in a clearly inflationary period. The years of the fat cattle had come to an end without reaching the biblical seven.

The bad years, however, were to last a quarter of a century for the corn producers. In 1964, twenty years after the end of the Second World War, a *carga* of corn at the moment of harvest was worth seventy pesos in the Morelos *oriente,* scarcely 40 percent more than in 1945. Many things had happened in those twenty years. Among others, the national price index rose more than 300 percent compared with 1945, and the exchange relation between corn and other products reached its maximum deterioration. Two great devaluations, one in 1949 and the other in 1954, had reduced the value of the Mexican peso to almost one third what it was worth in 1945 (Hansen, p. 68). Apparently, the second devaluation was excessive and was translated into an additional benefit for the manufacturers, who increased the price of their products, while the cost of some raw materials and of salaries decreased. The second devaluation and a policy of relative austerity during the Ruiz Cortines government, as well as a more intense flow of foreign capital, which took the place of a fiscal deficit as a stimulus to the economy, permitted relative control of inflation starting in 1955. Actually, they made it more selective. The average price increases were reduced from an annual 10 percent between 1940 and 1955 to 4 percent per year starting from the latter date. The prices of industrial products began to increase more rapidly than those of agricultural products during the period of stability (Solís, pp. 108–10), but against all the supposed laws of the capitalist market, agricultural production in general, including corn, continued to increase.

Ever since the Cárdenas period, the government has tried to control prices of agricultural products of primary necessity, especially of corn. In 1950 CEIMSA* took over the function of regulating agricultural prices, which several institutions previously shared, by means of direct acquisition at guarantee prices. Between 1950 and 1957 CEIMSA acquired corn at prices differentiated by region. In 1953 the average price was 517 pesos per ton, 592 in 1956, and 652 in 1957; in 1958 it established the single, national price of 800 per ton, which remained fixed for five years (Durán, pp. 142–43).

In order to have access to guarantee prices, certain requirements that no peasant could meet had to be fulfilled. The sale was made at the granaries, not in the countryside, and in order to get there, one had to go by truck. Not even those who cultivated an entire *yunta* obtained the volume necessary to fill or even to share a truck, which was the unit for sampling and weight in the official purchases. The trucks had to wait many hours and sometimes even a couple of days before unloading. The purchase procedure was complex, bureaucratic, and corrupt besides, to the point of becoming irrational for the small producer. Between the costs of selling to the government and the time lost in doing it, the peasants received less money than when they sold to the monopolist and

* Compañía Exportadora e Importadora Mexicana, S.A.

worked for a day's wage. However, for the boss who managed well in the bureaucratic labyrinth and even better in the corruption, all the barriers became advantages, in a system that set the small producers apart to leave them at his mercy.

The guarantee prices, set above international corn prices, made planting corn attractive for the powerful entrepreneurs from the large, national irrigation districts. Between 1950 and 1960 the area planted in corn on irrigated land almost tripled: it went from 194,000 hectares to 564,000, which represented more than one fourth the area of the national irrigated districts (CDIA, 1 : 134). Corn, which had turned into a miserable deal for the peasants, became big business for the entrepreneurs, who operated on a large scale thanks to the public resources invested in irrigation. The big entrepreneurs and the middleman bosses completely supplied the official market, which acquired between 10 and 15 percent of domestic corn production; the remaining 80 or 90 percent entered the open market and was consumed directly by its producers themselves.

The official supply was destined, and is still, to provide for the big industrial cities. In the sixties Mexico City received more than a half-million tons a year, at least a third and sometimes even a half of the total official purchases. Even so, it was occasionally necessary for CEIMSA to import large amounts of corn to supply the urban market. In 1957 and 1958 some eight hundred thousand tons per year were imported to meet urban demand and to prevent an increase in rural prices. The imported corn also had its disadvantages: It had to be paid for with foreign exchange, and it produced tortillas with the texture and taste of cardboard. The supply to the cities was always at lower prices than those of the purchase. Since 1963 the price of the corn delivered to the city mills was 75 percent of the purchase price in the countryside (Durán, p. 137)—less than half if the costs of transportation and storage are added. By reducing food costs in the cities, several things were achieved: wages of industrial workers and employees were lowered; part of their income was channeled toward purchase of industrial products; and they were kept quiet and submissive. Important statistical effects were also attained—like a reduction in the cost-of-living index, which includes food and is calculated by taking the cities as a base.

In the countryside the guarantee prices had much less impact. CEIMSA never sold corn in the rural environment. Open-market prices in the large regional markets have remained between 20 and 30 percent higher than the official guarantee price. In rural communities the old price relations continued in effect: the price at the moment of harvest is lower than that of the national market, while the price in periods of scarcity is higher. In the area, the price of seventy pesos per *carga* that was in effect between 1960 and 1964 was two thirds the average rural price that the statistics record; however, the price in times of scarcity was 30 percent higher than the average rural price and some 20 percent higher than the official guarantee price, that is, the same price as in the large regional markets like Cuautla.

The difference between the average rural price and the going price in the area at the moment of harvest widened again after 1945, and it stayed that way at least until 1965. This implied that in spite of the deterioration of prices—or, rather, because of it—the peasants were delivering a larger proportion of their harvest to the market, so that they necessarily had to increase their production. The moneylenders could export corn from the area in considerable volumes at the guarantee prices or at free-market prices with magnificent profits. In the fifties in Tepalcingo the most powerful boss in the *oriente* had a severe conflict with the municipal president, who tried to prevent him from exporting corn by alleging that there was great need in the village and that prices were very high. At a time when corn was the most important crop in the Morelos *oriente* and had attained its maximum dimensions, the prices for this grain were relatively the lowest that anyone remembered.

Between 1945 and 1965 changes in peasant consumption made the effects of the deterioration in the corn price more acute. Direct exchange between producers declined in intensity and importance. Many of the gathered products almost disappeared from the markets, and they were replaced by some industrial products: firewood and charcoal by oil, hard fibers by plastics, and even *pulque* by beer. The fields for gathering had become more distant from the villages as the cultivated areas had grown. Some species were used up through excessive exploitation. Others, like forest products, were "protected" by official action and remained out of the peasants' reach. In a few cases, but in some at least, the industrial substitute turned out to be cheaper and displaced the traditional product. Not only gathering lost importance, for exchange of some cultivated products did too. Many orchard fruits that used to be sold in regional markets disappeared because of pests or because the land was devoted to more intensive production for the outside market, and they left a hole that sometimes it has not been possible to fill. Even some regional manufactures declined—like pottery products, which lost importance because of competition from factory crockery, which was enhanced with a larger dose of prestige due in part to the influence of teachers, merchants, and communications media.

Although direct exchange between producers has not disappeared, it has been severely limited. The importance of industrial products in the regional markets, on the other hand, grew constantly. Ready-made clothing and shoes won the place of necessities, like kitchen utensils and plastic bags and containers in bold, loud colors. Even the diet was changed though without corn's losing its importance. Pastas, oils, sweets, even instant coffee—which replaced the coffee beans from the temperate country—and powdered milk became common, although they are still considered luxuries. Oil and, later, gas stoves appeared to replace wood-burning ones; beds in place of mats; chairs, tables; first radios and then, inevitably, television sets. As soon as the villages had electricity, light bulbs, electric irons, and perhaps even a blender were purchased. Even the houses changed with the times: first the adobe ones replaced those built of cane in the hot country, and straw roofs gave way to tile in the temperate country; but later cement appeared, along with metal structures and roofs of zinc or asbestos sheets. Even the doors and windows were made of iron—they offered a great deal of prestige and could be justified by the assertion that people had become more evil since the arrival of the movies, radio plays, and comic-book romances, which encouraged some men to feel like the Incredible Hulk after a few drinks.

All this became necessary, although, strictly speaking, it did not prove to be either vital or novel, since the functions that many of the new articles fulfill are the same ones that the regional products performed. Certainly, many of the new products save work; on the other hand, they are more expensive, which implies, contradictorily, that one has to work more to obtain them. A constant external pressure, subtle or overt, has made these goods into culturally and socially indispensable objects. The relative position of people in the group—status—is demonstrated more through the house and modern articles, which retain their identification with luxury, than through possession of land or ox teams, which circulate along routes that are alternatives to ownership.

Another type of industrial goods has become indispensable. Previously, very few factory-made objects were used for cultivation: plows and some tools. But, if necessary, even these could be replaced by local products without essentially modifying the agricultural system. It is more difficult to break the earth with the wooden plow, but it can replace the iron one. Moreover, the village smiths can make iron plows or machetes without the necessity of using resources from outside or resources that can not be exchanged directly with the producers. But the same thing does not happen with chemical fertilizers and tractors. Some of their functions can be replaced—as has actually happened—by local products, such as natural fertilizers like the ones the people of Hueyapan use or teams that are rented by the day, but above all by strenuous, ill-paid work. But the new technological arrangement is determined not only by the goods of production but also by the nature of the exchange. It does not make much sense to plant onions as a specialized crop if trucks, trains, selection and packing plants, international middlemen, and an infinite number of North Americans who prefer their hamburgers with onion do not exist.

Immersion in that sphere obliges the peasant to buy in order to produce. The new agricultural technology does not have a local rationale, but a world-wide one. The new agricultural system in the Morelos *oriente* is a combination of international and local resources.

Local resources are mixed with cosmopolitan, modern ones in peasant life, too. The corn yield no longer goes as far, although it made that mixture possible. In 1963 CONASUPO,* the successor to CEIMSA once the latter was dissolved for being corrupt and inefficient, established a national guarantee price of 940 pesos per ton of corn. This would not be changed for ten years, until at the end of 1973, after the year's harvest was brought in, a new official price of 1,200 pesos per ton was announced. Between 1964 and 1970 the general index of prices remained stable, rising only 4 percent annually. The stability represented a relative devaluation of 25 percent for corn. After 1970 effects from the international crisis began to be felt, combined with the no less severe effects of the internal crisis and the change of government. Prices went sky-high and are still continuing to climb, and corn is worth less and less, even though its official price rose to eighteen hundred pesos per ton.

All these indices reflect reality inadequately. On one hand, prices for the *campesinos'* production, foodstuffs, rise more slowly, in fact deteriorate. On the other, the statistics hide the fact that retail prices the peasant pays on products that he does not produce are double those registered in the index. In practice, the indices are used more to disguise what is happening than to clarify it.

When the government raised the guarantee price of corn in 1963, the price in the Morelos *oriente* started to climb slowly. In 1970 it had reached a hundred pesos per *carga* at the moment of harvest, a little more than 40 percent over the 1963 prices, while the guarantee price had only increased 17.5 percent. Once again, the difference between local and national prices was narrowed. In 1972 the local price reached 115 pesos per *carga,* a little more than 800 per ton, almost 90 percent of the average rural price in the country. The cultivators of the corn patch were fleeing the market; the region had shut itself off, and all corn exports were stopped. The peasants planted less and tried to keep the whole harvest. The rise in local prices indicates again that the peasants are not selling corn. The effects of this action, a kind of mute, disorganized strike, can be unpredictable.

The price of corn has many facets for the peasant. It represents not merely income through the sale of his production but also the principal expenditure for consumption. This multiple relationship has many implications that are altered not only by the relation between the price of corn and that of other products but also by the possibility the peasant has

* Compañía Nacional de Subsistencias Populares.

of obtaining autonomous production and keeping it. For the landless peasant, an increase in corn prices is not an advantage but a blow. For the peasants who cannot retain the production to meet their own needs for consumption, who sell at the minimum price and buy at the highest, it is not an apparent advantage, either, and it can be a determining factor in greater indebtedness.

This complex, ambiguous relationship in which corn is income and expense, commercial product and susbistence crop, is a determinant in the failure of this grain to behave according to the laws of the capitalist market: production is increased while the price declines, and can diminish when it climbs and it becomes rational to withdraw from the market. Independent of its formal valuation, corn is the country's most important crop. More than half the cultivated land sustains it, four fifths of the farming population grow it and all Mexicans consume it. The irregular behavior of corn, the exception that it represents in a market ruled by supply and demand, is one of the central phenomena for explaining the dynamic of the growth of industry, transfer of surpluses for its benefit, and capitalist accumulation in a corn-based, agrarian country.

Land Without Liberty. The majority of the *ejidos* in the Morelos *oriente* received little land after the first grant in the twenties. During the Cardenista distribution only one new *ejido*, Tenango, was created, and not all received the enlargements that they had so tenaciously requested. From that time until now, "the generation has grown a lot," but the number of titleholding *ejidatarios* has remained almost stable since the application of the law that ordered that the *ejido* be divided into parcels and that they be inherited undivided. At present, between half and two thirds of the area's adult men hold no title to land. They are the peasants with *derechos a salvo*, "rights without injury," the ones recognized as subjects of agrarian reform whose territorial claim cannot be satisfied. The rise of a group with exclusive rights over the territory, the titleholding *ejidatarios*, has led to the multiplication and diversification of the ways of obtaining access to *ejidal* lands.

The most common mechanism for giving access to the new generations consists of assimilating them into the original grant made to a titleholder. The young men work along with the titleholder and receive their support from him through their incorporation into an extended family or by receiving a share of the product obtained. In other cases, especially when the titleholder has died, the sons often divide the parcel among themselves so that each one works on his own. This arrangement violates the law, which does not permit fragmentation of the parcel and which establishes that the inheritance must pass to the first-born, to the wife, or to whomever the titleholder designates. To avoid this stumbling block, only one of the heirs appears as titleholder before the law, a fact that gives him certain rights. He is considered to have "loaned the land" to his brothers or his sons, who can exploit it permanently as they like but cannot sell it or transfer it without his approval. In these cases—assimilation and undivided or fragmented inheritance—access is obtained for free through kinship, through a social relationship. Although the words *free* and *social* are used here, there is no desire to suggest that economic implications are absent, but that they acquire a modality of their own: they are not specific, but imprecise, ubiquitous, and they establish relations involving intensive, generalized cooperation.

The free loan of land can acquire another modality and be extended outside the immediate family to co-parents and friends, from whom no payment of any kind is required, but a certain reciprocity is expected. In this case the loan is not perpetual, and it implies a specific use: planting corn, putting livestock to pasture, or making adobe. These loans are given on lands that the titleholder does not intend to, or cannot, use for the moment but over which he retains domain, and he can demand their return. In contrast, loans linked with inheritance are perpetual and independent of use. In the one the resources transferred are essential, and in the other, complementary.

The free loans outside the family also circulate through social relationships. They almost always seek to consolidate some previous relationship or to repay some past favor. At times they are used to establish new relations or even to avoid some potential conflict. One of the rich men from Zacualpan loaned his unused lands with the aim of recruiting clientele, a support group. After conquering a powerful competitor in a political dispute, he loaned land to the defeated man's nephew because "he was not going to be a devil about it."

All other forms of access to land imply a specific payment, a price established beforehand, which does not eliminate the social implications of the relation, and a remnant of obligatory reciprocity always remains after the deal is over, although it is weaker and confined to particular aspects. When there is a payment, lending land serves for the exchange of resources determined in advance; it is called a loan because it does not imply payment in cash. In some villages dry-farming land is loaned in exchange for water for irrigation, in others, in exchange for pastures or the use of a tractor. In this case, the loan has a fixed term and a fixed objective.

Mediania is one of the most common ways of obtaining access to the land, for redistributing it through production but not through possession. Many kinds of *mediania* exist, since each case is agreed upon individually according to the crop and the relationship between those who are going to undertake it, but in every case the agreement takes into account the traditionally established ideal norm of *going halves* on the corn. For this crop, it is considered fair for one partner to put up the land and the other the team, for the two to share the expenses and work equally so that the product can be divided in half. If one of them has something extra that the other needs, its equivalent in work is negotiated, but the proportion of the shares—half-and-half—is almost never altered.

Mediania turned out to be one of the most efficient mechanisms for adjusting corn production to the needs for consumption when the crop "ceased to be a business." The production of a *yunta* of three and one-half hectares of land proves to be excessive and yields a surplus for the market; besides, the cost and the effort involved in working an entire *yunta* are high, and few can do it without resorting to loans. Moreover, the rent of a tractor or a team by the day to work smaller areas is expensive and implies a preliminary cash payment. *Mediania* also legitimately eliminates the obligation to hire servants, since one of the partners acts as *gañán* and the other as *peón*. It also reduces the need to employ day-workers, since the two partners and their families can provide the greatest part of the labor. *Mediania* for cultivating a cornfield eliminates almost all the cash costs, except chemical fertilizers and insecticides, and it protects against indebtedness. However, it does not reduce the physical labor and the time that must be devoted to the corn crop, but intensifies it, although a good part of that effort can be transferred to the family.

Mediania is also used for undertaking commercial crops requiring minimal irrigation and without external sources of financing, like chile or irrigated corn. However, it is not used for rice or sorghum, for which official credit is available. The norm established for corn is adjusted when *medianías* of this type are attempted, but the distribution of the product is always by halves. In the case of these crops, *mediania* is an effort to reduce the cash investment and the need for financing. Double the labor is available, eliminating the hiring of peons, and cash costs are shared. The reduction of risk and, in the event, the attenuation of the consequences of a failure are important criteria in *mediania* established for planting commercial crops. With these advantages, *mediania* has also spread to the speculative crops undertaken by the peasants.

The partners do not join together by chance, but after many considerations and prolonged negotiations. *Mediania* serves, in its broadest sense, to concentrate dispersed resources, to make up for the lack of capital, as well as to redistribute access to the land through functional fragmentation. But possession of complementary resources is not enough for establishing *mediania;* mutual trust is necessary in order to ensure that all dealings are for "the benefit of the plant." Frequently the agreement is established between close relatives, father and son, brothers, or cousins; at other times, between *compadres* or close friends—always between people from the same *barrio*. Partners of disproportionate "fortunes" almost never get together: someone who has a great deal does not need *mediania,* and one who has too little has nothing to contribute. In general, *mediania* is a pact between equals. The risks of conflict are too high to run them with just anyone. The strict selection among those who share a network of social relations that establishes control over its participants makes it possible for quarrels, which do indeed occur, to arise quite infrequently.

Another way to obtain access to the land is by renting or buying, a common and frequent form of business in the *ejido,* despite the fact that it is prohibited by law. Rent for the land is paid in cash and in advance. The 1973 price varied according to the crop that was going to be introduced on the rented land: some fifteen pesos per *tarea* for corn or peanuts on dry-farming land, and between sixty and one hundred pesos per *tarea* on irrigated land, according to the duration and intensity of the cultivation. Rental of irrigated land arose when the corn "ceased to give" and the division of the *ejido* into parcels was already settled. Title to *ejidal* land had become a privilege exchangeable for money.

At first, land rental was only agreed to between people from the same village, and it was conducted as a substitute for *mediania,* in which the division was done in advance. It was a way of redistributing the land, but, unlike the others, also served efficiently for accumulating it, as happened subsequently. Redistributive rental can be recognized by the crop that is introduced and because the sharecropper works in it physically: the corn-field or commercial crops for the local or regional market that lack external financing, that is, the ones that are not a business but a means of surviving.

The sale of *ejidal* lots appeared immediately after the division into parcels. As the law required the titleholder to name his heir, the *transfer of rights,* inheritance during the titleholder's lifetime, became a customary transaction. This is done through a written contract, which in itself is illegal but is often used and is formalized by the involvement of the president of the *ejidal* committee. The national authorities have never punished this crime, a fact that is interpreted—and functions—as an endorsement. The prices for the transfer of *ejidal* rights fluctuate from seven hundred pesos per *tarea* of dry-farming land up to fifteen hundred pesos per *tarea* of irrigated land.

The resale of parcels has strict limitations. *Ejidal* rights cannot be sold to an outsider, and such a sale would not be permitted; all the transactions are conducted between members of the community, quite often between relatives. Excessive accumulation of parcels by a single *ejidatario* through the transfer mechanism is not permitted either, although it is indeed allowed when it results from inheritance. Transfer can be made by frac-tions of the original parcels, and possession of various tiny fractions is common. The control that restricts sale of the *ejido* is, above all, informal, but it is reinforced by the potential for application of the agrarian law. A census check would banish outsiders and strip property from those who accumulate, as has actually happened in some of the area's *ejidos*. But informal control through criticism and breaking off of relations with the one who breaks the rule is what, in the end, allows the sale of the *ejido* to be considered basically a mechanism of redistribution.

Many have sold their parcels because they have been unable to tend them because of a shortage of labor or capital, which obliges them to concentrate on smaller areas. Others have transferred their parcels to free themselves from old debts; and some because "they were up to no good," running away because of some crime; and a very few, they say, because of vices, drinking or women. The buyers of the land are considered *ejidatarios* with full rights and equality with respect to the original title-holders or their descendants in whatever involves the internal organization, although legally and before the outside world they can not defend their position. Through this mechanism, the size of the parcels has continued to shrink, and the real number of *ejido* members has continued to increase, although never at the same rate as the growth of the population.

All the forms of obtaining access to land that have been mentioned imply dealings among equals, among people who are acquaintances and from the same village, and they redistribute a limited resource among a growing population. They permit more intensive and efficient use of the soil and the fluid exchange of productive resources. They allow the assimilation of new generations, root them down, and favor a more regular, intensive distribution of the labor force in the region. Families with considerable labor power generally occupy more land and pay some compensation to families with fewer people. Under these conditions, the redistributive exchange produces the fractioning of the land, the *minifundio*, which appears in association with the intensification of production. Almost all the productive units possess more than one parcel, often tiny and separated from one another by several kilometers and even by a couple of hundred meters in altitude. They know the parcels thoroughly and use them according to their characteristic humidity, bulk and quality of soil, and climate to obtain increasing yields. Distributing the labor force and productive resources among these lands is a complex task; sometimes they make a mistake, but this does not happen often.

The forms that redistribute access to land are preferably linked to crops that are incorporated directly into consumption, whether as a product, like corn, or as money, like certain vegetables. However, they are less common, or appear less clearly associated, with crops that are entirely absorbed by the external market, that are dissociated from consumption, that are vaguely considered as an investment, as a risk. Access to the land through redistributive forms is based on horizontal, symmetrical social relations that are established within the limited framework of the rural community. Kinship and its extensions, belonging to a *barrio* or a village, behave in this case like relations of production that complement or make up for relations of property and give access to the goods of production. They also behave as channels for the exchange of resources that permit a momentary, synchronical concentration, which makes up for the absence of capital, of accumulation.

It is almost superfluous to say that the symmetry is never perfect. Even in the cases of nearest kin, someone always takes more away from the redistributive association, if it is measured only with economic criteria. When the redistribution takes place in the framework of a stratified community that is contained within a framework of relations dominated by capitalism, the precarious balance of the symmetry is often broken. Thus, some of the redistributive forms have become vertical, asymmetrical relations that encourage accumulation.

Land rental for planting commercial or speculative crops, especially onions, allows the concentration of the soil in the hands of the entrepreneurs. The latter, who have the capital resources to invest in agriculture but cannot acquire land, correct the imbalance by means of leasing *ejidal* parcels. This has been favorable for them, since they do not have to immobilize part of their capital, which they devote entirely to production. Rental of the *ejido* in order to establish commercial crops is not limited to people from the village or the region, although the first person who presents himself does not necessarily get the land, either. It is almost always necessary to have an introduction from someone from the village, an endorsement that allows one to deal with a matter that is, after all, illegal; not infrequently, the *ejidal* authorities are the ones who act as agents.

Thus, some entrepreneurs tied to the big national and foreign monopolists of the onion crop have managed to cultivate almost a hundred irrigated hectares, which implies an investment of at least a million pesos. But some people who rent *ejidal* lands are from the village or from close by. The administrators of what remains of the hacienda and other property owners from the zone often rent *ejidal* parcels to increase the scale of their operations and to maximize the use of machinery. Moreover, those who "have stopped" rent lands from those who have not been able to do so. Some "have stopped" so well that they rent not only in their own villages but throughout the area, establishing agricultural enterprises that have no precise locale but grow constantly and specialize in different crops according to changing conditions in the markets. These able, rustic entrepreneurs appear in four or five of their parcels in just one day, yet unlike the old Vizcayan, they need no pact with the devil to manage it, but only their cars or pick-up trucks. Even the magic has been lost!

By renting their land, the *campesinos* lose space for their own crops, but in return they receive money for the rental and for their work as peons, since the crops associated with the leasing generally require a great deal of labor. The exchange is onerous but necessary, since, despite everything, money and paying work can be scarcer resources than land when one does not have the capital to use the land intensively.

Asymmetrical rental of land also appears in the rice and sorghum crops, which are not speculative but commercial. In these cases, and in general, the person who rents the land is investing, not his own money, but the government's. Some people obtain official credit through personal or political contacts or through corrupt association with some functionary even though they do not have land. Since the credit is specified for one crop, they have to rent the land to introduce it; they risk nothing and can earn a great deal, especially if they do not pay off their debt to the bank, which often happens. However, the *ejido* holders lose not only the land area but the financing too. In the case of sorghum, the loss is more acute, since the land devoted to growing it competes with that for corn; moreover, sorghum is a mechanized, extensive crop that does not offer opportunities for employment. Those entrepreneurs who are not entrepreneurs succeed in accumulating up to 100 hectares devoted to sorghum and obtain production worth between 200,000 and 250,000 pesos, while for land rental they pay some 15,000 pesos in all.

The asymmetrical form of land rental involves the existence of areas under the liberal private-property system in almost all the old villages. The community cannot exercise any formal control over these lands. These properties are traded like commodities, and many of the entrepreneurs are settled on them. Some are owned by outsiders, like the Casa de Piedra, with fifty irrigated hectares, which belongs to one of the big monopolists from La Merced market in Mexico City; or the National Seed Producer, a decentralized government enterprise for the production of improved seeds, which are certainly not used in the area. Other properties have also been acquired by certain politicians through rather dubious procedures. The local entrepreneurs have also taken over properties that serve as a base for their dispersed and apparently disorganized, though highly productive, activities.

The coexistence of the two modes of land tenancy, the *ejido* and ownership, is and has been one of the factors that put pressure on the redistributive forms to change direction and to favor land accumulation. When nearby lands are rented and sold in order to earn money, it is not easy for the rest to be conceived of and managed as a social, collective resource.

But the pressure also operates in the opposite direction, and the agrarian community has created a force that certainly makes it difficult for privately owned land to pass into the hands of strangers, even if it does not prevent it. This pressure, redistributive to a certain extent, is exerted, paradoxically, through the capitalist mechanism of prices.

The prices of property have risen to levels noticeably higher than its strict commercial value. This tendency is more acute the smaller the size of the property. Acquisition of a small, expensive lot turns out to be a bad deal for an agricultural entrepreneur. However, for the local peasant trying to produce by replacing cash expenditures with his own family's labor and with resources exchanged through reciprocal social relations, the land's cost does not turn out to be so significant—especially considering that he would not be able to produce if uprooted from his community, his relatives and *compadres,* and even his moneylender. Thus, the absurd prices for land are not absurd in local terms; moreover, they are almost always paid on credit to a relative or acquaintance. The conversion of land into a commodity, the typical mechanism of the capitalist system, can behave in many cases like an onerous defensive system for the rural community, like a way to regain what belongs to one by playing along with the master's rules.

Liberty Without Land. Medianía and redistributive rental of land enabled more people to start crops on their own, but the generation had grown so much that many other people still remained without direct access to land, depending only upon their labor. For them, as for all the peasants, the basic strategy for survival is to obtain their own supply of corn. They obtain it through servitude, placing themselves as *peones* or *gañanes* with someone who is undertaking independent cultivation of corn. With all the changes in the use of land and access to it, the conditions of this servitude have changed, but it continues to be one of the most commonly used mechanisms for the readjustment of labor and land.

Around 1960, when the yield of the cornfields dropped and chemical fertilizers still had not been introduced, a new mode of servitude arose: the *peón por renta,* "peon by wage." In this system, the *gañanes* and *peones* did not receive a part of the land to plant for themselves, but a fixed amount of corn, independent of the crop's yield. The *gañán* was given seven *cargas* of corn and the *peón* five, in addition to being allowed to plant a *tarea* of one thousand square meters so that they could gather ears of corn in September, as well as being paid a weekly salary in cash and a corn ration during their ten weeks of service.

Peonage *por renta* did not replace peonage *por siembra;* instead, the two coexisted and still persist as different alternatives. In the *por siembra* mode, the decrease in yields was met by an increase in the area given to the servants; between seven and, most commonly, nine *maquilas* of corn are planted for the *gañán*, and between five and seven for the *peón*, so that they can harvest what the grain produces. This means that the servants' share has increased by almost half since 1940, when the *gañán* harvested six *maquilas*, and the *peón* four.

At present, the *gañán por siembra* or *por renta* receives between fifteen and twenty-five pesos a week in cash, more often the latter sum, and the *peón* between ten and fifteen pesos. This is less than a third what they would earn working as day laborers at fifteen pesos a day. In 1940 the *gañán* received in cash two thirds what he would have earned per day as a laborer. However, in 1940 the *peón* received a ration of four *maquilas* of corn a week, and the *gañán* six, while today they receive twenty and between twenty-five and thirty, respectively, four times as much as thirty years ago.

The modifications in payment of the servants are congruent with the effort to remove corn production from the market and to devote it to direct consumption. On one hand, the servants receive a larger share of their remuneration in grain, while, on the other, the *patrón* reduces his cash outlay. Even so, and giving corn the value of the going price at the moment of delivery, the *gañán* and the *peón* receive 50 and 20 percent more, respectively, for their ten weeks of work than they would earn as day laborers. The *patrón* also gains by using servants, since more than half the payment for their services is delayed until the harvest is obtained, while by taking on day laborers and asking for credit to pay their day wages, an almost inevitable consequence, his costs would increase by between a third and a half.

The spread of commercial crops, *medianía,* and mechanized cultivation of corn have removed some areas where servitude was practiced, while elimination of the fallow period and introduction of fertilizers has added new ones. Now it is common for the *patrón* to take a single servant in place of the two that tradition sanctions, whether because he cultivates an area smaller than an entire *yunta* or because he performs physical labor himself. The rough impression is that as a result of these changes, servitude is practiced less widely than thirty years ago, when it was a general norm. The rise of new alternatives for the *patrón* has emphasized the social character of the relationship of servitude even more. The servants are almost always chosen from among people of the same village and often from among relatives, while thirty years ago servants could be taken from other villages. "So that they give me 'recognition' afterwards"—that is, in order to strengthen reciprocal relations—is an explanation that the *patrones* give when they are asked for the criterion for selecting their servants. A line of defense for the peasant community is still established in this servitude.

Money, more and more necessary to the extent that the goods that are purchased are more numerous and more expensive, is not acquired through servitude but through peonage, through *el jornal,* as they put it, "the day's work." The very factors that limit the practice of servitude have made day labor the most common labor relation and the one depended upon not only by those without access to land but by the majority of independent cultivators who do not manage to meet subsistence needs with their own crops.

The most common form of the *jornal* is the hiring of peons by the day, generally for between eight and ten hours' work. For measureable jobs, especially those for the harvest, the peon *por tarea,* "by the task," is often used. He is paid by the unit of work—bags, furrows, bundles—whatever it may be. Working by the task, it is possible to make one and a half times and occasionally twice as much as by the day, but at least ten or twelve hours of very strenuous effort are necessary. Jobs by the task coincide with the seasons with the greatest demand for labor and permit more intensive use of it.

The usual daily wage in 1973 was twenty pesos per day during the rainy season, which offers more employment; at some points, it managed to reach twenty-five and even thirty pesos for jobs considered dangerous, like fumigating. In the dry season, however, the most common wage was fifteen pesos per day. In the temperate country, where there is less land and labor is abundant, salaries did not rise above fifteen pesos; the servants there were also paid a little less than in the hot country.

Between 1940 and 1970 the price of day labor increased almost ten times in the area. The corn price rose at the same rate, which seems to confirm that the price of labor is regulated in some fashion by the price of corn. But the two prices did not increase simultaneously: corn increased more rapidly between 1940 and 1945, while salaries did so after 1960; between 1950 and 1960 neither one climbed rapidly.

In 1940 the most common salary was two pesos per day; it was between three and five pesos in 1945, between six and eight in 1959, ten in 1960, twelve in 1964, and fifteen in 1969. Since 1944 the legal minimum wage has been established by government decree. For the state of Morelos, a minimum of 1.72 per day was set, considerably lower than the usual average salary that was then calculated for Morelos, 2.88 pesos (Whetten, p. 187). Setting minimum salaries below the rural averages in the entire country seems to be a government tactic for keeping salaries low in a period marked by high inflation and a meteoric rise in the price of corn. To top it off, it was said that in establishing minimum wages the revolution had fulfilled one of its social promises.

In the area, the average daily wages in the rainy season kept above the legal minimum wages until 1964, while those in the dry seasons remained a little below. Since that date the higher salaries have stayed below the minimum, and the difference continues to increase. This fact suggests a relative, constant decrease in the real daily wages within the area. If one adds to this that since 1940 real salaries have systematically declined in comparison with prices—almost one third between 1940 and 1950 alone (Hansen, p. 99)—the final result seems beyond doubt: current day wages are noticeably lower than those in 1940. Perhaps people earn more, but that requires them to do additional work disproportionate with the increase.

The low price of labor was one of the major attractions of planting speculative crops with a high labor requirement. The decline of real salaries was a condition and a consequence of the spread of these kinds of crops. This suited the entrepreneurs as much as it did the peasants. To the extent that tomatoes and onions have been adopted by peasants without capital, first on irrigated lands and then for dry-farming, day labor, like many other relationships the peasant establishes, strengthened its double character.

On one hand, day labor is a vertical, asymmetrical relation that enables the entrepreneur to obtain a high rate of earnings—in high-sounding terms, the appropriation of the peasant surplus labor. On the other hand, the cash salary is a symbol of a symmetrical, reciprocal social relation, through which work is exchanged without obtaining a profit. The awareness of this function is clear, and all the *patrones* of a commercial crop know that tomorrow they will be the peons of the men who work for them today. Through this mechanism, the labor is distributed without the expropriation of its product. This is expressed when the peasant who undertakes a commercial crop has to *ask* or *invite* people to help him, almost as a favor. The entrepreneur, however, offers work or gives it to those who ask him for it, which is interpreted as a limited contract that ends with payment of the salary. This double character is also expressed in the fact that when the labor supply is abundant, the entrepreneurs lower the salaries by as much as a fourth (or have to raise it in almost the same proportion when labor is short), while the peasants keep the average salary fixed and somewhat independent of supply in order not to upset the bases of reciprocity. This system is what enables the peasants without capital to be able to run the risk of planting onions or tomatoes, since they hope to receive as a daily wage all or a good part of what they pay out, which implies, in the end, almost no investment in labor, the most expensive item among the costs.

The reciprocity by means of the *jornal* is almost never direct or personal but is given through informal work groups, a type of squad. If a *patrón* is asked for help, he can send his son, nephew, or godson—who do not have their own crops—and expect the same in return. In a certain sense, the *patrones* are the leaders of teams that operate through *reconocimiento*, "recognition," and are the actual units for the practice of labor reciprocity. Like all social relations for purposes of production, this one establishes its boundaries at membership in the community, and, except in cases of close kinship, does not include people from the outside, even though they may be peasants, too.

The operation of the system of labor reciprocity also depends on the fact that the dates for planting and harvesting commercial crops, especially the speculative ones, are not as rigid as those for traditional crops, which permits rotation of the labor force. The flexibility derives from various factors—the use of irrigation in some cases, the brevity of the life cycle of these plants—but it is also supported by expectations that each *patrón* has about the market. There are those who hold that harvesting first enables one to get better prices, while others believe that the late prices will be the highest, and many prefer the middle period, which offers the illusion of security but happens to be the bad time for many others.

Despite the flexibility of the calendars, the demand for labor in the area, which continues to be basically a dry-farming zone, has very high seasonal variations. With the spread of commercial crops, the difference is so great that in the season of high demand, use of labor from outside the community is common; at times, these are migrant workers who have begun to arrive from the moutainous zones of the states of Puebla, Oaxaca, and Guerrero since the end of the sixties. Villages like Xalostoc, where onions are widely cultivated, employ the *oaxacos*, as the migratory workers are generically called, through almost the entire rainy season. Even Chalcatzingo, which has little irrigated land and is not considered one of the more flourishing villages, has to hire people from Tetelilla and Telixtac for the green bean and tomato harvests. Hueyapan, on the other hand, which is indeed considered flourishing, but Indian, and which grew in a different fashion, seems to be self-sufficient in the supply of labor.

Some of the largest entrepreneurs systematically hire outsiders for all the work on their crops because it can turn out cheaper, and even if it does not, it avoids conflicts and keeps it from occurring to the laborers that the land is theirs. This has created a tendency toward establishment of two parallel circuits of labor: one reciprocal, employing people from the village, and the other asymmetrical, employing people from outside. To an extent, the local entrepreneurs—those who have "stopped," who are still immersed in the local circuit—obscure this tendency; they hire people from the same village, but reciprocity is no longer expected from them. In spite of this, it is already understood that people from the locale go away to work outside, while people from other villages arrive, hired as day-workers. To some degree, this permits the more efficient functioning of both circuits and labor systems.

But in the dry season work is scarce for everyone, and many people from the *oriente* have to leave to look for it outside their villages and outside agriculture. In the area, no sizable labor force systematically resorting to migratory agricultural peonage has been created. Only very small groups regularly leave to work on the irrigated rice crop in the state of Veracruz. They are teams of workers who specialize in *aborde en seco* and manage to earn up to five times more than what a peon by the day makes in Morelos; they form a sort of aristocracy among the migratory laborers. But few of the peasants from the area know how to do *aborde en seco*, and when it is their turn to plant rice, they also have to call in the specialists and pay them well. No one else leaves the area regularly. There is nowhere to go, and "the truth is that one is not as desperate as the *oaxacos*."

Between 1940 and 1960 many *were* desperate, and they had to leave, forced out by debts and the lack of work. Some of them, very few, went as *braceros* to the other side, to the United States. Working hard, they succeeded in earning fifteen dollars a day picking vegetables for twelve hours. A good part of their salary they ate through, another they drank through and spent on blondes, but something was left over to send back to the village for paying off debts and continuing to eat; on their return they could even bring presents and some savings.

Seasonal emigration to the United States was formally begun in 1942, when there was a shortage of labor in that country as a consequence of the war. In fact, it always existed and represented an alternative. More than a million farmworkers are estimated to have emigrated to the United States between 1910 and 1935. With the crisis of the fourth decade, the emigration ceased, and many of the emigrants returned, sometimes repatriated against their will (Whetten, p. 188). At the end of the Second World War the legal hiring of *braceros* was limited considerably, but illegal hiring, of "wetbacks," increased noticeably. Between 1948 and 1957, 2.5 million Mexicans entered the United States legally as *braceros;* in the same period more than 4.5 million illegal emigrants were caught and repatriated (González Casanova, p. 301). Between 1950 and 1964 more than a quarter-million Mexicans crossed the border legally each year, but only 90 percent of them returned (González Casanova, p. 302). In 1964 the treaty was broken, and legal emigration was halted. At that time, people from Morelos ceased going to the other side, but others, more driven, kept going year after year. From 1970 on, the Mexicans arrested and sent back each year exceed 750,000; if those not caught are counted, the annual figure must be around one million. Between 10 and 20 percent of the population in Mexican agriculture resort to temporary emigration as wetbacks in order to survive after not finding work in Mexico. The other side of the coin is that the illegal Mexican workers probably increase the population devoted to agriculture in the United States by between 15 and 20 percent. The presence of a severe crisis in that country, which will affect the illegals first of all, can change these figures at any moment, with enormous consequences for Mexico.

Between 1940 and 1960 others went to Mexico City and stayed. The majority were young men who had no hope of getting land but had to help the family with cash. Those who were luckiest—a few—found jobs as industrial workers. Some found work in the soft-drink bottling factory administered by the hacienda heirs; they were trustworthy people of proven loyalty. The majority only found employment in incidental jobs, especially as unspecialized bricklayers. Others managed to place themselves as incidental workers with the city's street-cleaning and sewer services. In some way they manage to keep on living and even to return to the fiestas in their villages. They bring money and spend it generously. Their clothes and their manners arouse envy and are copied by the youths of the village. Relatives and friends from the village are put up in their houses on trips to the city, and often one of the younger brothers lives with them while he looks for work or studies.

But since 1960 the illusion of city life has been undermined little by little. Recently, some of the emigrants have returned, pushed in the opposite direction by the lack of work, which is constantly more scarce and more selective. One of those who returned remembers that "he didn't have the height" to work in a chewing-gum factory: they required a minimum of 1.7 meters, the same as for entering the Assault Batallion of the Presidential Guards, the most select corps in the Mexican Army. As soon as it becomes more difficult to find work, they begin to remark on the disadvantages of urban life. Now they say that they live fairly badly, "cooped up together like chickens," while in the villages, one never goes without "un petate y un pariente"—a place to sleep and a relative.

In the area, the geographic scope of the labor market for men has continued to shrink, and today it is, in fact, limited to each village and the neighboring ones. In the dry months, when there is no demand for agricultural peonage, it is not easy to find paid employment in the area. Some are employed "in the trowel," as bricklayers in their villages or those nearby. Others have artisanal specialties: they make saddles, mend iron pieces and make windows, bake bread, or cure people with herbs and prayers. The government offers the principal market for nonagricultural work in the area through public works, especially roads and irrigation, which appeared again in the sixties. In this case, they compete against machines that the private contractors have. The Benito Juárez Plan for building irrigation dams, administered by the ministry of agriculture, fell into the same trap (or shady deal) and imported enormous earthmovers, larger than anyone had ever seen, to do the work; paradoxically, the huge mechanical monsters do not seem to have speeded up the rate of construction. Fortunately, the archeological excavations that are being done in Chalcatzingo have not been mechanized, as has happened at other ancient sites, and the villagers work shifts in them for the legal minimum wage.

Many peasants spend the dry months without earning money or earning too little. It is a good thing that they finish harvesting the corn, which is sold little by little to keep getting the weekly expenses. The big regional fairs, particularly the one at Tepalcingo, are held during Lent, and some precious money is spent at them, further reducing the corn reserves. When it comes time to plant, the reserves have almost been finished off, and they have to begin asking for credit. Then there is work to do on one's own crop and on someone else's, although mechanized crops threaten it, and they have to establish a careful balance regarding the direction of their efforts.

The lack of work has also required looking for other alternatives, like reorganizing the family. To the extent that only men get salaried work but women and older people almost never do, it has become necessary to enlarge the proportion of people able to earn money. Many unmarried young women have emigrated for good to Mexico City or other nearby cities, where they are employed as domestic servants. Almost two hundred have gone from Hueyapan alone. Piously, Opus Dei has established a school to train domestics in what was the compound of the Santa Clara hacienda as part of its social work presided over by "realism." The servant girls send an important part of their salaries to their families; they contribute to supplementing the family's cash income, while at the same time their absence reduces consumption.

The great hope for some people is that one of their sons might become a teacher: a secure job and salary, fringe benefits, medical attention, pension. Many make sacrifices pursuing this ideal, since the students would indeed be able to obtain a salary; in fact, very few ultimately manage to. However, the sons of the villages' wealthy people, who have good political contacts, do get scholarships from the government, and some even go to the university.

Local agriculture and the intensification of it seem to be the most viable alternatives for confronting the labor crisis that threatens in the near future, which is, perhaps, already here.

Old Bosses, New Bourgeoisie. The old bosses, the corn and ox team lenders, are being finished off bit by bit. Between 1950 and 1960 it seemed that they had attained their maximum power and that they were not disposed to lose it. In the *oriente* there were a few who loaned out between fifty and a hundred teams each year and received as much as seventy tons of corn in payment; a good portion of that volume was doubled when they loaned it *a la dobla* or purchased corn on time. Some of them even had trucks for transporting the grain. The lesser bosses who loaned between ten and twenty teams each year were numerous: at least three or four in each village. These *caciques* of all sizes and levels of power appropriated perhaps half of the area's total production of corn, which at the time was the most valuable crop, the one that covered the greatest land area.

But the *cacique*-lenders were too narrowly linked to corn, to the autonomous cultivation of it by the peasants and its expansion, and that had reached its limits. They were too specialized, and conditions were becoming more complex and varied. The peasants began to look for new alternatives, to diversify their activity, and the bosses could not follow them in the adventure.

The golden age of the *caciques* had ended. The majority were already old and tired; they did not have the strength to renew themselves. Their sons, always numerous, were good at spending money but not at earning it. The inheritances carefully accumulated by the old men were divided up and squandered. Besides, these fortunes were not too big, and they were invested in goods that were losing their value: cattle, lots in the villages, rough lands in the mountains. The epidemics that reduced the livestock herds undermined the sources of their power and wealth. The incorporation of the pastures into cultivation made the livestock business more difficult and costly, and competition with the machines affected it profoundly. Cattle theft, which was begun, according to what people say, by the bosses themselves "with their ambition," ultimately took power away from all of them. They did not know how to unite, to share, and to divide; they even killed one another. They had been so secure that they did not pay sufficient attention to politics; they did not know how to tell the direction of the wind that was blowing from above, pushing them toward "modernization." They were losing the *ejidal* committees and the municipal presidencies, which passed into the hands of people involved in raising commercial crops. In 1964 the bosses made their last stand in the municipal elections. In some villages they tried to prevent candidates imposed by the PRI from taking office. The peasants vigorously supported them, but they lost or had to compromise, which was the same thing. They never recovered from that blow.

The corn and ox-team lenders have not disappeared, but they have ceased to be *caciques*. In every village there is a handful that continues to loan animals or buy corn on time. Many are old men, and all operate on a smaller scale. Those who had ten or fifteen teams are left with three or four. The peasants who try to keep their corn free of debts borrow from them less, although they may continue borrowing year after year, whether because they use tractors, go halves with others, or combine the tractor with the *macho*—a name they give, without any irony, to the mule —in a formula that seems to be advantageous. In many villages one even hears the complaint that now "there isn't anyone who makes loans like there used to be."

The rigid norms that regulated the loan continue to operate, but more and more exceptions are being made. The majority continue to loan corn *a la dobla,* but now there are those who make loans "by thirds": each *carga* loaned in a period of scarcity is paid with a *carga* and a half at harvest time, 50 percent interest in three or four months. The lender calculates it in another way: he considers the 50 percent as an annual rate, since while the corn remains in storage, it does not produce anything for him. The loan by thirds, which is still rather uncommon, adjust the interest rate to the seasonal variation in the corn price, which has become less pronounced to the extent that the crop is withdrawn from the national market.

Rent for the ox teams also shows exceptions. In some cases ten *cargas* of corn are paid for it, in others, eight (which seems most common at present), and sometimes even less. In the villages where the corn crop is dominant, like Amacuitlapilco or Tetelilla, the prices for rental and the interest rates remain high. In villages where commercial crops predominate, renting teams by the day is increasing; the fifty or sixty *pesos* daily includes the *gañán's* labor, which the lender values at the same price as the labor of each animal, so he gives him one third of the rental price as a salary.

A few bosses changed: they switched from lending teams and corn to lending money. These were the most avaricious, the ones who had given rise to the stories of mattresses stuffed with bills, but not the biggest and most powerful. They joined the merchants from the big villages or their rich widows, the principal lenders of cash. Some who had been minor but very frugal *caciques* moved to Axochiapan or Cuautla and became usurers. They almost always lend at 10 percent interest per month, the normal rate for cash loans. There are exceptions here, too: to people whom they trust a great deal, often close relatives, they make loans at 5 percent monthly. Some wealthy widows or old moneylenders also lend at 5 percent monthly, but they require very secure guarantees or pledges, which are often lost.

The cash loan is quite flexible. It can be used to finance production of corn or some commercial crop, as well as to meet the demands of consumption, from festivals and illnesses to whims and carousing. But lending corn and teams is not the same as lending money. The first are delivered on the basis of an established crop, in which the investment in work is always higher than the value of the loan; they are linked to production. The loan is made by people with whom there is a permanent relation, even though the debtor might not have desired it. This relationship is normalized and regulated by old rules. One is standing on firm ground, and recovery of the loan is easy. Failure to meet the terms threatens future production and can even end up making it impossible. Thus, neither papers nor pledges are needed; asking and lending are quick and simple.

With money it is another matter. Cash loans are considered something sordid, to be hidden, as one would hide something definitively immoral. The usurer is almost always an outsider in the community, although he might have been part of it at sometime, and they maintain distant, occasional relations with him. The loan's object itself, the money, is not tied to permanence in the community. One could ask for a loan to run away or refuse to pay, playing dumb. To collect would require violence or a long trial that nobody knows who would win, since the interest rate the usurers charge is illegal. Thus, to obtain a cash loan, it is necessary to leave the deeds of the land or some valuable property as security; one must also sign complicated papers that disguise the interest rate. The amount of the loan is regulated by the value of the pledge, which is always much higher. Many usurers have taken over cropland that they almost never work directly. For that reason, relatively few people receive money from the usurers, and almost always in very small amounts; the people have very little, or nothing, to mortgage, since *ejidal* land is unacceptable as security. Other people obtain loans through secret deals. Even so, the money received from usurers is a supplement or a last resort that everyone attempts to avoid. The cash loan, the most flexible in terms of its purposes, is not easy to get, and it is certainly the most expensive.

A very few of the old bosses or some of their children were able to join the new rural bourgeoisie. *Bourgeoisie* is used here in its oldest, local, village sense. It also implies the new meaning, but with some reservations. The bourgeoisie exploit the peasants but cannot be identified with the abstract bourgeoisie, inasmuch as the capitalist system is not contained in its totality in the country's rural villages.

The new bourgeoisie sprang up from the farmers and merchants, the owners of little stores or village saloons, or people who participated in the local markets. They had some money, but not enough to compete with the well-established, livestock-owning bosses. They also had some land that they cultivated as a support for their commercial activity. They had more extensive contacts with the cities, since through these ties they could reproduce their small capital, which could not enter the traditional activities controlled by the bosses. Their capital was smaller, but circulated more rapidly and was more flexible. It was money, not livestock, and it could be used to make loans or to hoard petroleum, salt, or sugar and to speculate on the increase in prices. By nature and vocation, they were speculators with imagination. They were tied to the peasants' complementary activities, from mercantile consumption to commercial planting to obtain money, which had become the most dynamic activities in accord with the country's development.

In the last fifteen years the new rural bourgeoisie ceased to be secondary and installed itself in the center of peasant life, at one of the points of articulation with the exterior that would become the critical one as peasant production intensified. A good part of their power derives from acting as lenders and promoters for commercial crops. These loans are specific and are given out not only in cash but also in kind. The worth of the chemical products and seeds loaned is always higher than the cash loan; the two amounts are regulated by the size of the commercial crop. The entire operation is apparently carried out without charging interest, but in return, the grower remains obligated to sell the lender the entire crop at the market prices in effect at that period.

The neutrality is deceptive. On one hand, the chemical products and seeds that are loaned prove to be more expensive than had they been bought in the store, whose owners are the lenders themselves. A sack of fertilizers, which purchased outright cost thirty-six pesos in 1972, was supplied by the lenders at forty pesos: an 11 percent difference, which sounds modest but is nothing to dismiss. If one adds on tricks the lender uses in buying—scales with kilograms of nine hundred grams or less, waiting until the seed is completely dry and weighs less, discounting for supposed deficiencies in the quality of the product—the interest on the money loaned rises to at least 20 or 25 percent.

This figure is considerably lower than that which the traditional lender or the usurer gets, but, again, it is misleading. The principal earning of the new lender rests in intermediation, in the difference between national price and the going price in the area, which is appreciably lower than the national price even after adding on the costs of transportation. It also rests on the volume upon which he is going to obtain the profit in the intermediation. The loan finances only a rather small part of the crop's cost, whose major component is the labor supplied by the family, but gives the lender control over the entire production. Thus, the profit on intermediation amply compensates for the absence of interest on the loan and enables the "modern" lender to obtain greater earnings for his capital than the *cacique* used to get.

In order to obtain these profits, the bourgeois has had to transform the character of the business of intermediation and its framework of relations. The old boss needed very few relations with the outside—a buyer for corn or perhaps a few of them—while the bourgeois basically depends upon them—an extensive network of buyers; broad contact with the wholesalers of fertilizers and chemical products and of the articles that he sells in his business, with haulers, machinery salesmen, and even with commercial banks now that credit cards, discounts, and loans are replacing the handling of the rolls of bills that the bosses enjoyed so much. Survival and success depend upon the manipulation of these types of relations.

The corn lender's profit rate remains fixed, independent of the number of debtors; for every ten units that he lends he will receive twenty, whether one person pays him or ten. However, the new lender's rate of earning increases to the degree that he lends less money to more people whose production he can control. For him, lending a thousand pesos to one peasant who produces a ton of peanuts is not the same as lending five hundred to two who produce seven hundred kilos each. This need to enlarge the clientele even at the cost of reducing the extent of their dependence obliges the new lenders to expand, to go outside of their communities. In order to recover their loans, barely protected in a brief document of doubtful legal value, the new bourgeois have had to establish a certain level of cooperation among themselves, which limits competition. The collaboration is grudging and never free of conflicts and frictions, but unlike the bosses, the new bourgeois have a tendency to die old or in automobile accidents.

The new bourgeoisie has extensive external contacts, operates at regional levels, moves its money rapidly, invests in machinery and trucks instead of in land and livestock. It has modernized itself, and some of these people total up their fortunes in figures close to a million pesos. In doing so, they have entered into contact and competition with enterprises that have the same character but much greater resources and political influence at the federal level, like the big foreign companies that export onions or the monopolists from La Merced, who have control or weight in national or international markets. At times the competition displaces the village bourgeois or corners him in an untenable position. It happened that way with the onion crop, when the big sharks swallowed up everything by giving credit to the peasants and buying directly from them. The area's bourgeois did not get so much as a crumb in that deal. They try their luck as producers on a more or less large scale; sometimes it is a gamble they lose. With the tomato crop, the La Merced *acaparadores,* who operate through a veritable plague of small middlemen, endanger the recovery of local credits and prevent the lenders from influencing the setting of the local price. In this case, the local bourgeois prefer to act as old-fashioned lenders, imposing high rates of interest. However, they totally dominate the peanut market, which, thanks to a state tax, is isolated from external competition.

They respond to these risks with flexibility. Sometimes, instead of fighting the external competition, the bourgeois join it and become its regional agents. They give credit and buy onions or tomatoes as well as sorghum on its behalf. In some way they manage to obtain a profit in addition to the commission they receive for their part as representatives:

they retain the differences from the art of weighing for themselves, grant additional loans tied to the principal loan, or even charge the peasant a second commission. The convenience of this arrangement for the big entrepreneurs rests on their being able to operate securely in an environment in which commercial guarantees do not exist, to recover their investments, and to avoid local conflicts that they do not know how to manage, all thanks to the acquaintances and relations that the local bourgeois has. In turn, they give him a commission and close their eyes to the rest, which the peasant pays anyway. Despite the modernity and pretensions of the local bourgeois, his existence and his rationale do not derive from his enterprise, but from his ability to keep in direct contact with the peasants, to know them, to shift languages and scope. These are people on the frontier between two worlds.

The national banks of credit for agriculture occasionally attempt to eliminate usury and intermediation. They have not done so, and to a great extent they have strengthened them. The banks lend very little money; they do so quite selectively—and between the corruption and the bureaucracy, quite badly. The National Bank of Agricultural Credit has practically never operated in this area. The National Bank for Ejidal Credit started its operations in the *oriente* in 1940, some years after its founding in 1936, but its activity was limited to financing the irrigated rice crop. Only toward the end of the sixties did it loan some money for planting peanuts, which it later stopped; since 1972 it has made loans in a massive way for the cultivation of sorghum. It never gave loans for corn or for fruits and vegetables, let alone for irrigation or livestock. The selection of activities that the bank supports is made in terms of national demands, which means international and urban markets, in that order of importance, and without taking into account the concrete needs or demands of the peasants.

Sometimes what the bank does is to undertake crops on its own in order to take care of national demands; in fact, it rents land from the *campesinos* in exchange for credit. That is what it did with sorghum, considered vital for the development of pig and poultry raising. In this case, the peasant does not take part in the cultivation, which is done with the machinery that the bank engages and controls. The peasants receive some money for performing some secondary tasks, actually a salary that is at the same time payment for the rental of the land. Because the fertilization is done mechanically, the fertilizer cannot even be used in order to save some expenses on the cornfields. The arrangement, which in certain cases would have been acceptable, ceased to be so because the bank did very poorly as a producer. The physical yields that the bank obtained were scarcely one or two tons per hectare in 1972, while those on the "small property," the largest fragment of the remnants of the hacienda, were three tons as a minimum and five as a maximum.

Apparently, the seed and fertilizers the bank used were inappropriate, and it applied them in insufficient quantities. Once the time for the harvest came, the bank could not or did not want to get threshing machines; the poor yield worsened as the ears of grain ripened and fell. Providentially, the active private entrepreneurs, many of them sorghum buyers, had threshing machines ready and waiting; they asked for half the crop in return for doing the little job, although they finally agreed to thresh for the usual price but to buy at a price much lower than the seven hundred pesos that a ton of sorghum was worth on the market. As a result, the peasants remained in debt because of renting their land. Worse yet, the bank insisted on planting more sorghum in the next cycle.

In the cultivation of rice, in which manual tasks predominate, this type of leasing is not possible. In this case, the *ejidatario* receives the credit in various *ministraciones,* or "installments," which cover the cost of specific tasks like preparing the soil, *aborde,* or transplanting. Part of the installments are delivered in kind, and others in cash to pay for the labor. Previously, as was logical, the money installments were received before the work was undertaken, but since, according to the bank, the beneficiaries were spending the money without doing the work, the credit is now given when the bank's inspector verifies that the tasks have already been done. At times the peasants have to borrow money from the usurers for some of the tasks. These things happen in the best of families.

Before the introduction of fertilizers even rice could fail, in the sense of yielding less than expected, and the *ejido* members remained in debt; for that reason, the bank has not maintained continuous operations in any of the area's communities. After a few years the debts end up accumulating, and the bank halts the financing. Here, the determining factor is the bank's method of operating. The *ejidatarios* have to form a local society for *ejidal* credit and choose a delegate member, who takes charge of negotiations with the bank. The latter insists that there be only one society for each *ejido,* which prevents natural associations between friends or relatives who trust one another. The bank always complains that the *ejidatarios* lack solidarity, a spirit of cooperation. The *ejidatarios* accuse the bank of wanting to protect itself at the expense of other workers. At the heart of this is the "solidarity clause," which obliges all the members of the local society to cover the unpaid sums, in spite of the fact that the credit—and in the event, the profits—is accounted for individually. Thus, few peasants receive official credit, but among them are various powerful entrepreneurs and many of the members of the new rural bourgeoisie.

The peasant has to combine several sources of credit, on occasion all of them, in order to bring off the miracle of continuing to produce without dying of starvation. He does it through a set of elaborate and sometimes convoluted strategies. Some people plant peanuts only in order to finance the fertilizers for the corn crop. Others use official credit to finance planting of the cornfield or for buying corn for consumption in the months of scarcity, while they resort to the local bourgeoisie or the big monopolists in order to finance a field of tomatoes or onions. Many turn to usurers to cover the costs of an illness or a fiesta.

The multiple combinations prove effective in many directions: The peasant can undertake crops that produce a higher surplus, which he consumes as much for production as for subsistence, but he can not, other than by exception, free himself from indebtedness. The growers accept this as a normal condition. At times they prefer to devote their scanty incomes to what would seem to be superfluous consumption if it did not have an important social function instead of keeping them to finance future crops. There are even people who borrow when they have money so that the lender "keeps up his trust," in order to strengthen his patronage. But the majority do not even consider these alternatives. Given what they produce in a year, what is left after paying the debts does not go far enough even for food during the dry season, much less for starting a crop on their own. For them, obtaining a new loan is a precondition for continuing cultivation, one that must be combined with the sale of labor if they are to hold out until the next harvest. Each year the effort necessary to maintain the precarious equilibrium increases, and it seems to be a spiral that constantly demands more work, as well as the daring and inventiveness to find it. Creating employment, inventing ways of working harder, is part of peasant leisure.

A Tiger by the Tail

Manifest Destiny. Beginning with the outbreak of the Second World War, the Mexican industrial plan received a boost from universal history, the history that the world powers make. Those nations reorganized their still-tottering economy around the conflict. They virtually halted the supply of industrial products for final consumption to the nonindustrialized countries; they created a vacuum in the dependent economies. At the same time, they bought all the raw materials that the agrarian countries produced at prices much more favorable than those of the Depression in the thirties. In a certain sense, the external juncture created the need for a local, native industry at the same time that it offered the opportunity for industrial investment to be rewarded with high rates of earnings in a market without competition. The substitution of imports had an open road and became a program of economic policy.

The small but influential industrial sector of the Mexican economy made good use of the juncture. With a few machines, often discarded in industrial countries as too old, they founded factories that produced an enormous variety of articles. They were often of poor quality and expensive, but they were the only ones, and the people bought them. The industrialists earned a great deal of money, which they used in founding new enterprises or enlarging the existing ones; they also used it to consume high-quality, imported articles instead of the current domestic substitutes. But certainly the change was noteworthy: at last the climate was favorable for capitalist investment.

In the forties manufacturers more than doubled the value of their production with a sustained growth of 8.1 percent annually; in the following decade they repeated the feat again with an annual average of 7.1 percent; in the sixties they outdid themselves with 8.9 percent per year (Reynolds, p. 40). Within thirty years manufacturing production increased almost tenfold in value and was statistically the weightiest sector in Mexico's obtaining an average economic growth of more than 6 percent annually for thirty years straight. The Mexican miracle was unleashed.

Mexican industry grew under the protection of a fiscal barrier that isolated it from international competition. A poor man's Monroe Doctrine was in effect: the internal market belongs to the local industries. When the war was over and international supply was reestablished, domestic production was protected by import taxes, which could exceed 100 percent above the value. The margin of protection was converted into a margin of profit by the entrepreneurs, who could raise their prices as a function of the tax. The artificiality of the prices enabled Mexican industry to obtain high rates of earnings even when it operated inefficiently. Since this situation was prolonged, the tax protection turned out to be inadequate, and thus import permits were adopted as an additional measure during the government of Miguel Alemán. A government authorization was needed to import commodities, independent of their price and of the tax; in clear bureaucratic language, doing so was prohibited. At present more than three quarters of import products require permits, among them almost all products for final consumption. The irrationality of separating profit from productive efficiency, a form of speculation, became a rule of domestic industry.

The variety of articles for final consumption whose importation could be substituted for by local manufacture was finite. Nylon stockings, English-style sweaters, imperial-style cutlery, and even Czech-like hand-cut crystal were already being manufactured. Radios, televisions, cars, and motorcycles were assembled with tax-free imported parts. Even an airplane factory had discreetly failed. On the other hand, work tools, fertilizers, tractors, and trucks were imported. The choice of the imports that could be substituted for was left in great part to the initiative of the entrepreneurs, who chose those items that implied lower investments and higher prices. Luxury articles appeared in the front rank, and prodigious refinements like the production of a Japanese-label Scotch whiskey were attained.

Toward 1960 the substitution of articles for final consumption ran up against a wall when no new alternatives were found. A new phase was begun: vertical growth through substitution of intermediate articles, the ones incorporated into those for final consumption, and substitution of durable goods. The government's action was definitive in this change, as well as a determining factor in choosing the automotive industry out of all the possible industries that might have been vertically integrated. The statistical effect of the process is noteworthy, and the automobile industry has become the most important one among manufacturers, even though it continues to be an inefficient branch, incapable of competing in international markets. Moreover, the enormous general distortion prompted by the preference bestowed on an industry that is the classic example of opulent consumption in a country that produced scarcely a hundred thousand cars and trucks in 1964 (Reynolds, app. E) and that continues to be a poor, peasant nation remains to be analyzed. In a slam-bang way vertical integration has followed its course, but national industry still falls short of becoming efficient and capable of competition in international markets.

Mexican factories use only a fraction of their installed capacity. After the end of the war the majority of the industrial plants worked only one shift. At this rate they meet the national demand, not because all the people buy their products, but because all those who can buy do so. The reduced character of the domestic market is not a result of the size of the population but of the number of people who can make purchases, who represent a very low percentage of the total for the majority of products. Under-consumption say the economists, but it is called poverty by the people who want to buy but cannot.

The reduced volume of production and the limited use of installed capacity, which depreciates and becomes obsolete just the same whether it is used or only put on exhibition, are causes of the industrial inefficiency. The great cost of the machines and the installations is distributed over a few articles. The obvious solution is impossible—there are no smaller machines. They are not produced in the industrial countries, and if they were produced, their operation would not be cost-efficient—paradoxes of the industrial system, which bases its existence on the massive scale. A curious situation, indeed, that requires squandering from those who have the least for the savings of those who have the most.

Once in the realm of paradoxes, one should mention others. The general productivity of manufacturing has not grown since 1950 (Reynolds, pp. 198–204). The increases in total production are in the same proportion as the increases in capital and in the labor force; put another way, if production increases 10 percent annually, the capital and labor invested have to increase in the same proportion—they have a constant yield. This obviously contradicts the premises of industrialization, but, curiously, it does not affect profits, which have grown at more than satisfactory rates in Mexico.

As a result of technological modernization, industrial growth has been based more on the investment of capital than on the absorption of labor. According to the censuses, the population active in industry grew from 640,000 in 1940 to 2,800,000 in 1970; it quadrupled, while the value of production grew almost tenfold, or in broader terms, employment grew half as much as production. It must be taken into account that in accord with the desire to show the success of industrialization, employment figures sin on the side of optimism, even to the point of becoming ingenuous. Thus, the tortilla-dough mills run by peasant children before they go out to work in the fields are considered industries. Of the people employed in industry, 14 percent worked *for themselves* and not for firms (Gollás and García R., p, 31). Even without apocalyptic intentions, it seems reasonable to affirm that in the short term industry will not be able to absorb the population working in agriculture, which is double the size of that employed in industry.

All the problems of this flourishing industry end up in its dependent nature, its subordination. The industry was born, grew, and may possibly decline as a deformed appendage of the industrial powers. From them it receives its machines, its technology, often its raw materials and intermediate goods, its organization, its rationale, and increasingly, its capital. All this must be bought abroad and paid for in foreign exchange, in the hard currencies of the industrial powers. In our case *abroad* means above all the United States, from which and to which more than three quarters of Mexican external trade comes and goes.

The illusion that industrialization would liberate Mexico from dependency was never realized. Since 1944 Mexico has bought more abroad than it has sold outside. Almost everything purchased abroad is destined to industry—80 percent on the average. However, what is sold abroad comes from agriculture and from livestock, more than half the exports of commodities and of the primary industries. The powerful, astonishing industrial sector provided barely 14 percent of the exports in 1969, although statistically it appeared much stronger, since processed food products, which represented between 10 and 15 percent of exports (Hansen, p. 78), were added to it. Almost all the exported manufactured goods are produced in Mexico by foreign industries of a multinational character—ITT, Heinz, Volkswagen, Olivetti—which makes Mexico's entry into international markets suspicious at the least. Actually, it is the result of the decentralization of multinational firms, ultimately generated by their own interests more than by local conditions.

As a result of the new industrial dependency, Mexico began to register negative totals in its balance of payments after the end of the Second World War. At first they were modest figures, but in the seventies they had reached magnitudes greater than a billion dollars a year. Since the value of Mexican money is regulated by the dollar, when the foreign exchange accumulated during the war was exhausted, the peso was drastically devalued on two occasions. To the instability of the currency was added inflation, severe in 1950 terms, 10 percent annually, which turns out to be moderate and even desirable in the seventies. In 1955, to overcome the climate of insecurity and discouragement among investors because of the devaluations and inflation, which meant splendid short-term deals for many of them, the economic policy of Mexico was reoriented, and fifteen years of growth with stable exchange rates and a moderate inflation of 4 to 5 percent per year on the average were obtained.

Growth with stability relied on the attraction of foreign resources in magnitudes sufficient to compensate for the draining away of foreign exchange. This was obtained by three routes: tourism, external credits, and direct foreign investment. In fact there are four routes, but the last is clandestine: the exporting of seasonal labor, illegal *bracerismo,* in which between 5 and 10 percent of the Mexican work force participates, but whose benefits are disguised, with considerable irony and a bit of truth, under the statistical rubrics of tourism and border transactions.

Tourism and border transactions, together with their hidden component, *bracerismo,* currently represent an entry of foreign exchange as great as the export of goods, but the real income from these activities is much lower. First because during the massive pilgrimages of devout Mexican consumers to the commercial shrines of San Antonio, Nogales, and San Diego, half the total is returned to its origin. A good part of Mexicans' expenditures outside the country is devoted to introducing contraband, which is ultimately a defensive strategy of the "consumer class" against the inefficiency and greed of local industry (it is also an example of consumer alienation, but that is another story). Furthermore, one has to consider that a good part of the real tourists' expenditures return to their origin by a much more sophisticated route: The majority of the largest firms that serve tourism are foreign—aviation, hotels, car rental, cafeterias, and even some folk artisanry. Moreover, tourism employs only 3 percent of the active population, a figure that is presumably inflated, but poor at that (Gollás and García R., p. 34). Light industry does not offer a long-term solution for the deficit of payments, although it constitutes an important relief.

Direct foreign investments quickly recovered from the scare of the Cárdenas expropriations. Their flow was slowly renewed once President Ávila Camacho negotiated the payment of indemnizations to the oil companies and of lapsed bonds on the public debt. Under the government of Miguel Alemán the current became more intense, and in the sixties stronger yet, until in 1967 it doubled the 1959 figure (Hansen, p. 79). The flow has not ceased, and today one can speak of a flood. Expropriations are a thing of the past, and the nationalizations that have replaced them, the purchase of foreign firms on the part of the government, are exceptional, at times originating in requests from the foreign companies themselves. In this case, too, *foreign* means basically the United States, which supplies three fourths of the total direct foreign investments.

The true magnitude and importance of direct foreign investments is quite difficult to establish, and one can even speak of a conspiracy to hide it, in which many people participate. The root of the concealment, but not its cause, is that in Mexico foreign enterprises do not exist legally: 51 percent of the capital of any enterprise has to be the property of nationals. Since control of currency exchange or of payments abroad does not exist either, firsthand information is not available. The indirect information, drawn from national accounts or from foreign statistics, which do not seem very trustworthy either, contributes little to one's peace of mind.

In 1972 direct foreign investment was estimated at a little less than $3 billion, 90 percent of which was located in manufacturing and commerce (Gollás and García R., p. 14). This figure is almost double the one for 1967, which, in turn, was double that of 1959; foreign investment grew more rapidly than manufacturing production. In the sixties it was estimated that direct U.S. investment generated a sixth of the total manufactured goods (Hansen, p. 79). When one shows a natural horror at these statistics, economists rush in to counterattack: scarcely a little more than 10 percent of gross fixed investment since 1940 has been financed with foreign resources, and of these only one third come from direct investments (Hansen, p. 58); in 1972 gross foreign investment represented only 3 percent of the total fund of capital, while the rest had been generated by internal savings (Gollás and García R., p. 14).

The overall, questionable figures do not consider the concentration and location of capital. While a good part of the internal capitalized saving meant that people bought a plow or a little electric motor, foreign capital comes concentrated and occupies strategic positions. In 1962, for example, it was estimated that 58 percent of the country's four hundred largest firms were controlled by foreign capital, against 9 percent in the hands of the government and 33 percent controlled by domestic capitalists; if only the hundred largest enterprises were considered, the breakdown was fifty-six foreign, twenty-four government, and twenty private domestic (González Casanova, pp. 257–58). The actual proportion of foreign enterprises must be much higher, to the extent that these firms have changed their method of investing. Until 1960 foreign capital funded enterprises, built new factories, created jobs. But to the degree that the most attractive lines of import substitution became more scarce, and in order to flee the competition that could decrease the privileges of protection, foreign capital began to buy existing enterprises. Its control, previously concentrated in the "modern" lines of industry, like automobiles, chemicals and pharmaceuticals, and electric appliances, spread into the traditional ones. The food industry, for example, was totally acquired by foreign business; the canned chiles that have proudly circled the entire world, the chocolates and the cookies, along with many other items, passed into the hands of the big U.S. conglomerates.

Moreover, foreign investment has another mode of operating that the statistics record only with difficulty: the concession of manufacturing licenses. In this case, the enterprise can be domestic by ownership but signs a contract to produce articles under a foreign brand name. The foreign enterprise provides the technique, the machines, the styles, and the prestige of its name, and it charges royalties on the production. The textile and fashion industry, among many others, illustrates this process in which formal ownership rests with Mexicans although the enterprise is a mere appendage of one abroad. This is one of the many forms of technological dependence that the whole process of capitalist industrialization implies. But in this case, it remains quite clear that the "progressive industrial bourgeoisie" does not go beyond being an agent for foreign interests, scarcely more sophisticated than the name-lender who figures as owner of 51 percent of the stock of the Mexican General Motors. Both are fictions that do not change the true, dependent character of national industry.

In the sixties 10 percent of the payments abroad from Mexico corresponded to services on direct foreign investments, that is, profits, and represented more than three billion pesos a year (Reynolds, app. D). That figure represented around 15 percent of the direct foreign investment, a more than acceptable margin if one realizes that these firms were reinvesting part of their profits in the country. New foreign investment hovered around the same figures (Hansen, p. 27), which implies that the extraction of profits was coming dangerously close to it, if it had not already exceeded it. If one adds to this figure the payment for transfer of technology made by national enterprises—calculated at more than a billion pesos—the balance turns out to be negative, and today it ought to be even more grave. The relief represented by foreign investment was exhausted and today its presence is a symptom of impotence, of national decapitalization.

Indirect foreign investment, the third route to make up for the deficit in foreign trade, the external public debt, is assumed and controlled by the government—the first considerably more than the second. After the Second World War, little by little, Mexico recovered access to international credit, from which it had been excluded after the petroleum expropriation. Credits from abroad became essential for financing public investment during the period of stability. Its total amount has continued growing constantly since then. Since 1960 the government and some State institutions have placed bond issues in the international market in order to complement credit from international organizations and private banks. The credits from outside, which reached some $100 million per year in 1955, approached $700 million in 1968. Payments on debts rose from $65 million to $550 million in the same period. New loans with higher interest are being borrowed in order to repay loans that have fallen due. Payment of the debt and interest takes more than a third of the total value of exports of goods and services each year (Hansen, p. 277). Even the most optimistic admit that the foreign public debt is reaching its limits.

The relative exhaustion of means for covering the deficit and the growing dependence abroad generated by the prodigious domestic industry pose a severe, urgent problem for the future. The idea of stopping up one hole by opening another, even bigger one has its long-term risks, and that term seems to have run out. Luckily, great stores of petroleum were discovered in 1974. Once this fortune is certain, Mexico will return to where it was in 1910 and 1940: selling raw materials. If the find does not have the magnitude suggested, and if gold is not discovered in its place, the comparison to 1910 seems to be more appropriate.

An Alliance for Profits. The development of Mexican industry can be narrated as a succession of responses or adaptations to economic junctures, among which those shaped abroad stand out, but it cannot be explained only by them, as is so often done. Taking advantage of the "opportunities" as not been a mechanical or automatic response but has been shaped by a deliberate policy. A primary role in formulating that policy has fallen to the Mexican State.

During more than thirty-five years the government has congruently and firmly kept economic development through industrialization as the central objective of its policy. The pursuit of this strategic goal has not been free of tactical contradictions, ambiguities, and even confusion, but its priority, its nature as an obvious and necessary path, has never been put in doubt. Nor do political opponents, whether on the right or the left, reject the goal; instead they criticize the implementation of it. In this case, *politics* is understood as the formalized activity that verbalizes ideological formulations and maintains specific institutions: parties. In that sense, development has not been confronted by different alternatives. The action of the government as a decisive influence in the politics of economic growth can be chronicled by following three principal lines, three aspects of a single subject. The lines selected are intimately related, and separating them is always arbitrary.

The first is the part that the State has played as investor, as a private agent in development. The revolutionary government was not going to commit the same error Don Porfirio did, and a good part of its action has set out to create an economic base of its own. The *caudillos* laid the cornerstones through foundation of institutions for promotion and control like the Bank of Mexico, the Bank of Agricultural Credit, and, later, the Nacional Financiera. During the Cárdenas era the government intervened directly in production, and from then on, it has been said— and is insisted today more firmly than ever—that the State will take productive activities into its own hands to complement or supplement private initiative. At present more than four hundred good-sized enterprises in almost all economic activities are government property or have strong government involvement. Beyond producing basic raw materials, the State has enterprises in fields as varied as aviation, film-making, newsprint, savings banks, sugar mills, hemp products, fertilizers, textiles, automobiles, mining, and many more.

The range is so broad and confused that it is difficult to discover the criteria that determine the government's direct investments. One is breaking up bottlenecks that threaten industrial development, which includes not only the production of raw materials and essential services but also the attempts to encourage the manufacture of intermediate goods. The second criterion is clearly political, in the sense of control of power, and is exemplified by the paper monopoly that serves in checking the press or by television and film-making. The government has acquired many of the enterprises that hold a critical position in mobilizing the people, in manipulating them. The third criterion is less clear and can be expressed as the rescue of the most resounding failures of domestic, and sometimes foreign, private initiative, independent of what they produce. In Mexico important enterprises that do not belong to the government never go bankrupt or close down. The ruined factories obtain official credit, and afterwards they sell the remnants to the government; in its preoccupation with maintaining employment and containing worker unrest as well as with preserving the climate of confidence among investors, the government puts in good money after bad and sometimes revives the enterprise. Corruption plays one important part in the application of this criterion, and politics another—through the pressure groups that used to be called, modestly, the "living forces."

The government's action as an investor creates conflicts, alliances, and dependencies with domestic private initiative. In some activities the government enterprises are absolute or virtual monopolies that produce for the benefit of the industrial sector as a whole. The fact of being sole suppliers of indispensable goods gives them enormous power, while their function of encouraging growth, which is sometimes translated into providing subsidies to industrial consumers, deprives them of excessive profits or makes them operate at a loss—all of which is translated into a clientele of industrialists on whom pressure can be exerted in some way. Yet, many State enterprises are not monopolies, but competitive. In these cases, the confrontation with private investors is severe. The latter accuse the government of disloyalty, of inefficiency and corruption, of communist tendencies. At times the government's enterprises lose systematically without obtaining any of the stated objectives but still persist in their undertakings. Joint control, association between the government and private initiative, has arisen in some activities; at times it is not even public knowledge, which leads to another type of dependency and conflict.

Despite all the problems and losses, the State industries constitute the most powerful coherent group in Mexican industry. This strength is increased by the position of an owner who is both judge and litigant and who is relatively less pressured by the need to obtain profits. In day-to-day practice the administration of the State's enterprises may be consistently contradictory and corrupt, but in the face of major crises or in dealing with projects over extended periods of time, they can react as a group with centralized direction. Under these conditions, the influence of the State enterprises in industrial development has been greater than that of other sectors. Moreover, by the very nature of some of their activities, like the railroads, electricity, or petroleum, the government enterprises employ a large proportion of the industrial work force and possibly the largest share of unionized laborers. If the organized bureaucrats are added to them, the government is the principal boss of unionized workers. The notion that Mexico practices a mixed economy, a blend of State and private capitalism, is based on these facts and is promoted by the government.

The domestic private enterprises statistically represent a much larger proportion in the manufacturing sector, yet they do not form a coherent or organized group, but one separated and torn apart by internal struggles. The number of private enterprises is much greater than that of the State firms, and the concentration of capital among them is much lower. The contradictions between the large and small enterprises in the competitive branches are acute. There are also severe contradictions between modern and traditional industries, the first intensive in capital, the others in labor.

The struggle is ending up in a polarization of the industrial sector, in a process of monopolistic concentration. Out of it have arisen some small but very powerful groups that are growing rapidly: Monterrey, Guadalajara, National Bank of Mexico, Jenkins and Heirs, and so on. These articulated groups, which generally have control over one or more financial institutions and over important manufacturing enterprises, have gained influence and a certain degree of autonomy in the face of the State. The powerful groups, linked among themselves socially, have vaguely agreed upon a certain specialization of effort, which eases the competition in some cases. They have also been able to act coherently in facing certain problems. They constitute a new oligarchy with powers restricted by the State. Some of the names of these oligarchs are the same ones heard a hundred years ago, but a considerable number are new and rang out for the first time in the government: these are the freebooters who are enjoying the justice the revolution did them.

Foreign enterprises have a special position derived from their high concentration of capital, their organizational coherence, and their ability to rely on vigorous external support. This grants them a high degree of autonomy, even arrogance, although not independence, before the State. Yet, this position prevents the foreign enterprises from participating directly in the factional struggle within the government, although their interests are always represented. The foreign firms establish a kind of implicit, condescending alliance with the oligarchic national groups with which they share a common principle: the maximization of concrete, immediate profit, the persistence of speculative conditions even at the cost of long-term total growth.

The second line of action of the government as a central player in the development process involves public expenditure and the collection of taxes. Since 1940 the government has carried out massive investment in projects that are a precondition for industrial growth. Between one quarter and one half of public investment has been devoted to industrial development; between 1960 and 1968 this last figure reached almost 40 percent (Hansen, pp. 62, 277). Even the private groups admit that the result of this policy is successful and that the country has available an infrastructure adequate for the functioning of industry. Besides making the industrial enclave possible, public works have had considerable effects on the growth of manufacturing. Completing these projects implies the creation of jobs, acquisition of inputs, an overflow of money that reverts to industry and that contributes to expanding the consumer market. Another, no less important effect has been the contribution to the formation of domestic private capital, which is invested or reinvested, although sometimes it also escapes abroad. Public works are carried out through concession to private contractors, most typically from among the freebooters, who obtain fabulous profits. The corrupt relation between supply and construction contractors and public functionaries is undoubtedly one of the integrating forces between private initiative and the government. Not a few of the outstanding members of the oligarchy owe their fortunes to association with or participation in the government. Another consequence of public works is the growth of the construction industry, one of the central ones in the process of industrialization and one of the most effective magnets for migration from the countryside to the cities.

Public works have basically been an incentive for generating and encouraging private investment in industrial activities. The policy has been so effective that the State has been left behind, and its relative weight has continued to decrease. In 1940 the government contributed half the raw capital that was formed in the country, while in the sixties its contribution represented one third. During this whole period public investment had not ceased growing, either relatively or absolutely, going fom 4.5 to 6.2 percent of the gross national product, but meanwhile the percentage of the product capitalized had gone from 8.6 percent to 20.7 percent (Hansen, pp. 61 ff.). Private initiative, both domestic and foreign, was free and unrestrained.

The government's investment and its consumption represent more than half the State's total expenditures, an achievement that contrasts positively with the behavior of other Latin American countries. This behavior becomes more noteworthy when one takes into account that Mexican public expenditure is quite low in comparison with that of other countries: around 10 percent of the national product, while in the majority of Latin American countries it is about 15 percent (Reynolds, p. 318). The feat has a simple explanation: Nobody has spent less on the social welfare of the population than the Mexicans; or as they put it, the human resource has received the least attention. Even education receives a smaller proportion than in the rest of Latin America (Hansen, pp. 115–16). Mexico has one of the lowest levels of taxation in the world, which in itself constitutes an enormous profit incentive. The attraction becomes greater if one considers that between 1940 and 1965 almost all tax revenues came from labor, exports, and consumption, while profits remained almost untaxed. Public expenditure has clearly served accumulation.

The Mexican government has systematically and constantly spent more than it collects in its effort to promote industrial development. Between 1940 and 1955 this was done through the use of deficit budgets. Inflation and the devaluations determined that external indebtedness would subsequently be preferred for covering the difference. In the sixties some efforts were made to increase tax collection, but the rate of indebtedness did not decrease (Hansen, pp. 133 ff.). As this debt approached insupportable levels, the need for profound fiscal reform became more urgent. The struggle to obtain it has distinguished the tone of relations between private initiative and the government during the regime of President Echeverría.

The private parties are not disposed to make concessions, and they have effectively resisted the government's confused attempts to obtain far-reaching fiscal reform. Their justification is obvious: the only conceivable reason for industrializing a country like Mexico is so that profit will be higher than it was and so that it will steadily increase. The government also has vital reasons for seeking tax reform: it is indispensable for maintaining the growth rate and for palliating the severe crisis that threatens the development model. Redistribution through the mechanism of taxation, even if limited in scope, is urgent not only for expanding internal markets but for checking the discontent and pressure that arise from those less-promoted human resources—many people have had it with all the statistical success. Moreover, the State, pushed by its own dynamic, has to keep growing. For reasons of state, tax reform is a necessity.

The tension between the private interests and the government has been heightened, and perhaps for the first time since the forties one can speak of opposition in referring to some groups. But the multiple ties that exist between the partners for growth seem to have the strength to keep the capitalist sector, of which the State forms part, integrated. In the conflict over fiscal reform there is no apparent winner, but losers are already in sight; indirect taxes, which are not redistributive or are so to a lesser degree, have increased appreciably and provoked the rage of the consumer class and the sadness of those who, like the peasants, do not form a part of this select group but who also consume. If the severe inflationary process is added to all this, it would be best if the oil discovery were a sure thing, and enormous besides.

The third line is the one of indirect effects of government action, which could be more precisely defined as the establishment of economic policy for the growth process. In this ubiquitous and complex action two levels can be discerned: the general orientation and the practical implementation. The direction of the first is more or less clear: to grow at any price through industrial capitalism. All resources, from foreign exchange to people, have been subordinated to this objective. Probably in few places has the model been imposed with more radicalism. The distribution of income has shown the extreme, accelerated polarization. In 1963, 70 percent of the families with the lowest incomes received less than 30 percent of the total income and made do with less than 1,250 pesos per month per family; in contrast, the 2.4 percent of the population with larger incomes captured 16 percent of the total income, above 7,000 pesos monthly; the 10 percent with the highest incomes were left with 41.5 percent of the total (Reynolds, pp. 104–5). Social-service demands have been postponed time and again, but profits have never been sacrificed. I cite Hansen: "It is the paradox of modern Mexico that such a development strategy has been devised and implemented in the only major Latin American nation to undergo a profound and bloody social revolution. In some other country the hard-nosed and unsentimental Mexican model of development might seem natural; in Mexico itself it appears incongruous" (p. 119).

The general orientation of Mexican development policy seems to emanate originally from the State. Obregón and Cárdenas, the two great designers of the model, acted in the face of relatively open historical situations that offered several possible alternatives. Obregón effectively avoided external pressure, and in a climate of conflict Cárdenas confronted it successfully. Neither of them ran into united internal opposition from groups with true autonomy and with a different, independent plan; on the contrary, the peasants and the workers were co-opted by the government, while the reactionary opposition was weak or did not essentially differ with the State model. Obviously, neither Obregón nor Cárdenas was personally the creator of the plan, and their decisions were shaped by pressures or influences that acted within the State. First capitalism and later industrialization—they seem to be creatures of the State. Concrete creatures, to be sure, explained not only by the ideology of their actors but by history. History here does not imply inevitable occurrence. History can help us to explain why something happened, but going from that to the past's being the only one possible, the inevitable one, requires a somersault; there is a bit of juggling when we are presented with a prediction of what has already happened as though it were a discovery.

The State is not, and has not been, a monolithic organization, free of internal contradictions. Its pendulumlike cycle, which lasts six years, suggests just the opposite: that contradictory forces are acting within it, seeking and finding support from different outside interests. But the State is not simply a constellation of multiple alliances, for it also has elements that structure it and make it different. One of these is its maintenance of power, which in itself provides cohesion; another is its creation of a plan that has essentially been compatible with the dominant interests.

The contradictions of the State are clearly exposed at the level of instrumentation. The practical implementation of the model requires actions in all fields of activity: legislation, institutions, declarations, physical repression, corruption, diplomacy, a method of measuring and calculating in order to grow—in sum, the acts of government. These are flexible, contradictory, absurd or disastrous, effective or counterproductive. They are marked by negotiation and by concession, by the cautious evaluation of the reactions of the affected parties, by give-and-take. In the government's concrete acts the different levels of dependent industrial capitalism are being brought together. In the last thirty-five years private enterprises have received all the advantages possible, and even some that were not, as a result of the government's action or passivity. This is neither a concession nor a show of weakness but a requirement of the model.

During the same period the government's influence increased appreciably. It won direct or indirect control in the most significant activities, and in some, it established undisputed dominance. It strengthened centralism and expanded its area of action. It added power without sacrificing authority. It established a mode of exchange with the entrepreneurs in which the surrender of tangible benefits was compensated for by the transfer of political autonomy. The government retained the hegemony won with such difficulty by the *caudillos* and consolidated by Cárdenas. It incorporated the groups participating in industrial development most effectively, and it passed over those who were paying the price. Obviously, it did not eliminate the contradictions, but it overcame them. The State has not been weakened. This surprising strength rests on the dominance that the State exercises over the country's majority group, the peasants, whose presence establishes a distinct balance of power. This uncontested control is another of the factors that structure the State and bestow upon it a character different from that of the other forces that sponsor the implantation and reproduction of dependent industrial capitalism.

The Mexican Miracle. The growth of agriculture was considered one of the pillars of Mexican development. Between 1935 and 1967 agricultural production increased at an average annual rate of 4.4 percent, which rather comfortably exceeded the growth of the country's population, and by a wide margin that of the country's agricultural population, although it was less spectacular than the growth of manufacturing. This permitted satisfaction of national demand, and imports of corn and wheat were resorted to only exceptionally, in especially bad years. On the other hand, agricultural exports grew in a sustained fashion, although at variable rates, until they represented half the value of the total export of goods, and in contrast with the behavior of manufactures, they generated a favorable balance of foreign exchange (CDIA, 1 : chap. 2). The value of land and livestock production tripled between 1940 and 1965, although its share of total production dropped from 24.3 percent to 17.4 percent in the same period (Reynolds, pp. 81–83). The land area harvested barely doubled in the same interval, which implied a net increase in physical and monetary yields per land unit. A severe underestimate of the population active in agriculture in the 1970 census makes analysis of growth in that aspect difficult. According to the census, the active agricultural population went from 3,831,000 in 1940 to 6,086,000 in 1960, scarcely a little more than a 50 percent increase, and was reduced to 5,132,000 in 1970; its proportion within the total active population decreased from 65 percent to 54 percent in 1960 and 40 percent in 1970 (Reynolds, app. E). Without giving excessive credence to these figures, it can be perceived that agricultural growth fell upon relatively fewer and fewer people, who necessarily worked more. In many senses, the true miracle of Mexican development is located in agriculture, in the countryside and in its people.

From the economic point of view, this miracle was performed with very little, which is the way it should be when one is talking about miracles. The tangible capital in agriculture was a little more than 10 percent of the tangible national capital in 1960; the capital per person employed in agriculture was one sixth the national average. If one adds to this that more than half the tangible capital in the land-and-livestock sector consisted of the value of the livestock, the proportions are much more surprising (CDIA, 1 : chap. 2). Public expenditure in agriculture also declined, from around 16 percent of the total in the forties to 10 percent in the sixties. More than three fourths of public spending on agriculture was devoted to construction of irrigation works in the northern part of the country.

Despite its poverty, or more precisely, because of it, the land-and-livestock sector transferred more than three billion pesos to other sectors between 1940 and 1960, counting only transfer by price mechanisms and the resources captured by the banking system and discounting the "profits" from agriculture through the fiscal mechanism (CDIA, 1 : chap. 2). The estimate turns out to be much more than modest, indeed almost ridiculous, since the greatest proportion of the transfers are performed through mechanisms not registered in the statistics. The miracle was not only performed with very little but with less and less all the time; agriculture suffered from a severe process of relative decapitalization. Thus, it is not surprising that the production per worker employed in the agricultural sector was six times less than that assigned to other sectors (Reynolds, p. 88) and that their earnings were yet more unequal.

The general decapitalization of agriculture does not affect equally all the people who cultivate, raise livestock, or live in the villages. Some are even getting rich; according to the statistics, they are few in number. In 1960 only 16 percent of agricultural properties attained production above five thousand pesos per year, which is not usually enough to get rich on. These properties generated 80 percent of the value of the total production; to do so, they accumulated 62 percent of the land area worked, 96 percent of the irrigated land, and 92 percent of the agricultural machinery. More than half of these ratios were accumulated on only 3.3 percent of the properties, which attained a production above twenty-five thousand pesos annually, representing 54 percent of the value of the total production with 43 percent of the land worked, 69 percent of the irrigated land, and 75 percent of the machinery. Looking yet again, and for the last time, more than half of these ratios were concentrated on some twelve thousand properties that produced more than one hundred thousand pesos per year and represented scarcely 0.5 percent of the total properties, the true *latifundios* (Reyes, pp. 392–93).

The owners of these properties and a few others received all of the advantages that statistically appear destined for agriculture. They appropriated or took control of irrigated lands, enjoyed official credit and guarantee prices almost exclusively, dominated the market for commercial products. Even agrarian reform, the distribution of lands, protected them and acted in their benefit. Ávila Camacho and Miguel Alemán not only slowed the rate of distribution but also issued some legal measures for the protection of the large agricultural enterprises. Statistically, Ruiz Cortines, López Mateos, and Díaz Ordaz gradually recovered the rhythm of the distribution to the point that Díaz Ordaz approached the figures for the Cárdenas period. But since Ávila Camacho the government's agrarian laws and actions have had very much the character of a farce that everyone applauds but no one believes. The best land is not distributed; what is distributed is not handed over; what is handed over is less than was granted; almost nobody is given documents; and despite everything, land continues to be given out. The *cerros*, the badlands, and the desert are cultivated with poor yields, but in the end they produce something. The final result is that the distribution of lands tends to be polarized and becomes more and more inequitable. This can be perceived even in the statistics, which reflect only weakly a process that in practice is considerably more intensive.

The great majority of the people dedicated to agriculture did not receive the "benefits" of growth. Public investment in land-and-livestock development did not reach them, although it affected them. However, the distribution of land was a decisive element for the participation of this group in agricultural growth and national development. The involvement of these people, the peasants, cannot be measured easily, not so much because of the intrinsic difficulty that this would represent but because the statistics do not bother to record it. These statistical practices were copied from the "modern" countries and apply their categories, so that they become an important instrument of external dependence and of subjugation. The method of measuring the economy takes the categories of capitalism for granted and as universals: the nature and objectives of the enterprise, the presence of capital and money markets, the exchange of all productive resources as commodities, and so on. Obviously, this leaves out the activities in which these conditions are not met or else records them only fragmentarily. Moreover, those who use and analyze the economic data generally suppose that what is unrecorded does not exist. Even so, some data permit outlining—as one might a black hole—the nature and magnitude of the participation of the peasants, who work 86 percent of Mexican agricultural properties.

In 1940 only 50 percent of the country's agricultural production was sold, while in 1950 and 1960, 80 percent of the total reached the market (Reyes, pp. 390–91). The higher degree of commercialization is necessarily linked to increases in the consumption of manufactured articles. Only part of the harvest of corn and its companion crops was retained by the producers, who had to buy everything else and became a considerable market for a very limited number of "modern" articles.

In 1940, 70 percent of the value of agricultural production came from crops destined directly for human nutrition; in 1960 the percentage had been reduced to 60. By the latter date cotton, sugar cane, and coffee, among the so-called industrial agricultural products, represented two thirds of the total, and they had grown more rapidly than the rest of agriculture (Reyes, pp. 387–88). Corn occupied more than two thirds of the land area devoted to raising foods and more than half the total cultivated land. The volume of this grain produced doubled between 1940 and 1960, but its share of the total agricultural production dropped from 38 percent to 28 percent in those years (CDIA, 1 : chap. 2). The products for self-sufficiency have lost neither their scope nor their real importance but instead their relative importance in regard to the market and exchange. The greater degree of commercialization has implied not only the delivery of a greater proportion of the harvests to the market but also diversification in the plants cultivated.

Between 1930 and 1960 the increases in land area cultivated, in capital, and in the size of the labor force contributed less than half of the real increase in agricultural production—which obviously contrasts with the behavior of the industrial sector in that aspect (Reynolds, p. 146). Put another way, there is an increase in productivity not explained by the growth of those factors. It seems that this mysterious element consists in great part, if not altogether, of a notable increase in the intensity of work, in a more extensive, more strenuous employment of the available labor. Only a part of this more intensive employment was absorbed by the properties that produce less than five thousand pesos per year, and another part was used on the larger properties through day labor, so that the growth that is generally attributed to the superior, "modern" sector originated in the majority peasant group. These conclusions are confirmed by data on productivity by type of property, according to which the most efficient use of resources corresponds to the smaller properties, not to the larger, capitalized ones (Reyes, pp. 394–95). This is to say that intensity of work explains productive efficiency but not profit or income, which move according to levels of accumulation.

But the peasants contributed more than intensive, diversified labor that was appropriated by others. Between 1940 and 1950 they sent six hundred thousand persons, 36 percent of the natural increase in the agricultural population, into other activities (Reyes, p. 395). Each year in that decade they provided the United States with a sizable number of seasonal migrant laborers, who, between the legal ones and the wetbacks, brought in foreign exchange and promoted internal consumption. In the following decade other activities admitted only 480,000 peasants, 28 percent of their population increase, as a result of the concentration of a greater density of capital in the other sectors (Reyes, p. 397). However, the seasonal migration to the United States grew until it exceeded possibly a million persons a year. Between 1950 and 1960 the number of *ejido* members' families that covered more than half their expenses with their own production dropped from 84 percent to 66 percent (Reyes, p. 397), so that more people had to work more intensively as domestic day laborers or as *braceros* and cheap, seasonal laborers. The minimum rural salary, which is not observed in the country, declined 6 percent in real terms between 1950 and 1960. People without nominal access to land constitute half the population active in agriculture, upwards of 2.5 million men.

The multiple effect of all these people on the industrial sector is enormous. On one hand, they consume, even though it might be only bit by bit. On the other, they exert pressure and make possible the availability of a work force that is ill-paid but does not make demands inasmuch as simple occupational mobility is conceived of as a benefit. They contribute capital and produce earnings, opportunities for speculation. They provide cheap foods, which contributes to checking the outbreak of insuperable conflicts in the "modern" sector. They also threaten by their very presence: they arouse fear and promote the formation of implicit coalitions against them, which contributes to creating a certain level of unity in the industrial sector. They deliver people with all the immeasurables that they bring with them. Moreover, they contribute initiative; they generate solutions, miracles. Ultimately, they were only given land that perhaps they would have taken anyway, and the rest they have done alone, against real, powerful forces. They have copied, invented, bought, imagined everything to permit the miracle of growth. They have contributed original, autonomous initiatives in order to coexist with unimaginative enterprises that limit themselves to poor copying of foreign models but have a good grip on things.

The combined effect of all these contributions that cannot be measured statistically but can indeed be captured (and that this essay attempts to describe) grants temporary viability to the model of growth through capitalism and industrialization, although it does not make it wholly rational. The majority peasant sector has been the creator of the conditions and the surpluses that permit the existence of a series of apparent paradoxes: while agriculture is relatively decapitalized, the entrepreneurial sector within it accumulates capital rapidly and intensively; on another level, it is the country that is decapitalizing, but the peasant surplus makes possible the appearance of sectors that grow rapidly and accumulate and reproduce capital; it enables nonproductive sectors to grow more rapidly than productive ones and allows their effort to be better remunerated. It makes it possible for a small group to practice consumption as a goal and to glory in extravagance and waste by simulating Western progress.

But the peasants not only deliver people, labor, commodities, forms of capital that are accumulated or consumed by different sectors; they also generate and confer power. This is almost undiluted—unlike commodities—but is concentrated in the hands of the State. The transfer of power is based in the first place on the reclamation of the original ownership of the soil, on the availability of a legal and institutional complex in order to exercise it, and on the control of a repressive armed force to impose it—all as exclusive privileges of the State that are denied to other groups. The original ownership does not have an economic character in its strictest sense, although its influence may be decisive in that area. It is not possible to treat the national territory as capital, much less as a commodity to be traded in the market, although some politicians have made serious attempts to realize this impossibility. Original ownership, exercise and imposition of it, is a domain that has a political character; it is a relationship of social power. Original ownership was only reclaimed for lands, waters, and subsoil, which granted the State the possibility of exercising a considerably more intense influence over the peasants and their production than it could wield over other activities. It granted the State a broader base of power.

The government, pressured by the peasants, exercised territorial domain for a redistributive purpose, as a restraint on accumulation. The land redistribution was and is conceived of as an exception and not as part of an integral redistributive process. Agrarian reform was the exception that proved the rule of accumulation that reigned in the total complex of economic activities. Redistributive action showed its possibilities for being the most effective instrument for supporting accumulation in the complex when another peculiarity was added to its character as an exception: subordination and the calculated manipulation of it according to the dominant rules.

The area of the subordinate exception, the *ejido,* enjoys a perfectly paradoxical position. It is not the only form of territorial possession recognized; rather, it coexists with classic ownership, although limited in its possible extent. *Ejidal* land cannot be traded as a commodity is traded, although its physical nature and its behavior as a productive resource are identical to those of land that is transferred in that way. This has enabled the *ejido* and the labor of its people to be devoted to production of commodities at the same time that they are devoted to producing foods for direct consumption, which are not monetarized. The *ejidatarios* are placed in the position of independent producers, but they have been plundered of the resources that make production possible, so that they are forced to sell their labor as a commodity. From a formal point of view, these multiple paradoxes function as conditions of the control derived from the presence of the State.

The agrarian law and the watchful presence of the government impose, on the other hand, a limit upon capitalist accumulation in the countryside. Beyond a certain limit, the growth of the agricultural enterprise requires qualitative changes in the composition of capital that imply investments in land, different criteria of investment in which security weighs as much as the rate of earnings, longer-term plans—in sum, respectability, solidity, security, and prestige. This cannot be attained in a Mexican agriculture always menaced by the agrarian law, by the peasants who know it, by the government that manipulates it. Thus, when the capital accumulated in agriculture reaches a certain magnitude, it is wholly or partially transferred to other activities in which it will be rewarded with satisfactory earnings and unlimited security. Capitalization in agriculture has a low limit, a real barrier that benefits the industrial sector as a whole.

But neither the law nor the State halts the obtaining of high profits in agriculture. The openings left by fleeing capital or the opportunities derived from new junctures are intensively exploited by new investors with a little capital who gamble in return for fabulous earnings. Private investment is highly speculative, expropriating resources without any restraint, given that continuity does not matter and is not possible. This constant circulation that transfers capital to industry, the frequent renewal of agrarian capitalism, is one of the central characteristics of the national economic system. The State is the only investor that continually accumulates in the countryside. Despite its niggardliness, public investment in the sixties contributed half the tangible capital, once the value of livestock is discounted. The government had a dominant position as producer, lender, and buyer. The State's direct action basically benefits the agricultural entrepreneurs in circulation, but it mobilizes all the people linked with agriculture. Private investment in the rural areas has neither the magnitude nor the articulation to do anything other than prosper in the shadow of the State, to constitute an appendage without autonomy. If it resists this destiny, the agrarian law becomes a pressure, a threat, an epitaph.

The real restraint on the accumulation of capital in the countryside leaves room for the survival of the peasants, although not many resources remain after the expropriation. The government administers this space rigorously, and with the aid of corruption, co-option, and repression, it establishes a rigorous, absolute dominance, a kind of bossism. The distributed land remains entailed to the State in the colonial sense of the word: perpetually assigned and amortized, isolated from the market, but managed in terms of it, whether directly or through agricultural entrepreneurs. But the government always wields the political control, without any concession or waiver.

Political dominance over the peasantry and the economic consequences of it constitute a principal source of the State's strength. The State's primary position among the forces that pursue development derives from it. But the primacy is further from autonomy every day because of the dependent nature of the growth. The strategic resources for the model sponsored by the State remain outside its control and authority, protected by stronger, more powerful states. This converts the State's program into a derivative product, subordinate to superior forces and without any possibility of being realized with internal resources. The State becomes the most important, most powerful, most effective external agent, the central bearer of dependency. Its existence depends upon service to the outside. To top it all off: far from God, but next door to the United States!

The model adopted has obvious advantages: speed, intensity, radicalism. It moves everything rapidly and effectively, gathers everything together, concentrates it, compresses it until it is graspable. The State never had more hegemonic power, but it has never had less mobility, fewer alternatives—it has nurtured a tiger and now has caught it by the tail.

Everything Useful Gets Used Up. The State's preeminence is manifest in a thousand ways in contemporary Mexico. One of them is that almost all the conflicts derived from the enormous tensions of growth end up in a confrontation with the government, whether because the government provokes it in its role of promoter or because it takes it on in its role as guardian of the development model. Conflicts with workers, students, entrepreneurs, bureaucrats, or intellectuals, each with their vested interests, lead to disputes with the government. Regardless of the concessions it may grant or the beatings it may give, the State has them all defeated to begin with.

The most numerous conflicts and the most frequent confrontations occur in the countryside, although they are the least known, as much because of their concealed location and their limited scope as because of a deliberate lack of attention, of publicity. A fiction of nonexistence envelops the frequent clashes in rural areas. The peasants are listened to mutely, as if they were undifferentiated background noise. The most violent clashes are sketched on the crime pages, but as simple acts of disobedience against the established order.

The majority of the conflicts in rural areas never exploded. They were resolved or dissolved within the bureaucratic apparatus with the support of corruption, economic repression, and, sometimes, individualized physical repression: personal threats, sudden imprisonment for an imagined or forgotten crime, death in a saloon brawl or in an alleged livestock theft. For better or worse, the elimination of dissidence is an important part of the good functioning of the institutions in the rural areas and permits conflicts to be confined to letters, to committees that come and go, to confused legal disputes that are resolved with promises, with visits from middling functionaries, with speeches and partial concessions that settle isolated, secondary problems. The political movements that broke out in the countryside were quite diverse in their expression and scope: armed uprisings like those of 1910, like the *bola chiquita* that rolled through the Morelos *oriente* in 1942, fierce, brutal riots like the one that took place in Temoac in 1974, guerilla warfare with a Guevara-like inspiration, strikes, marches on the cities, occupations of public buildings or transformer plants, and invasions of land. The political orientation was no less varied: tertiary, fanatical right; liberal Jacobinism; leftist of different stripes, lacking explicit ideological positions. However, all of the movements had a radical, disruptive character to the extent that the definitive solution for their demands was outside the rules of the dominant game.

The majority of the conflicts derived from territorial demands, but others emphasized management of the land more than ownership, and still others protested prices and the ways the production was acquired. But in all the causes and demands, a common element can be perceived: a call for greater autonomy, for a more extensive space for mobilizing the resources that the peasants have managed to retain. Autonomy, whether in management of the land or in politics, expresses not only an abstract anarchistic demand but also a concrete, specific need. To the extent that subsistence depends upon the free manipulation of resources, on their circulation outside capitalist relations, on reciprocal and redistributive exchange, autonomy is something real and concrete, even though it cannot be measured. The "guarantee" that the peasants ask for is to subsist as peasants, intensifying their activity for their own benefit, and what is more, increasing the transfer of it for the benefit of others. Peasant autonomy is the philosopher's stone of economic growth, the essential condition for the flourishing of dependent industry.

The diversity in the demands and tactics of the peasant movements expresses, on one hand, the variety in the conditions of peasant existence, but it also represents evidence of their political disarticulation. To a great extent, the atomization of the peasants, the co-option, and political alienation have been obtained. But in the seventies, signs of an acceleration of the outbreak of conflicts in the rural areas have appeared; in these one also perceives a certain tactical coincidence: a marked preference for invasions of lands, which have multiplied until they total several hundred. There is no evidence for attributing the mobilization to more effective political articulation. On the contrary, it seems to emerge from a heightening of the concrete pressures at a juncture in which repression has been controlled. However, it is apparent that the mobilization represents a fertile field for attaining political articulation, and many people are trying to sow in it.

The government has been outstanding in this attempt. Its actions in the countryside have multiplied in order to try to contain the mobilization of the peasants and even to direct and manipulate it. The Echeverría regime's agrarian deeds are numerous, although not so many as it claims: promulgation of the agrarian reform law, transformation of the Agrarian Department into a ministry of state, distribution of lands, and the initiation of an almost infinite number of development projects in the countryside. Thousands of promoters travel through the rural areas to offer, to organize, to teach; they keep a good cut of the government investment in agriculture. This has grown not only in absolute terms but also in relative ones, reversing a tendency three decades old. Although a definitive evaluation proves difficult, it seems clear that the agrarian spirit of the current regime surpasses that of its predecessors and comes close to that of General Cárdenas's government.

The very evident agrarian policy of the seventies is not motivated by peasant pressure alone. Severe problems in other sectors impinge powerfully on the design of the agrarian policy. It seems that industrial growth at any price has given what it had to give. The deterioration in the balance of payments that threatens the peso, government indebtedness, the necessity of importing food in unexpected volumes, slow growth of exports of goods and services, the flight of capital, insufficient development of the internal market, and many other factors have reached the threshold of the intolerable. The old symptoms became apparent and were unexpectedly aggravated as a result of a crisis in world capitalism. The international recession, or lack of tone, as it was discreetly called in Mexico, the imbalance of the monetary system and world inflation, are linked to the exhaustion of growth at any price. The external dependence that they had so painstakingly attempted to avoid showed its severity, its omnipotence.

The government reacted swiftly indeed in this case, and in a confused, hasty fashion it designed new tactics in search of a more stable growth through agrarian policy. In order to correct the most severe distortions, injecting new life into agriculture was held to be indispensable, making it produce and consume more, restoring its capacity to feed the population, to employ the labor force more intensively, to palliate the deterioration caused by insufficient capitalization or, depending upon how one looks at it, by the plundering. Put another way, the peasant surplus, stretched to the limit but over poor resources, no longer managed to pay for the unrestrained, speculative growth of industry and commerce. From the government's point of view, it was necessary to endow agriculture with some capital so that it would generate a new, generous surplus capable of stopping up the gaps left in the "progress." The new development tactic, described as a reformist strain in the revolution, as a resurgence of social justice, and spoken of in other such demagogic formulas, once again makes agriculture an activity subordinate to industrialization. The problems of agriculture are conceived of and expressed as results of low productivity, archaic technology, small scale, and poor organization of the productive enterprises. The poor level of well-being is explained by low, inadequate, and antiquated production. The actions are oriented toward improving production by introducing external factors: capital, technology, and even organization, all provided by the State.

The most radical project is collectivization, overcoming the fragmentation of resources in order to form enterprises of a reasonable scale. Brigades of young promoters armed with modern audiovisual equipment speed through the *ejidos* on a meteoric course. They gather the peasants together in assemblies and explain to them how backward they are, how lazy they are, and with words carefully evaluated for the psychological impact, they show them the benefits of union and of collective labor. They make them sign a certificate in which the *ejido* members agree to unite their efforts to seek credit, to buy fertilizers if someone lends them the money, or to sell their products in common if the government buys them; statistically, they remain collectivized, although they never agreed to work the land in common or to form an enterprise. After the signing of the certificate, which reiterates age-old practices, nothing happens, except that the brigades continue on their speedy way.

The efforts at economic promotion on the government's part aim at modernizing traditional agriculture, emphasizing capitalist relations, or introducing them into activities where they were not practiced. The State seeks the reduction of the autonomous area that gives meaning to peasant production. Official agrarian policy, guided from a quantitative perspective from which the increase of volumes is the principal goal, is suicidal inasmuch as it seeks the disappearance of the peasantry as an autonomous sector that produces according to its own rules, even though that might not be to its benefit. The suicide is not carried out because the new agrarian policy is inefficient and is running into severe resistance. It has not attained the scope, energy, and depth necessary to come near its explicit or calculated objectives.

The weakness of the agrarian policy can be seen as a result of the contradictions within the State. In its concrete actions, agrarian policy is confused and diffuse when not repetitive. It is surrounded by the vested interests within the government, diluted among the institutions that compete with and obstruct one another, bled by monstrous corruption, and smothered in a cushion of bureaucratic inefficiency. The new tactic for growth has been fought by the State itself, by the inertia of a bureaucracy that has spent many years dancing to the same old tune. The inefficiency of agrarian action is also a result of dependent growth. The country, which suffered recession and "domestic" and foreign capital flight in 1971 and 1972, has been affected since 1973 by a severe inflation that reached levels that were scornfully considered earlier as quite Latin American. Although it is argued that the inflation is imported and that the crisis is world-wide, its impact has been multiplied by internal phenomena.

As usual, agriculture suffered more acutely than other sectors, so that the effect of the public investment was possibly nullified or at least perceptibly diminished. Agricultural prices, especially for corn, rose much more slowly than the prices of modern articles and services. Petroleum derivatives that function as a cost in agricultural production, especially fuels and fertilizers, rose more disproportionately yet, so that the prices that the growers obtain declined in real terms. Some industrial crops—the cotton and sugar that the rural enterprises control—rose in price more than food products, but the peons' salaries increased less than the prices. Moreover, again agricultural enterprises were benefitted by a larger share of public investments; they received more consistent and more articulated support. The polarization in the countryside does not seem to have been restrained; on the contrary, it advanced in combination with the new agrarian policy.

A third line of explanation of the scant success of the Echeverría government's agricultural policy is the peasants' resistance to it—in this case, a passive, ubiquitous, and generalized indifference accompanied by distrust and even cynicism. When the minister of agriculture announced to the four winds that the antieconomical cultivation of corn would be replaced throughout the entire country by sunflowers, the peasants did not even get excited; it was an old, familiar story to them, although the latest new miracle plant might have been a novelty. The absence of participation and the lack of response are also forms of protest against an inadequate plan. Many of the promoters, ingenuous but arrogant, get exasperated over doing so much preaching in the wilderness to people who reject their own progress and salvation. Without perceiving it, they run up against the wall with which the peasants protect their autonomy.

The weakness of the agrarian program does not imply that it is unimportant or that it has no consequences. The investments and the development programs, combined with the crisis and inflation, have generated an additional pressure for increasing the intensity of the use of the land and the labor and of the reciprocal and redistributive relations that make this possible. Moreover, additional pressure was created to continue raising corn and the other subsistence crops, although these were withdrawn from the market, and even to keep on reproducing the social conditions of the peasantry. From that pressure are derived demands for a greater territorial, economic, and political area for the autonomous management of resources.

The State feels the pressure from the peasants but refuses to understand it. For it, the peasants do not exist as a category, as a distinct sector. It only recognizes the presence of poor, backward cultivators, ignorant besides, who ought to be eliminated for the benefit of society and themselves. It does not ask them anything because the erroneous character of what their opinion will be is already established. The arrogant vision of history as an inevitable development along a single road of progress, the triumph of industrial capitalism as a superior form of human existence, implicit in the State's model, has neither been criticized nor overcome. It seems cruel to observe that this realistic, serene vision of history is so far away from the absurd realities. The government has come up against peasants who do not understand it, who refuse to follow it in fulfilling destiny, and who, to top it off, make up almost half the population of the country.

The State has not lost control, direct power over the peasants, and perhaps in some respects it has even strengthened it. But there is an alarming symptom in this process: intervention by the army has never been more frequent. This is not novel or surprising, and in previous eras it was much more violent and bloody, while now it seems rigorously controlled. But the appearance of troops, of federal soldiers, has been more common and necessary. The tension grows, but no obvious solution is evident.

VI   AN INTERPRETIVE ESSAY

Material Conditions. Cultivate and *produce* are used as synonyms in this and many other studies. They are just barely synonymous and only in the broadest sense of using natural resources by means of work and in terms of human consumption. Apart from this, cultivating is a particular way of producing that utilizes specific resources and combines them in a particular way. To "cultivate" is to promote and direct a biological process of growth and reproduction self-generated by plants, just as "gathering" or "extracting," whether of wild produce or of precious metals, consists of making use of resources in whose formation one takes no part, although he may decisively influence the conservation of them. "Transforming" involves changing the manner of combining the extracted or cultivated resources, the raw materials, through a set of mechanical operations. A self-evident truth, so obvious that it is sometimes forgotten.

The cultivator creates the conditions for making use of certain forms of energy. Obviously, the most plentiful and important is solar energy, which is converted into plant tissue through the process of photosynthesis. The magnitudes of this type of energy are enormous and uncontrollable, so much so that the sun is worshipped as a god or is accepted as a given. From the cultivator's point of view, solar light is simply there or falls (according to the extent that he is convinced by theories about the roundness of the earth). Light is a constant flow without variations other than the seasons or night and day, changes that appear with absolute regularity. Moreover, it is an ubiquitous flow, perfectly dispersed, slavishly egalitarian, but perfectly rigid, inflexible, one over which no action can be taken, no appropriation claimed. This total rigidity cannot be interpreted as a lack of influence. On the contrary, the entire process of cultivation consists of adapting anything that can be moved in order to make better use of the perfect, regular dispersion of light. The source of energy most important to the cultivator is a constant element, a prerequisite before which the plants must be adapted, spread, and distributed as extensively as possible. Agriculture is basically a dispersed activity.

Water is not much more malleable. Rain, which the majority of cultivators depend on directly, is also a seasonal, ubiquitous flow, but an irregular and capricious one with far from perfect dispersion. It is the

266

starlet, the *vedette,* of agriculture, and though it may seem closer than the sun—thus, magic attempts to manipulate it—it is perfectly uncontrollable, and one must adapt to its seasonal recurrence in order to make use of it as extensively as possible by mobilizing other resources.

In certain forms—surface streams and natural reservoirs—water appears as a concentrated resource that must be distributed, dispersed. In these cases, it can be moved, directed, distributed, and even stored with considerable flexibility but within rather strict limits (Wittfogel, chap. 1). For example, and still within the realm of the obvious, water runs downward and refuses to climb except through very complex works that require enormous amounts of energy, so that irrigation can be used only in quite limited conditions, although it may cover very large land areas and play a central role in socioeconomic organization.

The construction, maintenance, and operation of hydraulic works require great amounts of work and complex ways of organizing it, which increase more than proportionately with respect to the scope of the project, to the extent that the latter approaches the physical and technological limits of possibility. This is the problem often faced by modern engineers, who know that the cost of irrigating a hectare near the limits of topographical possibility is considerably higher than the marginal utility that could be obtained from it. Large, modern irrigation systems are built quite far from the physical limits, heeding the slope, for instance, for cost-benefit reasons. The ancient systems, especially those of the so-called hydraulic civilizations, however, frequently approach the topographical limits, since the cost-benefit relation was applied in a different way and also because this relation is dynamic, so that a project that was irrational a millenium ago ceased to be so later on. The physical limitation in the management of water or other resources is not, then, a rigid barrier, but presents greater or lesser flexibility according to how it is combined with technology, including human labor and its organization, and with the orientation of the operative socioeconomic model. But among its conditioning factors the physical barrier is, in fact, a real limit.

The land is not a model of elasticity, either. In one of its aspects—its size or area—nothing can be done, and it must be taken as something fixed and invariable, definitively localized and limited. Only under very particular conditions and in the vicinity of the sea or of a lake, as in Holland or pre-Hispanic Mexico, is it possible to increase the area of the soil through human labor. In order to do so, enormous amounts of energy and a very complex organization are required, for which the principle of diminishing returns also holds as the scope increases and the limit of possibilities is approached.

In another of its aspects, as the substratum for the growth of plants, the land, can be subjected to limited manipulation. Its form can be altered, making it more even by leveling fields and constructing agricultural terraces in order to permit the more uniform distribution of other resources like water, plants, and labor; these measures also contribute to conservation through control of erosion. To a certain degree, the quality of the soil can also be altered, modifying its conditions to sustain certain plants better physically and organically through practices like periodic tilling of the crop or fertilization. Manipulation of the land in order to conserve it and to promote the selective, continuous growth of plants, crop specialization, has relatively strict limits and becomes rational in terms of other resources. Moving the earth obviously requires great efforts, although perhaps it does not necessitate very large, complex organizations.

The plants themselves, the natural result of the combination of the resources mentioned and many others, are at once a resource and the specific object of the cultivator's activity. He selects the plants in terms of his consumption. The choice takes into account not only the efficiency of the plants in using other resources but also their utility, basically their edibility, which is ruled and hierarchized more according to cultural preferences than for purely nutritional reasons. The preferences not only refer to taste, which is indeed a powerful influence, but also include ease of conservation, an essential requirement for production that is cyclical, not continuous, by nature; its combination with other plants and animals in the diet; and in certain situations, the possibility for exchange under favorable conditions, among many other criteria. This brings about the situation in which the cultivator is almost always encouraging the growth of plants that have disadvantages in comparison with other plants considered weeds, which seem to have a prodigious efficiency from the cultivator's point of view.

The cultivated plants have to replace or eliminate others in order to be able to use the other resources more extensively. Artificial selection, domestication, affects the equilibrium of the biotic community in which not only competitive functions occur but also complementary ones, like the formation of nutrients, among others. The breaking of the equilibrium must be compensated for with work, more intense the more profoundly natural conditions are contradicted. In order to become a permanent activity, planting requires work to maintain or create a certain balance in the biological population: the so-called cultural practices, from the fallow period, or rest, to irrigation and fertilization. Although more flexible than other resources, plants have a limited elasticity by their very nature, by their combinations among themselves and with other resources. They are vulnerable and capricious, make promises and may not keep them—they are living beings.

The limited flexibility of the basic resources for cultivation is used differently according to the relative proximity of the physical and technological limits that demarcate the accelerated decline in the yields of work. The manipulation of plants, which have a greater elasticity, is the most desirable, least onerous alternative; it is carried out in the long-fallow cultivation systems, especially the one called *roza*. In this system, the biotic community is prepared with the help of fire to permit the introduction of selected species; the soil and water are not touched. For the operation of this system, an abundance of land is indispensable, since it has to rest in order to restore the natural vegetation that makes the sporadic growth of cultivated plants possible. Under the long-fallow system the yield per unit of surface area cultivated is quite high, yet low if it is distributed across the territory necessary for the system's operation.

The short-fallow system, according to which the land rests at least one cycle for each one in which it is cultivated, is almost always associated with the use of work animals, given that the yield per hectare cultivated is lower, so that greater areas must be covered. However, the yield of the total area is higher than in the *roza* system. In the short-fallow system, the soil is manipulated; the plants are relatively unvaried and specialized, mostly cereals; and the partial restoration of the destroyed biotic equilibrium is one of its critical requirements, but one not always obtained. The introduction of irrigation water raises the yield per hectare and in the total area, since the land is used more constantly, almost continuously in some cases. With irrigation, the soil, along with the water, must be moved, leveled or shaped into terraces in order to favor the regular flow of the liquid, regardless of whether animals or only tools are used. The nutrients present in the water permit continuous specialized cultivation in some cases; a self-contained equilibrium is created in the system, like the one on the terraces where rice is continuously raised by flooding (Geertz, chap. 2). With irrigation, the elasticity of the other resources can be stretched to the maximum.

The different systems are not exclusive and can be combined in many ways by virtue of their mutual relation and in terms of the last resource, human labor—strictly speaking, people. They obviously have a peculiar position: they are at the same time an energy factor in production and the only reason that exists for the complicated, risky process of cultivation. This, too, as obvious as it is, is often forgotten. People are not the human resource for production as the supreme goal; people produce in order to live.

As a source of energy for agriculture people are very flexible and mobile. They can disperse their activity in order to capture solar energy or rain more extensively, or they can concentrate it to construct a terrace. They can share in the construction of a massive irrigation project or undertake something as delicate as a graft or a transplant. But along with contributing energy, people make decisions, choose the tactics for encouraging the growth of the plants in terms of themselves and their relation with other resources. They select the option that permits the highest productivity for their work and provide the energy to carry it out. They are a resource with autonomous movement, with initiative.

People do not seem to be one of the most powerful and efficient sources of energy. They eat a great deal and tire quickly. They have their own law of diminishing returns: the greater the quantity of work in a definite time period, the greater drudgery and fatigue for the worker will be in the last, marginal units of work he undertakes, Chayanov tells us (p. 81). Anyone can empirically validate this observation, which can also be expressed in another way: the productivity of work decreases as it approaches the limit of the worker's physical resistance. Or in a more personal fashion: the last tug on the rope brings less, and sometimes the cord breaks anyway.

To increase the efficacy of work, people have created instruments. Some—tools—permit concentration of energy for performance of specialized functions but are in themselves inert. However, others—machines and work animals—are reproducers of human labor that obtain their energy from another source. The reproducers of human work are generally more powerful but less flexible, more specialized and in many senses, more limited. Reproducers of human labor must be considered with certain reservations, since in the majority of cases they do not replace it, but distribute it more uniformly; they serve more for concentrating work in critical periods, imposed by the seasonal character of agriculture, than for eliminating it. Put another way, they enable people to cultivate more intensively in concentrated periods, but in return they demand complementary efforts that are apparently higher, although they are carried out across more prolonged intervals.

Draft animals offer a good example for this argument. Their strength is used only for traction or cargo. When some agricultural system that requires intensive manipulation of the soil, like the specialized raising of dry-farming cereal grains, is used, the animals' traction capacity and the plow enable a limited group of people to prepare a greater area than they would cover if they worked only with tools. But the beasts' energy is used only for ten weeks, and discontinuously. The animals, however, require care throughout the year. They need food, which in some cases implies expanding the areas cultivated and even introducing forage plants. When the livestock graze freely and occupy a specific territory, that area must be prepared in a different way: watering places, fences, vigilance. Finally, in the long term, tending the livestock requires more energy than the animals provide, but this is spread out over a greater span of time and in low-intensity units that can be entrusted to people who cannot fully participate in work during the critical period because they have little physical energy, like children or the elderly, or have other, simultaneous occupations, like the women. Having livestock proves to be rational: it is like borrowing energy credit that is repaid with interest, but in installments that those not totally employed in cultivation can pay.

At first glance, machinery seems to have a different character. Its goal and rationale rest precisely upon its possibility for increasing the productivity of work, and technical progress is a race in that direction. But under certain concrete conditions, machines fulfill neither their promise nor their objectives (perhaps, at a global level, the entire capitalist system does not do so either, but that is another story, barely an intuition at this point).

One of these "anomalous" situations is that of the peasants. Agricultural machinery is definitively immersed in the industrial mode of production and behaves according to its rules; its invention and development are results of the growth of capitalism. Machinery costs something, has a price, and even when it is not working it is losing its value through depreciation; it is a commodity that is acquired with money and represents an investment. By structural position, by definition, and in fact, precisely what the peasant lacks is capital. Each time that the peasant uses machinery, fuels, and the entire complex of capital that machinery requires in order to function he is exchanging his work against work and earnings valued above his own—in such a way that the peasants are borrowing energy with interest again, only in this case they cannot pay for it with anything but money, with their commercialized production, or with labor remunerated with salaries. Again, the energy that machinery provides turns out to be inferior to the work the peasants must collectively undertake in order to pay for its use over more extended periods of time. In this case, energy cannot be, nor should it be, measured in calories or horsepower but in terms of socially invested work and its valuation.

Out of the complex interaction between resources without elasticity (or with very little) and without autonomous movement, and work with its high degree of flexibility and autonomy, arises a relationship that appears to be a constant: more intensive use of land through cultivation corresponds to an increase in total production and a decrease in the productivity of work. Put another way, if the agricultural production of a territory doubles in a given period, the work invested to make it do so will increase in a greater proportion, inasmuch as there are increases not only in the quantity but in the complexity of the tasks that must be undertaken to extend the flexibility of the other resources. Or to put it yet another way, the more units of work invested in agriculture, the lower the yield from each one of them in general, and in particular from the last ones, those that explain the intensification.

The hypothesis obviously contradicts the widespread dogma that greater production, the scale that represents the model of capitalist efficiency, is a condition for raising the productivity of work. It also raises objections to measuring productivity from the capitalist perspective. According to the latter, the productivity of work is almost always measured per person and over prolonged periods of time, while in this essay, "productivity" refers to yield per unit of work actually invested, per hour of work, and by type of activity. In the first sense the peasant's productivity increases with intensification, but in the second it diminishes, since the real work performed increases more than the production. Sometimes it shows us that the introduction of modern technology, measured on one parcel or on one hectare during an agricultural cycle, makes work more productive, more profitable, better remunerated; at other times, however, it cannot even show that. As we make these calculations, this microeconomics of enterprise, data are hidden from us that can totally contradict the result—data concerning the duration and harshness of the day's work; what the people do when the agricultural cycle, which covers only part of the year, is over; what is happening on land unaccounted for; or what the money in which productivity is measured means in terms of subsistence, of the satisfaction of needs.

The decline in the productivity of work as the intensity of agricultural cultivation increases was established as a result of studies of "primitive cultivators," basically self-sufficient groups with little or no external exchange and in which no surplus is created. Studies that use ethnographic descriptions and comparative techniques extensively, like Boserup's in a direct way and Sahlins's indirectly, established that the more continuously the soil is used for cultivation, the more work each unit produced incorporates. "Primitive opulence" permits the survival of the group with relatively unintense, discontinuous efforts, while "progress" demands work that is more and more difficult and frequent in order to obtain the same end. Put in these terms, it seems that one is talking about a paradise lost, degraded by work as in the biblical curse. Neither of these authors—nor I myself—supports anything like this moral judgment; rather, they simply suggest that it costs the cultivator more work to obtain subsistence the greater and more complex the resources that must be mobilized for production. The contradiction between the lack of elasticity of two essential resources—light, which requires maximum dispersal, and the land, which is fixed and requires concentration—circumscribes the work that has to confront greater levels of complexity and sacrifices productivity in order to obtain the production necessary for subsistence.

The delimitation of the territory and the self-sufficiency of its inhabitants that appear quite clearly among the primitive cultivators are the analytical units that enable one to follow the decline in the productivity of work in more complex situations. Making use of the eco-system as an analytical unit, "which emphasizes the material inter-dependencies between the group of organisms that form a community and the relevant physical features of the environment in which they are found," Geertz analyzes the process of "agricultural involution" in Indonesia. In this process, a constant but very slow decline in the productivity of work appears as the intensity of the cultivation of the land increases, phenomena that appear associated with a demographic growth and a colonial dependency that are certainly quite remote from the world of the primitive cultivators.

Following another route, Chayanov uses statistical methods to estab-lish the decreasing productivity of work in families in Russia at the beginning of the twentieth century, another situation that does not have much to do with the primitive cultivators. Chayanov describes the declining productivity this way: "The peasant, stimulated to work by the demands of his family, develops greater energy as the pressure of these demands becomes stronger" (p. 78). In explaining this, Chayanov emphasizes the reduction of marginal utility and its subjective evaluation more than he does the actual decline of the productivity of work (pp. 81 ff.). Sahlins calls the formulation Chayanov's Law and expresses it in these terms: "The intensity of work in a domestic system of production for self-sufficiency varies inversely with the relative work capacity of the productive unit" (p. 91), which explains why in the families with a higher ratio of workers to members who only consume, work will be less intensive than in families with the opposite ratio and implies an inverse proportion between productivity and intensity.

These findings permit the tentative, rough application of this approach to the Morelos *oriente*. By heeding the data on population, technology, production, and standard of living or of subsistence, four distinct combinations can be distinguished, four different rhythms, starting from the final quarter of the last century.

In the first phase, the peasant crops, the *milpas*, seem static. There is no perceptible intensification: the yields per *yunta* of land appear constant, and the rest phase is rigorously observed; the technology does not show any modifications once the use of the iron plow became wide-spread. The area cultivated in cornfields is almost static, while the population grows slowly but constantly. The paralysis in the traditional crops is the result of hacienda dominance and is compensated for by the noteworthy growth of the cane fields—much greater than that of the population—which demand enormous amounts of work. The demand for labor grew more than proportionally with the increase in the area planted in cane, for the complex projects for expanding the irrigation system were being completed; at that time they planted in order to use the territory more continuously, more intensively. The decline in the productivity of work is present in this stage, but in a situation that defies measurement, since while the work was the peasants', the product and the profits were the landowners', and everyone reckoned differently. The peasant had to work more just to continue barely living without modifying his level of subsistence to a noticeable degree—this is the recurrent theme of the overview.

The hacienda's dominance broke down when it could not continue intensifying the use of the territory and tried to eliminate people in order to elevate the yield from labor; it wanted to modernize. The peasant saw his subsistence threatened but could not intensify his work; he lacked the land and the employment. The hacienda did not have employment for the peasants, but it could not surrender land to them without destroying itself, without liquidating the bases of its dominance. The revolution destroyed it but carried off half the peasants in the war. Once that conflict ended, in the second movement, there was more than enough land; the cornfields were restored and they grew, but the cane fields were never reestablished. Under those conditions—an abundance of good land and an effective agricultural system at that juncture—production grew more rapidly than the population, and the productivity of work increased, although the volumes of production prior to the war were not recovered. Nevertheless, the proposition remains in effect: the standard of living did not increase at the same rate as production, even though the peasant could sweat a little less in obtaining subsistence.

In the third movement, the area cultivated in cornfields grew, and small islands of more intensive systems sprang up. Insofar as the best lands were occupied and a level of intensity had been attained that was comparable to the times before the revolution when there was a similar population, production increased at the expense of productivity. On one hand, more land was occupied by traditional crops and the short-fallow system; on the other, continuous crops were established on the irrigated lands. The new lands were further away and poorer, required more work, and yielded less, although the plants and technology were the same. The productivity of work declined, and its total remuneration also dropped. In the irrigated crops the overall remuneration of work rose, but in a lower proportion than the increments of work: the new alternative was open. The standard of living was maintained, but consumption became more diverse, and work became much more intensive.

Up to that moment, the Morelos *oriente* could be analyzed as a productive ecosystem with a high degree of autonomy. All the production was derived from the combination of local resources, even though only a part of the harvests would be consumed in the area. But it was necessary to intensify even more, and in order to increase the volume of "exportation," energy was imported from outside: machinery, fuels, and, above all, fertilizers. The fourth movement, outlined above, has, then, another character and poses a different situation, yet the recurring theme not only continues but is more apparent. Never before has anyone worked so hard or produced so much, surpassing the rate of growth of a population that increases extremely rapidly.

In the specific case of the Morelos *oriente*, the intensification of agriculture implies the deterioration of the productivity of work, but this cannot be clearly separated from other processes. Even less can it be quantified with verisimilitude, not to mention accuracy. The central theme, the increase in the territory's total production compared with smaller increments in the population and much smaller ones in the standard of living, has, from my point of view, two central components: the decline in the per-unit productivity of work and the increase in the rate of exploitation. These can be isolated analytically, but they should not be separated, since they form a single, integrated process. Finally, it is suggested that the material conditions of agriculture are real and operative but that they do not by themselves determine the peasant's position or his relation with other groups.

Agricultural development and evolution, the history of the intensification of use of the soil, have been explained basically by three distinct determinants. One, the least consistent, makes the evolution a fated process, inevitable, external to humanity, and with an end in itself: the triumphal march toward progress or disaster—the optimistic and pessimistic versions of the same thing—as something independent of people and their specific situations. This version, which cannot be upheld except by faith and good will, infiltrates almost everything written on the peasants, who are treated as enemies of progress who march against history, against an obvious, unchallengeable destiny.

Another version, a variant of the first, explains agricultural intensification as a result of invention, of fortuitous, accidental technological innovation. However, it considers that technology and the productivity derived from it shape and regulate population growth; this factor, on acquiring a dynamic of its own, sets out on a collision course with the means of subsistence (Boserup, p. 7). This neo-Malthusian version, which is dramatically declaimed in apocalyptic tones today, apparently operates under certain conditions. In fact, what it does is to describe the most obvious aspects of a complex relationship, but without explaining them. This vision is apt for describing the situation of the Morelos *oriente*, where, overall, the production increases precede demographic increases, but does not help much in understanding it.

The third explanation, put forth by Boserup, makes population the independent variable. Demographic growth will be the determinant of the intensification of work and the drop in its productivity, which are considered adaptive responses to changes in population density. The underemployment of the territories occupied by the primitive cultivators contradicts this explanation. None of the known groups of primitive cultivators, the ones who enjoy primitive opulence and the highest productivity for work, is near the limits of the demographic load of their territory (Sahlins, p. 48), which suggests that demography does not have its own dynamic.

The case of the Morelos *oriente* also seems to deny that demography is an independent and determining factor. In this instance, it seems clear that the peasant intensifies his production to take care of growing external demands, to adapt himself to a more intense exploitation. The external demand multiplies for the peasant through the decreasing yield of his labor; for each new unit of value that the peasant transfers toward the outside, the demand of work increases in a greater proportion. It can be said, in a certain sense, that the peasant defends himself from more intense exploitation by reproduction. Of course, this long-term strategic response is combined with many others, but, finally, it makes considerable sense to suggest that in the face of increasing exploitation and decreasing productivity, the ultimate solution consists in augmenting the size of the work force. With this, a vicious circle develops, and a Pandora's box is opened: the peasant population must reach a magnitude sufficient to saturate the maximum labor demand of crops in a constant process of intensification. The maximum demand is generally of very brief duration, given the seasonal, irregular nature of agricultural production, and implies unemployment for the rest of the cycle, a remnant of labor without current use that is characteristic of peasant populations. From the dominator's point of view, the unused labor has a potential for exploitation. The "underemployment" becomes the determining factor in the fixing of a new surplus quota, which generates intensification again and, obviously, "unemployment" that must be eliminated—intolerable leisure time that the unthinking peasants devote to increasing their numbers.

The suggestion that exploitation is the factor with the greatest weight, with the greatest autonomy, in the process of the intensification of agricultural production—expressed here in its most oversimplified aspect but nevertheless, the central theme of the essay—does not imply that its determining force is mechanical or that it operates inevitably. Application of it is only possible in combination with other explanatory factors. Moreover, what is said here specifically for the case of the peasants is certainly not an original argument: the class struggle as the mover of history is, of course, an old and respectable idea.

The Peasant Family. The growth of the peasant population, subjected to a relation of increasing asymmetrical integration with modern industrialism, has led not only to the intensification of activity but also to its diversification. New productive activities have arisen, have been added to earlier ones, and have modified them in varying degrees. Along with tending cornfields, they now must take care of one or several commercial crops at the same time that they have to employ themselves as day laborers, without ceasing to perform the *faenas* for free or to fill religious *cargos*. The new activities demand more work and new resources that are organized differently, and when added to the traditional activity and its forms of organization, which are retained to a great extent, they increase the degree of variation and complexity of peasant activity.

The diversification is manifest not only in productive activities but in all peasant activities. In consumption, which has become one of the principal channels for draining off the surplus, diversification is expressed by the increasing acquisition of industrial goods, even though subsistence fundamentally depends on self-sufficiency in corn and beans. Unlike what occurs in production, in consumption the new industrial products are not always added to the traditional ones; instead, they frequently replace them.

The Morelos *oriente* peasants buy a greater variety of industrial articles, but few of these satisfy new needs; rather, the majority take care of the same needs they had before. From this results the paradox that the standard of consumption or living does not improve in proportion to the volume and variety of industrial goods acquired, and often it even becomes worse because of the substitution.

The relations that make possible the greater intensity and diversity in production and consumption have also become more complex and varied. Now the peasants have to resort to the bank, the usurer, and the monopolist, without ceasing to borrow from the old *cacique*. Many of the relations of exchange are carried on outside the community and even outside the area, and the external services that the peasant uses are more numerous. At the same time, he must move in the political realm to the extent that the presence of the State expands its arena of action and influence. The points of articulation between the *oriente* peasants and the outside world have become more numerous and specialized in their objectives. Credit, the markets, the peonage, politics, and transportation demonstrate the tendency for activities to become specialized for the capture of peasant resources. Each one of the channels for the specialized draining of resources is efficient and acquires its own dynamic of growth that demands the increase of the surpluses. Subjugation has become more intense through specialization and multiple articulation.

Peasant resources are not distributed or organized according to the specialized lines for draining of surpluses imposed from the outside. On the contrary, they are distributed in generalized units like the family, the *ejido*, or the community, which have all the resources available in small quantities. Within these units, the resources are not specialized but are integrated into a single system to permit the survival of the unit. The contradiction between dominance with a tendency to specialization and the generalized units that possess and manipulate resources provokes different types of conflicts and tensions, which are tempered by a process of mutual adaptation. The intensification of activity has not promoted specialization but, instead, diversification. The peasants have adapted themselves to subjugation in a way that is quite active and varied though generalized, diffuse, and flexible. This manner of adapting oneself contrasts with the specialized integration that is considered the normal response to modernization and that the panegyrists of development judge desirable and positive. The difference in the mode of integration with capitalism does not alter the central objective of this process—attaining more intensive exploitation, increasing the transfer of surpluses—but prevents integration from becoming absorption. On the contrary, the more intensively the peasant is integrated, the more he is differentiated, the more peasant he becomes insofar as he diversifies his activity to adapt himself to this process.

The diversification originates on a primary level in the family, the smallest unit for exercising territorial control and for the specialization of labor by sex and age, a unit linked together, moreover, because it obtains its subsistence as a group. Historically, the extended form of family organization seems the dominant one among Morelos *oriente* peasants. The males remained in their father's home after marrying and incorporated their wives and children into the production and consumption of the paternal home. However, daughters abandoned their parents' house upon marrying and were integrated into their in-laws' home. During the era of the hacienda, its permanent workers, the children of the hacienda who depended upon the meager salaries for their subsistence, opted almost as a matter of course for reducing the domestic unit to the conjugal family, in which all the children abandon the parental home when they marry. The extended family was not, then, the only form of organization and was even considered an Indian custom that it was important to abolish. Curiously enough, the plantation owners' families typically were extended, which enabled them to keep the enormous property undivided, but it never occurred to anyone to think that what *they* were practicing was an Indian custom.

As access to the land monopolized by the hacienda became more difficult to obtain, the extended family was strengthened as the most efficient unit for obtaining an independent supply of corn and for increasing income through salaries in order to meet the needs of peasant subsistence. It was the only form of organization that enabled the people to keep on living and to maintain a fighting force. But the death, emigration, and disorganization brought on by ten years of struggle profoundly affected the peasant families. When the war ended, almost no family was complete. The balance had been broken between the males, who contributed all the work in the cornfields and the money income earned through peonage, and the women and children, who undertook all the domestic work, including cultivation of the *calmil*, raising of domestic animals, and other activities that could be withdrawn from the cash economy, from gathering to the weaving of clothing. The extended family tried to recover its internal balance by joining together incomplete units, at times spilling over the boundaries of kinship. Once again the extended family was the most effective unit for grouping together dispersed and disarticulated resources.

During the first years of the distribution, when there was more than enough land and a shortage of the hands and means needed to cultivate it, the extended family served to concentrate and use productive resources more efficiently. It also enabled the greatest part of consumption to be covered by the family's autonomous production, inasmuch as the national markets were disarticulated. The law that established undivided inheritance of the *ejidal* parcel also favored consolidation of the extended family. But after the Depression, and especially during Cardenismo, when the transfer of a larger surplus was demanded of the peasant through the deterioration of prices for his corn production, which had no apparent possibilities of increasing yields per unit of area, multiplication of the number of productive units became necessary. Married young men undertook autonomous crops with more frequency while there were vacant lands to work. The extended family was modified with this tendency and granted greater independence, including separation of residence and consumption, to the conjugal families that formed it but remained united through control of the essential resources for production and survival, especially through control over the land.

At present, the extended family continues to be the fundamental unit for peasant existence, although its form has been modified in the last thirty-five years. The young men with families of their own have reduced the time of residence in the paternal home. Newly wedded men are totally incorporated into the consumption of their parents' home, and generally they work on the crops of the head of the family without receiving a specific share; however, they spend the money they earn in day labor independently, even while they are bachelors, although they are obligated to contribute a portion for family expenses. After four or five years of marriage, when they have their own offspring, the presence of the small children threatens the balance between producers and consumers in the extended family; at that time the young men begin to undertake crops in *mediania* with their fathers; from this, they receive a specific share, which obliges them to intensify their labor not only in the crops but in day labor as well. They begin to perform their consumption separately, preparing their own foods.

After some six or eight years the conjugal families establish their residence separately, whether within the family lot or outside of it. Even after the separation of residence, it is quite common for the father and son to remain partners in crops, although the latter begins to establish his own associations in order to intensify his activity. He can go halves with his father in cultivating the cornfield and undertake some commercial crop with a brother or cousin with the endorsement and support of his father. By the time the grandsons reach working age, the separation of the families is almost complete, and separate crops are begun. Then the inheritance is received, if it exists: a piece of land, an autonomous territorial base for founding a new extended family.

In this scheme, the work of unmarried young women turns out to be redundant as soon as the first daughter-in-law joins the family, for she covers the demand for domestic labor and contributes efforts for production and withdrawal from the cash economy. This has encouraged the female migration to domestic work in the cities. The young women send the greater part of their salaries home, which implies a double earning for the family—reduced consumption and increased cash income. The young girls return for the village festivals, captivate some young man, and many return to join the groom's family.

Males who are not first-born can delay or decrease the intensity of their labor or cash cooperation with the family. This delay is frequently associated with attending school, which they hope will prepare the boys to obtain a permanent, stable income outside agriculture. The majority do not obtain it and are fully incorporated into the family's agricultural work. The youngest among the males inherit the parents' house and the greatest part of the land; supporting the old people once their effectiveness in work is reduced also remains their responsibility. Definitive male emigration has been reduced considerably in the last fifteen years, in which more intensive crops have been undertaken. The outline suggests that the number of sons is almost infinite. There is some truth in this. The birth rate is quite high. Infant mortality is also great, and there is almost no family that has not lost a child. Even so, families with four children or more are the most common, and there are no signs that birth control is being practiced. The majority of the population is young, and children are the most abundant resource in the Morelos *oriente*.

The extended family has lost its strict localization and does not always coincide with the domestic unit. It is not precisely a unit of production, since it may contain various autonomous units or be part of a larger unit, according to the perspective from which it is observed. Nor is it strictly a unit of consumption, for it may contain various conjugal families with considerable independence in expenditure. It is not homogeneous, either, and the different conjugal units can be described as stratified within the family and with respect to the outside, with the highest position held by the principal family, the lineage bearer. But it is a permanent unit of close, symmetrical cooperation with recognizable boundaries that is integrated through the males. This unit for cooperation coordinates the use of resources and relations with dispersed or social possession. This coordination is actually a functional accumulation of efforts that makes it possible for people without previously formed capital to be able to produce by participating in a sphere dominated by capitalist relations, in which production is a function of capital. Moreover, the family provides resources that substitute for savings and compensate for the marginal nature of the national social-security systems. The family provides loans of money or corn without any type of interest, gifts, payment for fiestas or help in celebrating them, support during illnesses and their cures or in the care of children. This support is vital when one has neither savings nor permanent income and is earning a living day by day or losing it in the same way in a relation of dependency on outsiders. The family is primarily a permanent network of preferential social relations, based on kinship, that permits production without capital and subsistence without savings.

But the peasant family integrated into a capitalist society is first and foremost a unit that produces with unremunerated labor. The work of the children and women, which circulates only weakly as a commodity in capitalist Mexico, is one of the most important components of the peasant product. Women and children complete thousands of workdays incorporated into the peasants' autonomous production, besides undertaking tasks that are not strictly productive but save expenditure and enable them to go on living with incomes that, statistically, would be not merely insufficient but ridiculous. An additional amount is done by the men, who also sell their labor power to capitalist enterprises at prices lower than the cost of subsistence, since they obtain the greatest part of that from family production. When the days worked by the peasants are entered on the books as a function of the price of their product, it turns out that they are paid less than half the legal minimum wage. If these wages are compared with the index of prices, it can be seen that they would not suffice for the subsistence of a family. These calculations are a fiction, but the exploitation is not—it is an obvious, concrete fact that the peasants produce much more than they consume and that someone else is left with the difference.

The internal relations in the peasant families do not have specialized objectives, but general ones that are quite broad, although subjected to traditionally established priorities and rules. Each one knows in each specific case what he can expect from the family and what he must deliver in exchange, as well as how he has to do it. The norms of etiquette are important elements for family cohesion and to a certain extent contribute to smoothing over the conflicts that may arise from living together or to preventing them from breaking out. Moreover, a system of authority that is hierarchical, though concentrated in the family's central couple, contributes effectively to the conservation of the unit. These and other forces that pursue cohesion cannot guarantee it, and in the countryside, too, family conflicts abound, just as bitter or grotesque as those everywhere else.

Toward the outside, the peasant family's functions become more specific. The family is the real subject of the territorial possession that is formally ascribed to individuals. It is quite common for only the chief of the extended family to have title over an *ejidal* parcel, or several of them, and occasionally over some small property. In these cases, *small* is a real definition, one or two hectares, and not the euphemism used to refer to the *latifundista* agricultural enterprise. The area over which titular possession is exercised does not generally correspond to the territorial units of production. These have been modified by intensification in land use, which has permitted their fragmentation. Intensification also favored the fact that access to the land in order to produce could be attained through mechanisms other than formal possession. But a condition for access to productive lands is membership in a family, unless one has capital available, as in the case of the entrepreneurs. The resources that permit undertaking a crop in *medianía* or on rented land almost always rest with the family: the team, the implements, or, considerably more important, the labor. On the other hand, the lands worked by the family provide part of the corn supply, the minimal guarantee that allows one to undertake more risky crops.

Through belonging to a family and incorporation into the territory that it possesses, one's membership in the community is recognized. The tie with a permanent territorial base establishes a boundary between the inhabitants of the villages. The peons who emigrated from other regions and do not have land are considered outsiders, even though they might have lived in the village a considerable time; however, those who join a local family or manage to buy land are treated like residents with full rights. The family is also the unit of participation in the *cargo* system for religious celebrations, which also establish a subtle boundary. Generally, only the head of the extended family takes a *cargo* or a *mayordomía*, while the other members help him in performing it and thus are not pressured to participate directly. Moreover, through belonging to the family of a titleholder, one is given affiliation with the *ejido*, which, among many other things, bestows legitimacy on possession and production.

Belonging to the community and to the *ejido* is a precondition for establishing economic associations outside the family: *medianías*, rentals, or receipt of credit. In all these the family fills the vague but real function of granting endorsement, the guarantee of compliance. The fathers are the ones who introduce the sons to the moneylenders and *acaparadores;* with that action, they commit themselves, to a certain extent, to guaranteeing payment. "The family answers for one," they often say in describing the commitment that the unit as a whole acquires for the actions of any one of its members.

The family constitutes a work team, and it can form the nucleus of an even larger one for the circulation of labor on reciprocal bases. The circulation is established not only among the members of the team but also among the different teams that are formed in the community. With the introduction of labor-intensive crops, this organizing function acquired great importance. The intensive commercial crops that permitted survival in recent years have their rationale based on the investment of the maximum of work without payment of day wages. This includes family labor and work exchanged on reciprocal and very nearly symmetrical bases. The function that the family plays as the unit for the reciprocal exchange of labor is central and critical for the survival of the peasants.

Another critical function that the peasant family performs is constituting the unit for planning the actions that permit survival in an environment that offers multiple alternatives. The family is continually carrying out an inventory of resources, which are, of course, not very extensive, and of the social relations for mobilizing them. The strategy is designed in terms of the balance: to divide up into various productive units in order to capture more external resources or, on the contrary, to consolidate in order to gain autonomy; to decide on the variety of crops and their proportions; to establish calendars for improved circulation of resources and work. The choice of the strategy is almost always based on the composition of the family, on the ratio between the sexes and ages and their possible employments in the face of the necessities of consumption for survival; ultimately, it is based on the availability of labor, which is the most flexible, least specialized resource, the one with the most mobility, in order to allow the attainment of an income that is undifferentiated by its origin but diverse in its nature. It matters less to the peasant whether his store of corn is obtained through servitude or from cultivation, but having it available is indispensable and more important than earning money in certain conditions. In terms of these ratios, each family undertook the intensification and diversification of agricultural production when the overall availability of labor exceeded the possibilities of its being absorbed by the traditional activities, while the rate of the transfer of surpluses was continuing to increase and threatening the level of consumption.

The variation in the composition and in the resources of the family permits a great variation in strategies, which, when combined, offer the chaotic, disorganized image that bothers modern planners so much. But behind the option that each family chose, there is rational, careful planning. This is not formalized: planning meetings are never held, nor are future actions discussed overall in general terms. On the contrary, the plan is established through direct, specific, though quite frequent conversations with the head of the family and among those who are going to join together for production. Peasant planning is a complex, delicate process by virtue of the fact that all those who share in it lack resources to carry out a personal project independently. Some do not have land, others implements and animals; they all lack money, but only some can get credit, and they all depend upon reciprocally exchanged labor. With all the variables that come into play, peasant planning is, in the end, a surprisingly efficient process.

Women, who exercise control over consumption, play a central role in the planning of peasant activity and have a decisive influence in the choice among the productive alternatives that they know in detail. In groups located at a subsistence level through asymmetrical dependency it is quite common for consumption to precede production, which must cover increases in the costs or in the volumes of consumption retroactively and with interest. As the people of the *oriente* put it, "One lives on credit." When consumption is based on credit, it creates a potential surplus that must inevitably be realized with increases in production or in the sale of labor in order to restore the balance. In recent years many of the increases in peasant productivity were stimulated by consumption, and women have been the ones who have pressured for changing the traditional schemes in the productive arrangements.

As a permanent network of preferential relations, the peasant family is not in any sense self-sufficient, and it establishes multiple relations with the outside. Some of these are also permanent and preferential, and it is quite common for them to be formalized through co-parenthood. Co-parenthood, which expands the extent of the preferential relations, has varied motives and scope. In the *oriente* the most common type is the horizontal, which links persons in similar positions. Through it, they establish *reconocimiento,* the covenant of permanent reciprocity that includes not only the co-parents but their families as well. Recognition is also established through bilateral kinship or even through friendship, and in fact it is the mechanism that permits the functioning of the redistribution system. There is also another recognition that flows upward or downward and sets up preferential ties between the monopolist and the producer, the usurer and the debtor, the politician and his supporter, or the *patrón* and his client. Sometimes this recognition circulates through the same channels as the horizontal—through kinship, co-parenthood, and even friendship—but at other times it moves through its own channels, and this makes it different. The conscientiousness of those involved in the recognition also distinguishes it; there are co-parents and co-parents or relatives from whom "Heaven help us."

The form of the peasant family is not regular throughout the *oriente*. In Hueyapan and Temoac the period of residence in the parents' home is longer, and in Huazulco co-parenthood is more important than in neighboring Amilcingo, where the people are Protestants. Yet, not only do modifications occur between villages but they also appear according to position. Those who have no access to any type of land in order to produce and who depend solely on day labor to survive do so in conjugal families, since the money does not suffice to support more people. They are the poorest. Many of them are immigrants from outside Morelos or from other villages in the state. Others have fought with their families and are defiantly establishing themselves on their own and at their own risk. Their number has continued to increase, although they are still a small group, and in some villages their existence is almost impossible. Also, some of the richest people, specialized in commerce or entrepreneurial agriculture, shun the big families, which are only good for borrowing and threaten the process of capitalization. Such people, however, are less and less important, although they might be more numerous. However, the bosses and the new rural bourgeoisie, who rely upon their position as middlemen, on their ability to increase the transfer of surpluses through local channels, remain organized in extended families that enable them to expand the network of permanent relations that they take charge of converting into vertical, asymmetrical ones. There are, indeed, relatives and relatives.

The Agrarian Community. The family economy that the Morelos *oriente* peasants practice, with all the characteristics noted here, is only the smallest functional unit of a larger system: the peasant economy, or the peasant mode of production, with all the reservations implied by the use of concepts with a variety of definitions that are subject to debate. It is obvious that the family cannot maintain its position of producing without capital and without possibilities for accumulation and of subsisting without either reserves or saving in an environment dominated by capitalist relations unless it is supported by a larger entity that confers stable conditions on this contradictory situation. In the case of Mexico, the larger entity is expressed in the agrarian community, in which the peasant economy's relations of production can be observed in a broader, more complex fashion, though always a partial one.

The agrarian community in Mexico has traditionally performed three critical functions: to exercise corporate domain over the land; to constitute a political unit with a certain degree of autonomy, certainly never very extensive; and to serve as an organizing unit, or container, for the inter-action between persons and families that establishes more or less clear boundaries opposing the agrarian community to the outside or singulari-zing it with respect to the outside. In the colonial era (and presumably before as well), the three critical functions and many others were articu-lated in a single organization: the civic-religious hierarchy. The conquerors and their associates summed up the entire peasant group in a single identity—the Indians—and they established an ethnic boundary that set it apart. The peasants, however, did not recognize this all-encompassing identity and, even knowing themselves to be Indians, considered them-selves quite different from their neighbors. Local ascription and identity were the forms of integration of the peasant mode, or system.

In the nineteenth century the agrarian communities lost external recognition, first as political entities, then as possessors of land, and in many cases, even as human settlements. Nevertheless, the communities that managed to survive liberalism conserved and defended their integra-tion as organizing units, almost always formalized in the *cargo* system. Starting from this organization, they managed to retain or to reconstruct certain aspects of political representation and, in many cases, even terri-torial domain, by means of the prohibition against selling land to outsiders. Zapatismo struggled to return to the community all its functions and to integrate them in a single organization endowed with real autonomy. Through the recognition and strengthening of local identity, Zapatismo managed to expand the boundaries of ascription, and the peasants were identified as a group beyond villages and regions. The agrarian revolution obtained the legitimacy of the community but could not reestablish the organizing unit, and the functions were distributed among parallel insti-tutions that recognize different bases of ascription.

The *ejido* is the institution that exercises domain over the land in a corporate fashion, clearly distinct from private appropriation. The *ejido*'s land is a good of production, a means of subsistence with restricted possibilities for being converted into a commodity, capital. In some senses, *ejidal* possession has been exempted from the characteristic rules of the dominant capitalist industrial mode, and it represents almost half the arable territory in the country. The presence of this area of recognized exception has strengthened a tendency of private *minifundista* possession to withdraw itself from the capitalist economy and to circulate only within the communal limits, whether by means of the prohibition against selling to strangers or through the price of the land. To a great extent, the rural small properties have also lost some of their characteristics as commodities and have been assimilated into corporate possession. The national recognition of corporate possession is not a gratuitous concession over marginal territory but the sanctioning of the most important fact of the national system in the economic or political realms. Although different regimes have acted to encourage capitalist entrepreneurial agriculture and even to slow down the growth of the *ejidal* sector, none has threatened corporate possession or placed its legitimacy in doubt. The nation's potential is based on the existence of a peasant mode of production.

The communal possession of the land is one of the conditions that make the functioning of the familial economy possible. The associations that permit production without capital, and in some cases without technological autonomy, are established around the *ejido*. Assimilation, *medianía,* and even land rental upon redistributive bases, which permit the adjustment between territory and labor, can occur by virtue of the fact that communal land does not circulate as a commodity. The entire flow of the credit and technology that complement work is associated with the tying down of the people through corporate possession. To be eligible for credit, one must produce, have access to land, and be permanently tied to it. Even the organization of a cooperative for acquiring industrial inputs on credit, promoted by one of the area's priests, also established, in practice, *ejido* membership as a recruiting criterion. The granting of water and its management is also communal rather than personal, even in the case of individual *minifundistas,* and the organization for its distribution is one of the most important permanent organizations; it also produces the most conflict among the area's peasants. Some aspects of production, like the fencing of fields to prevent intrusion of livestock, selection of fields that are to be left fallow for grazing, and even the date of the corn harvest, are decided by the *ejidatarios* as a group. The *ejido* has become the central institution of peasant life.

Formally, the *ejido* is organized into a general assembly, an *ejidal* committee, and a council of overseers, the last two elected by the assembly every three years. Although the assembly is theoretically the supreme organ, the committee, in particular its president, exercises a power that considerably exceeds its formal prerogatives. In the *ejido,* as in many peasant organizations upon which a parliamentary democratic model has been imposed, the elections are mere formulas that sanction coalitions and alliances obtained through direct, personal contacts, through which the assignment of power flows.

The combination of parliamentary democracy and direct, participatory relations permits excesses in the exercise of power, and these occur frequently in the Morelos *oriente*. They are compensated for by the rotation of positions of power among the different bands and by the proliferation of parallel organizations that welcome those who are displaced. In the *ejido* the local society for obtaining official credit is an organization separate from the committee, with which it is frequently in conflict. Other informal associations that arise in the *ejido* are organized outside the committee and the credit society, and they are bound together with unofficial external resources. It is usual for one person or the members of one family to participate in more than one association at the same time, weaving a network that often includes all the producers, regardless of whether they are titular possessors of an *ejidal* parcel. Obviously, this arrangement implies enormous tensions and involves many conflicts.

Formal political functions have been separated from the *ejido* to be entrusted to the free municipality. This entity is composed of the residents of the rural settlements, independent of territorial possession. From the legal point of view, very few people are excluded from participation in the municipal system—those who are not natives and who have been residents only a short time—while it includes young people and women, who are formally excluded from the *ejido*. In practice, participation in the municipal system occurs through the heads of families and, again, by direct, personal contacts. In this case, election virtually occurs when some one of the slates obtains the recognition of the PRI and is nominated by that party. The formal election is almost always superfluous and often fraudulent, not always because opposition exists, but to facilitate the legal proceedings and to demonstrate massive support before party authorities. There are exceptions: in the 1964 and 1973 elections the *oriente* municipalities became arenas of struggle between factions that could not reach direct agreements; the state government gathered the office-seekers together and imposed one of them.

The rural bourgeoisie, which sometimes remains outside the *ejidal* organization, although influencing it, actively participates in municipal organization. The local merchants and agricultural enterpreneurs, the moneylenders and monopolists linked to the commercial crops, displaced the old bosses from municipal posts and have not let go of them since, although different factions take turns in filling them. However, the aspiring potential heirs to municipal power are already beginning to figure in the area. In recent years some of the sons of the village rich have gone to Mexico City for university studies. The university emigrants form associations that seek the improvement and modernization of their native region. They organize dances, raffles, and other events to raise money for construction of some project in the village. They work with the municipal authorities and in doing so, get into conflicts with them. Some of these associations are affiliated with the PRI and serve as a launching platform for a new political generation—young, dynamic, modern, and profoundly alienated from its origins.

The rural bourgeoisie, which does not practice a peasant economy, but, on the contrary, accumulates capital, acquires legitimacy thanks to the free municipality, to the separation of formal political functions from land tenancy. Based on residence and birthplace, the municipality permits existence of the nonpeasant enclave in the rural community. In a certain sense the municipality is an entity that legitimates the presence and power of the middlemen and takes power away from the agrarian community. But the existence of a local political institution is essential for the peasant community, since it permits the preservation and functioning of the peasant community's political mechanisms—direct, personal contact and the search for consensus—even though it may strengthen the rural bourgeoisie.

The municipality acts only weakly as an autonomous local government because it lacks resources of its own. Its income does not even permit preservation of existing public works, much less the construction of new ones. In that sense the municipality is an agent of the federal government. The governing boards of the *juntas locales*, "local councils," are elected in assemblies in which, theoretically, all those affected by a specific project participate. In fact, the meetings are poorly attended and often boring to the point of exasperation. They are formal rituals that only give the appearance of democratic process, inasmuch as the decisions are made in another way, with the involvement of the leaders of the most important factions. The councils for education, electrification, roads, material betterment (which sometimes add "civic and moral" to their title), and protection of childhood are more or less permanent, and others spring up for particular purposes. Each one is linked to separate federal institutions, and they nearly always have construction of public works as a goal.

Almost all public works are financed in a "tripartite" fashion: the federal government provides one third, the state government another, and the village the final one. The government's contribution almost always consists of industrial materials, machinery, specialized labor, and technical advice, often delivered through a private contractor. The village contribution consists of money and nonspecialized labor. The money is collected by establishing compulsory quotas among the beneficiaries. These funds are gathered slowly and laboriously, and sometimes it is necessary to jail someone to speed up his cooperation. The labor is recruited forcibly and for free, under the penalty of fines. The wealthiest people hire peons to perform the work in their place; the poorest cannot afford that luxury, but it is common for their sons, who are not subject to the tasks because they have no houses of their own, to work in their stead. The municipality and its boards administer the tasks, or *fatigas,* the communal work that complements and substitutes for capital, with which the villages contribute to their modernization.

The benefits of the public works are distributed quite irregularly within the villages and always in favor of the wealthiest people: drinkable water reaches the center but not the *barrios;* electricity illuminates shops and saloons and nourishes the mills but barely lights poor homes; in some houses there is a television set, and they charge those who cannot buy one for letting them watch. The benefits of the modernizing projects are even more irregularly distributed between the village and the outside: trucks that are not from the village arrive loaded with products from outside, but they leave twice as loaded with crops or with laborers. The pathetic, scarce little village lamps are the cover for big enterprises that are certainly quite well lit. But, above all, the public works justify a bureaucracy that would be tolerable if it were merely ineffective, but it is corrupt and voracious besides.

One of the most important aspects of municipal power is the disposition of an armed force, the police, which rarely has more than a half-dozen permanent members, and the control of the *defensas ganaderas,* the militia. This force is important and clears up any doubts that may exist about the legitimacy of municipal power, but it lacks autonomy and is supported and watched over by external elements. The most obvious and powerful of these is the Mexican Army, which maintains garrisons in some villages, where it clearly and specifically performs police functions, which are easily confused and turn into repressive functions.

The *cargo* system, the *mayordomías* to celebrate the feast days of the saints, exists and functions in the Morelos *oriente.* In some villages like Huazulco, Temoac, or Hueyapan, considered the most Indian and closed, the *cargo* system is very powerful, and it is quite probable that the same situation occurs in other villages. A good index of its strength is the violent conflicts that have erupted between the villages and the Catholic clergy. Under the leadership of the progressive bishop of Cuernavaca, the clergy are carrying out a modernizing effort, which is expressed in an attempt to make worship more rational: to clear the churches of images, to eliminate sumptuary expenditure on feast days, to decrease the importance of the saints. These elements are precisely the ones that constitute the specific goals and formal support of the *cargo* system. As one irritated *mayordomo* said, "The priests seem like Protestants." In some area villages the priests have lost physical control over the church and have to request the presence of the *mayordomos* in order to enter. In others the participation of the priests in the festivals is limited to saying Mass, but they cannot be involved in the organization of the celebration. Even so, the parish priests in the area have not had it as bad as those in other parts of the state, where priests have been run out of the villages.

The strengthening of the *cargo* system seems to be related to the absence or weakness of formal political organization, whether civil or religious. In the villages that are not municipal seats, the only formal political posts are those of municipal aide and commander in charge of maintaining order. All are elected once a year and must be ratified by the municipal presidency. Even external contracts to construct public works are channeled through the municipality and its boards. The political vacuum and the lack of formal power are partially and informally filled by the traditional *cargo* system. The *mayordomos* and the *diputados,* "deputies," as those who have performed all the *cargos* in the hierarchy are called in Hueyapan, have a decisive influence in village politics. Even the selection of municipal aides and presidents of the *ejidal* committees is sifted down according to participation in the traditional system, and these are positions to which one cannot aspire without having performed some *cargo*. The system, as a whole, acts as the central political organization.

In other villages, the organization and payment for the principal, general festivals have ceased to be subject to *mayordomía* and have passed on to a committee that is in charge of gathering voluntary but obligatory fees from among all the heads of families. At times, it takes work to find volunteers for the committee and even more work to collect the fees, so that some of the festivals have lost importance. The apparent weakening of the general *cargo* system coincides with the presence of a permanent priest, who in the area resides in the municipal seat. The formal political organization takes over the representation of the village and concentrates the arena of influence around itself, to the detriment of the traditional system. The same thing occurs with the priests, who with their permanent involvement take autonomy away from the *cargo* system but capitalize on its strength for power and personal influence. In the face of these dominant forces, the traditional organization withdraws and becomes less evident.

But the weakening of the traditional system is almost always in appearance only and has an effect only at the general level that involves the whole village. The *mayordomías,* which have been replaced by committees for the village-wide festivals, are at the same time strengthened for celebrating the *barrio* festivals. It happens that way in Tepalcingo, one of the larger villages, at whose shrine the Lent fair is celebrated. The organization of this event, which is a splendid business, has been taken over by the municipal presidency and the priests, who received large sums through taxes or offerings. However, the *mayordomos* dominate the *barrio* festivals. The same thing occurs in Zacualpan, where the neighborhoods compete against each other in the general festival, whose organization remains the responsibility of the parish church. The traditional organization has not been weakened, but it has been fragmented into several units, the *barrios*, in order to preserve the bases of its existence. One is autonomy, threatened by the control exercised by the business district, the municipality, and the priests. The other is the possibility of direct, personal contact among the participants in the system, a kind of kinship that serves for the establishment of boundaries threatened by demographic growth.

Other villages do not have a strong traditional system, despite the fact that they are not the municipal seat and do not have a resident priest. This occurs in Chalcatzingo and in Tenango, villages that were extensions of the hacienda compounds, where all political and religious authority was centered. The villages recovered the land but apparently did not manage to obtain even a minimum of political autonomy.

The *cargo* system has lost one of the functions that perhaps sustained it earlier. It is said that this function was to equalize members of the rural community economically by means of conspicuous, ceremonial consumption, halting the rise of exploitative relations within the community. The money and resources that the *cargo* system consumes are quite minimal if compared with the volume that is extracted through other mechanisms and drawn outside. Indeed, the people who take on a *mayordomía* almost never have a previous surplus available, but they agree to making a greater expenditure, which they will have to cover with production or more intense labor.

Those who already have something or who are in the process of accumulating generally refuse to take on a *cargo*, given that accumulation is linked to breaking the reciprocal relations that the *cargos* regulate and sanction. The wealthy endeavor to take part in the festivals in order to consolidate and legitimize a position within the village, but they do it in a distinct way in order to emphasize relations of dependency. It is common for them to make a donation for the festivals on the main plaza or for those that do not have a religious purpose, like patriotic festivals, or to add a distinctive expenditure to those the *mayordomos* make in the traditional festivals, like donating or lending bulls for the *jaripeo*, "bull-riding," just as the hacienda owner used to do. With this, they demonstrate their interest in and ties to the village but distinguish themselves from those who pay for a Mass or a band or who invite the other *mayordomos* to feast. A subtle, but definitive distinction. In this case the asymmetrical relations with the outside turn out to be more efficient than the *cargo* system for explaining the relations of reciprocity among the peasants. "Class" differentiation is not slowed by the *mayordomías* but by the monopolistic accumulation of capital and power by people who are not peasants.

The traditional festivals of the *oriente* villages are not very sumptuous and elaborate: a deluxe Mass, skyrockets, perhaps a band of musicians, food and drink for a large but select group, and running some bulls as the evening grows dark. Apparently, they were not more complicated in the past, either. Lately, in the most important festivals, "modern" dances are held, with an admission fee. For these, they hire well-known commercial bands that always specialize in Caribbean-style music, *música tropical*. This magnificent business is organized by the municipalities and their boards. The relative modesty of the celebrations is not, then, a symptom of decadence but one of survival.

The low cost of the public festivals does not imply that expenditures made for ceremonial purposes are reduced. In the area, the greatest proportion of ceremonial expenditures is devoted to the celebration of family festivals that can have religious justification, like Holy Week and in particular the Day of the Dead; work themes, like the festivals of the *acabada* and the corn harvest; or simply domestic ones, like weddings, christenings, and birthdays. All families hold various parties during the year in the presence of invited guests—relatives, friends and co-parents, and boarders. The expenditure on the fiestas is high and represents the most considerable expense item after food and clothing. But the people do not make this distinction, and the cost of the festivals is as indispensable as eating or recovering from illness. The fiestas consolidate a network of preferential relations that have vague, multiple purposes but are translated into reciprocal relations of various types and intensity; they give expression to the groups that are intermediaries between the family and the community or the *barrio*. Besides, they are entertaining, essential events in rural life. During them, people talk, drink, dance, and fall in love; information is passed on, and strategies chosen, alliances are established, and politicking gets done, among many other things.

Protestants, who do not participate in the *cargo* system, form groups similar to those established through the family festivals. Protestantism is fairly common in the area; in Amilcingo it is in the majority. In all the other villages, Protestants form an intermediate subsystem of social relations that is articulated by religious ceremonies but is not isolated from other subsystems or from the communal system. Many extended families have some Catholic members and others who are Protestants. Tolerance is high, and social participation is similar, if the public ceremonial expenditure is excepted. Familial ceremonial expenditure seems to be similar in both religious groups.

Among many other functions, the *cargo* system continues fulfilling one of demarcation, which ascribes the participants to one group and distinguishes them from others. It constitutes an imaginary formal boundary, an abstract container for concrete social relations. The presence of the imaginary boundary is indispensable as a frame of reference for the functioning of the intermediate systems that extend the family's relationships. The boundary that the *cargo* system establishes is not absolute, and there always are and will be exceptions like the Protestants and others who, although they are peasants, abstain from taking *cargos,* even though they may be integrated into intermediate subsystems. There are also people who participate in the *cargo* system but not in the reciprocal circulation that flows through the smaller groups. Even so, the *cargo* system is not sufficient to constitute the real boundary of peasant organization, although it is essential for the establishment of that boundary. Possession of lands, belonging to a family, celebration of festivals, affiliation with a political faction, luck, activity, and even sympathy and affinity are criteria that have a powerful influence in the establishment of reciprocal relations, but they are all marked by "being from the village," from the *barrio,* from "our people."

The various institutions permit integrating the community as an organizing container for social interaction that is distinct from the rural village and with which the village does not always coincide. The village is a spatial unit of residence, while the agrarian community is a way of organizing based on symmetrical, horizontal relations. The community makes possible redistribution through reciprocal relations through which circulate resources that do not become commodities, particularly land and work, the autonomous possessions of the peasants and the essential elements for their survival.

Articulation. None of the villages of the Morelos *oriente* can be seen as a socioeconomic microcosm of the nation, much less of capitalism. In the area, there are no banks or industries, chambers of commerce or foreign firms. The most exalted politican is the local deputy, and the highest ranking ecclesiastic is a parish priest. There are almost no professionals: a couple of doctors—without diplomas, it seems—someone who calls himself a lawyer, and primary-school teachers. The most important landholders are an ex-governor of the state of Morelos, a former manager of the *ejidal* bank in Torreón, and a powerful *acaparador* from the La Merced market, but none of them resides on his property. Unlike in the days of the hacienda, the members of the oligarchy do not reside in the area nor even visit it as tourists. The institutions of the federal government are not present either, with the exception of some local agencies, which need, at the least, a coat of paint. There are only a few rich people and many poor ones, enough to destroy any pastoral illusion of a simple, uncomplicated life.

This does not imply that local phenomena do not exercise or receive influences beyond the groups present. On the contrary, all are related directly, although not personally, to the stock exchange, the Congress of the [Mexican] Union, the National Palace, and the Capitol in Washington, D.C. Put another way, the facts that are observed in the area are integrated into a larger system and are only explained in that context. At first, we will use the social relations of production in order to try to establish a model for the articulation between local and national phenomena. We will take into account three aspects of the social relations of production: their objective, the nature of the exchange that flows through them, and the scope necessary for their objective to be met.

Thus, we can distinguish a first division, the crudest and deepest, which separates the peasant mode of production from that of industrial capitalism. In the peasant mode of production the internal relations are oriented toward symmetry, toward reciprocity, in order to obtain the subsistence of families, the smallest efficient units in the system. The community is the framework through which the reciprocal relations flow, filling the function of redistributing resources, of flexibly transmitting the use of the means that make possible agricultural production, the basic activity of the mode. Among the different peasant communities the symmetrical relationship is carried out through the direct exchange of complementary goods by the producers themselves. In order for the resources to be exchanged symmetrically, they must be under the domain and autonomous control of the peasants, independent of whether they are formally recognized as their property.

In another sense, the symmetrical relations of production among the peasants do not flow anonymously but are individualized. The redistributive symmetrical exchange is not one of equal values expressed in money nor of identical resources, but of similar equivalencies in terms of the resources that the units that establish the relationship have available or lack. For the establishment of equivalencies, it is necessary to have direct contact, previous acquaintance, and shared evaluation of the importance of the resource being negotiated: those well-known *face-to-face* dealings. The relations are not free from conflicts, complaints, grudges, and revenge, which are the more accentuated the more unequally the resources are distributed, so that they are regulated by a system of sanctions, a set of "traditional" rules that are constantly modified. The sanctions that tradition establishes are of a social nature, lack formal legality, and do not exercise physical coercion over the people and their property; however, they impinge on the possibility of continuing relations or of establishing new ones. Their efficacy and their severity rest on the fact that subsistence is derived from the establishment of personalized social relations for symmetrical exchange. They also have their limits and their failures, and from time to time, people end up fleeing or killing one another.

But the characteristics of the internal relations of production among the peasants are adjusted to the external relations, which are, on the contrary, asymmetrical, relations of subjugation, of exploitation. Through them the peasant is deprived of his production surplus, which is accumulated in the dominant capitalist sector. Beginning with certain conditions, with a degree of expropriation, the extraction of the surplus is carried out before the production is obtained. When extraction precedes production, it regulates it to a great extent, creating pressures for specialized or diversified intensification of it, or, on the contrary, limiting it and transferring it toward peonage or the labor force. The extraction of the surplus in advance is the mechanism that functions to regulate the amount of the rent fund, of the value that the peasant transfers to the outside (Wolf 1971, pp. 18–20). This form of subjugation bestows elasticity on a production that would vary only in terms of the population growth if it were analyzed only in terms of its internal characteristics, as, in effect, the economists of development, with their vision of a dual agriculture, have determined.

The transfer of surpluses or the payment of a rent fund is implicit in all the economic relations that the peasant maintains with the outside. Each time he sells or buys in the market, when he receives credit or uses some external service, when he works for a day wage or salary—each time that the peasant exchanges commodities, the rent fund, the exploitation, comes included in the price. The asymmetrical nature of the general exchange limits and offsets the elasticity that subjugation grants to peasant production.

Once subsistence requirements are satisfied, the peasant halts his production. On the one hand, the diminishing returns for more intense activity determine that all additional income above the subsistence minimum demands a disproportionate increase in activity. On the other hand, integration in the capitalist market implies that every increase in income gives rise to an increase in the transfer of surpluses. To exceed the limits of the culturally established level of subsistence, which includes the payment of the rent fund, implies increasing additional efforts with lower and lower remuneration. As long as the peasant does not manage to cover subsistence, he has no options and does all the work necessary without taking productivity into account, but obtaining additional income turns out to be an irrational activity. The constant growth of peasant production and its meager elasticity are shaped by this subjugation; they are two faces of the same coin. The agrarian sector's response to capitalist industrial development is an index of the degree of exploitation. The Mexican miracle is based on noteworthy agricultural growth, so noteworthy that it is on the verge of annihilating those who created it.

The asymmetrical exchange between the peasant and the outside is bilateral. The people of the Morelos *oriente,* for example, receive consumer articles and goods of production that are complementary but indispensable. The basic elements for subsistence—the corn and the land and the labor to cultivate it—are provided by the peasants themselves. The difference in the specific values of the goods exchanged, which are complementary for the peasant but vital for the outside, grants the peasant a strategic advantage that only materializes in widespread, total crises but usually does not manifest itself because of the scope and restricted character of the exchange. The goods and services that the peasant uses originate in many places and circulate through national or international markets; all his commercial production and even part of that for subsistence also circulate through these markets. The peasant does not take part in these sorts of markets directly but does business in smaller environments and through middlemen, or agents, who shape the social relations of the asymmetrical exchange. With the exception of institutional relations, the asymmetrical relations that the peasant establishes are based on direct, personal dealings, regulated by informal rules. But unlike the symmetrical relations, the vertical ones are backed up by external sanctions that imply physical coercion. This coercion, which is exercised as a last, but not exceptional, resort, is practiced as much through the legal system as through brutal repression.

On the other side of the division is the capitalist industrial mode of production, the beneficiary of the asymmetrical relations with the peasant mode of production, over which it exercises dominance. The internal relations within the capitalist industrial mode of production are also asymmetrical, relations of exploitation and competition for the permanent accumulation of capital, the goal of the system. The asymmetry and competition set up class and sectoral contradictions that tend toward the destruction of the whole system, toward its instability. One of the essential conditions for containing this destructive process is the permanent need to increase the productivity of work in order to permit, theoretically at least, the constant reproduction of capital without reducing the worker's income. The entire mechanism of production is oriented toward reproducing human work more extensively through the use of machines, of energy derived from other sources that diminishes the proportional cost of the labor in the goods produced. The use of machines, of increasingly powerful reproducers, leads toward the economy of scale, toward production on a massive magnitude as a model of efficiency. Since machines are expensive—quite expensive—the enterprise uses capital more and more intensively and labor less and less. From this results a spiral of growth, which is the inescapable, permanent condition of capitalist production, an unlimited, expansionist dynamic.

In the historical and the current practice of capitalism, the utopia of wealth that grows unceasingly through increases in the productivity of work has always been associated with domination over other modes of production, with imperialism. Capitalism needs natural resources and energy resources that are inscribed in other modes of production, foreign markets, and the more intense appropriation of surpluses produced outside its limits in order to increase the rate of accumulation. It needs to have certain products withdrawn from the rules of the system in order to keep its prices fixed or declining without massive increases in the volume of production. It requires capital goods obtained outside in order to maintain or raise the income of its workers without sacrificing profits. In Rosa Luxemburg's terms, capitalism can only realize surplus value or make it concrete through dominance over other modes of production. Confined within its own borders, capitalism has the same logic as a vicious circle. Its internal contradictions are smoothed over without being eliminated by virtue of the appropriation of resources produced under other rules, which act as a cement for a fragile and unstable structure. Imperialist domination is not an added feature or a phase in the development of capitalism, but one of its bases.

Obviously, this is an attempt, not to analyze capitalism, but to underscore some of its relations that contrast with those of the peasant mode of production that serves as a focus for this essay and that have an influence on the articulation between the two of them. The last we shall mention are the breadth and impersonal character of the social relations of production and exchange. Relations of ownership are established with commodities. Personal relations like kinship and friendship flow through channels distinct from those of production and are considered a different category of human relationship. In production, specialized functions are coordinated through a hierarchical order. Alliance and solidarity can be derived from capitalist production as forms of cooperation and collective action, but reciprocity does not come from it.

The articulation between industrial capitalism and the peasantry for the transfer of resources is quite complex. One of its forms appears when capitalism requires a particular resource under the peasants' control in order to exploit it according to its own rules. Earlier, force was used: if land was wanted, it was taken, and the labor enslaved. Although it might sound paradoxical, the peasants have won many battles since then— many of them without any weapons except physical disappearance or death en masse and others with armed violence, the same resource the conquerors used. In post-revolutionary Mexico a good part of the land, the water and forests, and the labor are recognized as peasant possessions. When the dominant mode requires one of these resources for itself, it acquires use of it by paying for it in money as if it were a commodity.

In this conversion there is something fictional that leaves the capitalist a profit. In the peasant mode the resource is not a commodity and is valued in a different fashion, as part of a complex whole. The capitalist pays a price equivalent to the satisfaction of complements for the peasants' subsistence, which is considerably less than the current price or the hypothetical price of the same resource within the capitalist system. The difference in the price, derived from the different nature that a single resource has in two distinct modes of production, actually becomes a real or potential transfer of peasant surplus. In order to perpetuate this difference, the resource must retain its double position and must be incorporated again, incidentally or partially, into the peasant mode of production. In the case of the land, this is managed through rental, which transfers temporary use but not possession; and in the case of labor, through the incidental day's wage, which prevents definitive proletarization—that is, maintaining and strengthening the separation between the two modes of production; joining them, but without mixing them together.

In the Morelos *oriente* there are two resources that are exchanged in this fashion: land, especially irrigated land, and work. Both are used preferentially, but not exclusively, by agricultural enterprises established in the area. These enterprises are units of production that possess capital, which they invest in order to reproduce it. But by virtue of the fact that they are devoted to agriculture, these enterprises are faced with a set of peculiar limitations. One is the impossibility of acquiring ownership of land in magnitudes sufficiently great to sustain economies of scale, which is compensated for by rental of *ejidal* land at laughable prices. This enables the enterprise to have a higher proportion of operating capital at its disposal and less fixed capital, which makes it possible to obtain greater production than would be obtained by operating under the rules of capitalism. The entrepreneurs invest fixed capital in machinery, not so much to increase productivity, but because of its speed, its ability to cover extensive areas in short periods. Machinery also fulfills an additional function: taking physical possession of the land, uprooting it from the peasant mode of production, and monetarizing its use. The functions derived from machinery, speed and monetarization, are more important than the increase in the productivity of work, in view of the fact that abundant incidental peasant labor is available and sufficiently cheap to compete with the cost of machines.

The *oriente* agricultural entrepreneur is faced by two different alternatives for the direction of his enterprise: one is to devote himself to speculative crops, and the other is to plant products sheltered by an official guarantee price—the first intensive in the use of labor, the second extensive in the same factor. The two options become attractive because of the presence of the *campesinos*, not because of the capitalist nature of the enterprise. In the speculative crops the possibility of success depends on the use of low-priced peasant labor and, to a great extent, on the rental of irrigated lands. The great risks in these crops, which offer a high rate of earnings, are in the market and in competition with the peasants, who encourage the depression of prices by producing the same vegetables on their own. To avoid the risks, one can choose crops with a guarantee price and accept a reduction in the rate of earnings. In this case, success is based on planting large areas of peasant lands, for which one pays a ridiculous rent: scarcely 5 percent of the production cost of sorghum, the crop most extensive in the use of labor. In either of the two alternatives, meeting the capitalist goals of the enterprise depends on its articulation with the peasants and on the use of their resources. In countries that are carrying out a forced process of industrialization, this articulation makes it possible for the exaction that agriculture as a whole suffers in favor of the industrial sector not to affect the agricultural enterprise, but to be passed on to the peasants.

When peasant resources like work and land are exchanged separate from their relations of production, the relations with the capitalist enterprise are direct. However, when products obtained through the relations of production that characterize each mode are exchanged, when it is necessary to convert products that are obtained through reciprocal relations into commodities, the articulation generates a specialized group that creates conditions that permit the fluidity: the middlemen.

The general functions of these intermediaries can be broadly outlined. The first is the physical adaptation of the product. The classic example would be that of the peddler who buys a pack of cigarettes in a store and sells them one by one right in front of the store's entrance. Physical adaptation is basically a problem of magnitude and secondarily a problem of presentation. When the product flows down from above, the magnitude is reduced, since industrial commodities circulate in units greater than those of peasant consumption. In the opposite direction the function is reversed, and the middleman is basically a broker who gathers together the peasants' miniscule harvests until he has made up units efficient for circulation in the capitalist market: a truckload, a railroad-carful, a shipment in terms of modern means of transportation. At times he also changes the presentation: he classifies the product by size and color, packs it in a certain way, in bags labeled "Better Mexican Onions."

The second is a symbolic conversion. When the product descends, this is almost unnecessary, since a "modern" abstraction is already imposed: *Fertilizer 10-10-0* or *methyl parathion*. Nor is this needed when the peasant raises a new product for which he adopts the "technical" terminology. But when the product is traditional, this conversion becomes indispensable. The corn harvest is computed in the countryside by volume and in national commerce by weight. The price of corn regulates many rural exchanges that also require equivalents. But this is a matter not only of metric equivalencies but of different sets of abstractions that determine norms for and regulate the exchange. The middleman sends invoices, has a record book, pays taxes or evades them; he complies with what are imposed as universal rules of commerce and accounting, which are not only that but also function as an instrument of dominance.

3   The third is the physical mobilization of the product. The channels for "modern" circulation are rather restricted and rigid. Paper factories do not buy a drove of pack animals with eighteen loads of wood, nor does the railroad reach the mountains of Hueyapan or even pass nearby. Nor do match factories send a truck to deliver two hundred packets to a little village shop that can be reached by a dirt path only in the dry season.

4   The middleman's fourth function is to extend the social relations of exchange outside the boundaries of the community and, in the opposite direction, from the capitalist enterprises to within the villages. He knows the buyers and sellers at both ends and puts them into real, but never personal, contact; that is his privilege and his defense. He establishes a bridge between personal relations based on ties to place and on mutual confidence and institutional relations based on the economic guarantee, on the possession of capital. Very much bound up with this last aspect is the middleman's final function: he is above all a moneylender who makes up for the peasant's lack of capital so that he can participate in the capitalist market as producer and buyer. The middleman is the actual agent of the expropriation, although he may not always be the beneficiary of it; he is the one who introduces the threat and then sells protection against it. He is the vehicle through which reciprocal productive relations can generate a surplus that becomes concrete as a commodity outside their system, in the capitalist mode of production.

The middleman is set up between two modes of production, manages two languages, two types of social relations and economic rationales, and he makes capital flow toward the dominant mode. He himself obtains a profit from all his acts, whether he is weighing to convert *cargas* to kilos or lending money for planting onions. Nevertheless, there are middlemen of differing strengths and characters, differences that derive from the type of relations they establish with the capitalist sector. There are middlemen who are free agents with some capital of their own available, sometimes ridiculously little, which they place in every possible juncture. Their success depends upon their flexibility and diversification, on being able to sell seven different things and receiving a hen in payment. No one merchant has that much flexibility, but the association of many of them creates an area of generalized exchange: the regional market and its satellite markets, the weekly marketplaces in the plazas, and the permanent shop that is established in their vicinity. In this system, a great variety of products for final consumption circulates, and the peasants' traditional crops, their animals and gathered products, are transformed into commodities.

The majority of the middlemen are retailers for the large regional commercial establishments and have no direct contact with the producing or distributing enterprises, so that they retain only a small fraction of the surplus. Many of these retailers are women who use commercial earnings to complement the deficit in their families' agricultural production. The established merchants, in accord with national rules, expand their operations through the retailers and keep a larger share of the profit, which they invest in modern activities. Broad participation in the markets, the generalized nature of the exchange practiced in them, and the personal character of the interaction between those who come together in them, as well as the fact that horizontal exchange between the complementary peasant producers is carried out in them, turn the markets into a line of defense for the peasant community (Mintz 1974*b*, p. 62), without their ceasing to be at the same time a field for expropriation.

The other type of middlemen is dependent. They are agents who do not necessarily have capital of their own available; instead, they operate as local representatives of large capitalist enterprises. They are *compradors* in Marxist terms and *coyotes* in the local language. Their activity is specialized, and the commercial crops destined for exchange in the domestic or international capitalist markets flow upward by means of it. In the opposite direction move the goods of production that make local production for the capitalist market possible: seeds, fertilizers, machinery, and credit. The activity of these middlemen is ubiquitous and does not have a locale like the regional market or market square. In the *oriente* their activity is carried on in vehicles—pickups, trucks, or tractors. But the *coyotes* know the people and the local environment. Moreover, in this case, many of them are agents for other *coyotes* who have contact with the enterprises that transform or distribute the products. Some of the *coyotes* are free agents who have a pickup and put up their own money to buy on behalf of the merchants at La Merced market in Mexico City. These merchants fix a price in the morning, and thousands of free agents go out in their vehicles to the nearby producing regions. The difference between the price fixed in La Merced and the price that they pay the peasants is the profit. These thousands of *coyotitos*, "small time *coyotes*," are vital for the functioning of the intricate urban markets, veritable prodigies of efficiency that operate at very low costs.

The areas and modes of articulation broadly defined are general types, theoretical modes of the accommodation between two modes of production that do not constitute successive historical stages. The modes are not exclusive but complementary, and together they contribute to creating the general conditions that permit the individual development of each one of them. But the coexistence and complementarity are at the same time competition and limitation, a clash over the capture of larger shares of a single surplus. The level of constant tension that exists between the different modes of articulation reflects the contradictions between the distinct sectors of capitalism and their struggles to appropriate the surplus, since the number of leashes that can be attached to the collar around the peasant's neck is not infinite. In the opposite direction, the level of tension and competition offers the peasants varied and diversified junctures of insertion, all of them costly indeed.

The State is the most general system of articulation and the one that establishes the conditions for the rise and development of the modes suggested, the ones through which commodities flow. Many of the State's actions can be inscribed within the types described—from the sorghum crops of the Ejidal Bank, which in this case acts as an agricultural enterprise, to the purchases at guarantee prices, which are a kind of *coyotaje*—asymmetrical exchanges that despoil the peasant of surplus or oblige him to create it. But even the purely economic actions of the State have a distinct accent, not only because they cannot be ruled by the pursuit of profit but because they are taken by the entity that distributes the land, imposes taxes, issues laws, and has an army, acts of a distinctive nature, although they, too, generate relations of production.

The political actions of the State that shape peasant existence run through channels of their own, like the *ejido*, the municipality, the government offices that impose or collect taxes, the agencies that construct public works, the omnipresent bureaucracy, the schools, and the almost nonexistent public services. They also flow through the elections, the political parties—strictly speaking, the PRI and the National Peasant Confederation—which can still mobilize the peasants but cannot always contain or discipline them. The courts, the police, and federal troops also articulate the peasant with the rest of the country and with the outside. Just as when commodities are circulating, the exchange that flows through political channels is bilateral and unequal. The peasants increasingly surrender power in return for guarantees for their survival. They give the government backing and support: they serve it as a political base in order to retain autonomous control over the resources that enable them to survive. Like many of the asymmetrical exchanges, this one is also deteriorating.

The State's presence delimits an arena for symbolic exchange. Concepts and facts of an ideological nature also shape peasant existence.

Language; religion; nationality and its derivative, ethnicity; the image of oneself and of progress; communication and the monopoly on information—all unite the people and at the same time separate them into groups with different consciousnesses, with distinct affiliations. Words and ideas actually connect the modes of production and shape their relations toward the inside and toward the outside. The symbolic flow is again bilateral and asymmetrical, despite that arrogant and overbearing vision that sees the peasant as an object to be taught, educated, guided, but never as a subject from which to learn.

Ultimately, the State does more than that: it establishes the general conditions for the plundering of the peasants. It establishes the prices of the things that circulate, which are set more in terms of power relations than of the laws of supply and demand. The prices are expressions of a broader system of appraisal and accounting—even including the value of the money and of the people's labor—that the State imposes as a function of its plan and for the benefit of the urban population. The State redistributes the national wealth, readjusts it independently of those who created it. The peasants, who are the majority and produce more than anybody, receive the smallest cut.

Affiliated with the capitalist industrial mode of production, the State performs certain functions for its preservation. One is to subdue and control the contradictions that arise in the capitalist sector: fragmentation into classes; competition among similar enterprises that have different sizes and wealth or that produce the same things in alternative ways, between the "traditional and modern" sectors, between all the forces that, driven by their own dynamic, try to grow at the expense of others or of the stability of the whole. It is also up to the State to accumulate capital that is not reproduced in order to provide general services, the infrastructure that makes the system of exchange possible. In this dimension the State can be seen as a level of integration of the capitalist industrial mode of production in its own terms that creates the conditions so that the enterprises, the basic productive units of the mode, can carry out the accumulation and reproduction of capital.

But the stability of industrial capitalism requires dominance over other, different modes of production in order to expropriate their real surpluses and to actualize the potential ones for the same purpose. The dominance is a direct function of the State and has a political nature protected by the power of physical coercion, armed repression; force is one of the sources of the State's legitimacy, although use of it is rarely actualized, and the usual dominance is exercised through other mechanisms that create an economic and technological dependency. Some countries have banished the other modes of production from their interior or have confined them to secondary positions. Many of the great industrial powers and some of their extensions have done just that through colonization. But the industrial powers are the ones that most need control over those who produce on different bases. In this case, the State's function of dominance is exercised toward the outside, as an external relation, through barbarous and discredited direct colonialism or through the subtle and sophisticated but no less brutal system of alliances with dependent, subordinate sovereign governments.

International capitalism has created an international division of labor in which the great powers monopolize the strategic sectors, most especially science and technology, as well as the capital. Unequal relations are set up among the distinct areas, and the metropolitan areas are developed at the expense of the others. In this sense, the State encompasses a viable area, the nation, for the exercise of its political power. Purposely passing over history, the state-nation is a social and human spatial segment that acts as the effective unit, adapted to concrete conditions and to controllable magnitudes, for the integration of the capitalist industrial mode. As it was observed of the Morelos villages, not even the most advanced industrial power contains the capitalist mode of production in its interior. This mode is integrated ubiquitously, without precise localization, and the effects of its action extend outside its boundaries and areas of dominance. The State acts as the effective unit that makes possible the international circulation of commodities and capital and the concentration and reproduction of capital. The State is not, then, a superstructure, but a basic, essential force for the development of industrial capitalism. It is an organization with a high degree of autonomy. It is the bearer and guardian, a specific unit of the capitalist industrial mode of production.

The State that has called itself pro-development acquires peculiar characteristics, inasmuch as it has to articulate in a single domain two or more modes of production in hierarchized positions, at the same time that it maintains dependent, subordinate relations with the industrial powers and cannot give up containing the contradictions that arise in the local capitalist enclave. The level of tension that this generates makes government a refined art or an apelike exercise of brute force. In these cases, parliamentary democracy seems an impossibility, a luxury for rich countries that have banished other modes of production from their interiors.

Mexico is an agrarian country not only because of the composition of its population but especially because of the specific weight that the peasants' activity has within the whole. This essay suggests that the essential contradiction in this case is established between the State as the central bearer of capitalist industrial domination and the peasant mode of production that sustains it and makes it possible.

Despite having emanated from an agrarian revolution, the Mexican State did not encourage the peasants' development nor the growth of their productive efforts in accord with their own dynamic. In the face of multiple, complex outward and inward contradictions, the State tried to restructure the country upon alien bases and in terms of its integration with the capitalist industrial mode of production. The State does not want to govern the country but to remake it; it wants to manufacture a people who serve "progress and modernization." It remains to be known whether this is desirable, a problem that cannot be separated from change, much less from revolution, but especially whether this is possible. The State does not act in a void, in profound solitude, as it wants to pretend. The peasants were strengthened throughout the process that was seeking to annihilate them. They defended themselves by growing in numbers. In the end, the peasants, organized on their own terms for autonomy and for freedom, have the last word.

GLOSSARY

acaparador	A monopolist, commonly a moneylender (*acaparador* is often a pejorative term); a middleman who buys (and sometimes hoards) products in order to control prices or to sell at more favorable prices.
barrio	A neighborhood or so-called ward in the villages.
bracero	A seasonal migrant agricultural laborer, especially one who goes from Mexico to the United States to seek work.
caballería	A unit of land measurement equal to 42.795 hectares.
cacique	A local boss, usually with financial and political power.
calmil	A cornpatch raised on a house lot.
carga	A measure of volume equal to 181.629 liters.
cargo	An office in the system of stewardships formed among the Indian villagers around the cults of certain saints.
ejidatario	A person who holds title to a portion of the communal land, which is, however, owned by the State.
ejido	Land collectively assigned to each village, or the association for the administration of such land. Ownership of this land actually rests with the State.
encomienda	Estate granted in trust by the Spanish crown during the period after the conquest.
faena	An obligatory, unpaid task performed for the plantations or for the village.
fundo legal	The minimum landholding guaranteed each Indian village by the Spanish conquerors. Originally, this common land was a square 1,000 *varas* (each .838 meter) with the village church at the center. Subsequently, the size was cut to 600 *varas,* and ultimately disregarded as landowners usurped the villagers' lands.
gañán	One of two laborers usually hired for sharecropping. Originally, the *gañán* drove the ox team.
jornal	Wage paid for a day's work; in some cases, the day's work itself.
latifundio	A large agricultural estate employing laborers from outside the owner's family.
mayordomía	A stewardship; an office in the cargo system.
mediania	A form of sharecropping in which each partner, or *mediero,* receives half the crop.

merced	A land grant from the Spanish crown.
milpa	Cornfield.
minifundio	Farm without enough land to meet the subsistence needs of a family.
naborío	Indian laborer on the hacienda. Originally, in the period after the conquest, a villager who provided tribute labor to a Spanish landholder.
patrón de la milpa	Patron of the cornfield; the chief figure in cultivation, especially sharecropping. He provides the land and resources and hires the laborers, the *gañán* and the *peón*, whom he may pay with a share of the crop, with corn rations, a portion of the land for their own use, and/or a wage.
peón	The laborer who assists the *gañán* in sharecropping.
realeño	A resident hacienda laborer.
repartimiento	Allocation of lands after the Spanish conquest. Certain lands carried rights to tribute labor from Indian villagers.
tarea	A unit of land measurement equal to 1,000 square meters when referring to lands planted for corn, and 2,500 square meters when referring to lands planted for sugar cane. A cane *tarea* can also be called a *suerte*.
tlacolol	A field cultivated on a mountain slope during the Zapatista revolution in order to protect crops from marauders.
yunta	An ox team; by extension, a measure of land that can be worked by an ox team over a year, ranging from 2.0 to 3.5 hectares, according to the location and quality of the land.

BIBLIOGRAPHICAL NOTE

All the material referring to the Morelos *oriente* in this study was gathered in the field by those of us who formed the Seminar on Peasant Societies of the Center for Advanced Research of the National Institute of Anthropology and History (CIS-INAH) between October 1972 and October 1973. The information collected was indexed and classified in accord with the *Guide for the Classification of Cultural Data*, better known as the "Murdock guide," and the general index is preserved in the CIS-INAH. Except for annotation to the contrary, all the data used come from this source and are not specifically cited. Textual references are presented within quotation marks.

The seminar is producing a series of publications under the general title *Los campesinos de la tierra de Zapata*, published by the SEP-INAH.* Two volumes appeared in 1974, a third is being printed,† and the fourth is in preparation. The first volume, subtitled *Adaptación, cambio, y rebelión*, contains a study by Sinecio López Méndez, "Hueyapan: Un pueblo de la tierra fria," which analyzes the surprising adaptation of a community generally considered conservative; one by Laura Helguera Reséndiz, "Tenango, metamorfosis campesina," which studies the transformation of the children of the hacienda into peasants as a consequence of the agrarian distribution; and that by Ramón Ramírez Melgarejo, "La bola chiquita," which chronicles and interprets the peasant uprising in Zacualpan in 1942.

In the second volume, subtitled *Subsistencia y explotación*, Alfonso Corcuera Garza deals with "Dominio y dependencia del campesino temporalero" in present-day San Gabriel Amacuitlapilco; Jorge Alonso, with "Disolución de la hacienda a la consolidación del neolatifundio" in the case of the hacienda of Tenango and Santa Clara; and Roberto Melville analyzes "Una familia campesina y el cultivo de cebolla para exportación" in the village of Jaloxtoc. In the third volume studies by Elena Azaola, "La dependencia política en un municipio de Morelos," and by Esteban Krotz, "El poder político en un pueblo de Morelos," will appear. In the fourth volume studies of family organization and strategies for peasant survival by Germán Neira and Alejandra Valenzuela will appear. Neither these studies nor other manuscripts and reports from the Seminar on Peasant Societies are specifically cited. This essay is part of this collective effort and rests, not without disagreements, on all the projects of the seminar. The complex experience of collective work is doubtless one of the most gratifying; again, I express my gratitude to those who shared in it.

* Secretaria de Educación Pública, Instituto Nacional de Antropología e Historia.
† Volume 3 appeared in 1976.

This essay is based on field work. I believe that anthropology has a rationale to the extent that it retains its capacity to produce its own information through field work and does not limit itself to elaborating secondhand data gathered for purposes differing from those of the researcher. A great deal of social research condemns itself by accepting as valid the criteria according to which information is gathered by government organizations; in doing so, it legitimates a system of dominance that it wishes to criticize. Social interpretation, sociological theory, is fundamental and an undeniable part of anthropological research, but it is not exclusive to it; however, field work certainly is. In this study I attempt to set out from new information, from the small item gathered in the field, to pose broader problems to myself. I try to learn from the peasants. At times, by following this path, I attempt to contradict some interpretations that are considered self-evident truths. I try to describe and understand concrete things practiced by real people in a world that is not organized according to abstract concepts.

I use few additional bibliographical references—the minimum that decency permits, I would say. I do so consciously and for several reasons. The apparatus of erudition separates the believers from the infidels. It establishes a very elaborate formal barrier that makes comprehension difficult for those who are not members of the club. I tried to write a book that nonprofessionals could read. I do not know if I managed it; I am up to my eyebrows in the academic trade.

Moreover, as is apparent, not all the information used was collected by us in the field. There is, then, a fundamental debt of honesty to those who did that work. There is also an advantage: sharing the risks and the blame. I sought to make it possible to identify the source of all information that comes from published studies, placing the author's last name in parenthesis in the text and the title of the work in the bibliography. When the citation is textual, it appears within quotation marks. Many other data are public knowledge; or, incapable of remembering where I read or heard them, I consider them that and do not relate them to any specific work. I regret involuntary omissions, and I beg pardon for any unconscious appropriation of information.

Yet I appropriate not only data but also complex propositions, an entire book, or the theories developed by an author. In many cases, these authors and their works are not tied to the text of this study; thus, they do not appear mentioned in it, although their work was definitive in the conception and development of this book. I will mention them shortly, and the complete titles of their works appear in the bibliography. I am afraid that there will be omissions, and I ask forgiveness when that is the case; again, unconscious appropriation is responsible for the error.

For the first chapter, "Origins," the *Títulos de la hacienda de Tenango y Santa Clara* were very important. This collection of documents on the ownership of the hacienda is under the control of the descendants of the owners, who generously permitted consultation of them. The transcription of some documents from this magnificent collection was incorporated into the archives of the Seminar on Peasant Societies. The numbers of the documents and the pagination cited correspond to these transcriptions. Chevalier's splendid book on land ownership in the colonial era provided the general framework; the study by Enrique Florescano was used for the same purpose. Eric Wolf's book *Pueblos y culturas de Meso-américa* supplied the dynamic model that ties the colonial epoch to the pre-

Hispanic past and to the republic in its various, agitated stages; his book *Los campesinos,* which was used in this chapter in discussing colonial dominance, has a great influence upon this study. The studies by Ángel Palerm, some in collaboration with Eric R. Wolf, allowed me to perceive the importance of irrigation in the history of the *oriente,* one of the central themes of this book. Ward Barrett's book on the cane hacienda of the descendants of Hernán Cortés in the neighboring valley of Cuernavaca, from the sixteenth century to the nineteenth, afforded an understanding of the hacienda's structure and its operation. The studies by Andre Gunder Frank and Immanuel Wallerstein aided in the brief discussion on the controversial theme of capitalism in America in the colonial era.

The study by Eric Wolf and Sidney Mintz on haciendas and plantations, Sidney Mintz's book on the Caribbean, and the studies of the Seminar of San Juan, Puerto Rico (which appear in the bibliography under the Pan American Union) provided the theoretical framework for analyzing the hacienda not only as an economic enterprise but as a sociocultural system. This model was very important for the first two chapters of this book. Andrés Molina Enríquez's study of social structure in the Mexico of peace, order, and progress facilitated understanding of the agrarian problem and the role the hacienda played. The history of Anenecuilco, Zapata's village, told by Jesús Sotelo Inclán, was quite important for reconstructing the regional history of Morelos in the nineteenth century, and the specific memories of the people of the *oriente* are placed in that context.

John Womack's extraordinary book on the Zapatista revolution made possible the preparation of the third chapter. It is a book that has always aroused my envy, one that I would have liked to write. Friedrich Katz's work on Villa, of which he has barely offered us a few hints, should provide us the history of the other branch of the agrarian revolution in Mexico. Much has been written on the Mexican Revolution with capital letters, but Gilly's book on it provides novel and healthily polemic conceptions. Recently, people have begun writing on peasant revolutions, and rightfully so: they are changing the world every day. In that sense, I used these studies a great deal: Eric R. Wolf on the peasant wars in this century, as well as those by Eric Hobsbawm, Barrington Moore, Landsberger, and Alavi. I believe that the great lessons of twentieth-century history are in this field, which has barely been opened. I do not know if these lessons are going to please us.

The history of Mexico after the revolution, most especially that of the agrarian distribution, is yet to be written. It is not that books on the theme are wanting, but we have yet to hear the version of those who fought but did not win. In this sense, the books by Jean Meyer on the Cristeros and by Luis González on San José de Gracia—another of the books that stir my envy—are drawing aside the veil; Paul Friedrich's book also provides a great deal that is novel. The book by Arnaldo Córdova turned out to be quite useful for contending with the ideology of the victors. Redfield's book on Tepoztlán, those by Lewis on the same village, and Friedlander's book on Hueyapan were used extensively to enrich and to compare with the data obtained by our seminar.

For the recent years, I employed many statistical compilations on the agrarian problem and interpretations based on them. I mention three: The most extensive, although not the most manageable, is from the Center for Agrarian Research;

those by Reynolds and Hansen were quite useful—the latter has the additional advantage of referring to politics. Among the interpretations, I note those of Stavenhagen, Huizer, Bartra, and Gutelman. The reading of a good number of recently written or published monographs by Mexican anthropologists, which I shall not mention on this occasion, was of great usefulness. Perhaps the sum of this effort can exercise some influence in modifying the arrogant and perhaps somewhat racist vision that dominates in Mexico when one speaks of the problems of the countryside.

In the conclusions, I obviously became a jack-of-all-trades. I mention the studies that to me seem most significant for their theoretical contributions. I divide them rather arbitrarily into four groups, since the majority of the works cited go beyond their placement. I utilized the first group of authors in relation to the general conditions of agricultural activity and its specificity: Ester Boserup on population and agriculture; Marshall Sahlins on the domestic mode of production; Clifford Geertz on ecological analysis; Roy Rappaport on energy flows; Karl Wittfogel on irrigation and, obviously, on political power; and Ángel Palerm on agricultural systems and productivity. The second group I used in relation to peasant economy; it includes Chayanov, who provides a general theory; Kautsky, who expresses the more orthodox point of view of Marxism regarding the theme; and Teodor Shanin, Eric Wolf, and Sidney Mintz, who link theory with anthropological work and contemporary peasants. The third group I used in relation to articulation and dependence. In first place I mention Rosa Luxemburg, then the group that has more recently developed the so-called dependency theory, including Frank, Amin, Cardoso, and Wallerstein; and Assadourian as compiler of various studies on modes of production in Latin America. The fourth group I used in relation to power and the State, and it includes Richard Adams on power; Gramsci, Miliband, and Poulantzas on the State; Barrington Moore on political systems; and Gluckman on politics.

Many authors were consulted so that I could clarify my own theoretical position. Many did not help me; others I have already mentioned; and for others who were quite important I found no place in the sequence of this listing, for which reason I shall mention them right away. I believe that my basic positions derive from Marxism as broadly understood, and I cite, besides the authors already mentioned, some works of Marx that I reread, making discoveries for myself. The conception of a multilineal evolution that grows like a tree without obligatory convergences or unavoidable stages owes a great deal to Julian Steward, among those whom I have not yet cited, and to many of those already included. The conception of economies that operate with laws differing from those of capitalism, central to this essay, owes much to Polanyi and John Murra, and to many of those already mentioned. A reference to cultural ecology as a method should additionally include Barth, who also helped me to understand inter-ethnic relations. Although I see a real continuity and a possible integration among all the authors who can be assigned to these approaches, this has not been explicitly formulated or named; fortunately, it does not represent a formal school of thought in the sense that the academic world gives these words, which makes me suppose that there is still a living current of thought. From my point of view, if anyone has come near this integration, it is Eric Wolf, who, as the perspicacious and punctilious reader will have noted, appears quite frequently in this listing. His influence goes beyond the works included in the bibliography, and it is superfluous to add that some of his studies, too, make me envious.

The omissions from this list are infinite. Many are due to the unconscious appropriation of ideas. I am sure that I stole many of them from the peasants, not in the abstract but from specific people who said wise things to me carelessly, in passing and as if by accident, things that I believed forgotten and that, nevertheless, I surely have used. A thousand pardons for them.

I would not want to leave the impression that I agree with all the authors mentioned or used. The very idea! Not even with those whom I respect or admire most. But I remain grateful to all of them, and I leave them free of blame. The heresies are mine, even though I might not have invented or discovered them but have only repeated them or expressed them differently.

BIBLIOGRAPHY

Adams, Richard M. "El poder: Sus condiciones, evolución y estragegia." *Estudios sociales centroamericanos* 2, no. 4 (1973).

Alavi, Hamza. "Peasant Classes and Primordial Loyalties." *Journal of Peasant Studies* 1, no. 1 (1973).

Alonso, Jorge; Corcuera Garza, Alfonso; and Melville, Roberto. *Los campesinos de la tierra de Zapata*. Vol. 2, *Subsistencia y explotación*. Mexico City: SEP-INAH, 1974.

Amin, Samir. *El desarrollo desigual: Ensayo sobre las formaciones sociales del capitalismo periférico*. Translated by Nuria Vidal. Barcelona: Editorial Fontanella, 1974.

Assadourian, Carlos Sempat, ed. *Modos de producción en América Latina*. Córdoba, Argentina: Ediciones Pasado y Presente, 1973.

Barrett, Ward. *The Sugar Hacienda of the Marqueses del Valle*. Minneapolis: University of Minnesota Press, 1970.

Barth, Frederich. *Ethnic Groups and Boundaries*. Boston: Little, Brown and Co., 1969.

Bartra, Roger. "Campesinado y poder politico en México." Mimeographed for Tenth Latin American Congress on Sociology, Santiago, Chile, 1972.

Bassols Batalla, Narciso. *Obregón*. Mexico City: Editorial Nuestro Tiempo, 1967.

Bataillon, Claude. *Las regiones geográficas en México*. Mexico City: Siglo XXI Editores, 1969.

Boserup, Ester. *The Conditions of Agricultural Growth*. Chicago: Aldine Publishing Co., 1965.

Cárdenas, Lázaro. *Ideario politico*. Mexico City: Ediciones Era, 1972.

Cardoso, Fernando Henrique. *Dependencia y desarrollo en América Latina*. Mexico City: Siglo XXI Editores, 1969.

Censos nacionales. Mexico City: Gobierno de la República Mexicana, 1900, 1910, 1921, 1930, 1940, 1950, 1960, 1970.

Centro de Investigaciones Agrarias. *Estructura agraria y desarrollo agrícola de México*. 3 vols. Mexico City: CDIA, 1970.

Chayanov, A. V. *The Theory of Peasant Economy*. Homewood, Ill.: Richard D. Irwin, 1965.

Chevalier, François. "La formación de los grandes latifundios en México." *Problemas agrícolas e industriales de México* 8, no. 1 (1953).

Confederación Nacional Campesina. *XXXV años sirviendo al campesinado mexicano*. Mexico City: CNC, 1973.

Córdova, Arnaldo. *La ideología de la revolución mexicana: La formación del nuevo regimen*. Mexico City: Editorial Era, 1974.

315

————. *La política de masas del cardenismo*. Mexico City: Editorial Era, 1974.

Diez, Domingo. *Bibliografía del estado de Morelos*. 2 vols. Mexico City: Secretaria de Relaciones Exteriores, 1933.

Durán, Marco Antonio. *El agrarismo mexicano*. Mexico City: Siglo XXI Editores, 1967.

Flores, Edmundo, ed. *Lecturas sobre desarrollo agrícola*. Mexico City: Fondo de Cultura Económica, 1972.

Florescano, Enrique. *Estructuras y problemas agrarios en México, (1500—1821)*. Mexico City: SEP-SETENTAS, 1971.

Frank, Andre Gunder. *Capitalism and Underdevelopment in Latin America: Historical Studies of Chile and Brazil*. New York: Monthly Review Press, 1967.

Friedlander, Judith. "What It Means to be Indian in Cualpan, Morelos: A Study of Symbolic Exploitation." Ph.D. diss., University of Chicago, 1973.

Friedrich, Paul. *Agrarian Revolt in a Mexican Village*. Englewood Cliffs, N.J.: Prentice-Hall, 1970.

García, Bernardo. *El Marquesado del Valle: Tres siglos de regimen señorial en Nueva España*. Mexico City: El Colegio de México, 1969.

Geertz, Clifford. *Agricultural Involution: The Processes of Ecological Change in Indonesia*. Berkeley and Los Angeles: University of California Press, 1963.

Gibson, Charles. *Los aztecas bajo el dominio español (1519—1521)*. Mexico City: Siglo XXI Editores, 1967.

Gilly, Adolfo. *La revolución interrumpida*. Mexico City: Ediciones "El Caballito," 1972.

Gluckman, Max. *Politics, Law, and Ritual in Tribal Society*. Chicago: Aldine Publishing Co., 1965.

Gollás, Manuel, and Garcia R., Adalberto. "El crecimiento económico reciente en México." Mimeographed for Fourth International Congress on Mexican Studies, Santa Monica, Calif., 1973.

González, Luis. *Pueblo en vilo: Microhistoria de San José de Gracia*. Mexico City: El Colegio de México, 1968.

González, Casanova, Pablo. *La democracia en México*. Mexico City: Editorial Era, 1975.

González Navarro, Moisés. *La Confederación Nacional Campesina: Un grupo de presión en la reforma agraria mexicana*. Mexico City: Costa-Amic Editor, 1968.

González Ramirez, Manuel. *La revolución social en México*. Vol. 3, *El problema agrario*. Mexico City: Fondo de Cultura Económica, 1966.

Gramsci, Antonio. *Notas sobre Maquiavelo, sobre la política y sobre el estado moderno*. Buenos Aires: Ediciones Nueva Visión. 1972.

Gutelman, Michel. *Capitalismo y reforma agraria en México*. Mexico City: Editorial Era, 1974.

Hansen, Roger D. *La política del desarrollo mexicano*. Mexico City: Siglo XXI Editores, 1971.

Helguera Reséndiz, Laura; López Méndez, Sinecio; and Ramírez Melgarejo, Ramón. *Los campesinos de la tierra de Zapata, I: Adaptación, cambio y rebelión*. Mexico City: SEP-INAH, 1974.

Hobsbawm, Eric J. *Rebeldes primitivos*. Barcelona: Editorial Ariel, 1968.

————. "Peasants and Politics." *Journal of Peasant Studies* 1, no. 1 (1973).

Huizer, Gerrit. *El potencial revolucionario del campesinado en América Latina.* Mexico City: Siglo XXI Editores, 1973.

Jaramillo, Rubén, and Manjarrez, Froylán. *Autobiografía y asesinato.* Mexico City: Editorial Nuestro Tiempo, 1967.

Katz, Friedrich. "Agrarian Changes in Northern Mexico in the Period of Villista Rule, 1913–1915." Mimeographed for the Fourth International Congress on Mexican Studies, Santa Monica, Calif., 1973.

Kautsky, Karl. *La cuestión agraria.* Paris: Ruedo Ibérico, 1970.

Landsberger, Henry A. "The Role of Peasant Movements and Revolts in Development: An Analytical Framework." *Bulletin of the International Institute of Labor Studies,* no. 4 (February 1968).

Lewis, Oscar. *Pedro Martínez.* Mexico City: Editorial Joaquín Mortiz, 1966.

———. *Tepoztlán, un pueblo de México.* Mexico City: Editorial Joaquín Mortiz, 1968.

Libro de Tasaciones de pueblos de la Nueva España. Mexico City: Editorial Grijalvo, 1972.

Luxemburg, Rosa. *La acumulación del capital.* Mexico City: Editorial Grijalvo, 1972.

———. *Introducción a la economía política.* Translated by Horacio Ciafardini. Mexico City: Siglo XXI Editores, 1974.

Magaña, Gildardo. *Emiliano Zapata y el agrarismo en México.* 5 vols. Mexico City: Editorial Ruta, 1951.

Marx, Karl. *El capital.* 3 vols. Mexico City: Fondo de Cultura Económica, 1959.

———. *Precapitalistic Economic Formations.* New York: International Publishers, 1965.

———. *El 18 brumario de Luis Bonaparte.* Translated by O. P. Safont. Barcelona: Editorial Ariel, 1968.

Medin, Tzvi. *Ideología y praxis política de Lázaro Cárdenas.* Mexico City: Siglo XXI Editores, 1972.

Meyer, Jean. *La cristiada.* Translated by Aurelio Garzón del Camino. 3 vols. Mexico City: Siglo XXI Editores, 1973.

———. *Problemas campesinos y revueltas agrarias.* Mexico City: SEP-SETENTAS, 1973.

Miliband, Ralph. *El estado en la sociedad capitalista.* Mexico City: Siglo XXI Editores, 1970.

Mintz, Sidney. *Caribbean Transformations.* Chicago: Aldine Publishing Co., 1974.

———. "Sistemas de mercado interno como mecanismos de articulación." In *Los campesinos y el mercado,* ed. Enrique Mayer. Lima: Pontificia Universidad Católica, 1974.

Miranda, José. *Vida colonial y albores de la independencia.* Mexico City: SEP-SETENTAS, 1972.

Moore, Barrington. *Social Origins of Dictatorship and Democracy: Lord and Peasant in the Making of the Modern World.* Boston: Beacon Press, 1966.

Molina Enríquez, Andrés. "Los grandes problemas nacionales." *Problemas agrícolas e industriales de Mexico* 1, no 5 (supp.) (1953).

Murra, John V. "Una apreciación etnológica de la visita." In *Visita hecha a la Provincia de Chucuito por Garci Diez de San Miguel en el año 1567,* pp. 421–42.

Documentos regionales para la etnología y etnohistoria andinas, vol. 1. Lima: Casa de la Cultura, 1964.

———. "El control vertical de un máximo de pisos ecológicos en la economía de las sociedades andinas." In *Visita a la provincia de León de Huanuco*, ed. John V. Murra. Huanuco, Peru: Universidad Nacional H. Valdizán, 1972.

Navarrete, Ifigenia M. de., ed. *Bienestar campesino y desarrollo económico.* Mexico City: Fondo de Cultura Económica, 1971.

Palerm, Ángel. *Productividad agrícola: Un estudio sobre México.* Mexico City: Centro Nacional de Productividad, 1968.

———. *Agricultura y sociedad en Mesoamérica.* Mexico City: SEP-SETENTAS, 1972.

———, and Wolf, Eric R. *Agricultura y civilización en Mesoamérica.* Mexico City: SEP-SETENTAS, 1972.

Pan American Union. *Estudios y resúmenes de discusiones celebradas en el seminario de San Juan, Puerto Rico.* Washington, D.C.: Pan American Union, 1960.

Partido Nacional Revolucionario. *La cuestión agraria mexicana. Ciclo de conferencias organizado por la secretaria de acción agraria.* Mexico City: Partido Nacional Revolucionario, 1934.

Polanyi, Karl. *Primitive, Archaic, and Modern Economies,* ed. George Dalton. Boston: Beacon Press, 1971.

Poulantzas, Nicos. *Poder político y clases sociales en el estado capitalista.* Mexico City: Siglo XXI Editores, 1969.

———. *Sobre el estado capitalista.* Barcelona: Editorial Laia, 1974.

Rappaport, Roy A. "The Flow of Energy in an Agricultural Society." In *Energy and Power.* San Francisco: W. H. Freeman and Co., 1971.

Redfield, Robert. *The Little Community, Peasant Society and Culture* (2 books in 1 volume). Chicago: The University of Chicago Press, 1965.

———. *Tepoztlán, a Mexican Village.* Chicago: The University of Chicago Press, 1973.

Reyes Osorio, Sergio. "El marco macroeconómico del problema agrario mexicano." In *Lecturas sobre desarrollo agrícola,* ed. Edmundo Flores. Mexico City: Fondo de Cultura Económica, 1972.

Reynolds, Clark W. *La economía mexicana: Su estructura y crecimiento en el siglo XX.* Mexico City: Fondo de Cultura Económica, 1973.

Ronfelt, David. *Atencingo: The Politics of Agrarian Struggle in a Mexican Ejido.* Stanford: Stanford University Press, 1973.

Sahlins, Marshall. *Stone Age Economics.* Chicago: Aldine-Atherton, 1972.

Sanders, William T., and Price, Barbara J. *Mesoamerica: The Evolution of a Civilization.* New York: Random House, 1968.

Sandoval, Fernando. *La industria de azúcar en Nueva España.* Mexico City: Universidad Nacional Autónoma de México, 1951.

Shanin, Teodor. "The Nature and Logic of the Peasant Economy." *Journal of Peasant Studies* 1, nos. 1 (1973) and 2 (1974).

Silva Herzog, Jesús. *El agrarismo mexicano y la reforma agraria: Exposición y crítica.* Mexico City: Fondo de Cultura Económica, 1964.

Simpson, Lesley Byrd. *Los conquistadores y el indio americano*. Barcelona: Ediciones Península, 1970.

Solís, Leopoldo, *La realidad económica mexicana: Retrovisión y perspectivas*. Mexico City: Siglo XXI Editores, 1970.

Sotelo Inclán, Jesús, *Raíz y razón de Zapata*. Mexico City: Comisión Federal de Electricidad Editorial, 1970.

Stavenhagen, Rodolfo, et al. *Neolatifundismo y explotación*. Mexico City: Editorial Nuestro Tiempo, 1968.

Steward, Julian H. *Theory of Culture Change*. Urbana: University of Illinois Press, 1973.

Wallerstein, Immanuel M. *The Modern World-System: Capitalist Agriculture and the Origins of the European World-Economy in the Sixteenth Century*. New York: Academic Press, 1974.

Whetten, Nathan L. "México rural." *Problemas agrícolas e industriales de México* 5, no. 2 (1953).

Wittfogel, Karl A. *Despotismo oriental: Un estudio comparativo del poder totalitario*. Madrid: Ediciones Guadarrama, 1966.

Wolf, Eric R. *Pueblos y culturas de Mesoamérica*. Mexico City: Editorial Era, 1967.

———. *Peasant Wars of the Twentieth Century*. New York: Harper and Row, 1968.

———. *Los campesinos*. Barcelona: Editorial Labor, 1971.

———, and Mintz, Sidney W. "Haciendas and Plantations in Middle America and the Antilles." *Social and Economic Studies* 6, no. 3 (1957).

Womack, John, Jr. *Zapata y la revolución mexicana*. Mexico City: Siglo XXI Editores, 1969.

Zavala, Silvio. *La encomienda india*. Madrid: Centro de Estudios Históricos, 1935.

Arturo Warman is director of the Centro de Investigaciones del Desarrollo Rural in Mexico and professor at the Universidad Iberoamericana. Stephen K. Ault teaches at the Massachusetts Institute of Technology.